PRIMORDIAL
BORSCHT
75¢ BOWL
W/ BREAD

PHOSPHATE

PH

AMMONIA

HYDROGEN
SULFIDE

In the Midrash, the Creation is compared to "milk in a bowl before a drop of rennet falls into it. It quivers, but as soon as the drop of rennet falls into it, it immediately curdles and stands still. Similarly, 'the pillars of heaven quiver' [Job 26:11] then the solidifying substance was infused into them . . . God's handiwork was liquid and on the second day it congealed." [From the Midrash: Genesis. Rabbah 4:7 and 14:5; Lev. Rabbah 14:5]

JEWISH ENCOUNTERS
Jewish Encounters is a collaboration between
Schocken and Nextbook, a project devoted to
the promotion of Jewish literature, culture,
and ideas.

>nextbook
PRESS

Library of Congress Cataloging-in-Publication
Data

Name: Katchor, Ben, author.
Title: The dairy restaurant / Ben Katchor.
Description: New York : Nextbook / Schocken
Books, 2020.
Identifiers: LCCN 2019022798.
ISBN 9780805242195 (hardcover)
Subjects: LCSH: Kosher restaurants—New York
(State)—New York—Directories. Cooking (Dairy
products)
Classification: LCC TX907.3.N72 .K25 2020 |
DDC 641.6/7—dc23 | LC record available at
lccn.loc.gov/2019022798
www.schocken.com

Cover: Imaginary view of Kampus's Milkhiger
Restorant, NYC, c. 1900

Printed in the United States of America
First Edition
2 4 6 8 9 7 5 3 1

The Dairy Restaurant

Ben Katchor

NEXTBOOK · SCHOCKEN · NEW YORK

The "Garden" in Eden is the first private eating place open to the public that's mentioned in the Bible.

Rather than be totally honest, admit their ignorance, and be left without a story, the authors of this best seller cloaked the origin of the human condition in terms of an unpleasant incident in a fifth-century BCE Persian fantasy of a 3000 BCE Sumerian pleasure garden.

A naked man, devoid of all iconographic markings of rank, arises out of the dust of a parched road. The spark of life is kindled in him by the scent of a garden. He's permitted to enter this walled garden as a sort of unpaid employee/guest, to work it and watch it, but is also encouraged by the owner to enjoy all the fruit that grows within. This is possibly the greatest narrative invention of the story: to postulate the existence of a man before the existence of social and class categories — a new, yet unnamed, category of guest or unpaid employee — not a slave or a guest of royalty or a family member, and not a god, just the first man who's permitted to enjoy the fruits of a private pleasure garden.

Within the Garden is an orchard of date palms. A fountain of fresh water produces a cool atmosphere, the first air-conditioning. The light is filtered through the fronds of the date palms, the first indirect lighting. In later legends, the Garden is described in greater detail. The trees retain their leaves all year, it is a perpetual spring — the model for artificial plants as decor. The water of the fountain is flavored with ginger — the first mixed drink. They were not trying to describe a state of unspoiled nature, but a paradise, or enclosed park, in the midst of an arid desert world.

The choice of food is already limited to the fruit that grows in this enclosed garden, but, in a gratuitous display of proprietorship, the owner points out one date palm, growing in the center of the Garden, and tells the lowly employee, who until then thought he had the run of the Garden, not to eat the fruit of this one tree under threat of death. This one palm is called the Tree of Good and Evil. He says that death will occur on the same day he eats the fruit but does not say whether these particular dates will cause death through poisoning, or whether he will be put to death by another agency in punishment for eating the dates, nor does he mention that the visitor will die eventually whether or not he eats from the tree — it is the prototype of all nebulous threats. In fact, later in the story we learn that this guest/employee lives to be one hundred. A threat made just for the sake of establishing a hierarchy of power, ownership, and control. As the Garden is filled with other trees bearing similar dates, there's no reason for the visitor to take this threat to heart. This one tree is hereafter off-limits, but that in no way hampers his enjoyment of paradise.

   With the words "Behold, I have given you every herb bearing seed, which is upon the face of all the earth, and every tree, in which is the fruit of a tree yielding seed; to you it shall be for meat," the proprietor establishes a vegetarian menu.

All pleasure gardens built in the midst of a desert were for the enjoyment of royalty and their court. This pleasure garden, "Eden," was open to the public and naturally attracted a crowd. Adam awakens from a nap to discover that he has company — a woman — perhaps an employee, a dancing girl, or just a visitor.

To be closer to the cool of the fountain, they both gravitate toward the center of the Garden and sit in the shade of the Tree of Good and Evil. An upright creature approaches and begins to taunt them. "So, you're not allowed to eat the fruit in this garden," he says. The woman corrects him by explaining that they are guests/unpaid employees and can eat from every tree in the Garden except this one Tree of Good and Evil — this tree, they are forbidden to touch, much less eat.

The creature goes out of its way to make the same tree seem more appealing than the other date palms in the Garden. He is the first waiter: an intermediary between the fruits of nature and the eater. This is the second great moment of narrative invention: a middleman in the business of human nourishment. Through the sheer power of verbal description, without so much as giving them a taste, the so-called deadly quality of the fruit is transformed into a beneficial quality. He appeals to her sense of status. The fruit will imbue the eater with "wisdom" — a nebulous concept — but, more important, make him an equal to the owner, a veritable god, capable of constructing and owning a garden.

The woman is convinced and her excitement infects the man and they both eat the dates from this tree. The date is known to be a powerful aphrodisiac. To further stimulate their growing lust for each other, they partially cover themselves with palm fronds — the first account of dressing for dinner. This scene is depicted in a Sumerian seal from 3000 BCE.

In this cryptic account of an afternoon in the Garden in Eden, the relationship between patron, proprietor, and waiter is established. The model of the sole proprietor is transformed into a god. Rather than having to appease a different spirit dwelling in every bush, river, and rock, man can make a simple contract with a sole proprietor of nature.

What becomes of the act of eating when a benevolent mother is replaced by two middlemen of questionable character? A fig is imbued with special, extra-nutritional qualities. The contemporary restaurant eater can appreciate Adam's dilemma: the certain, but distant, threat of death linked to a particular dish on the menu. The very food that nourishes us is, in turn, killing us, yet that doesn't stop us from eating. In the Genesis story, we have the strangely anachronistic threat of death made to a couple unaware of death's existence. Laws of decorum and propriety are established and beg to be broken.

There's no question of them paying extra for the special dates of Good and Evil. The fixed, table d'hôte–style menu was not good enough for them, or so they were led to believe by a lowly waiter who had it in for his boss. In Genesis 3:6, we have the first recorded instance of a couple splitting a single dish.

The proprietor, feigning no interest in the dangerous business of piquing and satisfying human appetite, strolls through the garden in the cool of day just waiting for trouble to occur. And when his first two custom-ers stray from the menu fixed for that day all he can do is curse everyone involved. In the absence of currency, the eater cannot settle his bill or pay for damages. The curses are mere words; the real tragedy is being physi-cally thrown out of the establishment.

In throwing them out, the owner makes another show of proprietary be-havior. Not only have they been thrown out and forbidden to come back (he doesn't have to depend on their busi-ness as it's not yet a business), but they won't be able to enjoy the fruit of "the tree of life." Only now, after this unpleasant incident, does he mention that there was yet another "special" date palm in the Garden, whose fruit gives its eater immortality — the first form of health food, complete with an exaggerated claim of efficacy.

Sumerian cylinder seal depicting Adam and Eve (c. 2200 to 2100 BCE) in the British Museum

According to one Biblical scholar, only a few hours were spent in the "Garden."

In his shame at having broken the rules of the Garden, the man puts the blame on the woman, but as we can see in the Sumerian seal, he was present all along. He, too, fell for the waiter's recommendation.

As they leave the Garden, they see the entrance flanked by two cherubim of Sumerian design and a rotating sword of flames — the first illuminated signage marking an exclusive and unattainable place of eating.

They must establish their own home in the world, which by comparison to the "Garden" will seem small and cramped, and reek of the sweat of their own hard labor.

This story has nothing to do with the concept of original sin, or the so-called fall of man — it's simply the description of an incident in the first private eating place open to the public. The consequences of their actions in the "Garden" set the model for our present condition, but it's impossible to say that these actions were worse or better than countless other actions made by man since that time. The course of human life is no more, or less, altered every day in countless restaurants and cafes, by people ordering the "wrong" things, waiters and bouncers waiting to do their job, and owners looking on with a mixture of motherly love and proprietary scorn.

Instead of being seen as a source of original sin, the act of eating was considered by some Hasidim to be the highest form of prayer.

A few thousand years later, with the invention of the restaurant, ordering à la carte, according to one's personal whims, would be an accepted form of behavior. In this early garden of pleasure, it was grounds for being thrown out.

In this little narrative compote we're given all the details of future public eating culture — specifically of a meatless variety.

As we read through the pages of Genesis, we realize that the same sole proprietor who operates the Garden of Eden operates the entire world — the first worldwide enterprise. Adam and Eve are expelled from one "garden" into another, larger place of business operating under the same management. The proprietor is known under different names, depending on when and where he's called. To protect the value of his name, he forbids it to be used in oaths and promises. To maintain the force of his signature, he forbids it to be defaced or erased, or to be mentioned outside of his earthly headquarters: the temple. In time, its pronunciation is forgotten and we're left with a string of consonants — YHVH — an early brand name recognized by his "people" or customers.

Eve and Adam, age 500, eating at home

Although the Garden was a vegetarian eating place, we soon learn that its owner enjoys meat, or at least the smell of meat in the form of a burnt, sacrificial offering. Adam and Eve's children suffer the consequences of YHVH's taste. Cain, a farmer, makes a sacrificial offering of grain. Abel, a shepherd, offers the firstborn of his flock and the fat thereof.

The offering of grain was not "respected" by YHVH, but the meat was. According to legend, the grain offering displeased YHVH for two reasons: first, he had cursed the ground itself, in the act of expelling Cain's parents from the Garden in Eden, and so this grain was the fruit of that cursed ground; and second, as though the first reason was not bad enough, he was offended by the paucity of its quantity. This gives us a sense of the complexity of "taste" and its development.

Cain blames YHVH for causing him to murder Abel. YHVH, realizing the element of truth in his words, partially forgives him for this act — and so begins the long slide into human depravity associated with the generations of Cain.

This story also shows us that the maker of a vegetarian offering, a farmer not accustomed to slaughtering animals, is capable of murdering a man.

This incident over a matter of taste led to YHVH's eventual decision to throw everyone out of the world and start again — this time with more prohibitions in place: the Seven Laws of Noah.

The covenant made between YHVH and Noah is sealed with a sacrifice of every clean beast and every clean fowl — a restraint on the slaughter of living things.

It is not a coincidence that the animals required for sacrifice later became the animals fit for human consumption. In a gesture of equanimity, YHVH allows man to partake of the pleasure he derives from the smell of roast animals and announces that "every moving thing that liveth shall be meat for you; even as the green herb have I given you all things."

His only limitation is placed on eating blood, or flesh still filled with blood.

The worship of many gods in the ancient world resulted in the wholesale sacrifice of animals and the subsequent eating of their flesh. The pleasure of a meat meal became confused with the necessity of a sacrifice. We can see a direct correlation between the increased meat eating of polytheistic worshippers and aggressive forms of behavior: the development of kingship, warfare, the building of fortified cities, and slavery. In the narrative of the Torah, the vegetarian-based Garden of Eden continues to exist in some inaccessible place — an alternative to the appetitive history of mankind.

And so began the mythology of an inaccessible or lost paradise: similar to a defunct eating place that one can know only from memory, or postcard images, but can never again visit.

Abraham and the Font of Hospitality

In the figure of Nimrod, a warrior king, we are given the epitome of depraved human behavior. "A mighty hunter of men and beasts, and a sinner before God."

In this world of ruthless competition, Nimrod had a dream that foretold his eventual downfall at the hand of a male child·

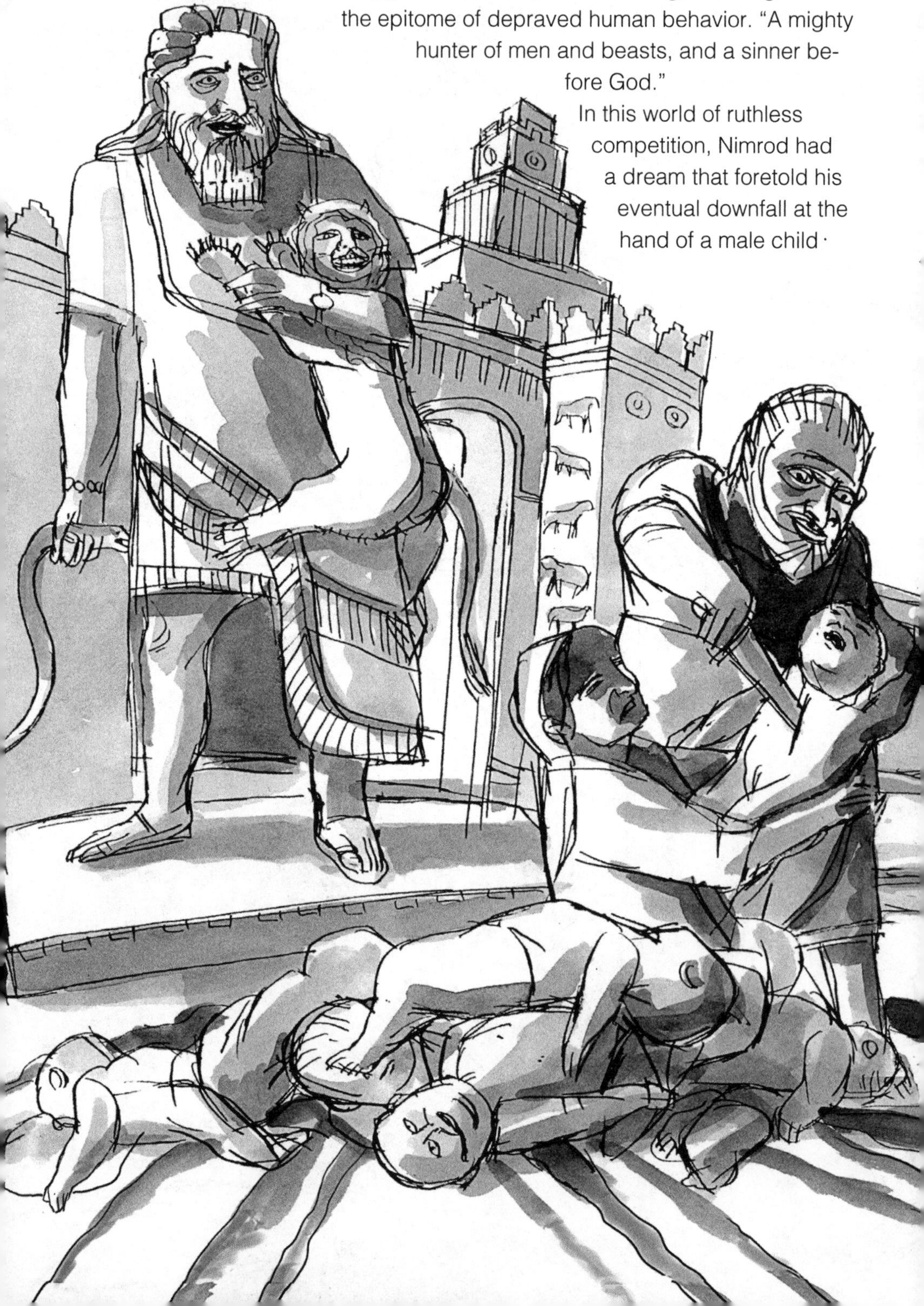

soon to be born. And so, he ruled that all pregnant women would report to a building where all births would be monitored. Male infants would be slaughtered on the spot.

To save her soon-to-be-born child, Emtelai went to a cave to give birth secretly. The male infant was left in the cave to fend for itself, and from this extreme and unnatural situation, public eating took a new and miraculous turn.

The angel Gabriel transformed the infant Abraham's right hand into an all-purpose dispenser of food and drink. From his little finger the child could suck milk, from a second finger water, from a third honey, from a fourth the juice of dates, and from his thumb butter. This miracle is today re-created in the common bar-gun or soda-fountain console.

Only a child suckled on his own hand would have grown into a man filled with the superhuman urge to offer hospitality.

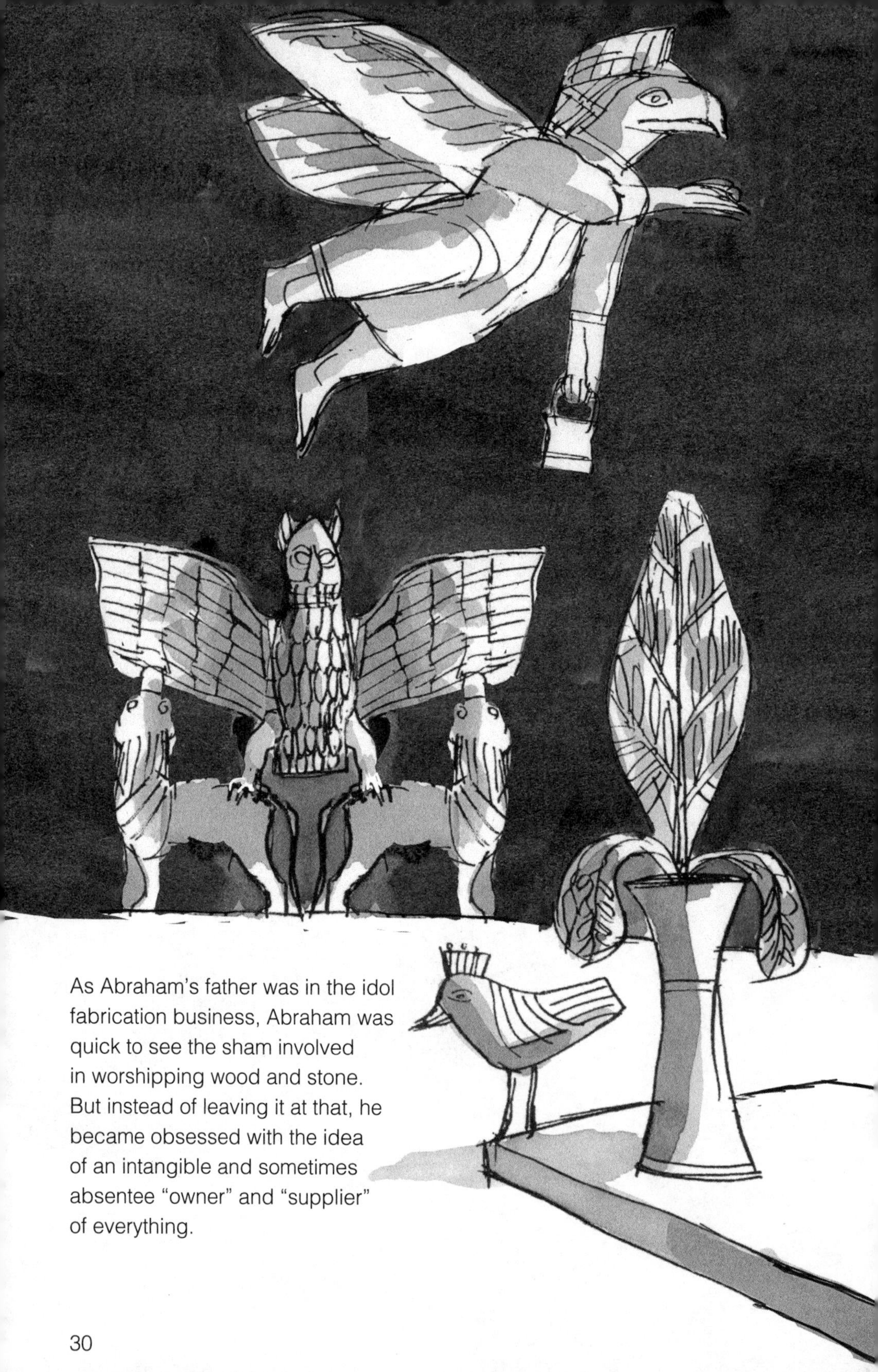

As Abraham's father was in the idol fabrication business, Abraham was quick to see the sham involved in worshipping wood and stone. But instead of leaving it at that, he became obsessed with the idea of an intangible and sometimes absentee "owner" and "supplier" of everything.

Like all men after him, he looked down at his own nipples, from which no milk could flow, and was reminded of his nutritive impotence. He was driven to control animals and the labor of men and women to provide nourishment. And this drive to provide nourishment was masked by an extravagant display of hospitality. And his hospitality was masked by an imaginary owner of all his food and drink. He was reduced to a mere conduit of nature's bounty. He left Babylon and with his wife and small tribe of shepherds went to proselytize in the wilderness of Canaan.

Abraham's tent, of Bedouin design, was positioned on the crossroads of a busy trade route somewhere in Hebron. Boys were hired to tend his sheep and goats, so that Abraham could give himself over to the practice of hospitality — which was to offer a place of refuge to those wandering souls who, for one reason or another, have cut their cultural moorings to travel on the path of darkness and folly.

The tent was constructed of strips of woven goat hair. The flaps could be adjusted on all sides to catch breezes. When it rained, the hair swelled to become a waterproof covering. The tent was divided in two: a woman's section, where cooking was done, and a men's section, for the entertaining of guests.

Abraham positioned himself at the flap of the men's section and waited for wandering souls in the desert. He'd leap from his seated position and rush to intercept them. He'd offer to wash their feet and prepare a small banquet in their honor.

This almost pathological generosity was manifest among the Bedouins up until the nineteenth century. It was said to be a natural outgrowth of desert life, where each person was dependent upon others for survival. Three days of unstinting generosity was the norm.

Abraham, at the age of one hundred, sat in the blistering desert heat, nursing his recently self-inflicted wound of circumcision, and, as ever, still preoccupied with entertaining wayward souls. At that moment three travelers appeared before his tent.

He ran to meet them and called to his wife to prepare a meal of round, flat cakes and laban and cheese.

This time, sensing that these were special guests, he himself ran to fetch three kids. The creatures were slaughtered and dressed with the speed and ease that one would today open a shrink-wrapped portion of meat from the supermarket. With the kids' entrails still quivering with life, they were placed on the fire.

In short order, he was able to set a "tongue with mustard" before each of his guests.

The guests ate and drank as much as they wanted; the host touched nothing. When the guests retired for the night, the host made his dinner from their leftovers. The women, in turn, made their dinner from the host's leftovers.

The diet of the ancient desert nomad was largely vegetarian. The sheep and goats were kept alive to provide milk and wool.

When his guests thanked him for his hospitality, Abraham would explain that he was just a middleman and that everything he had offered actually belonged to someone else and that thanks should, in all rights, be offered to this ultimate provider of all food and life. Why posit an ultimate absentee proprietor — a proprietor like himself, only on a grander scale? To diminish the value of his own property, and thus defuse the envy of the others? To diminish the value of the work of his wife and shepherd boys and thus defuse labor unrest? To reduce the pantheon of gods to the one personally responsible for his own welfare? To understand the complex workings of the natural world and the relationships of human labor would take thousands of years. The act of hospitality was, in fact, a technique for proselytizing one particular god over the many others.

These guests, it turned out, were angels in human garb. Their meal of milk and meat was to repeat on them in the next chapter of the Torah.

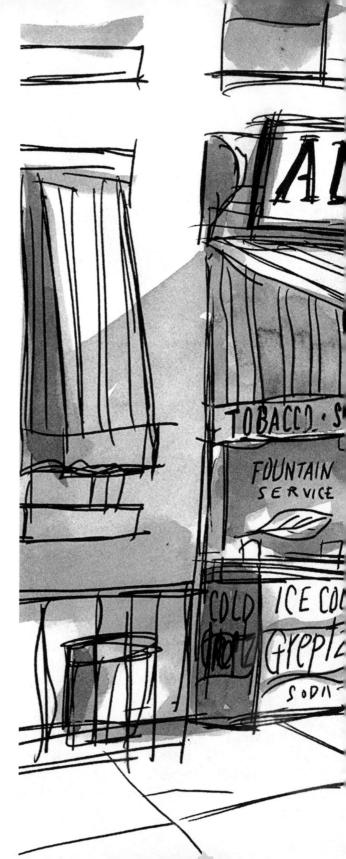

Abraham's tent, situated on a busy crossroad, prefigures the desirable corner location for urban eating places. The tent flaps become the adjustable awning. The powerful urge to feed strangers runs its course. Hospitality becomes a business and its original purpose is forgotten. By the 1950s Jewish restaurateurs use their earnings to send their children to college, thus guaranteeing that they won't follow in their parents' business.

YHVH, now in temporary residence in the clouds around Mount Sinai, summons Moses to receive the terms of a full contract. According to legend, the host of Angels of Terror that surround the Throne of Glory tried to scorch Moses with their fiery breath. They asked YHVH, "What does he who is born of woman want here?" When they were told that Moses had come to receive the Torah, the angels argued: "O Lord, content Thyself with the celestial beings, let them have the Torah, what wouldst Thou with the dwellers of the dust?" YHVH then reminded the angels that during their visit to Abraham they had eaten a meal of meat with milk. In punishment for this transgression of the law — a law not yet established for man, but apparently in force among celestial beings — he would not give the Torah to the angels, but to Moses.

משה

41

MOSES
↓

How Moses was physically able to carry the two sets of stone tablets — each set weighing approximately 2,000 pounds — is a matter of debate among scholars. The best explanation is that the words engraved upon the tablets, like the words of a work song or other verbal distraction, somehow reduced the stone's perceivable weight. Upon reaching the encampment, Moses discovers that many of his people couldn't wait and have reverted to the worship of an animal god, a calf. He breaks the first set of tablets, containing the ethical commandments (the well-known ten commandments), in a fit of anger and instigates a tremendous slaughter of those thousands of impatient idol worshippers.

Moses ascends the mountain a second time to take direct dictation, in stone, of the ten ritual commandments. These commandments deal largely in the specifics of placating, or feeding, YHVH through ritual offerings. The tenth of these commandments has been translated to mean: DO NOT SEETHE A KID IN ITS MOTHER'S MILK.

Having been transcribed at first hand from the proprietor, this text carried great weight among the early scholars of the Torah. The choice of each letter, its form and position within each word and phrase were loaded with a fathomless significance. When people read not only between the lines, but between the letters and graphic elements of the letters, the contemplation of this text led to an ongoing commentary on the proper handling of milk and meat that affects public and private eating to this day.

Anthropologists tell us that this prohibition echoed ancient Orphic mystery rituals and Canaanite fertility rites. In the Orphic ritual, a kid was cut into seven pieces (the parts of the soul) and then boiled in its mother's milk (a return to the original state of bliss). Zoroastrians in Persia in the sixth century BCE also made use of milk libations in their meat sacrifices. In retrospect, we see these formulations in the practice of sympathetic magic as a balancing of male and female, or life and death qualities — the alchemical idea of a balanced diet fit for a particular god. A kid boiled in its mother's milk placated a god in such a way that the natural world would continue to function as it had or better. If these primitive chemical works were directed to a god with some human appetites and desires, then the priest is preparing a meal for a supernatural diner and so the sacrificial preparations should appeal to the taste of the god. The logic of food combinations, like modern nutritional concerns, will be discarded if the god is not satisfied. In this way, the workings of sacrificial offerings partake of the mystery, and unaccountability, of taste.

The specificity of YHVH's taste in sacrificial offerings set him apart from other "gods" and gave him a fully fleshed-out set of human attributes — a fully anthropomorphized god.

We can also say that this male god had a preference for roast meat, well done almost to the point of being burnt, as opposed to a stew of milk and meat, in which the two tastes are merged into a third flavor. Cooking meat in milk adds a degree of milk fat to the already present animal fat, resulting in an overly rich dish. "Dishes" involving milk, and female deities associated with milk, were not something he would savor. A burnt sacrifice, in which little meat remains to be eaten by the officiating priest, might seem like more of a sacrifice, in the modern sense of the word, than a stew in which all the ingredients are cooked to tender morsels and are not literally consumed by the fire.

The Torah text recounting the Revelation on Mount Sinai was compiled around the ninth or tenth century BCE. From that time until the redaction of the Mishnah (189 CE) the prohibition was largely confined to sacrificial practice. Otherwise, as demonstrated in the story of Abraham and the three angels, if someone chose to serve an honored guest roast meat it might be served with laban and bread. The Bedouin specialty mansaf, made of lamb or goat meat cooked in dried yogurt, and the Greek katsikaki gamopilafo, kid goat cooked in yogurt, are still eaten today. Rashbam explains that kid meat is routinely cooked in milk by Muslims in Spain, Africa, Persia, and Palestine simply to make the otherwise dry meat tender.

Among the people that followed Moses through the desert and survived the slaughter on the first day of revelation at Mount Sinai, a different taste

developed. Here we have the first inklings of the meat/milk prohibition affecting human culinary practice. How could the taste preferences of a "god," whether through smoke or aroma, not influence the taste of the priests performing the sacrifice and, by example, the common man? The remains of flesh sacrifices should be eaten within the three days, a Passover sacrifice within the same day, and the "leftovers" burnt to ashes and discarded. As there were few sacrifices of meat boiled in milk, the taste for this combination would not develop. To get around the prohibition, for the purpose of placating other local gods, sacrifices of non-goat flesh seethed in the milk of non-mothers from other species were made.

The prohibition was eventually extended to include seething all flesh in all milk. To further squash the practice of meat-in-milk sacrifice, the eating of such a combination was also prohibited. The leftovers were worthless as human food.

From the time of the Tabernacle through the destruction of the Second Temple, the act of animal sacrifice was put into the hands of a priesthood: those individuals descended from the Levitical tribe. The procedures for animal and vegetable offerings, as outlined in Leviticus, specify which parts of the sacrifice might be eaten and by whom. With the immolation of fat, nothing would remain but a sweet aroma. With the immolation of an entire carcass, some portions of meat were set aside as sacrificial meals for the priests. In private "thank you" offerings, the right shoulder was given to the priest, the breast to the Aaronites, and the rest to the family making the offer. Before the offering was placed on the fire, the blood was removed and sprinkled around the altar. The culinary specificity with which these offerings are to be made — the salt, oil, and fine flour required of "meal offerings" depending on how they're cooked, avoidance of making smoke with leavening and/or honey; that the offering of first-fruits should not be made through burning on the altar, the details of butchering of lamb and goat before placing on the fire, etc. — make one think that these texts were written with the taste of the priests in mind. In each verse, we are reminded that it's food to be savored by YHVH. Through these Temple practices, a complex culinary tradition for certain meats, baked goods, and methods of preparation must have developed.

Here we see a place for the slaughter and burning of flesh on a grill whose flame burns 24/7. The first all-night food preparation establishment, albeit for the preparation of divine meals: Paschal lambs, first-born bull oxen, calves, lambs for daily offerings, goats and kid for sin offerings, turtledoves and pigeons for sin offerings for poor people — only fish were never used. The first-fruit offerings were ears of corn or the finest-quality wheat. Barley flour for wives suspected of adultery; honey, frankincense, olive oil, and wines for others.

Twelve square loaves of unleavened bread, the "showbreads," were stacked between golden tubes (presumably bearing warm air to keep them hot) on an ornate golden table bearing two cups of frankincense. The breads were simply on display for the delectation of YHVH and replaced each Sabbath with fresh loaves. The stale loaves were eaten by the priests. Many of the mechanisms of modern food-handling were in place in the ancient world. The thermopolium of Pompeii c. 79 CE prefigures the design and function of the modern cafeteria steam table.

53

Meat eating, in a climate and economy in which meat was not part of the daily diet, except perhaps for the priestly class, thus became a special occasion imbued with intimations of vital power.

In the Vienna of the 1890s, after a night of debauchery, a young Arthur Schnitzler and his friend routinely went to a favorite restaurant for a meat dinner. Bowery men of the twentieth century, after visiting commercial blood banks for money, went to have a cheap dinner of beef liver to replenish their strength.

Even in the ancient world, the wholesale practice of animal sacrifice in the hands of a hereditary class of priests seemed excessive, cruel, and worst of all exclusive. Such sacrifice was a hardship on people who lived on a largely vegetarian diet and who valued their sheep and goats more as an ongoing living source of milk than as a single meal. Other ways had to be devised for the common people to communicate with their god. With this democratic impulse came the belief that through study of the sacred text one could partake of the divine inspiration behind the text of the Torah. The human mind was meant to flesh out the written law through an ongoing process of reasoning. Moses was, in retrospect, given the title of rabbi, and considered the first scholar of the Torah. In this development were sown the seeds for the future of Jewish religious observance.

The long and complicated history of cultural antagonisms, economic power struggles, and theological differences between the numerous Jewish sects that arose in the centuries before the Common Era resulted in the rise of a class of scholars, scribes, and lawmakers. With the destruction of the Second Temple and beginning of the current diaspora, the Temple priesthood and the rituals of sacrifice needed to be reinterpreted in such a way that the ethical and ritual commandments could be observed in routines of daily life — including eating and household management. The dietary laws concerning milk and meat are part of a great interconnected scheme of 248 positive and 365 negative mitzvahs or commandments. The observance of these commandments by necessity involves every action of human life. A silent, or vocalized, prayer precedes and follows every action during the day, beginning with a prayer upon waking. Before eating a meal — a meal including bread, as opposed to a snack without bread — one washes one's hands ("Fill a large cup with water. Pass the cup to your left hand and pour three times over your right hand. Repeat by pouring on your left hand"). As you dry your hands you recite a blessing ("Blessed are

You, Lord our God, whose mitzvot make our lives holy and who gives us the mitzvah of washing our hands"). A short prayer precedes eating or drinking dairy ("Blessed are You, HaShem, our God, King of the Universe, through whose word everything comes into being") and a longer prayer follows the meal. In some Orthodox communities the hands are washed before reciting this prayer. This prayer thanks Moses in gratitude for the manna the Jews ate during the Exodus from Egypt; thanks Joshua for leading the Jewish people into Israel; thanks David for establishing the capital of Jerusalem and Solomon for building the Temple; and finally thanks God's goodness. These hand-washing rituals are adaptations for the home of the ritual hand-washing that preceded a sacrifice in the Temple. One effect of these prayers is to heighten one's awareness of one's place in history, perhaps to a debilitating degree.

In the next section, we see how a specific ritual prohibition was transformed into a dietary law and then a culinary style.

The Rabbinical Scholar

We read of the gradual rise, over fifteen centuries, of a class of scribes, law-makers, and scholars who began to influence the manner in which the priests conducted their Temple rituals. With the first Jewish-Roman war and destruction of the Second Temple in 70 CE, the practice of animal sacrifice was interrupted and the power base of the hereditary priesthood destroyed. The scholars left Jerusalem and established academies in Yavne and Babylon.

Although priests continued to receive vegetable tithes into the third century, their position as religious authorities had ended. The rabbinical academies established a new form of authority based upon study of the Torah. The rabbis offered healing powers, the resolution of problems through legalistic reasoning and/or magic amulets and spells. They operated in, and around, established customs. No law would be maintained if the majority of the people were unable to observe it. The law could wait until the time was right for its introduction. The rituals of sacrifice had to be reinterpreted in such a way that they could be observed in routines of daily life: eating and household management. Through analysis and observation of the routines of daily life, they saw the possibility of fulfilling the ritual and ethical commandments of the Torah. In time, the commentary on the Torah overwhelmed in volume the original text. The collected teachings of these scholars became the Oral Law — an expansion and clarification of the Written Law of the Torah. The Oral Law covered household and marketplace. The early rabbis had something to say about every human eventuality. The laws, as they applied to the eating and handling of food, were simplified for the benefit of laypeople, but to the scholar, the logic of observance was a skein of the subtle differentiations. There was a reason for and an acceptable manner of dealing with almost any human appetite.

Today, the kosher food industry has created artificial bacon and non-dairy creamer. With the advent of "clean meats" grown in the laboratory from stem cells, we have the possibility of pareve "meats" and actual kosher bacon. Anyone who chooses to do so, can violate, in name, the most basic dietary laws while still observing them.

The contemplation and reasoning of the rabbinical scholar was required to complete the Written Law. YHVH, the male sole proprietor of the Garden, had effectively taken on innumerable partners. The enjoyment of earthly pleasures, through the aroma of burnt offerings, or strolls in his own garden, was now left to the rabbinate. These rabbinical innovations served to de-anthropomorphize YHVH.

One tractate of the Babylonian Talmud, Chulin (Profane Things), deals with the slaughter and eating of meat for non-sacred purposes. The complex culinary laws derived from the sacrificial prohibition of cooking a kid in its mother's milk are considered in exhaustive detail. The complexities of this law may have been no more than a method of consolidating the limited power these early rabbis had within their community. Under the political jurisdiction of other nations, their lawmaking was limited to the home and internal Jewish matters. Each Jewish sect had its own idea of religious observance: Essenes of various stripes, from vegetarian to meat eating, Pharisees of varying orders from Temple priests to Jesus, Ananites and Karaites who rejected the Talmud, the Isunians who had

their own Messiah, the Malikites, and others whose names have been forgotten under the gradual consolidation of Rabbinical Judaism. In the early years of the twentieth century a power struggle over the specifics and certification of ritual slaughter and dietary observance took place among rabbis of New York City — and continues to this day.

That the prohibition against cooking a kid in its mother's milk is mentioned three times in the Torah was not understood as an instance of sloppy editing, but as a directive to the law's three applications: not to cook meat in milk, not to eat a combination of milk and meat, and not to profit from the cooking of meat in milk. The exact meaning of each of these prohibitions is defined and clarified to an obsessive and fascinating degree, what constitutes meat, milk, and "cooking."

The dietary world was divided into three spheres: milk, meat, and neutral foodstuffs — grains, eggs, fruit, vegetables — that can be eaten and mixed with either milk or meat. In Yiddish: fleyshik, milkhik, and pareve.

The milk under consideration is the milk of one of the animals considered ritually "clean" either as understood by Noah or as precisely described in Leviticus 11:1–8 as those animals with split hooves that chew their cud: cows, sheep, goats, camels, and deer. These animals should be milked and the milk bottled under the supervision of an observant Jew, to ensure that it has not been mixed with milk from an unclean animal. With this law, we encounter the ques-

tion of trust. How can one be sure that the supervisor of milking and bottling is being honest?

Poultry does not qualify as a "meat," but, according to early rabbinical advice, should be considered a meat, to avoid possible confusion, and not eaten or combined with milk.

It is the custom of certain observant Jews, in parts of North Africa and Spain, to eat chicken with milk.

Around the question of cooking meat and milk together, a great fence of protective laws was erected. Not only is cooking prohibited, but the mixing in of any quantity over a sixtieth part was prohibited; as was the mixing of utensils, pots and pans, and preparation surfaces. The transmission of taste by steam vapor must also be avoided. These laws are highly nuanced. Should a smooth piece of raw meat fall into a bowl of unheated milk, it could be washed off and eaten, as no mixture has taken place. Should a rough piece of raw meat fall into a bowl of milk, the outside can be removed and the piece still used, but should a piece of cooked meat fall into a bowl of milk, their flavors will mingle, rendering both substances forbidden.

For an udder to be eaten, some rabbis felt it must be cut open and its milk removed by cutting it in its length and breadth and then pressing it against a well. Others maintain that it's not necessary, as only that milk which has passed through the udder of a live animal qualifies as milk under the meat/milk prohibition. The milk found in the udder of a slaughtered cow is not milk under this law. Similarly, an infant is permitted to drink its mother's milk via a nipple of flesh, as the milk in the breast is not yet considered milk, but pareve.

Yaltha, the wife of Rabbi Nahman, explains that God has balanced the deprivations imposed by the Torah with permitted pleasures. The brain of a fish called shibuta has the taste of pork; sexual relations are permitted with a non-Jewish female if she is a captive of war; and an udder roasted on a spit so that the milk would not fall on the meat, but retain the flavor of milk, is permitted. Other, so-called boundary cases involved types of meat. One may not eat or boil a fetus in milk, but one may boil and eat a placenta, skin, veins, bones, and claws with milk. Liquids that have the appearance of milk, but are not milk, are permitted. These liquids include milk water, male milk (the secretion of a male mammary gland), stomach milk (milk found in the stomach of a suckling calf), and, of course, non-dairy creamer.

Mixture can also occur in the human mouth, and so after someone has eaten a meat meal, six hours must pass before eating dairy. The flavor must be

completely gone from the mouth and no particles of meat should remain in the teeth. Meat can be eaten one hour after a dairy meal, or, according to some rabbis, as soon as the mouth is cleaned of cheese particles or milk taste. These waiting periods differ according to local customs and personal choice.

The question of wiping clean the inside of the mouth after a dairy meal is thoroughly considered. It should be wheat bread, not barley bread, as this crumbles and cannot effectively wipe away the cheese residue. And it should be cold bread, as hot bread sticks to the palate. And it should be soft bread, as hard bread is not as effective. The Gamara says that wiping can be done with any food except flour, dates, or vegetables. "In summation: One who ate cheese and wishes to eat meat must wash his hands or check them, eat a solid food other than flour, dates, and vegetables and rinse his mouth with a liquid. There is no specific order in which these acts must be performed; one may first 'wipe' and then 'rinse,' or first 'rinse' and then 'wipe.'"

Hand-washing between meat and milk meals was made a required act: another aid in alerting oneself to the fundamental rules of separation.

The punishment for mixing, eating, or benefiting from mixing milk and meat was lashes. In communities where corporal punishment was difficult to enforce, a monetary fine might be levied instead. The violator is punished, in addition, by knowing that he broke the covenant with YHVH and in so doing jeopardized the well-being of his community. According to Deuteronomy, the violator and his descendants will be cursed in town and field, in their basket and kneading bowl, the issue of their womb, and the productivity of their soil.

And were the Jews the only people to observe this culinary prohibition? Milk/meat prohibitions exist among the Maasai, a semi-nomadic people of Kenya and northern Tanzania. According to a folk belief, if the milk were to touch flesh the udders of the cows would become diseased and no longer give milk, and so they have separate containers for each substance. They furthermore do not permit the mixing of milk and meat in a person's stomach. Blood, from a live animal, however, may be mixed with milk and consumed. To them, both blood and milk represent life. The rarity of the milk/meat taboo led to speculation that the Maasai had been in contact with the Mosaic laws in the distant past.

Jewish dietary laws in North Africa and Spain developed independently. Fowl and milk can be eaten together, and waiting periods between meat and milk are generally shorter.

The Effects of the Mosaic Laws Are Widespread

The Muslim avoidance of blood, carrion, and food that had been offered to idols stems from the Mosaic laws. Muslims can, however, eat milk and meat combinations. The Jews, they say, were given the more stringent rules as punishment for distorting the Torah.

Seventh-day Adventists and the Molokans (a sect of sixteenth-century dissenting Russian Orthodox peasants) avoid shellfish and pork and encourage a vegetarian diet.

Christ's teaching that "there is nothing from without the man that going into him can defile him: but the things which proceed out of the man are those that defile the man" evolved as a rejection of the Mosaic dietary laws.

No explanation of the milk/meat dietary rules is given in the Talmud. These prohibitions fall within the category of Chukim — laws for which no explanation is available to the human mind. Yet, throughout time, philosophers have attempted to offer rational explanations.

Philo, an Alexandrian Jewish philosopher (20 BCE–50 CE), explains it as a form of God's compassion in line with prohibitions such as sacrificing an animal during the first seven days of its life, sacrificing an animal and its young on the same day, and taking a young bird from its nest without first chasing away the mother bird. "The person who boils the flesh of lambs or kids or any other young animal in its mother's milk, shows himself cruelly brutal in character and gelded of compassion." The limited and proscribed nature of these rules calls into question the idea of compassion. Why is it less cruel to cook a kid with the flesh of its father? Or chicken fat?

Moses Maimonides (1135–1204) explained that prohibited foods were unhealthy or associated with filth. Also, the milk/meat prohibition originated in a desire to avoid the practices of idol-worshipping cults.

Abraham ben Meir ibn Ezra, twelfth-century philosopher/poet, attributes the law to culinary practicality: Certain meats become tender when cooked in milk. The meats eaten by the Israelites were fatty enough to supply their own moisture. Certain meats eaten by non-Jews were cooked in milk to make them tender. He also points out that meat and milk are difficult to digest together.

Early Christian expositors attributed the law to the desire to avoid wiping out a race of animals by killing both mother and child. Augustine saw the young animal as Christ and the seething as the passion and tribulation surrounding the fact that the infant Christ would not be killed by the Jews when Herod sought him.

Although other religious sects have adopted some portion of the Mosaic laws of diet, only the early rabbinate extrapolated these fragmentary laws into a complex system of household management and culinary practice that affects every aspect of one's daily life. The degree of sensitivity to the countless possibilities of defilement reminded modern psychologists of the manifestations of obsessive-compulsive behavior. The web of avoidance knows no bounds, the danger of contamination lurks in every routine action — a psychiatric disease justified as religious law.

The mystery of two perfectly acceptable foodstuffs, milk and meat, becoming a forbidden substance when combined, serves as an object lesson in the effects of spatial proximity and chemical interaction. The prohibitions against yoking two types of animals together, sowing diverse seeds, and mixing wool and flax are examples of YHVH's obsessive-compulsive need to keep diverse things separate. Qualities can only be understood in relation to their surroundings. The prohibition linked the act of eating with ethical behavior. The reasoning and subtlety of thought required to see through this one prohibition in the countless possibilities of eating served as a model for analyzing behavior in the physical world. To the modern intellectual Jew, the dietary law is of value as a pure exercise of human discrimination and choice — the particulars of the choice are a matter of "cultural tradition." For non-observant Jews it can be explained as an act of culinary choice.

The segregation of milk- and meat-eating utensils and kitchenware is equally complicated. To simplify the housewife's life, separate dishes, eating utensils, and today entire kitchens are recommended. The detailed questions of contamination are thus avoided. In Sholem Aleichem's story "The Pot," a woman visits her rabbi with a question. As a preface to her question, she presents her life story. The question, we learn on the last page of the story, has to do with the possibility of her only fleyshik pot being made unfit for use as her boarder spilled a pot with a dairy dish — buckwheat with milk — in the oven. The dietary transgression is the result of a lifelong web of tragic circumstances: early widowhood, poverty, lack of food, and illness. The laughs are all based upon a tragic situation. The rabbi, grasping the futility of his ruling upon the minutiae of a ritual in the context of a lifelong tragedy, succumbs to a fit of despair. The reader is left with a sense of how dietary laws played out in real life — the tip of a precariously balanced world of poverty, anger, fear, and hunger.

Eating Out

The observance of dietary laws in the home is left largely to women: wives, mothers, and daughters. In public eating places, the observance of these laws is in the hands of businessmen, their families, and employees. The laws are internalized by the community and, except for accidents or cases of deception, can be followed with some degree of ease by each individual. A visit to a glatt-kosher pizzeria in Borough Park will reveal that the eating and the enjoyment

of food is not necessarily diminished, just circumscribed. The operation of a non-kosher restaurant several blocks away is equally circumscribed by health-department laws and cultural taboos against cannibalism and other culinary possibilities.

Within the Council of the Four Lands, that vast federation of Jewish self-government in Poland and Lithuania, there was a steady decline in the power of the rabbinate from the sixteenth to the eighteenth centuries. In what became the largest Jewish community in the world, political power was in the hands of the monarchy and the elites of the Jewish lay community. Rabbis were left to deal with such questions of Halakhic law as contaminated cookware.

The moment an observant Jew leaves his home and community, problems can arise surrounding the simple act of eating. Fortunately, the problems of the traveler are considered in the Talmud.

The unstinting hospitality of Abraham was only possible in the desert of the ancient world. In towns and on trade routes of the Middle East, the resources of individuals would be overtaxed by the volume of travelers. Providing a place to sleep and eat became a business. Since, by choice or historical necessity, exile and travel were defining aspects of Jewish life, somewhere a Jew was always eating out.

For a traveler in the ancient world to observe the dietary laws outlined in the Talmud was a matter of selection and abstinence. They could subsist on an antediluvian diet: the entire range of vegetables and fruits. Eggs, clabbered milk, hard cheese, and dried meats, derived from ritually "clean" animals, could be carried with them. The personal procurement of meat and fish was dependent upon an individual's knowledge and proficiency in the techniques of ritually correct slaughter. Although an observant community relies upon a trained specialist, the shoykhet, anyone who knows what they're doing can perform the task. We read of early Jewish travelers subsisting on such portable food, sometimes in painfully small quantities, until they came upon a community of Jews in which an observant kitchen could be found. The trade routes of the ancient world were dotted by oases and caravansaries — latter-day versions of the Garden in Eden — a walled enclosure offering water and a place to rest and escape the heat of day. Travel in the warmer climates was confined to the night.

Should a traveling Jew, without family or friends, arrive in a strange town, the well-to-do Jews would vie for the opportunity to invite him into their home to enjoy a meal prepared in accordance with dietary laws and spend the night — a holdover of Abrahamic hospitality in service of YHVH. The traveler would not be forced to patronize a public eating place even if one existed.

It was for the guest to determine whether his host's kitchen and home are up to his standards of observance. If the blankets on his bed are made of wool sewn with linen thread they are in violation of the law of sha'atnez (Lev. 19:19, Deut. 22:11). Who's been in charge of the preparation of foodstuffs? Have the leafy vegetables been thoroughly examined for insects, or has this job been left to careless servants or old women with poor eyesight? Who's in charge of drawing the water from the well? Have their hands been washed before performing this duty? If not, everything the water touches will be defiled: the foodstuffs, the cooking vessels, the utensils. Has the meat been prepared in accordance with the rules of Kashruth? The possibilities of violations are countless. Are the milkhik pots and pans kept separate from the fleyshik ones?

Once the invitation to have a meal in the home of another observant and knowledgeable Jew is accepted, one should eat it and not question the degree of care with which the laws were followed. Here, we see how travel might promote a degree of laxity that might lead to further disregard for ritual observance.

Seventeenth-Century Vegetarian Renaissance

In their migrations and travels, the Jews were subject to the anti- or philo-Semitic fantasies developed in the larger Christian culture. These fantasies were based upon a combination of research into ancient texts and the promulgation of legends that arose from limited observations of living Jews.

In England, the Edict of Expulsion issued by King Edward I in 1290 forced virtually all of the island's two to three thousand Jews to emigrate to the Continent. In the popular imagination of English Christians over the next 370 years, an entire culture was built upon historical imaginings concerning the various qualities of Old Testament Jews and their unwitting role in fulfilling a New Testament prophecy.

In 1655, Menasseh ben Israel, a Portuguese rabbi, diplomat, and printer working in Amsterdam, attended a conference in England to discuss the future of Jews in that country. His recently publicized discovery of a lost tribe of Jews living in South America excited the Millenarian Christians of England, who believed that the Messiah would return only when Jews were present in every country of the world. This theological argument neatly bolstered Oliver Cromwell's desire that the wealthy Jews of Amsterdam relocate their trading base from Holland to England. The Edict was lifted in 1659.

The project of establishing a New Jerusalem or prelapsarian civilization in seventeenth-century England obsessed a portion of the Christian population.

The radical Puritans of seventeenth-century England — the Diggers, Shakers, Ranters, and Quakers — reasoned that the first step in this project was to adopt the imagined

Menasseh ben Israel at the Herring Market

An eighteenth-century *English Jew* encounters two *philo-Semites* of the *Adamite persuasion*

diet and lifestyle of the Jews before the flood: abstinence from meat and alcohol, the adoption of communalism, egalitarian politics, pacifism, and a return to agrarian labors. Fealty to the king was seen as a form of idolatry.

Their repugnance toward bloodletting was not just a reaction to the violence of the Civil War, but, they argued, in accord with the Jewish prohibition on blood eating.

In 1652, Roger Crab, a haberdasher and herbal doctor, gave up his worldly possessions, lived in a rude hermitage on homegrown vegetables (having renounced butter and cheese), and through a folk-medicine practice offered others a way to spiritual enlightenment. According to him, God had permitted meat eating to Noah after the flood because vegetable life of the earth had been destroyed — it was meant as a temporary solution until the plant life was regenerated.

Dr. John Pordage (1607–81), also known as "Father Abraham," was the founder of the Philadelphians, a pantheistic society that recommended fasting as a way to achieve communion with angels.

Dr. John Pordage

[This history is detailed in Tristram Stuart's *Bloodless Revolution: Radical Vegetarianism and the Discovery of India* (Harper Press, 2006).]

The philo-Semitic, or Judaist, impulse among these radical Puritans was not directed to the recently returned Jews of England. The contemporary Jews were distant and degenerated descendants of the tribe of Judah. The Second Coming of Christ could be hastened by either uniting the dispersed tribes of

Israel, converting the Jews, or by arranging their presence in all countries of the world.

John Robins (fl. 1650–52), an English Ranter and self-proclaimed reincarnation of Adam, proposed parting the waters of the English Channel and leading his lost tribe of 144,000 people to the Holy Land. In preparation for the revival of ancient Jerusalem in England, some studied Hebrew and had themselves circumcised, while others adopted the nudism of Adam and Eve.

For the radical Puritan sects, a vegetarian diet was meant to be a protest against the luxury and violence of the Royalists during the Civil Wars. Animal slaughter was an outgrowth of warfare; alcoholic beverages a spur to intemperate behavior. The Church of England maintained that the dispensations of the New Testament made the dietary taboos of the Jews invalid. To the dissenters, a dietary revolution was needed, if not in England then in the New World.

Reexamined accounts of Brahmin court life in India by Alexander the

SARASWATI RIVER

PYTHAGORAS

Great, Marco Polo, and Vasco da Gama confirmed the existence of an alternative dietary world in glowing terms. The Brahmins, a Hindu priest class, lived in harmony with nature, on milk, fruit, and bread, and were unaware of Christianity. They valued animal life as equal to human life — not just to be used by man. A new sense of cultural and species relativity arose among European thinkers.

Isaac Newton (1642–1727) maintained that Christianity might remove the Mosaic food taboos, but the taboo against eating blood was of Noahic law and therefore universal and to be upheld for all time. He theorized that the Brahmins were the descendants of Abraham and his second wife, who were sent off to live in the East. Pythagoras had traveled in the East and based his philosophy upon the learnings of the Brahmins. When he returned to Greece he brought with him a "secularized version of Noah's original religion" stripped of literal belief in reincarnation, along with a heliocentric system of astronomy, which Galileo (and Newton) simply recovered. Adam and Eve's partaking of the date was an allegory for meat eating, which brought upon man disease and early death.

Orientalist Sir William Jones (1746–94) believed that the similarities between Indian, Greek, and Hebrew cultures were the result of their arising from a common source — a settlement of Noah and his three sons in Iran. The descendants of Ham spread these ideas of the ur-religion through India, Italy, and Greece. The similarity of episodes in the Hindu scriptures to the Bible — the flood, the tower of Babel, etc. — could thus be explained.

Baron Franciscus Mercurius van Helmont (1614–98), Flemish chemist, studied the process of reincarnation in the kabbalist texts of Solomon Luria and Chaim Vital. He struggled to incorporate reincarnation into Christian theology and escape the "mental tyranny of hell." He maintained that the Brahmins learned of gilgul (the Hebrew word for reincarnation) from the Jews and not the other way around.

The direction of influence was hotly debated: Did Pythagoras learn from the Brahmins or teach them these ideas? Did the ancient Jews bring these ideas to India and Greece or did those ancient pagan philosophers inherit their

Physiocrats in a chestnut orchard

doctrines from Moses? In either case, Christians, Jews, and Brahmins at one time all followed the one true Religion. Over time, the Christians and Jews had corrupted these teachings, leaving only the Brahmins still in touch with this ancient philosophy and living in a culture of the Golden Age.

And this living proof of the benefits of a prelapsarian diet agreed with the most advanced scientific studies of nutrition. The longevity of Biblical figures might be attributed to their meat-free diet. With the Noahic dispensation to eat meat, the life span was reduced to seventy years. The human digestive system and human teeth might not be suited to meat eating. Does man not shrink from eating raw meat? Man was not physically equipped to hunt and kill other animals. Descartes (1596–1650), Francis Bacon (1561–1626), and Pierre Gassendi (1592–1655) all wrote treatises arguing that man was intended to live on vegetables.

The tradition of radical vegetarianism that arose during the English Civil War continued through revolutionary France of the 1790s. Diet could be used to cleanse the corruption and evils of modern life. Eating became a political activity.

Conversions to Hindu religion and vegetarianism occurred within the upper classes of England and France in the eighteenth century. Abraham Hyacinthe Anquetil-Duperron (1731–1805), the first French scholar of Indian culture, traveled to India, became a disciple of the sacred laws of the Hindus, and then returned to France with a collection of Oriental manuscripts to live in voluntary poverty.

Voltaire used the example of Indian vegetarianism to critique the cruelty of European culture and Christianity. "The Indian books announce only peace and gentleness; they forbid the killing of animals: the Hebrew books speak only of killing, of the massacre of men and beasts; everything is slaughtered in the name of the Lord; it is quite another order of things." His writings established the connections between radical liberal thought and vegetarianism. The rise in Indophilia helped popularize the simple vegetarian diet proposed by Jean-Jacques Rousseau.

The principles of universal sympathy encouraged the emancipation of slaves and the idea of political rights for all men and women. It was Jewish and Christian anthropocentric thought, with its concepts of sacrifice and eternal punishment, that suppressed the possibility of universal sympathy and human perfection without the agent of a God.

As most people could not afford to eat meat, vegetarianism was also an act of solidarity with the working poor. Enclosing land for animal grazing deprived the peasantry of their source of vegetables and grains. The French Physiocrats attempted to solve the food shortages before the Revolution by introducing chestnuts, a staple of the ancient Gauls, into the contemporary diet. All through the eighteenth century, Spartan simplicity of life and food was in vogue.

Meat eaters among the revolutionaries explained that active and contemplative modes of life required differing diets and so they sometimes indulged in flesh. This fact, according to Percy Bysshe Shelley (1792–1822), was the cause of the Revolution's failure — people became ferocious beasts. Meat eating "turned man into the tyrant of the world and introduced inequality into both natural ecologies and human society." A vegetarian diet could reverse this behavior. Charles Pigott's satirical *Political Dictionary Explaining the True Meaning of Words* of 1795 defined Adam as "a true Sans Culottes, and the first revolutionist."

It was argued that eating a vegetable diet made men weak, lazy, and effeminate. Meat eating produced courage, energy, and vitality. The Yiddish expression, "Er blaybt oyf der milkhiker bank" (He remains on the dairy bench or counter) reflects someone being left behind, for whatever reason, while the meat eaters take an active part in worldly affairs. During the Napoleonic Wars, the French nicknamed the British troops "les rosbifs." Beef eating as a national trait was personified by the character of John Bull — vegetarianism was a near-traitorous pursuit.

Erasmus Darwin (1731–1802) claimed that humans were omnivorous, that vegetable diets made people feeble, but the inefficiency of beef production should be curtailed. The amount of food offered by a bullock is small in comparison to the vegetable matter he consumes.

Sir William Lawrence (1783–1867), the radical materialist and president of the Royal College of Surgeons, insisted that "vegetarianism was inherently a primitivist attack on civilization and society." He ridiculed the idea of a Golden Age in which "man was as innocent as the dove . . . and always in peace both with himself and other animals." Vegetarianism was based on a misunderstanding of the workings of nature. Mass death was necessary for producing and sustaining the greatest possible diversity of flora and fauna. Mass death was responsible for the variety of life on earth. Charles Darwin's (1809–82) realization that natural selection was the driving force of evolution came after reading Thomas Robert Malthus's theory of mass death in 1838. The emphasis upon competition as a driving force in evolutionary processes led to the acceptance of competition among humans as being natural and inevitable. As Karl Marx pointed out, under capitalism competition leads to monopolies of large capital. "The necessary result of this competition is a general deterioration of commodities, adulteration, fake production and universal poisoning, evident in large towns" [Karl Marx, *The Competition Among the Capitalists* (1844)].

Asceticism and the Jew

A well-fed and inquisitive eighteenth-century Jew might want to get involved in the intellectual excitement of this revolution in eating. The majority of poor people, Jews, Christians, and Muslims, spent their days struggling to have anything to eat. For the Jews of Eastern Europe, the question was not only about killing animals, but killing tavernkeepers. In response to the frequent murders of Jewish tavernkeepers and commercial travelers in Romania, the victims were given the status of martyr

in the religious struggle to provide "kosher" food for their fellow Jews. The sons of these murdered tavernkeepers were called to the Torah as "Ben ha-Kedoshim" or Son of the Saints.

A solution arrived at in the monasteries of Europe was a diet designed to regulate the human passion for food. Chapter 39 of the Holy Rule of Saint Benedict of Nursia (c. 480–547) prescribed simple dining rules: "Making allowance for the infirmities of different persons, we believe that for the daily meal, both at the sixth and the ninth hour, two kinds of cooked food are sufficient at all meals; so that he who perchance cannot eat of one, may make his meal of the other. Let two kinds of cooked food, therefore, be sufficient for all the brethren. And if there be fruit or fresh vegetables, a third may be added. Let a pound of bread be sufficient for the day, whether there be only one meal or both dinner and supper. If they are to eat supper, let a third part of the pound be reserved by the Cellarer [the house steward] and be given at supper.

"If, however, the work hath been especially hard, it is left to the discretion and power of the Abbot to add something, if he think fit, barring above all things every excess, that a monk be not overtaken by indigestion. For nothing is so contrary to Christians as excess, as our Lord saith: 'See that your hearts be not overcharged with surfeiting' (Luke 21:34). But let all except the very weak and the sick abstain altogether from eating the flesh of four-footed animals."

These meatless meals were taken in the Refectory, a room with a long table at which the monks ate communally. Conversation was limited during meals. Meat eating took place in the Infirmary, a separate structure reserved for the sick. It was located outside of the cloister, sometimes divided into private rooms and often equipped with its own kitchen.

Asceticism practiced outside of the monastery led to more than half the days on the Russian Orthodox calendar being marked as fasts of some kind. Those who did not aspire to these heights of spiritual purity turned with great energy and invention to the preparation and endless combinations of foodstuffs that characterize the Christian European culinary traditions.

During Lent — those six weeks leading up to Easter Sunday, in which the believer prepares himself through prayer and forms of self-denial to commemorate the death, burial, and resurrection of Jesus Christ — this self-denial took the form of fasts (one day, one meal, etc.) and prohibitions of certain foodstuffs: All meat and dairy during the Middle Ages, to just meat in recent years. On Ash Wednesday and Good Friday, both fasting and no meat; on other Fridays just abstinence from meat. A menu of pancakes, noodles, and cheese and other dairy dishes evolved by the adherents to Roman Catholicism.

The tradition of eating dairy dishes on Shavuot is commemorative, not an act of self-denial. When the ancient Israelites returned to their camp after receiving the Torah with its laws concerning ritual slaughter and Kashruth, they could no longer eat the meat they had prepared, and so, instead of preparing new meat in newly kashered pots and dishes, they chose to eat a simple dairy meal. Dairy foods, symbolizing modesty or humility, also seemed to be the appropriate cuisine to follow the receipt of the Torah. Other reasons for eating dairy on Shavuot include King Solomon's reference to the Torah being like milk and honey lying under the tongue, and numerological connections between cheese and the giving of the Torah.

As for the Yom Kippur fast, great attention is paid to the meal preceding the fast and the meal that breaks the fast, so as to minimize the suffering. The other five fast days in the Jewish calendar are no longer widely observed.

The Talmudic rules for dining maintained a middle path: reconciling the

wide range of human appetites through a system of food handling that could be implemented by every household. Operating under, and around, these rules, a cook had a wide scope for culinary invention.

The Ba'al Shem Tov (c.1700–1760), founder of the Hasidic movement, opposed asceticism of all kinds. "Since every act in life is a manifestation of God, and must perforce be divine, it is man's duty so to live that the things called earthly may also become noble and pure, that is, divine" [*Jewish Encyclopedia*]. At one point, he operated a tavern and enjoyed discourse with peasants and drinkers.

Rabbi Abraham Isaac Kook (1865–1935), who argued that Talmudic dietary law was a form of modified vegetarianism, recommended that one partake of a piece of meat occasionally, so as to dampen the dehumanizing effect of asceticism. Jews can express their misanthropy within the world through complaint and argumentation, not mortification of the flesh.

Ironically, the very thing that anti-Semites cited as a physical confirmation of their disgust — the smell of Jews and their food — became for Jews a way of describing that ineffable, yet ultimate, distinguishing quality of their culture — a yiddisher tam — a Jewish flavor, or taste.

Travel and Food

Trade, and the travel involved, spurred the growth of towns and cities and, in turn, the development of inns offering a place to sleep and eat. At a common table (the table d'hôte, or host's table), a set meal was served at a fixed time to the guests of the inn.

At some point in the early nineteenth century, many of the inns in the Pale of Settlement were operated by Jews. This occupation established the Jew as a middleman between the peasantry and landowners. Like the occupation of banking, the Jewish tavern became a locus of anti-Semitic feeling. The Jew was accused of encouraging drunkenness among the peasantry by selling alcoholic drinks on credit. Since it was known as the place where stories were exchanged and current events transmitted, the uneducated peasants saw the Jewish owner as part of an international web of knowledge and influence. After a few drinks, they fantasized that the taverns were literally interconnected by subterranean passageways.

Sholem Asch describes a nineteenth-century Jewish tavern as being open for business seven days a week. The Sabbath was observed in the owner's living quarters, but in public rooms business went on as usual.

Among the laws on handling foodstuffs for travel we read: "A person may wrap meat and cheese in one cloth, as long as they do not touch one another. . . . It is permitted for two strangers to share a table in an inn, one eating meat, the other dairy. The chance of their sharing one another's food is unlikely. Two companions sharing a table cannot partake of dairy and meat. Among companions, the accidental sharing of food may occur."

The division of a table between milk and meat stuffs is matter-of-factly mentioned in the autobiography of I. L. Peretz. In the year 1870, at the age of eighteen, Peretz was coming home from an arranged marriage ceremony. The wagon filled with his family and new bride stops in the rain at a Gentile inn. They carried their food with them but wanted a hot tea. His aunt is worried about drinking water boiled with unclean utensils. His uncle examines the kitchen and approves of the samovar. They begin to unpack an assortment of meat and milk stuffs and Peretz's mother shouts: "Leave half the table for dairy."

Here, among the members of family, meat and milk stuffs are eaten without mixture. The table may have been physically divided by a tablecloth, or a loaf of bread serving as the boundary line.

The Talmudic ruling is stretched as members of the same family partake of a mixed meal on a single table. A hundred years later, in a restaurant in Berkeley, California, a restaurant is arranged in which half the room eats milk and the other half meat. According to Talmudic law, there is no need for a public eating place devoted to one or the other category of food.

The floor of a tavern in nineteenth-century Poland is similarly divided with chalk marks into "private" sleeping quarters. Once the physical division is established, the strength of the barrier is unimportant. It's recommended in the Talmud that breads made with dairy products should be given an identifiable form, so as not to be confused with pareve bread made with vegetable shortening. In Catskill Mountain resorts, dairy dishes came from the kitchen identified with plastic covers as opposed to the metal covers placed over meat dishes, to keep them warm.

The difficulty arises when Jews have to eat with non-Jews. For non-Jews there is no problem other than social and cultural differences of taste.

The Talmud deals with the question of having non-Jews prepare food according to the dietary laws. Accidental mixtures are judged as somewhat less stringent — one-sixtieth part or the transmission of a discernible flavor — and in that case a Gentile is required to make the taste test. The danger of having a non-Jew prepare one's food is that you will become too familiar with them and possibly marry them. To live in compliance with dietary law, it is preferable to eat in one's own home. Eating in taverns or hotel dining rooms in which the obser-

vance of Kashruth, if it is observed at all, is dependent upon employees and so open to transgressions.

It has been observed that dietary laws have, over history, been one of the major factors in Jewish cultural cohesion. Before the modern age of travel, food, language, and clothing were the most visible declarations of belonging to a sect or clan. To deviate from the norm was to cause a serious rupture in the worldview of the clan.

The experience of moving away from one's mother's cooking gives us a sense of the power of taste within a clan or sect. In a close relative's cooking, there was an animal sense of familiarity, but the first meal eaten in the stranger's kitchen was filled with sickeningly strange flavors — the very substance of the forks and plates seemed to impart a powerful flavor to the food. Ten minutes into the meal, this flavor became palatable and possibly agreeable. It might form the basis of a new, enlightened sense of the possibilities of eating, or, for some unfathomable psychological reason, remain forever wrong. To move on to the cuisines of other nations involves a serious reappraisal of one's taste. Some people can make this leap; some, otherwise highly cultured individuals, remain fixated to the hamburgers and french fries of their youth. This process can explain how Jews came to adopt and adapt the cuisines of their host nations.

In time, it is possible that a fuller picture of Jewish-owned-and-operated eating places in Eastern Europe will be possible. The search through Yizkor books, memoirs, newspapers, and obscure journals has been made easier through digitalization. The visual reconstruction of daily life in the shtetlach of Eastern Europe is being made by picture-postcard and photograph collectors. Otherwise, the texture of everyday life was recorded by chance and to a limited degree. In the case of dairy eating places, scant historical records exist; mentions in fictional accounts of the Old World are few.

The impulse to return to the first foods of infancy was intertwined with a desire to experience a sense of the world in its infancy. That history of attempts to re-create a model of paradise on earth is well documented.

The Pastoral Impulse

To understand the European concept of the pastoral and its relation to dairy culture, a brief, and broadly sketched, history of garden design is here necessary.

During the second and third centuries, we hear of a strange social phenomenon: thousands of young men retreat from the civilization of the Roman Empire to live in the Nitrian Desert of Egypt. Others sought isolation in the countryside outside of Rome and other urban centers. Some were professed Christians fleeing persecution, others were simply fleeing their fellow man.

Many came from wealthy families and tried to outdo one another in the harshness of their self-induced deprivations. They felt the devil tortured them by boredom, laziness, and lascivious thoughts. Macarius of Egypt fled a paternity charge. Saint Pishoy tied his hair and hands to the ceiling of his cell to stay awake for his night prayers. Saint Onuphrius wandered in the desert for seventy years, enduring thirst and hunger. Anthony the Great went so far as to close himself in a vacant tomb and depended upon the local people to feed him. Other young men formed small communities built around prayer and, in emula-

tion of the first man, the cultivation of small walled gardens.

In the sixth century, Benedict of Nursia, the son of a wealthy Umbrian nobleman, who fled the licentious life of the city, stumbled upon a nearby community of misanthropic anchorites. The monasteries he came to establish were built upon the ruins of Roman villas. The wealthy Romans had fled the heat and social pressures of the city to lead an idealized rustic life of leisure and erotic freedom. The ruins of their colonnaded peristyles were planted as gardens by the monks. The peristyle was a Roman adaptation of the walled Persian garden introduced in 60 BCE by the great general and legendary big eater Lucius Licinius Lucullus. As these Benedictine and other monastic orders spread through Europe and North Africa, the walled garden followed.

The images of the Garden of Eden, painted and drawn by these monks, retained the original Persian design. The surrounding wall and entranceway were carefully delineated. Details of the local flora and fauna were used to flesh out the invented Oriental landscape.

The local nobility modeled their gardens after this form of paradise garden. The geometrical division of the plot allowed for a systematic arrangement of nature, provided protection from theft and intrusion, and allowed one to enjoy a scale-model of paradise on earth.

In the fourteenth century, a renewed interest in ancient Greek and Roman culture led certain Italian painters and philosophers to conflate the Garden of Eden story with the Greek myth of the Golden Age of Man — the earth in its unspoiled infancy.

The final Hellenizing, and subsequent Christianizing, of the Garden of Eden story was put into motion by Giovanni Pico della Mirandola (1463–94), a philosophy student who, while recuperating in Perugia from physical injuries suffered at the hands of a jealous husband, came, by chance, across a collection of ancient Chaldean books of philosophy and magic. In Perugia, he was also "introduced" to the Kabbalah. He studied the Hebrew language and texts with the help of conversos and other Jews who had settled in the Italian Peninsula. His syncretic approach, the examination of a theological belief from different points of view, would lead, he thought, to the revelation of a universal religion. Marsilio Ficino (1433–99), a vegetarian philosopher/astrologer of the Florentine Academy, searched for a single ancient theological tradition linking the teachings of the Egyptians, Hebrews, and Greeks. Jewish learning became part of European culture.

Their imagery was based upon Arcadia, a remote mountainous region of Greece where man was reputed to still live in harmony with nature. The visual details were gathered from a study of the local landscape. This earthly paradise was inhabited by shepherds whose children were suckled by willing goats. Animal milk as a form of human nourishment became central to the idea of an

אוֹדֶה

Ficino studying Hebrew grammar

earthly paradise — thus dairy eating entered the myth. The garden wall disappears, and the geometric plots of soil are subsumed by the surrounding Italian or Northern German landscape.

Under the influence of Theocritus, Virgil, Petrarch, and Garcilaso de la Vega the pastoral dream was kept alive in France and England. The rustic setting of Philip Sidney's (1554–86) *Arcadia* allowed him to explore the erotic love through rural decor, costume changes, etc. In *The Shepheardes' Calender* (1579) of Edmund Spenser, the pastoral drama is used to denounce the extravagance of both the Anglican Church and Rome and praise the rustic life. This mixture of didactic and erotic poetry remained popular for over a hundred years. They wrote of milkmaids with Greek names whose diction was unlike that of any living milkmaid. The action took place in a countryside that was a composite of England and Arcadia.

The Jews became mythologized. In England from 1290 to 1657 they were not present but seen in a mythological light as representatives of the ancient world who lived in harmony with nature, until their rejection of Christ cursed them to wandering the earth and engage in usury. The few Jews they saw epitomized man's removal from the pastoral dream, living in urban squalor and operating as an unproductive middleman in business and trade.

The production of printed versions of the Hebrew texts — the Shulhan Arukh and the Mappah, among others — in Venice in 1565 diminished the influence and development of local Jewish traditions and local commentaries

by living rabbis. The Christian Hebraists who had access to these books professed to have a knowledge of Jewish thought surpassing that of the living Jews. The Zohar and other esoteric kabbalistic texts — divine secrets not meant for wide dissemination — were first printed and edited by Christian Hebraists in Mantua and Cremona. It has been noted that the interest of these scholars in Jewish books did not nec-essarily extend to contemporary living Jews. The estab-lishment of Jewish ghettos throughout Italy was standard policy by the six-teenth century.

The emphasis of the Garden of Eden story was shifted from a partic-ular mistake to the tragic and inevitable sense of loss caused by the advent of civilization and original sin. By comparison, the unpleasant incident that occurred one evening in a private Persian pleasure garden was hardly worth discussing. The Jews, living in the midst of the European traditions of picture making, were left to illustrate and contemplate a text-based version of the Torah and their own pastoral tradition, but on a physical and sensual level, it could not compete with the crypto-pagan artists working in the employ of the Church. Through their life in the diaspora, Jews had to come to their own terms with the allure of the physical world or join the Christian majority.

The history of Christian Europe forcing Jews into a largely urban life based on banking and trade has been well documented. When Catherine the Great imported foreign groups to introduce dairy farming into Russia, Jews were the one group excluded. The economic reality of the pastoral life in much of Europe involved a Christian upper class using Jews as middlemen to deal with Christian or pagan peasants.

The impulse to strip these stories and paintings of Christian dogma is the history of the Enlightenment in Europe. Thomas Hobbes's view of life in a state of nature as "solitary, poor, nasty, brutish, and short," argued for mutual contracts between society and government. The invention of the microscope in 1595 allowed for a rational explanation of the unseen forces of nature. A view of the world in a drop of water beggared the idea of the Garden of Eden as a scale model of a celestial paradise. The discovery of the New World seemed to offer Europeans a chance to begin history again.

The formal monastic garden seemed artificial, lacked a sense of grandeur, and was linked to the Roman Church. The model for English landscape gardeners of the early eighteenth century was the Roman landscape as seen in the painting of Claude Lorrain and Nicolas Poussin. The idea of having a bit of untamed nature in one's own backyard was irresistible.

The archaeological researches of Poussin and his Roman circle were in-

"The Nurture of Jupiter," after Poussin c. 1637

Adam and Eve
in an Arcadian
landscape
after Poussin

fused with a study of the local landscape. Over time and space, these images devolved into the clichéd toy theater sets of English pastoral drama — the adoption of secondhand literary and visual conventions instead of observation from nature. The so-called English garden style of Charles Bridgeman, Lancelot Brown, and Thomas Whately spread throughout Europe.

A number of public pleasure gardens opened in London to capitalize on this taste for the picturesque Italian garden. On a modest plot of land, the plausible replica of the garden of an Italian villa was erected — complete with ruined statuary, grottoes, fountains, shady walks, and rustic refreshment halls serving tea, bread and butter, syllabubs (a cold wine-and-frothy-cream concoction dating from the sixteenth century), ice creams, and other bucolic dishes. Each May Day, at the London Spa (Rosoman and Exmouth Streets) milkmaids and their swains danced to the accompaniment of a fiddler. Sadler's Wells, a tearoom and medicinal spa, offered cakes, milk, custards, stewed prunes, and performances by "Jew" Davis, a character actor and singer known as the best stage Jew. At the Adam and Eve Garden at Tottenham Court Road in 1718, cows were kept expressly for the making of syllabubs. The Shepherd and Shepherdess Ale-house and

Garden on the City Road was frequented by invalids for the pure air of its neighborhood and its frumenty (a pudding of cracked wheat, cow's milk, eggs, and sultanas). The Marylebone Gardens in 1751 was renowned for its cheesecakes made by the owner's daughter, Miss Trusler. In addition to its medicinal waters, Pancras Wells in 1769 was described as a "genteel and rural tea garden that served hot loaves, syllabubs and milk from the cow." The White Conduit House and Gardens offered milk directly from cows who were guaranteed to "eat no grains." The fashionable and sumptuous Ranelagh Gardens in Chelsea, where the eight-year-old Mozart performed in 1764, was called "the Bread and Butter Manufactory." A French visitor described the "bad music and bread and butter" as the most insipid form of amusement that he could imagine.

The Florida Gardens in Brompton, owned by a German florist, Mr. R. Hiem (or Haym), featured cherries, strawberries, and flowers that visitors could gather "fresh every hour in the day." A specialty of the refreshment room was Bern Veckley, described as "an elegant succedaneum [substitute] for bread and butter ate by the Noblesse of Switzerland."

From 1752 to 1756, the Jew Naphthali Hart (aka Nathan Hart) was the proprietor of Marble Hall on the Thames at the southern abutment of Vauxhall Bridge, where he taught music and dancing in the season. In the winter, he conducted Hart's Academy at Essex Street, Strand, where "grown gentlemen are taught to dance a minuet and country dances in the modern taste, and in

a short time. Likewise gentlemen are taught to play on any instrument, the use of the small Sword and Spedroon. At the same place is taught musick, fencing, French, Italian, Spanish, Portuguese, High German, Low Dutch, navigation, or any other part of the Mathematicks. A sprightly youth is wanted as an apprentice." Naphthali went on to have a career, in partnership with Duncan Urquhart, as a silversmith. In 1807–8, he acted as the treasurer of the Hambro Synagogue, and later joined the Western Synagogue. He died a bachelor in 1828.

In a history of London's pleasure gardens, only one, the Jews' Spring Garden in Stepney, is mentioned as being frequented by wealthy Jews who lived in the neighborhood of Goodman's Fields. An adjoining tavern was run by Dove Rayner, a man of "agreeable mirth and good humor" who was also a prosperous clockmaker. He died in 1743.

The pastoral tradition in literature was given an injection of new blood by the publication of Daniel Defoe's *Robinson Crusoe* in 1719. Here was the story of a contemporary man forced, by accident, to confront the basics of life in a natural world. The novel is credited with having inspired Rousseau to reconsider human education and the social contract.

Jean-Jacques Rousseau, a native of Geneva, situated his ideal human nursery in the rustic simplicity of the foothills of the Alps. In *Emile, or On Education* (1762), he advocates a diet for children of bread and milk or rice cream.

As our first food is milk and we should "preserve the child's primitive tastes as long as possible; let his food be plain and simple." "On the other hand, the more nearly a man's condition approximates to this state of nature the less difference is there between his desires and his powers, and happiness is therefore less remote. Lacking everything, he is never less miserable; for misery consists, not in the lack of things, but in the needs which they inspire.

"Yet I do not exhort you to live in a town; on the contrary, one of the examples which the good should give to others is that of a patriarchal, rural life, the earliest life of man, the most peaceful, the most natural, and the most attractive to the uncorrupted heart. Happy is the land, my young friend, where one need not seek peace in the wilderness! But where is that country? A man of good will finds it hard to satisfy his inclinations in the midst of towns, where he can find few but frauds and rogues to work for. The welcome given by the towns to those idlers who flock to them to seek their fortunes only completes the ruin of the country, when the country ought really to be repopulated at the cost of the towns. All the men who withdraw from high society are useful just because of their withdrawal, since its vices are the result of its numbers. They are also useful when they can bring with them into the desert places life, culture, and the love of their first condition. I like to think what benefits Emile and Sophy, in their simple home, may spread about them, what a stimulus they may give to the country, how they may revive the zeal of the unlucky villagers.

A State of Nature

"In fancy I see the population increasing, the land coming under cultivation, the earth clothed with fresh beauty. Many workers and plenteous crops transform the labours of the fields into holidays; I see the young couple in the midst of the rustic sports which they have revived, and I hear the shouts of joy and the blessings of those about them. Men say the golden age is a fable; it always will be for those whose feelings and taste are depraved. People do not really regret the golden age, for they do nothing to restore it. What is needed for its restoration? One thing only, and that is an impossibility; we must love the golden age."

In a milk shop in Piedmont he recalled eating giunca (a fresh cheese) and sour milk with local bread and that meal he considered, in retrospect, one of the best meals he ever had. Rousseau firmly established the spirit of the Golden Age in an attainable geographic location: the foothills of the Swiss cantons with its thriving communal dairy culture.

The Enlightenment agenda was clear — reconciliation of urban and rural economies, diet and health, and freedom of individual taste within a social contract. There arose two approaches to the realization of this idea. The modest solution was the establishment of a pleasure garden, or resort, modeled after the self-contained, walled paradise garden within which social relations and eating could be controlled. The second, and far more complex approach called for the wholesale reorganizing of the world according to this agenda.

How to Milk an Animal

In the ancient world, a simple act of sympathetic magic was performed by every dairyman and milkmaid. The processes of collecting milk involved a certain level of cooperation between the milker and the milch cow.

The very fact that a cow, or goat, gave milk was seen as a sign of divine favor, for at any moment, an animal might suddenly go dry.

In Sholem Aleichem's "Der Farkishefter Shnayder" ("The Haunted Tailor"), the delicate balance of nature is upset by nothing more than a lack of enthusiasm on the part of a tailor. His wife urges him to buy a milch goat to supplement the family's meager diet, and after repeated pleas he finally gives in and agrees to buy one. The seller demonstrates, before his eyes, the milk-producing prowess of one particular goat, but as soon as it's brought to his home, it loses its ability to give milk — it literally loses its sexual characteristics.

It was the husband's half-hearted attitude that caused the female goat to refuse to give milk. His wife's desire for the family to have a steady supply of milk was not enough; everyone had to wholeheartedly agree for nature to take its course.

Dairy management was an uncertain endeavor; its success depended upon the farmer's esoteric knowledge and the observance of mysterious rules of conduct. If the rules were not followed, the animal would give less milk, milk of poor quality, or milk that would quickly spoil.

The animal must be handled gently and not rushed from pasture to barn. It should not be excited by loud voices. It should be milked by the same person at the same time twice a day. Women seem better suited to perform the job in a gentle and clean manner. There should be no gossiping among milkers in the stall.

"Cows should always be treated with great gentleness, and soothed by mild usage, especially when young and ticklish, or when the paps are tender; in which last case, the udder ought to be fomented with warm water before milking, and touched with the greatest gentleness, otherwise the cow will be in danger of contracting bad habits, becoming stubborn and unruly, and retaining her milk ever after. A cow never lets down her milk pleasantly to the person she dreads or dislikes."
[J. Anderson, *On the Management of the Dairy* (London, 1798)]

Goats, in order to be milked, were literally embraced by the milkmaid. The animal itself was to be brushed and curried like a horse, the udder washed before milking, its tail docked to reduce the splashing of mud.

Attention was directed toward the cleanliness and dress of the milker. Farmhands should not be allowed to go from other dirty chores to milking without first changing their clothes and washing. Clean water should be provided for hand-washing.

The act of milking by hand, or forcing the milk out of the teats, is a skill that requires practice. "Take hold of the udder with the whole hand so that the small finger will be held just so low that the stream of milk coming from the teat cannot wet the finger or the lower part of the hand. The hand is then lifted, opening it at the same time so that it takes hold of the teat very loosely, with a quick but soft pressure, and is then lowered so far that the teat is stretched just to its natural length. At the same time as the hand is brought downward, begin to press the teat from above downward, and end with squeezing the milk out with an increasing pressure of the whole hand. The movements must not be violent, however, but soft and at the same time as energetic as possible.

"The milker must always be quiet and deliberate in his movements in the stable, and on approaching a cow ought to speak gently to her." [Gösta Grotenfelt, *The Principals of Modern Dairy Practice* (1894)]

The cow should not be fed while being milked, as dust will be stirred up and coarse fodders may contaminate the milk. At least one and a half hours

should
be allowed
for the cow to
digest its meal before
milking begins.

There seemed to be a connection between presence of impurities that fell into the milk pail and the rapid spoilage of the milk. Before the milk was strained, it might contain manure particles, fodder particles, molds and fungi, cow hair, particles of skin, human hair, parts of insects, down from birds, small wooden shavings, woolen threads, linen threads, soil particles, and cobwebs.

On larger farms it was advised that the animal be removed temporarily from its natural surroundings during milking to reduce the presence of impurities in the pail.

Specially designed milk houses were constructed to minimize the presence of airborne particles. The windows were fitted with screens and air baffles; the floors and walls were ideally made of stone or glazed tile. The benches upon which the milk pans were placed were made of stone or slate. The ceiling should be at least eight feet high and finished like that of an ordinary dwelling house. The woodwork should be regularly whitewashed. A stream might be directed through the building to cool the interior in summer. The milking room must be well lit so that milkers were not groping in the dark in winter.

A milking house in Naples in 1795 is described as being "very commodiously arranged and consists of an oblong, arched room, in each of whose two sides are four apertures like doorways, leading on either side into an enclosed court. At milking time, the sheep are driven into one of these courts, and successively passed through one of the apertures, where a man waits to milk them, which being done, they are let through the opposite opening into the other court, and are thus speedily milked." [Karl Ulysses von Salis Marschlins, *Travels Through Various Provinces of the Kingdom of Naples in 1789*]

The sanitary milkhouse of glazed tile was to become the model for the modern dairy store and eventually the sanitary dairy restaurant.

And then, most important, the milk, after being manually removed from the udder, was to be quickly removed from the vicinity of the animal. This action was taken not only to prevent the bucket from being accidentally kicked and its contents spilled, but to prevent the milk from spoiling. It was noticed that the longer the milk was left near the animal, the more likely it was to develop a variety of "diseased" conditions. Warm milk, just drawn from the udder, is particularly susceptible to spoilage.

Several days after milk was drawn, it was not uncommon for its surface to be covered with spots of red, blue, yellow, or green pigmentation of varying degrees of toxicity. Milk would suddenly turn bitter for no apparent reason, or it might form long viscous threads, so-called ropey milk. Although all milk will gradually turn sour, some dairies were cursed with rapidly souring milk of an unpleasant and odorous nature.

It was as though the speedy removal of the milk spared the animal the knowledge and agony of its position in the food chain. Should the milkmaid tarry in the presence of the animal, she would be punished by having her milk spoil. All of these precautions were in place long before the discovery of bacterial contamination.

118

In the seventeenth century, Antonie van Leeuwenhoek's explorations of the microscopic world revealed animal activity hitherto unknown to man. The invisible forces of nature attributed to gods were perhaps just animals operating on a scale too small to be seen by the naked eye. Still, Ignaz Semmelweis's recommendation in 1847 that doctors should wash their hands between handling a cadaver and a living patient was rejected by the medical establishment. The transference of the essence of death via touch was considered pure superstition.

This natural law demanding the physical separation of milk from animal was, and still is, universally observed by successful dairymen regardless of race or religion. The milk, separated from the animal, is cooled from the body warmth of the animal, strained to remove all gross impurities connected with the animal, and then processed for drinking or cheese. The animal, once its milk production ends, joins the other cattle in

the slaughterhouse. The technical necessity of separation led to the development of two distinct trades, guilds and modern industries: one dealing with milk, the other with meat.

The so-called steam dairy with its smokestack, stands in the distance on hundreds of picture postcards from the late nineteenth to the early twentieth century. Steam was used to sterilize the dairy equipment — cans, ladles, etc. — but contamination might still occur in the handling and transport of the milk.

To provide Cholov Yisroel, or milk produced according to Talmudic dietary laws, the milking must be supervised, or performed, by a Jew who can attest to the fact that the milk was, in fact, from a "clean" animal and not intermixed with the milk of an "unclean" animal. Otherwise, from a technical point of view, the Jewish dairyman was subject to the still-undisclosed laws of bacterial contamination. The last remaining dairies in metropolitan areas were ones that provided such "kosher" milk.

Once the milk leaves the dairy, its purity and quality are dependent upon the ethics and business practices of the milk seller. These people were experts at "cooking up the milk" for resale. The strong flavor of fresh milk was routinely watered down. The opaque fluid was commonly adulterated with chemical whiteners and anti-spoilage agents.

This understanding led consumers to go to the countryside to obtain truly fresh milk. The small farmer had a better chance of producing a bacteria-free product through milking in sunlight and careful handling of small quantities of milk — something impossible to duplicate on an industrial scale.

If that was not possible, consumers would put their trust in a reputable milk seller who guaranteed fresh daily deliveries.

Rousseau's recipe for human happiness was played out in the private gardens of the nobility. Marie Antoinette's garden at the Petit Trianon was remodeled in 1783 to resemble a petit hameau, complete with a functioning dairy. The queen and her attendants, costumed as milkmaids, went through the motions of milk production. The interior of the dairy was decorated with casts of the queen's own breasts. The rapid turnover in costumes needed to enact these passing fashion trends fueled the used-clothing business of Paris — left, by default, in the hands of the Jews.

The economic theories of the Physiocrats — that government should not interfere with natural economic laws and that land was the source of all wealth — were spurred by the pastoral impulse. The Jews, as urban middlemen, were confirmed to be unproductive parasites.

For the French philosophes of the eighteenth century, the line was drawn between the Hellenic and Oriental cultures (Judaism, Christianity, and Muslim). The Oriental current had polluted the Hellenic. The fallacy of these pure cultural lines is most evident in the fact that the Enlightenment was stimulated and grew directly out of the transplantation of Turkish and Arabian coffeehouse culture to Europe.

Coffee, as a mental stimulant imported from Turkey and the Middle East, as opposed to the European ale-and-wine culture, was the drink that helped shift public thought in new directions. That the first coffeehouses in England were run by Jews and the beans cultivated by slave labor did not disturb the Enlightenment discourse held within them. A look at the history of organized religion's opposition to coffee drinking demonstrates its disruptive influence on the status quo.

This fantasy of becoming an organic whole with the earth of one's motherland led to the disastrous revivals of nationalism and anti-Semitism in the nineteenth century and the debates of nature vs. artificiality and rationalism, rootedness vs. rootlessness, and altruistic authentic cultural expression vs. commercially contrived product.

A practical scheme for providing the most sophisticated mechanism for public eating in the eighteenth century was the invention of the restaurant.

On the Invention of the Restaurant

The invention and history of the restaurant intersects with the history of Jewish dietary law on the Right Bank of Paris in the year 1766. In the opinion of the advanced thinkers of the time, the social sicknesses of mid-eighteenth-century France were intertwined with the eating habits and diet of the people. A rift had developed between the ancient and modern methods of cooking. The over-refinement of modern cooking made the urban population morally and physically weak. The spices of the Orient had corrupted the simple and wholesome taste of the ancient Greeks. The traiteurs and cookshops of Paris offered mutton in rich sauces, heavy pâtés, highly seasoned sausages. This overstimulation of the palate led to an imbalance among all aspects of life. The connection of Jews with the chocolate and spice businesses confirmed the degenerative effect of their Asiatic presence in France.

In the larger context of the struggle for the rights of man, the time had come to assert the biological and gustatory rights of the individual within the French Republic. Mathurin Roze de Chantoiseau was an enthusiast, an economic theorist, and a publisher who signed his writings "The Friend of All the World." In his ratio of cogitation to action he can be considered a milekhdike personality avant la lettre.

In between proposing schemes for the permanent eradication of

the national debt, Roze de Chantoiseau compiled and published a business directory of Paris. His overview of the public food suppliers and seven hundred eating establishments of the city — the traiteurs, the wine shops, the cook-caterers, the taverns — enabled him to see the need for a new sort of public eating establishment that appealed to the upwardly mobile merchant class, the entrepreneurs of the Ancien Régime: intellectuals, actresses, dukes, and minor officeholders; an establishment that crossed the rigid boundaries set by the monopolistic food-handling guilds and corporations; an establishment that catered to the individual who desired to eat in public, but at the privacy of his own table, satisfying the unique demands of his own digestive system according to the latest scientific discoveries of nutrition and food preparation.

He opened his place in the courtyard of the Hôtel d'Aligre (current numbers 121–125) on rue Saint Honoré, and listed himself under a new category of business — Le Restaurateur, a new category somewhere between a medicine supplier and food seller.

Other entrepreneurs followed Roze de Chantoiseau's lead. These "maisons de santé" (houses of health), as they were called, served "restaurants" or restorative dishes, aimed to reconcile the decadence of modern cooking with the simple, unadulterated foods of the peasant through the latest scientific ideas of food preparation. The diner was presented with a written menu, an extensive list of the available dishes with a separate price attached to each, from which he'd choose exactly those items desired. Other innovations in service were modeled after the cafe: diners were seated at individual tables, not the

communal table of the tavern, and talking to one's neighbor was discouraged. A meal could be ordered at any time of day, not according to the set time of a table d'hôte, and the hours extended late into the evening beyond those of the traiteur or cookshop. The "restaurants" were based upon the cuisine of the Swiss village depicted by Rousseau in *Emile* and his other writings. A selection of bouillons, rice creams, porridges, semolina, macaroni, eggs, fruit compotes and preserves, Burgundy wine, capons (castrated young roosters with dense, delicate meat), butter, cream, and cheeses could be ordered, according to the appetite and physical disposition of each patron. These mild white foods were the foods of women, children, and highly strung intellectuals. The dark-brown and blood-red foodstuffs eaten by laborers and warriors had no place in these maisons de santé. Through scientific preparation, foodstuffs could be reduced to their essence and so put less of a strain upon the digestive system. The diet of the peasant, in its natural state, was difficult to digest and thus stultified the body and mind.

The maisons de santé offered the pleasures of an Alpine meal without having to leave Paris: "The restaurant offered many Parisians what they believed to be a Rousseauian opportunity for shared, frugal melancholia, for the semi-public display of sensibility." The food was served in an elegant, high-ceilinged room. The walls were decorated with mirrors (so that the diner could enjoy the sight of himself in public), clocks, and paintings of pastoral scenes. On the wall was inscribed in large letters:

Hic sapidé titillant juscula blanda palatum,
Hic dater effaetis pectoribusque slaus.
[Here one judiciously titillates the sense of taste,
Here is realized the sense of well-being.]

Voltaire and the Encyclopédistes were disgusted by this "nouvelle cuisine" because of its tampering with the food of the ancient world and because of its high price.

In 1798, a "Dutch dairy" established near the Jardin des Plantes served entire meals based upon dairy products. The dairy diet was prescribed as a cure for the physical ills of debauchery — it also claimed to re-arouse the body in anticipation of further debauchery.

The "restaurants" offered were of a medicinal nature (not the food itself, but an essence of the food) and so even Talmudic law might see these "dishes" in another light.

Within twenty years, the delicate and healthful menu was expanded to include the hearty culinary inventions of the famous chefs of the Ancien Régime, but the name, style of service, and ambience were retained and popularized. The influence and movement of culinary fashions from the nobility to the merchant class to the working poor occurred in both directions. [Rebecca L. Spang, *The Invention of the Restaurant*]

With the return of Louis XV to Versailles in 1722, the once fashionable residential neighborhood of the Marais began a slow transformation into a business district of notaries, lawyers, and artisans. Into this district and the adjoining Saint-Merri settled the thousand or so Jews who came from Metz, Alsace, Lorraine, Germany, and points east. By the mid-eighteenth century, the nearby open space around the Church of Saint-Paul and Saint-Louis, known as "the old Jewry," was again a locus of Jewish activity, as it had been, between expulsions, since the thirteenth century. Although they were just a ten-minute walk from Roze de Chantoiseau's restaurant, poor and working-class Jews of the area could not afford its high prices. They were more likely to eat at the Cafe du Commerce, nicknamed Cafe des Juifs, on rue St. Martin or in the private apartments of widowed Jewish women who served kosher meals.

In Paris of 1766, with seven hundred or more traditional eating establishments, it's unlikely that a poor Polish Jew would dine at one of the

new restaurants, but one such poor Jew, Zalkind Hourwitz (1738–1812), an intellectual and follower of Moses Mendelssohn, might have ventured into such a place as the guest of a wealthy friend.

In 1774, Hourwitz found himself at the center of the debate concerning the regeneration of the Jews and their place in the French Republic. It was alleged that the Jews comprised a nation unto itself existing within the French Republic. Its laws and customs were designed for the purpose of separation and so, short of conversion to Christianity, integration was impossible. In addition, their disdain of Christian society allowed them to practice the antisocial business practice of moneylending for profit. Hourwitz, and other enlightened thinkers, argued that Jews were first human beings and secondly Jews. They were forced into various unsavory businesses because the denial of full citizenship barred them from participating in the wider economy. Their private religious beliefs in no way conflicted with full citizenship and participation in the national life of France. Christians, he explained, must renounce the practice of referring to all Jews when condemning one. Jews do not form a single sect. He

Imaginary portrait of Z. Hourwitz

believed that religious belief should not be subject to rabbinical or communal rulings. The idea of excommunication was abhorrent to him.

In the words of Clermont-Tonnerre, "One must refuse everything to the Jews as a nation but one must give them everything as individuals; they must become citizens." [*Moniteur*, vol. II, 455–56, in Arthur Hertzberg, *The French Enlightenment and the Jews*]

The popular idea of the Jew was based largely upon limited or mistaken observations and half-baked mythologies. The final, and damning, proof offered for the impossibility of Jewish integration into French society was that Jews were forbidden to share a table with Frenchmen. According to Voltaire, "The supreme expression of Jewish hatred of all men is that they, unlike all others, refuse to eat at the same table with other men." [*Oeuvres complètes,* vol. XX, 525–26]

This claim was dismissed as nonsense by Hourwitz. "Jews are not forbidden to eat with 'foreigners.' Legislators, officers and public functionaries dined at the homes of Parisian Jews and they in turn dined at theirs — on fish, dairy products, vegetables and eggs. . . . Judaism prohibited Jews neither from eating nor socializing with others. In fact, Jews were no worse table companions than Muslims, or, for that matter, Catholics during Lent. Anyone asserting the contrary was merely seeking a pretext to deny them their full rights as citizens." On January 17, 1790, Hourwitz dined in the Parisian home of Cerf Berr in the presence of Roederer, Grégoire, Thiery, and Godard. In that same month, the delegates of the Jewish community of Bordeaux to the National Assembly dined with Brunet de Latuque. Abraham Furtado, on his visit to Paris (1799–1800), dined at the homes of Madame de Condorcet and Helvetius, and enjoyed the Jardin des Plantes and the works of art in the Louvre.

For an account of how dietary laws were observed by a Jewish visitor to Europe in the late eighteenth century, we can turn to the diaries of Rabbi Ha'im Yosef David Azulai. In his two trips across Europe to collect funds for his school in Palestine, Azulai recorded the day-to-day details of eating. Many nights were spent in Gentile inns, taverns, and hospices where carefully chosen foodstuffs were eaten. For the most part, he avoided meat and subsisted on bread, fruit, wine, and chocolate in the form of a drink.

In the villages of Alzonne, Tavo, Labouheyre, Carbon-Blanc, Saint-Andre-de-Cubzac, and many others he ate his midday meals in Gentile hospices and inns — a diet consisting of dairy and pareve foodstuffs, or fish examined and prepared by his assistant. In Ferrara he enjoyed a meal entirely of cheese dishes.

In several Jewish communities, he abstained from eating meat because of doubts concerning the knowledge and practice of the local shoykhet (ritual slaughterer). In Italy he was warned "not to eat of the shkhite of David Morpugo: for thus had R. I. Fomiggini declared: He is not expert and not sensitive to test the knife, and they should not rely on the credentials of a shoykhet where the

Hakham (endorsing these) is not himself a shoykhet of the peqia [fraternity or society of licensed shokhtem]." At a banquet, he refrains from eating meats. In Bordeaux in 1755, he refuses to eat meat in the home of Benjamin Gradis because he doubts the knowledge and practice of the local shoykhet. Among the oldest and most assimilated Jews of France, the dietary laws were less strictly, or not at all, observed. In Toulouse, "the shoykhet there was from Rodriguez (Spain) and I did not want to eat of his shkhite." When Azulai became sick, a dispensation was made so that he could eat "(just) a little meat and toasted bread soaked in wine."

In the diary of Azulai, we can see that in the case of foodstuffs that fall outside of the practice of shkhite, or ritual slaughtering, one might rely upon common sense and observational fact. Fruits and vegetables without obvious insect infestation were permissible; eggs of domesticated fowl, without visible blood spots; fish must have fins and scale that are easily removable without damaging the skin. Bread, and other precooked foods, present some Halakhic

Preparation
of a bouillon
d'essence de lapin

problems, but through smell or questioning, one can determine whether the bread was prepared with non-kosher fats.

Azulai remarks upon the beauty of Paris in 1777–78. Everything is expensive, "except for harlotry which is cheap, and flagrant. They say there are thirty thousand common whores, inscribed in a register, besides tens of thousands that are not for the passing public." He saw the rabbi of Avignon in a Gentile tavern drinking wine.

Azulai noted the admiring attention he received from Christian women of the upper classes; in his exotic garb they saw a figure from the pages of the Old Testament. Among the young affluent Jews of Europe, who would have been more generous had not the American Revolution upset their finances, he notes countless faults: non-kosher eating, reading of Voltaire, shaved faces, European dress, speaking French, and socializing with Gentiles.

A number of well-known Jews in Paris were known to live in flagrant disregard of Jewish law and kept Christian mistresses. Not long after their invention, the restaurants of the city featured private dining cubicles for the satisfaction of appetites beyond food. Erotic freedom became associated with the pastoral atmosphere of a restaurant interior. The visiting wealthy Portuguese Jews of Bordeaux and Bayonne, like David Gadis, would appreciate the idea of the restaurant. They had rejected the Mishnah and the Talmud and practiced a literal or commonsense reading of the Torah. By discounting the interpretive traditions of the Oral Law, they were free to eat forbidden foods in public. To such Jews, the prospect of a scientific system of eating in an elegant environment made perfect sense. What better place to mingle with the most forward-looking people who saw beyond race and historical accidents.

As a community, the Jews struggled against the commercial limitations of the guild and corporations that monopolized many businesses. "Le restaurant" disregarded these limitations in the name of human need. The idea that each individual required a particular diet at a particular time is something that even the most casually observant Jew would understand. In the restaurant, each diner could indulge in the satisfaction of his own appetite at a table separate from, yet situated in the midst of a semi-public room filled with, other congenial individuals — a model for learning to ignore the private religious beliefs of others for the good of the Republic.

Christian Wilhelm von Dohm, an economist in Berlin (1781), explained that human character was not innate, but created by climate, food, and conditions of the environment. "The Jew is more of a man than he is a Jew."

The Idea of the Restaurant in Industrialized Europe

The same currents of scientific inquiry used to substantiate the health dangers of a meat diet led to the industrialization of the world that began in the late eighteenth century. Over the next two hundred years, textile production, the steam engine, iron making, machine tools, and chemical production increased the world's average per-capita income tenfold; the population increased sixfold. That this revolution in industrial productivity emanated from England reaffirmed the connection between beef eating, productivity, and the production of wealth.

The growth of an affluent middle class in need of luxury dining and working-class requirements for quick, inexpensive food led to the attendant growth of restaurant culture. Gaslight, introduced in London in 1812, allowed nightlife to flourish. The perfection of sheet glass in 1832 and continuous-sheet paper in 1798 provided the possibilities of retail food display, packaging, and a popular press to advertise these dining places. Industrialization came more slowly to the Continent.

The machinery that drove the agricultural revolution of the eighteenth century had already caused a shift of population from the countryside to cities. The Jews, a minority population, followed this drift. In Poland, many Jews already forced into an intermediary class between the nobility and peasant populations were a de facto middle class. Through industrialization and urbanization, the middle-class businessmen and industrialists wrested political and economic power from the landed gentry and nobility.

In 1800, only 3 percent of the world lived in cities. By 1890, 35 percent of the population of Western Europe was urban and by 1950, 63 percent. By the late nineteenth century, 70–90 percent of the urban population was infected with tuberculosis bacillus. Eighty percent of those who were infected died.

An 1853 account of the Rotonde du Temple (built 1788, demolished 1863), near the rue du Temple, describes a circular cloister whose outer circumference housed forty-four arcades where Jews specialized in the selling of old clothes: out of fashion, property of the dead, theatrical wardrobes, out-of-date military uniforms, etc. The thousand or so inhabitants of the inner court "drink and dine at the neighboring wine-shops and cafes, known as the Elephant, Two Lions and kindred names. At these, brandy is eight sous the bottle, a ragout three sous and a cup of coffee one cent. There are resorts still cheaper and lower, such as the 'Field of the Wolf,' frequented by the most brutal of the denizens of this quarter, who in their orgies not infrequently mingle blood with the blue fluid that they swallow for wine. The greater part of these dram shops add to their debasing occupation that of usury." [From "Life in Paris," *Harper's New Monthly Magazine*, June 3, 1853, 38–50]

The spread and growth of restaurant culture was a direct result of this worldwide industrialization. The restaurant represented a French idea of freedom of dietary choice and social style. From the seventeenth century, French was the international lingua franca spoken by the elite of Europe. French royal style set the tone for European fashion from the reign of Louis XIV — the Enlightenment Monarch. France was the epicenter of luxury-good production and established the very idea of changing fashion and haute couture. The restaurant was a visible symbol of the personal liberty associated with the reforms of the Napoleonic Code and found a receptive audience in even the poorest shtetlach of Eastern Europe.

The rise of industrialization and its attendant human cruelty — child labor, pollution, an impoverished working class, chronic hunger and malnutrition (a norm for most of the world until the late nineteenth century) — led to a revival of the pastoral dream, a reconsideration of vegetable diets, and the escape to the countryside among the educated middle class who could afford such luxuries.

Jacobson's
school for boys
Seesen 1889

Reform Judaism and Eating

The interconnections between eating and prayer in the mind of an Orthodox Jew can become complex, and potentially paralyzing, questions of logic. For instance, the question of drinking coffee before Shabbos morning davening in order to fully focus on one's prayers consists of three problems: (1) one shouldn't be eating or drinking before morning davening, (2) the prohibition of eating and drinking in a shul, and (3) the problem of heating water on Shabbos. Without first having the coffee, would one not be fully cognizant of the words of the prayers, or in danger of falling asleep while praying? Would it be permissible to install an automatic coffeemaker with timer outside of the men's section of the shul? And what of adding sugar and/or milk to the coffee?

Mordecai Schnaber (1741–97), Berlin doctor and philosopher, wrote that the mitzvah of belief in God was timeless, but that all other mitzvot could change over time as they were offshoots of the fundamental belief. The laws concerning diet, priestly purity, and dress were anachronisms that, in fact, prevented the expression of contemporary ethics and spirituality.

Israel Jacobson (1768–1828), one of the founding fathers of the Reform movement in Judaism, accumulated a small fortune and in 1801 established a free school for Jewish and Christian children in Seesen, near the Harz Mountains. It remained in existence for a hundred years.

On the school grounds, he built a temple in which he endeavored to put into practice his ideas of religious reform. It was equipped with the first organ in a Jewish house of worship. The ceremony of becoming Bar Mitzvah was replaced with a confirmation for Jewish boys.

With the creation of the model state of the Kingdom of Westphalia by Napoleon in 1807, a constitution granting equal rights to all was imposed. Serfs and Jews were emancipated and Jacobson was appointed president of the Jewish consistory. Jacobson established a house of prayer organized along the lines of his temple in Seesen. References to the coming of a Messiah were removed from the services. Bareheaded men and women worshipped and studied together ethics and Enlightenment reason. The Sabbath was moved to Sunday and traditional restrictions were lifted, services were conducted in German, and dietary laws were declared repugnant and abandoned. Is it any wonder that the model of the French restaurant that granted each diner the freedom of eating exactly what they wanted, and what their biological mechanism required, gained popularity among the forward-looking Jews of Europe?

With the fall of Napoleon in 1815, Jacobson moved to Berlin, where he established a hall of prayer and lecture in his own house where the proponents of the Jewish Enlightenment delivered sermons. Because of his collaboration with Napoleon, the Prussian authorities forced this institution to close, but other Reform temples were built in Hamburg (1818) and Berlin.

Isaac Mayer Wise, a Reform rabbi from Bohemia, arrived in America in 1846 and hoped to reconcile the theological differences among Jews. In 1883, Gus Lindeman, a local Jewish caterer, was hired to provide a celebratory banquet for the first graduating class of Wise's Hebrew Union College in Cincinnati. Lindeman was told to provide a kosher banquet, and so he excluded pork from the menu but included clams, crabs, and shrimp as he usually did

for banquets held by the affluent German-Jewish Allemania Club, the local sponsors of the event. The menu was an affront to the Orthodox guests. Blame for the thoughtless blunder was placed on the lay organizers — Rabbi Wise insisted that he kept a kosher home — but the Reformists' lack of interest in dietary law was evident. The most radical reformers dismissed Kashruth as "kitchen Judaism."

In reaction to the scientific and rationalistic renovation of Judaism there was set into motion a fierce movement led by Rabbi Moshe Sofer (1762–1839) to conserve traditional Jewish culture through a wholesale freeze on the evolution of rituals and laws — including dietary law. These eternal laws maintained the only outward signs that differentiated and segregated Jews from the Christian majority. Dress was the other element seized on by Orthodox and Hasidic communities to help maintain their cohesion. Going against the logic of scientific understanding, traditionalists set themselves upon an untenable course of obsessive-compulsive behavior.

In contrast to the legendary wealth of a few celebrated Jewish bankers and businessmen, the majority of European Jews lived under oppressive conditions: subject to blood libels, capricious taxation, and expulsions and confined to crowded ghettos and muddy villages. The diet of most Jews in the Pale of Settlement consisted of grains, vegetables, water, and a small quantity of milk and cheese. Countless stories and reminiscences involve the weeklong concern with being able to afford a piece of fish, chicken, or beef for their Sabbath dinner.

According to the *Journal du Nord* of 1892, most of the proletarian Jews of Russia lived in semi-starvation. "There are in Russia only 10,000 to 15,000 Jews who possess any certain means of existence. As to the masses, they possess nothing; and they are far poorer than the Christian populace, who at any rate own some land."

As a gymnasium student in Dvinsk in 1879, Simon Dubnow, recorded, "It is more than one and one-half months since I have had any meat and live only on bread, herring and tea." The government liquor monopoly of 1896 drove thousands of tavernkeepers out of business and into the crowded cities, further exacerbating the conditions of poverty.

Meanwhile, the idea of the restaurant had spread throughout Europe. To adopt a sophisticated French name for a place of public eating was a good business decision. As the restaurant offered its diners a freedom of choice based upon physiological need or whim, it can be seen as a step in the emancipation movements of the time — the culinary equivalent of the Napoleonic Code. The idea of the restaurant (in its post-medicinal stage) followed the spread of French Empire and culture throughout the world. By the early nineteenth century, it was an established idea that flourished at all socioeconomic levels and in all but the most anti-French pockets of Europe.

The missionaries of the Scottish Episcopal Church unwittingly left a record of public eating in the Pale of Settlement. To these missionaries, a village with a large Jewish population was immediately recognizable by the degree of commercial activity. In their mission to convert Jews to Christianity, they discovered that the tavern or eating house offered the most conducive atmosphere. In these places, Jews were most open to discussion and possible conversion. A degree of communal restraint was temporarily removed.

The idea of the "restaurant" transplanted to a poor Jewish town is described in Sholem Aleichem's "Dos Naye Kasrilevke" ("The New Kasrilvker," part 3, "Kasrileveker restoranen," 1901). In this fictionalized version of his Ukrainian birthplace, Voronkov, a hungry traveler, is delighted to see a sign announcing a "A Kosher Restaurant" with the motto "Our food is fresh and

Karnatzlach

cheap" and the name of the proprietress: Sore Indik. Within moments, the traveler learns that the original proprietress is dead; after six years the signboard has not been updated. The current owner appears and there begins the pretense of a perusal of countless menu possibilities: What do you have? What would you like? In this poverty-stricken establishment anything can be requested, but its delivery is impossible. The husband of the proprietress grows tired of the game and says, "Just fetch the food and let's have no more talk," to which she responds with the munificent restaurateur's answer — "You've got to know what to fetch, don't you? Every man to his whim" — and proceeds to enumerate the particular whims of Kasrilevkean diners. When she leaves to fetch the one thing available, a herring, the husband describes his wife's glorious state of mind as a restaurateur: "As bad as the business is just now, it's still a restaurant. To look at Rokhl, when she dresses up and goes out for a stroll, you'd think she was a countess!"

Sholem Aleichem's restaurant story evoked the impossibility of restaurant culture existing in anything but name among the impoverished towns within the Pale of Settlement. Generations of near starvation resulted in the development of the big eater who, when he could at last afford to eat to his heart's content, required seltzer water and bicarbonate of soda to alleviate his indigestion.

The history of the Yiddish theater is linked to European restaurant culture. Early performances took place in the garden cafes of Iasi, Romania; the London restaurateurs Sonnenschein and Moishe Kibin were patryotn (supporters and devotees) of the wandering Jewish actors in that city; and actor Ludwig Satz operated his own cafe in New York City. Only in these semi-public spaces could actors freely live outside of traditional communal restraints.

Living among Christian majorities, Jews must have always felt the temptations of non-kosher foods and non-Halakhic combinations of food and must have occasionally given in to them. The Reform movement effectively removed dietary concerns from the sphere of Jewish law and moved it into a larger question of scientific ethics. A Jew could eat shellfish and pork, mix milk with meat, and still live within a Jewish community.

Those who chose to eat traditional Jewish dishes did so as a culinary choice, surrendering to a momentary craving, or, in some cases, as a culinary expression of their national identity.

Heinrich Heine (1797–1856) is an example of a converted and assimilated Jew who despised both the Jewish and Christian cultures of Europe yet maintained a taste for traditional Jewish cuisine. In his *About Ludwig Börne* (1840), he muses over a Sabbath meal of tsholnt at a friend's house in Frankfurt.

"This dish is really first-rate and it is deeply to be regretted that the Christian Church, which borrowed so much that was good from ancient Judaism, should have failed to adopt tsholnt as its own. Maybe it has put it off for some future day when it will fall upon hard times, when its most sacred symbols, even the Cross, will have lost their power, then it will seize upon tsholnt! Whereupon, the backsliding nations will once again and with new appetite return to its fold. When that will happen the Jews, at the very least, will adopt Christianity out of conviction . . . because, as I clearly see it, it is tsholnt alone which holds them together in their old faith. . . . No sooner will the renegades who will go over to the new faith get a whiff of tsholnt than they'll begin to feel homesick again for the synagogue, that tsholnt was, so to speak, the cowherd's melody of the Jews."

The wonders of Jewish cuisine have been attributed to the fact that Jews had few other cultural outlets and so put tremendous energy and ingenuity into cooking and food preparation.

In Sholem Aleichem's monologue of 1903, "Milkhigs," a fictional member of the Kasrilevke Fressers Club — a frum, as opposed to free, Jew — expresses a clear preference for milkhiker cuisine over fleyshiks. "With meat there's meat and there's bones; with dairy one has milk, and

MILK
BUTTER
SOUR CREAM
SMETENE
SOUR MILK
KREPLACH
KUGEL
FARFEL W. MILK
KASHE W. MILK
VARNITSHKES
BLINTZES
TSORES KNEYDLEKH
FRIED FISH
VARENIKES
NOODLES W. MILK
KNISHES
BALABESHKE W. MILK
BORSCHT
TEYGLECH

cheese, and butter, and sour cream, sourmilk . . . Consider all the delicacies that one can make dairy.

"From meat you have a soup, a roselfleisch, an esikfleysh, a roast . . . and that's it. . . . From milk, however, you have milk, cheese, butter, sour cream, pid-smetene, whey, kasha with milk, noodles with milk, rice with milk, and teyglekh with milk, and balabeshkes [boiled in water dumplings] with milk, and farfel with milk . . . the delicacies from cheese and butter . . . including kreplekh, and varenikes [pirogen], and varnitshkes [fried noodle with buckwheat], and kugel . . . and knishes and blintzes, tsores kneydlekh [dumplings]. . . . And how dear are the delicacies that one can not remember! For example: Korzh [dry buckwheat cakes] with cheese, maslinkes [buttermilk] kasha, and fish fried in butter, and a dairy borscht, and raisins and buttermilk. . . ." The monologue is a paean to the endless possibilities of dairy eating.

Milkhiks, he also points out, are more affordable than fleyshiks, and when one can't afford even the milkhiker ingredients, one can at least enjoy standing around a fish market talking about them.

Food historians have puzzled over the origins of various Jewish dishes: which are adaptations of the cuisine of the Christian majority and which are uniquely Jewish inventions. According to Hasidic lore only kugel, or noodle pudding, is an authentic Jewish dish — all others are preexisting dishes adapted by Jews according to the possibilities of their dietary law. I've eaten a large Pakistani potato samosa that, except for their triangular form and spices, recalled the texture of a potato knish. Upon entering a Korean barbecue-and-bone-soup restaurant,

I've been struck by an aroma reminiscent of a Jewish delicatessen in Brooklyn c.1960. Have we overlooked the intimate and direct connection between language, speech, and food? A native Yiddish speaker transforms whatever he puts into his mouth by naming it as he eats it.

Every combination of dietary observance was possible: The radical socialist who, brought up eating traditional Jewish cuisine, still craves it. The strictly Orthodox Jew who works in a laboratory contriving artificial versions of forbidden foods. The Jew who eats "kosher" at home, but treyf in restaurants. The Jew who eats treyf at home, but "kosher" for social reasons among co-religionists in public. The Jew who eats Jewish dishes when the mood strikes him, but is indifferent to their preparation.

The separation of Jewish cuisine from religious practice leads to the dilemma of the "Jewish-style" restaurant. In Sholem Asch's *A Passage in the Night* (1953), the Orthodox father of a young Florida resort developer is angered by the idea of a "Jewish-style" restaurant in his son's new hotel. Traditional Jewish dishes prepared and served with no regard to Jewish dietary law were, to him, an affront to Judaism. In fact, all Jewish eating establishments offer a "style" of Jewish cuisine prepared and served somewhere within the wide spectrum of dietary observance. The so-called culinary Jew — someone whose only connection to Judaism is through food — tends to be more concerned with the gustatory quality of a particular dish, rather than the chef's understanding of dietary law. Between the modern "culinary Jew," and the practitioner of "kitchen Judaism," there stands the question of taste.

For that poor child disgusted by food prepared in a stranger's home, the restaurant offers a neutral field for eating removed from the physical aura

of any individual. The food appears from behind closed doors and is carried in the clean hands of a professional food-handler free of emotional involvement. Franz Kafka described the restaurant as the perfect social gathering: no one is expected or excluded, you can leave at any time without offending the host, you can keep to yourself if you choose to, you can eat the food of your choice, and, as the cost of the festivities is shared by all, you do not feel beholden to the host.

The range of reactions to the food of one's childhood — at home and at local restaurants — is wide. To some that food is part of a lost paradise that they strive to return to for the rest of their life. To others, it represents a family bondage and provincialism, the escape from which they mark as a day of liberation. To others, that food represents a period of economic and social failure to which they never want to return.

Xenophobia, in its most basic form, is based on a visceral repugnance to the smell and sight of foreigners. The smell is a direct result of the stranger's diet. And so Jews who've renounced all other forms of observance may still feel an attraction to the food of their family and immediate ancestors. This olfactory bond can be irreparably broken in a single generation.

An empirical logic was already inherent within Talmudic law. In cases of sickness, any food that served a medicinal purpose was admissible. Sholem Aleichem's sister was dutifully fed slices of ham upon the recommendation of a doctor. When Moses Mendelssohn had a physical breakdown in March 1771, the court physician treated him with bloodlettings, leeches, footbaths, and a largely vegetarian diet. The idea of restoring health through a resetting of biological functions and a return to the food of infancy fit comfortably within the dietary laws of Judaism.

The Milk Cure

Milk-drinking culture was formed by two diametrically opposed ideas: milk as a foodstuff with nutritive and curative powers and milk as a vehicle for the transmission of disease.

Consumption, phthisis, scrofula (terms used to describe tuberculosis), and various "milk sicknesses" were associated with drinking of milk that had been tainted after leaving the cow, or from a diseased cow. Diseased milk was blamed for epidemics of diphtheria, scarlet fever, typhoid, and even tonsillitis. Cows are particularly susceptible to tuberculosis and, while not displaying symptoms of the disease, can spread the disease to other animals and man. The microorganism that causes tuberculosis was discovered in 1882 by Dr. Robert Koch. One method of controlling the spread of the bacillus tuberculosis is to maintain a tuberculosis-free milk supply.

Because these outbreaks of disease often occurred in warm weather, when the bacteria grow more rapidly, the public became concerned with the quality and freshness of its milk supply. Affluent people who consumed more dairy products were more likely to contract milk-borne disease than the poor —

women and children in particular because of their affinity for milk and cream. By 1912 tuberculosis was the most common and widespread infectious disease, responsible for 30 percent of all deaths between the ages of fifteen and sixty. Human tubercle bacilli also enter the milk supply through improper handling of milk. Because milk is composed of water, protein, and sugar, it's a perfect medium for the growth of bacteria. Being an opaque white liquid, it's easily adulterated.

Many cases of typhoid bacilli being transmitted through milk products handled by infected milkmaids and milkers in contact with cows were recorded in the early 1900s.

The careless production and handling of milk was directly related to the incidence of disease. Outbreaks of disease followed the route of a milk deliveryman. In Germany, special milk institutes monitored small herds of their own milch cows to guarantee purity. The retail sale of milk was handled by shops specializing in dairy products. Specialization permitted an attention to handling and storage. In the public mind, it was desirable to procure milk as soon as it left the udder of a healthy cow. For this reason,

Milk seller in St. James's Park, 1763

at many milk-cure institutes the milk was served directly from a live animal. At dairy shops and Milchhallen (milk pavilions) one would have their glass of milk on the premises, and so a few tables and chairs were often made available for customers. In this way, the dairy shop crossed into the field of public eating.

The milk cure consists of a diet exclusively of milk, in varying quantities, over a prescribed number of days. The curative power stems from the correcting of a common vitamin deficiency. The return to a human's first food signaled a kind of resetting of the organism to restore one's health.

The curative powers of milk were noted in the ancient world. Galen of Pergamon (129–c. 200/216) recommended milk from Stabiae, a resort town near Pompeii, as a cure for the viral plagues of the first century. The itinerant physician Paracelsus (1493–1541) prescribed sour goat's milk for its healing powers. Maimonides prescribed the milk cure: one glass in the morning and one in the evening.

The milk cure is mentioned in the Talmud. It was one of the medical discoveries brought to Europe by Muslim and Jewish doctors in the sixteenth century. Francis I (1515–47) sent to Constantinople for a Jewish physician, who introduced into France the use of she-ass's milk. It was Francis I who also founded a chair in Hebrew at the Collège de France in 1538. In cases of medical urgency, the non-kosher status of the animal was disregarded as the saving of a life supersedes the laws of kashruth.

The renowned diet-and-weight-loss expert of Bath, England, Dr. George Cheyne (1671–1743) discovered that a milk diet was able to cure epilepsy and other nervous conditions. Milk was "just semi-digested vegetables, the milk and vegetable diet should theoretically be the universal remedy" [Stuart, *Bloodless Revolution*, p. 166]. Copulating with and suckling the breast of a young nurse had been proven to revive sick old men.

A revival of interest in the milk cure was sparked in 1749 when a Dr. Meyer cured a hopelessly ill tubercular patient with goat whey. The whey, or liquid portion of milk, from a particular herd feeding on the grass in the Gais district of the Appenzellerland possessed startling curative powers. The cure was further popularized by Dr. Johann Heinrich Heim (1802–1876), who established a successful institute and resort in the area. The sublime views combined with the health-giving qualities of fresh milk products made the Alps into the first tourist destination in Europe.

To correct the inability of the heart to "irrigate" the lungs, it was advised that tuberculosis patients be moved to a location high above sea level where the atmospheric pressure was reduced. By 1830, visitors complained that the natural beauty was overwhelmed by tourists and sanatoria. A hybrid of the Tyrolean and the Alpine milk house, with its rough-cut timber and wide, projecting roof, evoked the ideal place for escape from the industrialized world and has influenced resort architecture worldwide until this day. The hotel buildings of the Catskill Mountains in New York State suggest this form on a gigantic scale.

Dr. Johann Heinrich Heim 1844

Gais

Dining-room activity also took place on a gigantic scale, fresh air and heavy eating being the main attractions.

Little Switzerlands and milk-cure resorts were established in other parts of Europe. The efficacy of the Alpine milk cure was due, in part, to the change of scenery and fresh air. The milk cure was one of many drinking cures around which health resorts were established in Europe and Russia in the nineteenth century. Each resort specialized in one cure, but offered the full range of mineral waters, grape juices, kefir made from mare's milk, wheys, and whole milks.

The famous Molkenkur (whey cure) of Heidelberg was developed on the site of an inn that sold goat's milk whey in 1852. In numerous postcard views we can wander through the dining rooms and terrace cafes, ride the funicular railway, enjoy an aerial view of the town, and admire the Tyrolean structure of the hotel and cure house.

Dr. Philipp Karell, physician to Tzars Nicholas I and Alexander II, published c.1866 an account of the milk cure through history and his own success with it when applied in a strict scientific manner and to the exclusion of all other kinds of nourishment.

Lenin and his wife take the Milchkur 1916

Dr. Philipp Karell

A *New York Times* ad of November 26, 1871, offers "Howe's Arabian Milk Cure for Consumption. The only preparation of the kind in the world. Sold by druggists. John F. Henry, New York, Wholesale agent."

In 1916, Vladimir Ilyich Lenin and his wife spent six weeks at the Tschudiwiese nursing home in the mountains of the Swiss Canton of St. Gallen, where she was put on a dairy diet for her thyroid problems. "In the morning we had coffee with milk and bread and butter and cheese, but no sugar; for dinner: milk soup, something made of curd-cheese, with milk for a third dish; at four o'clock we had coffee with milk again, and another milk meal in the evening. This milk cure had us howling at first, but after a while we reinforced it with raspberries and bilberries that grew all around in profusion. . . . We lived a carefree existence, spending all day rambling about the mountains. . . . Ilych did no work at all there." [*Reminiscences of Lenin*, Nadezhda Krupskaya (1933)]

The milk cure described in 1922 required six weeks of perseverance. The curist would live on six quarts of milk a day. The patient was encouraged to rest and expend as little energy as possible. The day before the cure begins one takes a dose of castor oil. On the first day, as much fruit as desired can be eaten. On the second day, the six quarts of milk per day are started. "One-half pint glass of milk every half-hour from seven in the morning till seven at night. An enema is performed each night followed by a quick hot bath. Sweating spells

Sholem
Aleichem
In MARIENBAD

are normal. After each glass of milk, a few drops of lemon or grapefruit juice are taken. This assists in the curdling of the milk in the stomach. The milk is to be consumed slowly, in small sips or through a straw. Nausea can be prevented by taking a bit of lime water. Feelings of uncomfortable bloating and heart palpitations are to be expected and endured. After six weeks, the quantity of milk slowly reduced and fruit slowly introduced into the diet. Immediately after the cure, one feels weakened, but in a week's time, the patient feels like a new person." [*The Genuine Milk Cure* (1922)]

The affluent urban dweller driven for health reasons to a rural location where he, and/or she, was forced to interact with the rural milkmaid and cowherd spawned a literary (see Ulrich Hegner's *Die Molkenkur*) and visual genre. The intention of regaining one's health and strength at all costs, in the course of which one might seduce, or be seduced by the milkmaid or cowherd, and the class-based jealousies involved, naturally lead to dramatic situations. The dyspeptic businessman and his neurasthenic wife were seen as sapping the healthful life force from the rural laborers.

In 1836, Dr. Huber, a physician to the nobility of Vienna, set up businesses in Merano in South Tyrol, offering milk cures in the spring and grape cures in the fall. Sigmund Freud and his wife took the cure in the summer of 1900. In 1912, the milk cure was offered in Baden-Baden, the Black Forest resort.

Sholem Aleichem's novel *Marienbad* (1917) portrayed middle-class Warsaw women and daughters looking for husbands in a cosmopolitan spa setting. The water-and-milk cure was taken for the purpose of being seen; more as a cure for loneliness and bourgeois despair than any physical illness.

In 1929, the spa town of Zakopane, in the Carpathian Mountains, was largely populated by wealthy Jews who could afford the first-class hotels and expensive mediocre restaurants. Some of these Jews were proud Polish nationalists. They spoke Polish or German and dined in French-influenced Polish restaurants. The history of these resorts recorded in comic postcards always featured the overweight Jewish parvenu, in a tight English suit with gold pocket watch and chain.

"The Polish Jews still in kaftan or Chasidic garb take their cure in Szczawnica, six hours away by car. The thermal bath establishment is dominated by black garbed consumptive Jews who wander the manicured lawns and gardens. They walk slowly to save their breath. All of them carry a glass mug containing a vacillating, whitish liquid. It is a mixture of water and kefir. In the glass there is a glass straw. As they walk, they occasionally suck in a mouthful of this beverage.

"Their hands tremble; thin, bluish milk splashes kaftans that are already pretty dirty. I shall remember this sight as one of the saddest of my life.

"It was a Saturday. A rabbi who had come to be treated had donned his Sabbath hat, decorated with tawny foxtails. He was completely surrounded by his coreligionists. He was speaking. They all listened, swaying slowly. They stopped to drop their heads to drink a few drops of kefir and again took up

the rhythmic
movement.

"Naturally, the rabbi was
speaking in Yiddish. So does the whole
town of Szczawnica. . . . I fled from both this
depressing establishment and from this dreadful
park. Below, in a steeply sloping avenue, I saw an
old Jew who had vomited blood onto his kaftan. He was hanging onto an iron
rail which ran the length of the street to help those who did not have the strength
to make the climb on their own. He asked me something in Yiddish in a very low
voice. I did not know what to reply; I said a few words to him in Polish. He did
not understand me. He was from a generation of Jews who spoke only Yiddish
and German." [Édouard de Pomiane, *The Jews of Poland* (1929)]

The front page of the Warsaw *Haynt* in the 1920s carried a small
standing advertisement for fresh kefir.

During a 1916 visit to Marienbad, Franz Kafka was fascinated to follow the Belz rabbi ("He looks like the Sultan in a Doré illustration of the Münchausen stories") and his retinue as they wandered around the spa. "I can detect this peaceful, happy confidence in the eyes of everyone in the group."

Otherwise, his days revolved around a vegetarian routine: "Breakfast at the Dianahof (fresh milk, eggs, honey, butter), then quickly to the Maxxtal for a snack (sour milk), quickly to the Neptune where Headwaiter Müller presides over lunch, to the fruit vendor to stock up on fruit, a brief nap, then a bowl of milk at the Dianahof (place your order beforehand), quickly to the Maxxtal for sour milk, and on to the Neptune for supper, then sit awhile on a bench in the public park and count over your money, then to the pastry shop." [Franz Kafka, *Letters*]

A number of urban milk spas existed in the major cities of Germany. A lavishly illustrated 1909 invoice from the Berliner Milchkur-Anstalt (milk cure institute), directed by L. Cohen and E. Weimann and formerly Friedrich Grub, depicts a three-story neoclassical building surrounded by a garden in which curists can be seen lingering over glasses of milk. A river passes in the background; in the foreground carriages bearing prospective curists and

Dresden
Milchkur
1883

solitary pedestrians suffering from various illnesses fill a rutted dirt road. Surrounding the vignette are seven gold and silver medals awarded to the institute for the quality of its milk. Friedrich Grub is recorded as the founder of this institute and other urban milk spas of the 1890s.

An engraving of 1883 depicts the central room of the Wille'schen Milchkuranstalt in Dresden. Within a large wooden barnlike structure, twenty live milch cows — some standing, some reclining, one happily being milked by a handsome young man — surround a central cafe with hanging flowers and a fountain. Curists sit at delicate tables enjoying their milk. Children and adults with tall glasses of fresh milk wander about the barn admiring the cows.

Milchhallen, Meierei, and Crémeries

In those countries where the population was able to digest fresh milk, a complex culture of milk drinking developed. The business of providing a simple glass of milk, in the days before modern refrigeration, depended not only upon its taste and freshness, but also upon the pastoral connotations of the act and its health-giving benefits.

In the streets of nineteenth-century European cities, vendors were allowed to deliver fresh milk directly from the udders of their goats and cows. In

of Vienna. The Meierei in the Bürgerpark, Bremen, built in 1881, included a barn for thirty-six cows (also one for swine), a cheese dairy, and a large restaurant building in the Swiss style. A cage with monkeys was added in 1886. The farm was closed in 1900, but the restaurant continued in business, survived the Second World War, and still operates. In 1897, a Meierei in popular Tyrolean style began operating at Lake Emmasee in Bremen complete with a music pavilion.

By studying the image of a Milchhalle, such as the one in Maschpark, Hannover, from the early years of the twentieth century, we can get a sense of the urban inhabitant striving for a taste of the pastoral life. They sit on a delicate folding chair inertly staring at their glass of milk; a bored child casts a distracted look off-camera; the server poses behind her counter in a modified milkmaid's costume, hands clasped in anticipation of the next customer. Did these places offer any satisfaction, or just cast one's discontent with urban life into higher relief?

On June 16, 1914, Franz Kafka sat in a Prague park to write a letter to Grete Bloch. His routine of insomnia, headaches, swimming, and then a walk in the park ends with a stop at the park's milk pavilion for a glass of sour milk. This was part of his self-imposed regime of light, air, and water.

In I. L. Peretz's 1903 short story about a Jewish writer in Warsaw entitled "Stories," the narrator notes a deserted dairy stand in the Krasinski Park of Warsaw.

Milchhalle im Brucker-Lagen 1907

In 1927, the architect Walter Gropius designed a Milchhalle for the Törten Estate, a housing development in the city of Dessau. The drawings exist, but it was never built.

The suburbs of German and Austrian cities were dotted with Meiereien, or dairies — eating-and-drinking establishments partaking of the pastoral atmosphere of a dairy farm but offering beer, cold cuts, and other delicate foodstuffs (delicatessen). The 1782 Edict of Toleration allowed Jews to settle in Vienna and, within a generation, many became assimilated Austrians. As a young man hiking on the outskirts of Vienna, Arthur Schnitzler stopped for a beer in a shady Meierei. Some of these were actual defunct dairy farms converted into garden-style establishments for food and drink. The most elaborate in scale and structure were self-contained resorts offering lodging, music, food, and dance.

Anti-Semitism expressed through acts, not necessarily written texts, manifested during the summer months in Germany. During the Vormärz Period (the years before the revolution of 1848) the Sommerfrische, an escape from the urban environment to the quiet and fresh air of the nearby countryside, was an annual ritual of working-, lower-middle-, and middle-class German life.

The lively tourist industry that developed in these locations is well documented in picture postcards — graphic advertisements for and handwritten

Meierei in Wiener Stadtpark

Heidelberg
Molkenkur

testaments to the enjoyment of these resorts. As more Jews became part of the bourgeois urban culture, they too partook of these resorts located in mountain villages and seaside towns. The health-giving purpose of the summer vacation was central to the spa towns of Europe. The desire for total calm, rest, and quiet was disturbed, in the eyes of some sections of German society, by the very presence of Jews.

Through the Weimar Period, this friction grew and found expression through signage and cartoon depictions. In the U.S., several notable cases of wealthy Jews being denied rooms at hotels in Manhattan Beach, Brooklyn, and Saratoga Springs made the news. For many Jews of the late nineteenth to early twentieth century, this expulsion from the paradise of vacation resorts was a wake-up call to the more virulent forms of anti-Semitism to follow. [Jacob Borut, *Anti-Semitism in Tourist Facilities in Weimar Germany*]

The term "Milchhalle" was also applied to an urban retail dairy pavilion or shop where a glass of fresh milk could be enjoyed. At least one Jewish milk shop in Vienna housed a live cow as proof of the freshness of its milk.

"In the newer parts of the city," according to an 1855 account of Munich, "may be found milk shops, where milk and all its preparations are sold, and there may be met students and others making a cheap and substantial supper of rye bread and milk, of which a very satisfactory quantity may be obtained for 4 kreuzers, or less than 3 cents." [*The Cultivator,* January 1855]

The Parisian crémerie is described in Charles Dickens's 1882 *Dictionary of Paris* as a dying institution: small shops with whitewashed walls selling milk, eggs, butter, and cheese that, through the addition of a kitchen, expanded into cheap restaurants. They were popular in the student quarters of Paris, where regulars would relax from seven to half past nine over a coffee, chocolate, and bread. The name "crémerie" was also adopted by low-priced table d'hôte restaurants offering "omelettes, and bifstecks, or cotelettes de mouton" in the business districts.

Located across the street from the Académie Colarossi, at 13 rue de la Grande-Chaumière, was Madame Charlotte's (Caron) (1849–1925) crémerie, a popular eating and meeting place for art students. The Académie Colarossi was established as an alternative to the official

from Juden in der Sommerfrische, 1895

government-sanctioned École des Beaux-Arts and attracted a number of Russian and Polish students. The Polish artist Władysław Ślewiński (1856–1918), then studying at the school, introduced August Strindberg to the crémerie in 1890. Charlotte Caron was an Alsatian who had transformed her dairy shop into a small restaurant seating about ten people. Meals cost 1 franc (about 3 euros today). A small garden in the back was shaded by acacias. She extended credit to artists or fed them in return for paintings. Other regulars were Paul Gauguin, Paul Sérusier, Zadkine, Modigliani, and Frederick Delius. Alphonse Mucha lived for a time above the crémerie and with Ślewiński decorated the crémerie's facade. Two acts of Strindberg's play *There Are Crimes and Crimes* are set in a fictional crémerie, probably based upon Charlotte's. Ślewiński returned to Warsaw from 1905 to 1910, was active in the Young Poland movement, and was present for the birth of mleczarnia in that city.

Krasinski Park WARSAW

C. Lewis Hind's 1906 *The Education of an Artist* described a visit to a crémerie off Boulevard Montparnasse:

"They . . . entered an unpretentious shop exposing in the window a cabbage and a dish of stewed prunes. A woman, elderly and gracious, sat behind a counter on the left of the entrance. Facing her was a long table. The floor was sanded; table-cloth and napkins were considered superfluous; but the place was clean and wholesome. An inner room was thick with tobacco smoke. Half a dozen voices were talking and shouting. . . . Their dinner consisted of a soup, a succulent 'biftek,' a dish of prunes, half a bottle of wine apiece and coffee. The joint bill came to two francs fifty. 'We've been extravagant,' said Lund: 'you can dine excellently in the quarter for a franc.'"

In *Purple Tints of Paris: Character and Manners in the New Empire* (1854), Bayle St. John describes the crémerie in the first half of the nineteenth century as a place that sells milk, cheese, and eggs "all nicely arranged in the window, or on marble slabs running round the shop — the crémière sold certain fruits, as apples, pears, and oranges, in their season, with various kinds

of liqueurs — brandy, cassis (made of black currants), anisette, and Jamaica rum, manufactured in Touraine; and behind the shop, separated off by a glazed partition, was a little parlor with two tables, wherein the morning breakfasts, consisting of cafe au lait, bread and butter, eggs, omelettes, and even chops and steaks were served up. Wine and beer, also, were supplied. This was the state of things when I first went to the place. The crémerie was transformed into a morning eating-house." At some point a customer was given the privilege of having an evening meal there, as well, at six o'clock. The hostess "had come to an agreement that no new persons should be admitted to dine without their consent. . . . The table was only large enough for six or seven; and each guest had a right sometimes to bring a friend. . . . We had always a good soup, the boiled beef, some roast meat or poultry, vegetables, and dessert, with wine and bread ad libitum, for from fifteen to twenty pence." The "club" members soon discover that the crémerie is the petite maison in which a wealthy businessman was keeping his mistress, their hostess.

The dairy business appealed to intellectuals and revolutionaries on the run. The loss of his teaching position coupled with the poor critical reception of his book *Der Einzige und sein Eigentum (The Ego and Its Own)* in 1845 drove the German philosopher Max Stirner (1806–56) to go into the dairy business.

Using
the inheritance
of his second wife,
he financed a cooperatively
run and elegantly decorated milk
shop in Berlin. Local dairy farmers agreed
to supply the milk, although they were suspicious
of the motives of the intellectuals involved. Neighborhood
customers felt uncomfortable shopping there because of its
elegant decor. The dairy failed and Stirner's wife, angered by the waste of her
inheritance, left him.

After fleeing Russia, the Marxist revolutionary Pavel Axelrod settled in
the Russian colony in Zürich, Switzerland. In the 1880s, to support his family,
Axelrod began producing his own kefir for the Russian community. According
to Lunacharsky, he was torn between tending the fermentation of his kefir and
his theoretical writing. Within ten years, the company grew to have offices in
Geneva and Basel, as well. The income from the kefir business supported his
family and went to help poor revolutionaries in his circle.

My Milkshop in Vienna (1934) by Alja Rachmanova describes the life

Pavel Axelrod with his kefir pots.
Geneva 1875

of a White Russian couple who fled the Bolsheviks to Vienna in 1925. The husband looks longingly at the proprietor standing at the door of a milk shop, selling a variety of cheeses, butter, eggs, and fresh milk. "Do you know," said Otmar, "that's an idea, a shop like that! I don't imagine that the work is very complicated. Furthermore, there is a flat over the shop, you buy your food cheaply and you have enough time to attend to other matters." They end up renting a milk shop. The husband continues his scholarly work

while the wife discovers the routine of running such a business: "measuring milk, cutting sausage and counting pastry." Milk is sold by the glass for 13 groschen. One table is provided for customers to sit and eat pastry (zucker kippl), a roll, or sausage.

A Russian "prince" who also fled the Bolsheviks comes in and is asked if he'd like a glass of milk. "Schnaps," he replies "is the only thing that can give me anything like self-confidence. Do you think milk can do that?"

People gather in the milk shop to discuss a recent murder case or talk of romance. She sells thirty liters of milk in a day for a profit of 4 groschen. (An Austrian schilling contained 100 groschen.) The wife is caught up in the desperate lives of her customers and the day-to-day struggle to keep the business afloat.

The galaktopoleia of Crete, the gwala of India specializing in lassis and curd- and cheese-based desserts, the pudding shops of Istanbul, and the latteria of Italy are all part of this worldwide milk culture. With the addition of a table, or two, any milk shop can be transformed into an eating place.

Out of this complex milk-drinking and dairy-eating culture in Europe there arose a specifically milekhdike personality. A type of person who in their demeanor expressed the qualities of the dairy culture.

In early-twentieth-century photographic postcards of the shtetlach of Poland and Russia we see Jews in, and around, marketplaces at makeshift tables selling various drinks, tea, milk, and kefir. A few benches set up nearby would constitute a dairy eating place without the ideological structure of a restaurant.

The Milekhdike Personality

The young Sholem Rabinovich married into, and lived with, a family that could afford to eat meat on a daily basis and exercised this privilege. Meat eating was a mark of success. His mother-in-law, who kept a kosher home, continued this luxury even after the family's wealth declined.

The ethical ramifications of meat and poultry production, possibly sparked by indigestion after a particularly heavy meal, led the writer to produce one of the most effective pleas for vegetarianism. "Dos Porfolk" ("The Pair, or Married Couple," of 1909) describes the brief nightmare of existence seen through the eyes of geese being prepared for slaughter. There's no evidence of Rabinovich becoming a vegetarian; acknowledging the cruelty involved in meat production was enough.

Under the pen name of Sholem Aleichem, he invented two great characters of Jewish dairy fiction. Tevye is the best-known. The nickname bestowed upon this figure by the narrator of the stories was "the milkhiger," or "the milky one." According to the writer's daughter, the term "Der Milkhiger" was consistently mistranslated over the years as simply being a trade — the milkman or dairyman. Harkavy's dictionary of 1910 gives "milkh-man" or

"pakhter" (the lessee of a farm, or dairy farm) for the trade and "milkh treger" for the deliverer. Other native speakers have confirmed this understanding of the term as an example of the Yiddish tradition of nicknaming. Only in Weinreich's 1968 dictionary was the word translated as milkman — a neologism, one of many introduced by this dictionary.

Tevye (meaning in Hebrew "the goodness of YHVH"), a man who happened to deal in milk and cheese, also embodied the myriad connotations of milk culture. He was the embodiment of the milekhdike personality. Some of these milekhdike traits derive from the technical necessities of dairy practices that have been described: an aura of purity, at least at the moment the milk leaves the udder; the desire to establish a benevolent relationship with an animal so that it gives its milk willingly; and milk as a source of health and nourishment.

The stories are set in the villages and countryside around Anatevka, between Yehupetz and Boiberik, fictionalized versions of Kiev and the nearby resort town of Boyarka during the years of revolutionary activity leading up to the assassination of Alexander II in 1881 and the Kishinev pogroms of 1903 to 1905.

Tevye is not a vegetarian or a farmer; he falls into the dairy business by chance. He's given a cow that's mysteriously stopped giving milk, as part of a reward for returning two lost vacationers to their dacha in Boiberik. He sells his cheese, cream, and butter in Boiberik during the summer and in Yehupetz during the winter.

Tevye embodies the ruminant behavior of a milk-giving animal. Unlike the proverbial Buridan's ass, which dies of hunger unable to choose between of two equal stacks of hay, Tevye sees and devours both sides of every argument with absolute and equal relish. In a single sentence, he can go from revolutionary zeal to religious resignation.

The well-to-do Jewish vacationers of Boiberik are engaged in the pursuit of the pastoral. They fled the heat and dust of Yehupetz, with its industrialized steam-dairies and rumors of adulterated milk, for a taste of unspoiled nature. The countryside around Kiev was known, through postcards and popular prints, for its peasant milkmaids of Amazonian stature. Having their milk products delivered by a bearded Jew with a bedraggled horse and wagon

may have been a disappointment, but at least they were assured of quality. His products were homemade in small quantities by his Jewish wife, Golde, and, most important, they were delicious and well priced.

The Tevye stories were sparked by the character of an actual milkman in Boyarka. Vacationing there in the summer, Sholem Aleichem saw the black humor of a poor Jew supplying the demands of a European pastoral fantasy in late-nineteenth-century Russia. The actual milkman knew of the stories and derived some local celebrity from them. A 1920s issue of the Warsaw illustrated magazine *Der Stral* ran an article on Jewish farmers in the Pale, extolling the fact that the ancient Jewish pastoral tradition was still alive.

Tevye brags of the superior quality of his produce — his customers await his arrival like the Messiah — and yet he dreams of striking it rich, selling his horse and wagon, and moving to Yehupetz, where he can enjoy the luxuries of urban life.

The stories remind us of the wide range of dairy dishes: the potato knishes, the milkhiker borscht, the cheese kreplekh, the varnishkes, the pirogen, blintzes, buttermilk, and for dessert pudding and poppy cakes — the food of a Jew's pastoral dream. Sholem Aleichem depended upon a reader capable of filling in the specific qualities and flavors of these foods. Can these stories make any sense to a reader without this common culinary background?

In "Tevye Strikes It Rich," a meal offered to Menachem Mendl, an obscurely distant relative who can't "remember when he had last eaten such delicious dairy food," leads to idle after-dinner talk and a disastrous investment in the stock market of Odessa. Tevye rationalizes his lost wealth: "God was

trying to tell me, 'You should have stuck to your cheese and butter.' " [All quotations from Hillel Halkin's translations.]

In "Today's Children," the milk/meat taboo is given human form when Layzer Wolf, the wealthy butcher of Anatevka, asks to marry Tsaytl, the milkman's daughter. At first, Tevye mistakenly believes that Wolf is interested in his cow, a sale he would never allow; the man's actual desire leaves him dumbfounded. His natural repugnance, the idea of someone smelling of the meat counter mixing with a family in the dairy trade, is quickly overcome by the economic advantages of the match. Tevye sits and thinks. "The greenery gave off a smell like Paradise." In his mind he overthrows the established economic order. "Where does it say in the Bible that Tevye has to work his bottom off. . . . Where does it say that the rich Jews of Yehupetz must have fresh cheese and butter each morning. . . . When will justice be done, so that Tevye too can spend a summer vacation in a dacha in Boiberik! Who, though, you ask, would bring him cheese and butter? Who would milk the cows? Why, the Yehupetz tycoons, of course!" At this thought, he stops and laughs and recalls the proverb "If God were to listen to what each fool has to say, He would have to create a new world every day." On the next page, we learn that Tsaytl has already arranged her own marriage to a poor local tailor. Political, economic, and theological theories are overthrown for love.

In the next story, Tevye meets a young man, an intellectual on the road, and invites him home for a dinner of borscht and knishes. "If you'd like to wash your hands and say the Lord's blessing, go ahead, and if not — that's fine with me too. I'm not God's policeman. No one's going to whip me in the next world for your sins in this one." Tevye enjoys the conversational mix of Bible, Talmud, and philosophical ideas. The young man, nicknamed Pepperkorn, disappears and then shows up again at mealtime for Golde's irresistible dairy dishes. It's arranged for the young man to take meals with them in exchange for tutoring Tevye's daughters. Suddenly, Hodl, the next daughter in line for marriage, announces that she's engaged to Pepperkorn. After a joyless, "official" marriage, Pepperkorn disappears for mysterious political reasons with a group of young Kasrilevkite revolutionaries, "one, wearing his shirt down over his pants and looking more like a Russian than a Jew." Next, Pepperkorn is in prison and Hodl prepares to join him in Siberia. Tevye is crushed by the prospect of losing his daughter for a theoretical benefit to mankind. This milkmaid in a Jew's body tries to hold back his tears by repeating, "Tevye is no woman." And so a delicious dairy dinner is a prelude to political and personal tragedy. "Let's talk about something more cheerful," says Tevye to the narrator. "Have you heard any news of the cholera in Odessa?"

"Whatever God does is for the best. That is, it had better be, because try changing it if you don't like it." The effort, Tevye realizes, is a waste of time as the world can't be remade. In this story, he confronts Christian culture as it exists in his village: a town priest, who insists that he knows the Scripture better than Tevye and recites it in "a Hebrew that sounds like a Frenchman talking Greek," and the town scribe, Fyedka Galagan, the son of a peasant who his daughter Khave has befriended. She insists on seeing him as an individual and considers him a second Gorky. Arguing over Gorky and the basic value of literature, they are suddenly called to dinner. Tevye shouts back to his wife, "Here we are talking about the universe and all you can think of is your borscht." Golde responds with "Better my borscht without the universe than the universe without my borscht." Khave puts herself in the hands of the priest who will arrange her conversion and marriage to Galagan, and her family mourns her as dead. In the forest, Tevye encounters her, or an image of her, begging to

speak, obstructing the passage of his horse and wagon, but he refuses to stop. He pushes onward, his mind filled with thoughts: "What did being a Jew or not a Jew matter? Why did God have to create both?" One day he sets off to take a train to Yehupetz, where he knows Khave lives, only to be stymied by a ticket seller who's never heard of the place. He begs the narrator not to recount these events in his books, or, if he must, attribute them to a fictional character. He realizes that his suffering can make a worthwhile story.

Tevye evokes his favorite quote from the Ethics of the Fathers: "Regardless of thy will thou art conceived, and regardless of thy will thou art born, and regardless of thy will thou livest, and regardless of thy will thou diest."

Tevye befriends Ahronchik, the son of a rich widow, a customer of his in Boiberik. The boy cared only for fishing and horses and fun, but Tevye was attracted to his generosity of spirit and so invited him and his friends for dinner on the first day of Shavuos. He promises blintzes fit for a prince. On that perfect day, Tevye arranges an outdoor feast — a pastoral idyll with an endless supply of hot blintzes. Sphrintze, the next daughter in line, helps serve the food. Ahronchik cannot take his eyes off her and within a few pages announces their

engagement. The prospect of Tevye's daughter marrying into a wealthy family must, at last, be signaling a change in his fortune.

For a few days, Ahronchik fails to appear; Sphrintze is distraught. Tevye goes to Boiberik, to see what's happened and to seal the marriage. The boy's uncle answers the door; the widow and son are gone. He asks Tevye how much it will cost to cover his nephew's breach of promise. He accuses Tevye of setting his nephew up by luring him to his home with blintzes. "Where does a sensible Jew like yourself get off thinking that a dairyman, a common cheese monger, can marry into a family like ours?" One evening, soon after, Tevye comes home to discover that Sphrintze has drowned herself. He asks the narrator, "Have you ever seen a drowned man? Never? Well, mostly one dies with one's eyes shut, but a drowned man's eyes are always open. I just thought you might know why that was." Tevye fixates on a technical detail of the tragedy in the hope that it will enlighten him in some way. He is a bystander to his own experience.

At certain moments Tevye allows himself to equate the countryside between Anatevka and Boiberik with paradise, but quickly catches himself.

Tevye's youngest daughter, Beilke, agrees to a loveless marriage with Padhatzur, a wealthy Yehupetz builder and army contractor. In her misery, Tevye occupies himself with trying to differentiate between "crying" and "weeping."

He's invited to the newlyweds' home in Yehupetz and imagines that he'll be asked to join the business and spend his declining years in the wealth and luxury of the big city, but these thoughts are interrupted by a realization of the worthlessness of these luxuries when all he wants is "to enjoy a peaceful old age in which I can study a bit of Mishnah now and then and recite a few chapters of Psalms."

Over a sumptuous dinner filled with business and other worldly talk, Tevye recalls the saying of Rabbi Simeon, from the Ethics of the Fathers: "Three men who eat together at the same table and speak no words of Torah may as well have eaten the flesh of a pagan sacrifice."

Tevye lives in an eternal present, while his daughters feel themselves victims of "the Age of Hodl," or "the Age of Beilke" — each with utterly unique ethical and social rules.

Padhatzur confides in Tevye: "With a business like mine, with a reputation like mine, a public position like mine, I can't afford to have a cheese monger for a father-in-law." He offers to set him up in another line of business, or better yet, ship him off to Palestine, "where all the old Jews like to go to die."

In the last story of the series, Tevye assumes the role of narrator to his own history. Sholem Aleichem hardly recognized his own creation as Tevye's hair has turned white.

"I'm still Tevye, though I'm not a dairyman [or "milky one"; here the word "milkhiger" is used] anymore; I'm just a plain everyday Jew. . . ." He is still in Russia, prevented from traveling to the Holy Land by the sudden death of Tsaytl's husband. Beilke's millionaire husband has gone bankrupt and the couple has fled to America, where they make socks in a sweatshop. Finally, he recounts how, "just like in one of your books," Chava has returned home to her father and her God.

He recounts being ordered to leave his village in accordance with the May Laws and equates it with God telling Abraham to hit the road. A mob of peasants arrive at his house and, in a friendly way, explain that it's expected of them to join the wave of pogroms by sacking and looting his house; in fact, it would be suspect if they didn't. In the end, the peasants agree to leave it to Tevye to smash his own windows, "as long as those damn officials can see there's been a pogrom," and they all sit down for tea. He no longer apologizes for going on too long, realizing that his tales will give Sholem Aleichem something to write about. Tevye "remains on the milkhiker bench."

The animals around Tevye share his pleasure and pain. "Even a cow grieves when her calves are taken away." The selling of his horse is poor thanks due to a beast of burden.

To what can we attribute the great popularity of these stories? The linguistic particularity of the dialogue, the familiarity of the situations, the sense of the absurd, the matter-of-fact tragedies. For the Yiddish audience, the taste of blintzes, peppered with eroticism, was fresh in their mouths. These were variations on a Yiddish pastoral: intimations of paradise intruded upon by the cruelty of modern European culture. But most of all, the stories present a vivid portrait of a perfect type: the milekhdike personality, a personality composed of rare traits, a few of which each reader could see in himself. Readers and listeners came away feeling that they could appraise the events of their own life with the impartial eye of a good storyteller and thus better appreciate their own hardships and pleasures.

Khoskl Kotik's Mleczarnia

After being diagnosed with pulmonary tuberculosis, Sholem Aleichem spent
the winters of 1908 to 1913 in Nervi, on the Ligurian coast of Italy, and summers
in the clinics and sanatoria of Lausanne and Berne in Switzerland and Baden-
Baden in the Black Forest of Southern Germany. Treatment of pulmonary
tuberculosis at that time involved a combination of dietary and climatic
adjustments — one without the other was useless. It was while shuttling between
these restful and picturesque locales, undergoing a milk or whey cure himself,
or observing others on this regime, that Sholem Aleichem discovered his second
great milekhdike character.

A copy of *My Memories* by Yekhezkel Kotik was sent to him by the
author in 1913. Sholem Aleichem was deeply taken by the literary talent of this
unknown writer and a lively and encouraging correspondence ensued. He
was surprised to learn that the author was a sixty-five-year-old man who ran
a mleczarnia, a type of dairy cafe, or restaurant, in Warsaw at 31 Nalewki, the
central business avenue of Jewish Warsaw.

The use of the word "mleczarnia," or dairy, as the place where milk was produced, handled, and/or sold, was gradually extended from the pastoral location to an urban business where milk was sold to an eating place where milk-based foods were sold and served.

Kotik's was a well-known literary cafe located in a courtyard behind a glass door. The cafe figures in contemporary accounts of literary Warsaw. It was described as "sooty" and unusually well stocked with Hebrew, Yiddish, German, and Russian newspapers and literary journals; it had the atmosphere of a reading room. It also had a telephone — unusual for public eating places in Warsaw at that time. The inexpensive food and drink was served on credit.

Kotik came to run this cafe after a long series of commercial failures. From the age of twelve, Kotik was a compulsive social organizer. His mind was involved in the planning and composition of bylaws for a dozen nascent organizations, and rarely on the various schemes he undertook. In the early 1870s he leased a dairy and tavern near Białystok and had some success selling butter, cheese, and milk. All along, he displayed a lack of interest in business. "What I sought was a peaceful life; easygoing, modest, without undue wealth, so that I would be able to devote time to intellectual pursuits. Moreover, I always hated those people who devoted themselves entirely to business, their miserliness, their one-track thinking about money, their inability to find anything else of interest." From there, he managed an inn on the banks of the Dnieper

near Kiev, ran a grocery store in the city, dealt in dried fruit, managed a bakery, had some success making and selling raisin wine. The pogrom in Kiev following the assassination of Alexander II, drove him and his family to Warsaw. There he was active in social and religious organizations for the support of Lithuanian Jews recently arrived in Warsaw. The antagonism between the Polish Jews of Warsaw and the Lithuanians is legendary. To make a living, he ran the dairy restaurant. Kotik was one of those intellectuals, like Pavel Alexrod, who looked upon the dairy business, in this case a dairy cafe, as a painless way to subsidize other, more important work.

The mix of businesspeople, political activists, dreamers, and literary figures sparked lively arguments. The mild tumult disturbed Mr. Kotik, who did not

hesitate to call for quiet. Whether he was worried that the noise might attract the police or simply felt that such behavior was not fitting for a mleczarnia, is unclear.

Kotik's time and money were spent writing and publishing the charters and bylaws of his various proposed organizations. His most successful organization was "Akchiezer," to provide aid for the sick of Warsaw. He organized a synagogue committed to doing away with special seating, honorary readings, and other abuses.

He organized soup kitchens for the poor, societies to assist orphans, and a large community center. He organized Warsaw's first old-age home and in 1909 tried to organize a Jewish housing project in a forest twenty miles east of Warsaw. Most of these projects remained in the organizational stage — the stage Kotik most enjoyed. His obsessive attention to the minutiae of organization made him difficult to work with. In 1912, his son convinced him to take time from this frantic activity to write his memoirs.

When Sholem Aleichem came to write a second series of epistolary stories about Menachem Mendl (his famous luftmensch would now be based in Warsaw working as a journalist c. 1913), he wanted to insert a slightly fictionalized version of Kotik and his dairy cafe and wrote to secure his permission. The course of this strange relationship was soured when Sholem Aleichem responded with little enthusiasm to the second volume of Kotik's memoirs.

In the second letter of the series, Menachem Mendl refers to Kotik's cafe as *his* mleczarnia, implying that there were others to choose from. It was the place he frequented for coffee, conversation, and a light meal. There's little description of the place — was it assumed that readers were familiar with the physical setup? — just tables at which Mendl could have a tête-a-tête with Kotik.

During the 123 years of Poland's partition and occupation by Prussia, Austria, and Russia (1795–1918), mleczarnie or dairy-style eating establishments became linked to nationalistic aspirations, questions of Polish identity, and aesthetics.

A traveler in Warsaw in 1833 describes "a pleasure garden [the Saxon Kempe] on an island in the Vistula. Principally inhabited by Dutch, who were planted here by Augustus, the Strong, Elector of Saxony, and the King of Poland. They have excellent cattle, and you there get delicious milk and butter, which the Warsaw world, on Sundays, makes great trial of." He notes "the noble gardens [adjoining the Saxon Palace] to which every one, except a Jew, has free access." [Peter Diedrich Holthaus, *Wanderings of a Journeyman Tailor Through Europe and the East*]

By the early nineteenth century, Swiss confectioners from Poschiavo ran over sixty well-known cafes or coffee houses and confectioneries in Poland. There were fourteen such "Swiss" eateries in Warsaw. Family names such as Semadeni, Maurizio, Vassali, Zamboni, Zappa, Tossio, Lours, and many others were known all over Poland. Each year, young men with an expertise in sugar baking would leave their Alpine homes to find work in European cities. After accumulating sufficient money, they'd often return to the Tyrol to build sizable homes.

These "Swiss" eateries featured pastries and other confections. The traditional cuisines of Poschiavo, including buckwheat noodles smothered in vegetables and local cheeses, spinach dumplings, and other pasta dishes with raisins and cream, may have entered the menu of their Warsaw eating places.

In the Saxon Gardens of Warsaw, while under Prussian rule, an

Mleczarnia
in Saxon Gardens
c. 1838

actual working dairy (mleczarnia) offering koumiss treatments and dairy dishes was established alongside an artificial mineral-water pavilion as early as 1838. These cafes and confectioneries were part of the garden's redesign in the English style in 1816.

Cukiernie were described in George Anson's (1697–1762) eighteenth-century account as "something like the French cafes, where many Warsovians breakfast and lounge in the morning." Already at that time, he explained, "the whole business of the country is in the hands of the Jews [thirty thousand out of a population of 140,000], and all the useful and mechanical arts are practiced by strangers [German, Italian, and French]. I did not find a Pole in a single shop in Warsaw; the proprietors of the hotels and coffee-houses are strangers, principally Germans. . . . Society consists altogether of two distinct and distant orders, the nobles and the peasants, without any intermediate degrees. I except, of course, the Jews . . . whose long beards, thin and anxious faces and piercing eyes, met me at every corner of Warsaw." The 1929 Warsaw directory, with its categories translated into French, lists cukiernie as confiseries, confectioneries in English, and cross-references to herbaciarnie, kawiarnie, and mleczarnie. The Polish nobles, called the French of the North, were fond of amusements, lounging in public and averse to the practice of any profession. In 1900, there were 32 hotels, 67 pensions, 269 restaurants, and 727 places licensed to sell alcoholic drink. The 1929 directory lists 200 cukiernie.

"Herbaciarnie" are confectioners' shops like the cafes of Southern Europe, where tea is the primary drink. Translated into French as "Debits de thé" (after "debits de boisson," a drinking establishment or taphouse), 240 such

182

establishments were listed in 1929, many with Jewish names. Kawiarnie, or "cafes" in French, served coffee and were possibly differentiated from cukiernie by the serving of alcohol.

Mleczarnie existed within the rich public eating culture of Warsaw. Food historians trace the origins of the widespread popularity of mleczarnie as eating places in the late-nineteenth into twentieth-century Poland to Stanisław Dłużewski (1865–1935). Stanisław was the scion of Polish gentry whose estate was in Dłuzew, near the bridge over the Swider River, fifty kilometers from Warsaw.

Upon the death of his father in 1875, Stanisław left his chemistry studies in Riga to manage the family estate. Through a scientific approach to cross-breeding along with improvements to irrigation and drainage, he managed to greatly increase the estate's production of dairy products.

In 1896, in a move to bypass the intermediaries involved in the selling of milk, he established a company, the Mleczarnia Nadswidrzanka, to directly distribute milk from his estate at several locations in Warsaw: Bracka 22, at the Summer Theater in Łazienki, and one at Nowy-Siwak 11 (New World) and the corner of Jerusalem Alle that included a cafe/eating place. Built on the grounds of the former Opalinski Palace (built 1762, demolished 1928), it was a long,

one-story pavilion set back from the street within a large garden with chestnut trees. Metal railings separated the garden from the street. In warm weather, the popular garden was furnished with iron tables, painted white. There was a pool with a non-functioning fountain. The pavilion was decorated in the rustic Zakopane Style of the Polish highlands. The waiters were young boys and girls, aged twelve to fourteen, dressed in peasant costumes.

The menu included unique preparations of kefir and koumiss, along with Warsaw kaiser rolls, crescent rolls, rural-style breads with black caraway seeds, "country style" coffee and cocoa, dumplings with cheese, sour milk (or cream) with buckwheat groats, and young potatoes with kefir [Angnieszka Jez, *Interwar Years Cuisine: What and How It Was Eaten*]. Intelligensia of the Young Poland movement took their "second breakfast" there at 11 am.

The novelty of a pastoral environment on a busy commercial thoroughfare attracted the fashionable public, the demimonde, bohemians, and especially the intelligentsia associated with the Young Poland movement looking for an alternative to the bourgeois cafes and restaurants of Warsaw. The bohemian crowd dressed in a purposefully discordant combination of colorful peasant vests from Kraków and Zakopane, cartwheel hats, bowlers, high stiff collars, bows, and wide plastrons above their well-worn upper shirts. [K. Pollack, *From the Memoirs of an Old Journalist from Warsaw*]

A dairy-styled eating establishment in the 1890s is late in the history of such places in Paris and even the United States. Dłużewski's business scheme may have been based on foreign models, such as the Parisian crémerie or the Milchhallen of Germany and Austria. The dairy-style eating establishment turned out to be the perfect gathering place for the young intelligentsia in Poland.

Reacting against the previous generation's desire to cultivate a Polish identity within the occupied status, those associated with the Young Poland movement aspired in their writing and art to be part of the supranational art world of Paris, London, and Vienna and advocated making art for art's sake. Along with imported art and writing, the dairy as cafe would connect them with Parisian and Viennese culture. They argued that this impulse could coexist with a natural expression of Polish culture through gestures of language and painting that symbolically referred to the dilemma of Warsaw's occupation by Russia since 1867. These feelings were part of an ongoing "peasant mania" — the raising of the image of the peasant to an idealized vision of an uncorrupted, pre-industrialized pure Poland of the past. In the mleczarnie both impulses could coexist. These questions of Polish identity concerned members of the intelligentsia, not the peasants themselves. The Jews in Poland who did not exhibit the markings of Polish ethnicity were excluded from this "natural" expression of Polish ethnic identity.

The popularity and atmosphere of the Mleczarnia Nadswidrzanka inspired three kefir producers, K. Życki, S. Giżyński, and Elżanowski, of the "Udziałową" cafe ("Joint Ownership" or "Shareholder's" opened in 1884) just across the street, at number 15, to rename their place the Pierwsza Warszawska Mleczarnia Udziałowa (First Warsaw Shareholder's Mleczarnia). By 1906 they had opened three branches.

The interior decoration of "Udziałową" seems to have been a discordant

amalgam of mahogany-paneled walls, overstuffed magenta sofas and an Art Nouveau mural that appealed to the young intellectuals who gathered there from morning to late at night. It became the meeting place for members of the *Chimera* (1901–8), a small-circulation but influential avant-garde art-and-literary journal whose offices were nearby. Its editor, Zenon Przesmycki, was instrumental in introducing Polish readers to modernist artists and writers from around the world. Among the contributors were two Polonized Jews: the poet, philosopher, science-fiction author Antoni Lange, and the poet and prose writer Bołeslaw Leśmian. Other habitués of the "Share" were the novelist and Nobel laureate Władysalw Reymont, the novelist and dramatist Stefan Zeromski, the erotic poet Kazimierz Tetmajer, the writer and cabaret organizer Kazimierz Wroczyńiski, and the dramatist and writer Włodzimierz Perzyński.

It offered a wide selection of local and foreign newspapers and journals; in the evening, an orchestra provided music. The menu featured kefir and other dairy-based dishes along with an assortment of regional meat dishes, sausages, etc.

The decision to call the place a "dairy" may have been made, in part, to avoid the surveillance that literary cafes were subjected to, or to avoid the licensing requirements of a cafe as opposed to a dairy or food shop.

Stanisław Dłużewski went on to engage in various nationalist activities, such as agricultural training for peasants and the advancement of Polish language in schools, for which he spent some time in jail. Otherwise, earnings from his successful mleczarnie in Warsaw helped finance the design and building of a splendid manor that still stands today in Dluzew.

A 1907 directory of Warsaw lists nine mleczarnie. The Mleczarnia Salvic at Alle Jerozolimska 68 is "always stocked with the latest dairy, cake and bread" and reminds readers that "consumption on the spot" is possible. The Mleczarnia Polska at Krucza 16, at which "consumption on the spot" is also possible, features facilities for playing billiards. Others seem to be wholesale and retail shops for dairy products, with no advertised eating on the premises. The popularity of the mleczarnia, as a dairy cafe/eating house, spread through Warsaw. A 1914 Baedeker of Russia lists the Udziałową cafe "with dairy restaurant" and recommends that "good milk can be obtained in the larger Dairy Restaurants (Mleczarnia)."

Business directories of nineteenth- and early-twentieth-century Poland carefully differentiate and cross-reference the various shades of public eating and drinking establishments. Businesses dealing in milk products are listed as "mleczarnie i nabial" (milk and kefir) or "mleczarskie zaklady" (milk-processing plant).

A 1929 Warsaw business directory lists about 350 restauracje or "restaurants," many using the French word in their names, others using the English words "bar," "lunch," and others evoking a cosmopolitan air with

names like Liverpool Bar, Mikado, Central, Ritz and Victoria, Ch. Hirszfeld's Piccadilly, "Les Establishments Duval," and "Louvre."

According to Edouard de Pomiane's account of Polish restaurant culture in 1929, the Warsaw middle-class restaurant was totally French in tone. The restaurants with clearly Jewish names in the Jewish district include Chaim Blumenfeld (Grzybowska 16), Rachmil Judaszko (Nalewki 29), Anszel Osma (Mila 52), S. G. Pszczola (Nalewki 37), Sura Ryfka Weinsztadt (Gesia 105), Szmul Rotenber (Sierakowska 1), Icek Reinerman (Prozna 7), and S. Goldblatt (Nalewki 43). To experience a Jewish-style restaurant, he recommends traveling to Kraków.

The literary and journalistic history of Jewish Warsaw is peppered with mention of countless cafes and restaurants. Chaim Finkelstein in his history of *Haynt: A Jewish Newspaper, 1908–1939* recalls the Piccadilly on

Bielanska Street and Schultz's Restaurant at the corner of Carmelicka and Nowolipki, "a tavern where people would drop in for a little schnapps chased by a piece of herring or a serving of chopped liver." These were all places of shelter for writers and activists engaged in underpaid work.

The 1929 Business Directory of Poland lists 119 mleczarnie in Warsaw. They are cross-referenced with cafes (kawiarnie), tea rooms (herbaciarnie), and pastry salons (cukiernie) to distinguish them from dairy plants (mleczarski zaklady), places to buy milk (mleko), and various dairy products (nabial or cremiers). By name of owner and/or location, twenty-nine can be identified as Jewish businesses:

Ch. Ajzenwaser, Pawia 4;
M. Akerman, Karmelicka 13;
Krajndla Apelblass, Nowolipie 27;
Chaim Bedzak, Zabkowska 11;
Leib Berenhole, Grojecka 45;
Chaim Borenstin, Pawia 38;
M. Charazinska, Sliska 1;
Szymon Charazinski,
Sliska 6;
Chuna Eisenwasser,
Tamka 17;
Felicja Figat,
Krochmalna 86;
Jakob Flam,
Dzika 13;
Icko Forek and Jankiel
Pominowski,
Franciszkanska 24;
Moszek Frydman,
Grzybowska 5;
Markus Glocer, Nalewki 26;
Eljasz Goldstejn,
Chmielna 54; Moszek
Grinhaus, Ceglana 10;
Sz. Grzesz, Sliska 31;
I. Gutgold, Dzika 41;
"Higlena," Estera Goldberg, Dzika 44;
Anna Horowicz, Zelazna 31;
R. Jachimowicz, Muranowska 17;
Bajla Koper, Pawia 19;
M. Laubsztajn, Krzyska 28;

M. Montak, Nalewki 42;
Abram Rutman, Jerska 24;
Abram Sztejnberg,
Bonifraterska 11–13;
Pinkus Wajnsztejn, Nowomiejska 2;
S. Wajsbaum, Dzika 30;
Abram Zylberman, Mila 30.

Whether these were literary cafes in the style of Kotik's or dairy shops with one or two tables remains to be discovered. Kotik had died in 1921. Some have names like "Health," "Hygiene," and "Truth." Others are named after pastoral regions of Poland. Most are simply listed in the owner's name. The same directory lists 25 mleczarnie in Kraków, 48 in Lovov, 53 in Lodz, and 30 in Wilno. The 1932 Bialystok business directory lists 22 mleczarnie.

From photographic evidence we can see that some of the mleczarnie in Jewish neighborhoods were small operations occupying narrow storefronts. From the better financed businesses that could afford to advertise in newspapers, we can see that they featured menus based around dairy dishes made in accordance with Jewish dietary law.

In a 1921 ad in *Der Moment* Sh. Haltzberg, "a longtime gastronomic expert asks you to acquaint yourself with the newly opened Mleczarnia 'UNJA' at Tlomatzkie 13, Warsaw. He especially recommends that you take note of fresh dairy midday meals." (See ad opposite.)

In June of 1921, "the elegant Jewish restaurant" Piccadilly at Bielanska 5 announced the opening of the Large Veranda and a summer-menu of cold and hot milkhiger foods rabbinically certified. (See ad on page 193.)

Menachem Mendl, a compulsive but ineffectual schemer himself, is infected by Kotik's organizational mania. Sitting in Kotik's mleczarnia — itself already a lively gathering place for Jewish writers — he asks why there is no place in

Warsaw for Jewish writers to congregate, why they must depend upon Polish cafes. In interwar Poland, 74 percent of Jews considered Yiddish their first language. He was thinking of the great literary cafes of Vienna and Berlin, not a lowly mleczarnia. With Kotik's help, he begins to devise a grandiose plan for a cooperative Yiddish writers' cafe — a complex social center with library, restaurant, clothing supplies, and housing facilities. And why, he further asks, does not each profession in Jewish Warsaw have such a cooperative cafe of its own? In the face of recent Polish boycotts of Jewish business, he argues, the Jews would, at least, be able to patronize their own cafes. Within moments, he's diverted from his original plan to an even more grandiose scheme involving all Jews in Warsaw.

The growing cultural rift between Jews and Christian Poles during the

interwar years can, in part, be attributed to Polish nationalists blaming Jews, who composed one-third of Warsaw's population, for the overcrowded and disease-ridden condition of the city. Jewish political ideologies leaning toward socialism and anarchism, and, in the arts, the attendant attraction to Tolstoy's call for a didactic art that would impart moral values, as opposed to the modernist idea that pure art should lack any responsibility to society and simply reflect the naked soul of the artist, further separated the two intellectual cultures.

Kotik is at hand to advise Mendl on the intricacies of the bylaws for this new Jewish organization. With superhuman facility, he begins to dictate, off the top of this head, the detailed charter and bylaws for the cooperative cafe.

In drawing his portrait of the "fictional" Kotik, Sholem Aleichem relied upon the fact that the "real" Kotik was a well-known figure in Jewish Warsaw. Through correspondence with other Warsaw writers, he had learned of the full range and peculiarities of Kotik's behavior. A kind of mental rumination gone wild.

Like most of Kotik's plans, the organizing of the plan is an end in itself — there's no energy left for its realization. The cafe of Menachem Mendl's dream is a paradise of pure rumination; a social structure in which a writer could work free from material concerns, free from the pressure of having to finish or publish.

Several scenes in Louis Begley's semi-autobiographical novel *Wartime Lies* are set in his grandfather's mleczarnia of choice, sitting over tea and cheese pierogen or nalesniki (cheese-filled crepes).

Milk was covertly delivered into the Warsaw Ghetto by a pipeline temporarily laid across the ghetto wall. In December of 1950, a second portion of the important Emanuel Ringelblum Archives, documenting life in the Warsaw Ghetto, was found in the cellar of a ruined house at 68 Nowolipki Street — the documents were preserved by being hidden in two large milk cans.

Polish food historians see the later bar mleczny, or milk bar, a type of inexpensive, state-subsidized eating place with a largely non-meat-based menu, as the descendant of the mleczarnia. In 1950s communist Poland there were 40,000 subsidized milk bars in Poland serving a full-range of Polish dishes including dairy and meat. Today, 140 remain in business.

The surviving facade of an early-twentieth-century mleczarnia in the shadow of a Wrocław synagogue, today operating as a youth-oriented cafe, consists of three heavy archways topped with Jugendstil signage frames of delicate copper. A contemporary Polish milk-bar enthusiast reported that his Christian grandmother would not mix milk and meat in a single meal simply because it seemed to be a good thing for the Jews to do.

If the saloon was a place for workingmen to fall into an alcoholic stupor, and the cafes of Paris, coffeehouses in London, and tearooms of Russia were caffeinated hotbeds of radical thought and action, the mleczarnia, or dairy cafe, was a place of ferocious rumination.

193

The Vegetarian Restaurant and Radical Politics

In contrast to Tevye's questions to God: "Would it hurt for me to be rich? Upset a larger plan of nature?" the anarchist Alexander Berkman (1870–1936) advocated murdering capitalists who refused to give up their property. If an "employer should refuse to yield to the demands of his employees . . . he would go straight to the employer and shoot him down."

Through the selective breeding and improved feeding of cattle, the weight of a bullock increased from 370 pounds in 1710 to 800 pounds in 1845. The consumption of meat had almost doubled over the first half of the nineteenth century.

In Nikolay Chernyshevsky's (utopian socialist, 1828–1889) *What Is to Be Done?,* the character Rakhmetov, the model of the "new man," "eats huge

194

quantities of raw beef and sleeps on nails, thus acquiring enormous strength and hardiness for revolutionary tasks [Chernyshevsky himself was frail and bookish in appearance]. Aside from raw beef, he would not eat food that poor people could not afford." [Adam Bruno Ulam, *The Revolutionary Tradition*]

With his dictum "Man is what he eats," the German materialist philosopher Ludwig Feuerbach (1804–1872) explained the dilemma of workers lacking the energy to overcome the beef-eating aristocracy; similarly, if they ate beef, they would emulate them. He recommended shifting their diet from potatoes to beans.

Still, a number of early socialist and anarchist thinkers turned to alternative eating systems, convinced that it was the meat diet that produced the callous and aggressive behavior of the tsar and ruling classes. Olinde Rodrigues, the Portuguese-French-Jewish banker/mathematician and supporter of the Comte de Saint-Simon (1760–1825) may have been instrumental in attracting Jewish followers to the scientifically based ideas of utopian socialism. Working on his *Memoir on the Science of Man and Work on General Gravitation,* Comte de Saint-Simon lived on bread and water.

The modern vegetarian movement in Europe and America was organized by individuals from the upper and middle classes, who could afford to eat meat but chose not to for ethical reasons. In fact, many prominent vegetarians adopted this diet for reasons of personal comfort — they suffered from digestive problems and only found relief through a meatless diet. Gandhi discovered vegetarianism in this way in a London restaurant.

The earliest vegetarian promoters, as we have seen, linked their behavior to the Hebrew Bible: fruitarians following an Edenic diet of things that naturally fell to the earth. Others equated vegetarianism with the diet of the Jews being led through the desert by Moses.

A number of socialists and anarchists in Russia adopted a vegetarian diet as a way of differentiating their behavior from that of the ruling class.

Mandelkorn's Adventures in Odessa and America

Israel Mandelkorn (1861–?), born in Dubno, a city in Volhynia, Ukraine, in his unpublished memoir, *Recollections of a Communist*, offers an interesting piece of this history. The twenty-year-old Mandelkorn was working as a teacher in a kheyder in Odessa. He awoke in his bed on March 14, 1881, and felt that something momentous had occurred. Between classes, he ran to the corner of the Preobrazhensky, where the city's official newspaper, *Odesskye Vedomosty*, was pasted on a wall for public reading. Alexander II had been assassinated the day before in St. Petersburg.

In 1880, Yuri Bogdanovich, a county surveyor and medical student of noble heritage, became an executive member of the Narodnaya Volya (the

People's Will), a political group whose program included the assassination of Tsar Alexander II. After a number of failed attempts, they had to operate with increased ingenuity.

On December 2, 1880, under the assumed name of Yevdokim Kobozev, Bogdanovich and his "wife," Anna Yakimova, rented a three-room basement space at 4 Malaya Sadovaya (Little Garden) Street in St. Petersburg. On January 8, 1881, they moved in, opened a dairy shop in one room, and lived in the other two. A dairy shop, with its associations of pastoral calm and well-being, was the perfect cover for this violent plan. In the basement shop, a tunnel was being dug under the street that the tsar regularly passed. A bomb was to be planted there and detonated as he passed. They sold cheese and dairy

products at suspiciously low prices for two months while their coconspirators arrived at night to dig the tunnel. A local police officer reported these suspicious activities. An investigator was sent and saw the numerous wooden barrels containing earth from the excavation but did not think to ask what they held. The dampness of the floor was explained as being due to spilt milk. On March 13, the tsar's entourage took a different route and alternative plans for the assassination were put into successful action. In the investigation following the assassination, the dairy shop plot was uncovered. [Avrahm Yarmolinsky, *Road to Revolution: A Century of Russian Radicalism* (1956)]

Mandelkorn usually spent the afternoon at the public library, but on this day, he feared going there. Instead, he explains: "I went into a dairy restaurant and ordered some light lunch. The proprietor did not bear his accustomed smile, so important in his business. After putting the food before me he turned to me in Yiddish (usually he spoke in Russian), 'Some news . . . Better not to discuss here? What do you say? . . . We will pay for it?' I nodded but did not enter into further discussion. He handed me the newspaper. I looked at it but had to read it over and over, so nervous and excited was I. The meal somewhat steadied my nerves."

The possibility of removing oneself from the reality of this momentous event by going to a Jewish dairy restaurant and the calming effect of the food comprise an otherwise unrecorded aspect of life in that city. The history of this restaurant and its place in the dairy restaurant culture of Odessa remains to be written.

In those years, Odessa was the fourth-largest city in the Russian Empire and second, only to Warsaw, in Jewish population. It was built upon and around an eighteenth-century Romanian colony, the Moldavanka, known for its pastoral atmosphere, vineyards, and gardens. By the appointment of Tsar Alexander I, the free port of Odessa was designed and organized by the Duc de Richelieu, who had fled France during the Revolution. From its conception it was cosmopolitan in nature. By 1897, Jews comprised a third of its population. The Moldavanka had become the center of Jewish brothels and crime. In 1841, the Reform Jews of Brody in Galicia moved to Odessa and built the first Reform synagogue in the Russian Empire.

The Italians of Odessa, importers of wine and dried fruit, established a cafe-and-confectionery culture including the Zambrini cafe and pastry shop, where Chekhov ate ice cream. The French colony produced the best chefs and restaurants and Parisian-style cafes. A Swiss colony was occupied with wine cultivation. The German colonists introduced advanced agricultural technology to the Black Sea region and ran bakeries and beer halls. Jews were central to banking, commission stores of international companies, as well as wine cellars and delicatessens. Pushkin frequented the Greek and Turkish

coffeehouses. It was referred to as a Little Paris. [Nicholas V. Iljine, *Odessa Memories*]

It was also a destination for Jews escaping from the economic and cultural oppression of the Pale of Settlement. Isaac Babel recalled its "free and easy atmosphere." "To live like God in Odessa," was an expression used by poor Jews in the Pale of Settlement.

Sholem Aleichem lived there from 1891 to 1893 and his fictional journalist/luftmensch, Menachem Mendl, enjoyed the Swiss ice cream of the Cafe Fanconi. An old, rusty 10-unit token from the Confiserie Fanconi attests to its actual existence. In summer Odessa was a seaside resort with a lively restaurant culture as seen in the picture-postcards of the Buffet in the Alexander Park and a cafe on the Boulevard Nicolas. A vegetarian restaurant meal with Stalin is matter-of-factly mentioned in F. F. Raskolnikov's *Tales of Sub-Lieutenant Ilyin: The Fate of the Black Sea Fleet* of 1918.

An 1890s entry in Simon Dubnow's diary of life in Odessa describes "the shores of the Black Sea, where nature was richer and sunnier, despite all the political disabilities and outbreaks of violence against Jews, a rich, pulsating and colorful Jewish cultural life was in the exalted state of initial creativity." He mentions "meeting in the summer with other intellectuals of Odessa in the beautiful suburbs. Up late, drinking wine, singing folksongs in the sleepy German colony." A pleasant change from his life as a gymnasium student in Dvinsk.

In the afternoon of March 14, 1881, after his dairy lunch, Israel Mandelkorn proceeded to give private lessons at the home of Kabatchk, a saloonkeeper. In the malodorous and dirty home, discussion of the repercussions continued. "They say we will have to pay more for patents [licenses to keep saloons] and that they would not admit Jews to the gymnasia."

The assassination failed to trigger the hoped-for peasants' revolt. Instead the conspirators were linked to the few Jews involved: two young women, Hesia Helfman and Vera Figner. The Catholic Pole, Ignacy Hryniewiecki, who threw the bomb that killed Alexander II, was falsely rumored to be a Jew. This was enough evidence for the tsar's anti-terrorist secret police to publicize the connection between Jewish wealth, power, and revolutionary activity. The assassination was seen as part of the Tartar impulse to destroy Western civilization and return to a nomadic and communal way of life. A series of pogroms were incited across the Pale of Settlement. This crackdown on Jewish life triggered the first of many waves of immigration to Western Europe and America.

In the following days, Mandelkorn decided, on a whim, to have his beard shaved off — perhaps to move more comfortably in the advanced social circles of Odessa, perhaps to look less like a Jew. This fashion choice cost him a prospective appointment at an Orthodox kheyder. He returned to his hometown of Dubno, where two brothers he knew were saving their money to travel to America.

Mandelkorn joined an Am Olam (Eternal People) group waiting in Brody for permission to go to America. Am Olam was a socialist back-to-the-land movement that saw a future for Jews in America as opposed to Palestine. Their discussions focused upon what to raise on their farm in America ("hogs, and whether we were going to use them for food in the colony"). They left for America in January of 1882.

Mandelkorn found work on a model Swiss-owned dairy in the suburbs of Boston and then, in August of 1882, joined his thirty-four comrades in Portland, Oregon. They had purchased a large tract of land on which to establish the colony of New Odessa under the uncompromising leadership of William Frey (Free). Frey, the reborn Vladimir Heins, a "gentle Russian

nobleman and mathematician," had emigrated to America in 1875, had one failed utopian colony in Kansas behind him, and professed his own form of Comtean positivism involving personal regeneration through a vegetarian diet. He already had a following among the young Russian socialist intellectuals on the East Side of New York City. He and his wife, a practitioner of hydrotherapy, concocted a bean soup that was legendary for its regenerative and unpalatable qualities. Because of his charisma and supposed experience running an agricultural colony, he was chosen to lead the colony of New Odessa. The fifty young colonists subsisted on the latest scientific vegetarian diet: the bean soup and hard baked biscuits of unbolted flour "called after that wretched dyspeptic Graham [of cracker and flour fame]." The bleak agricultural life, the lack of women in the group, and the strict vegetarian diet led to the colony's demise.

In Mandelkorn's words, "We had by this time all accepted vegetarianism, under the influence of Frey's preaching. We also agreed to abstain from tobacco, and even tea and coffee. (In liquor we never indulged.) Instead of tea we drank water and milk, and for coffee we used a substitute of ground roasted bread crust. We called it community coffee. It tasted like

Postum. The food was not bad. Quantity however took the place of quality. We did not like it, but the authority of Frey was so great with us, that we consented to give this diet a fair trial. Frey was to us 'the last word on science.'"

A bedroom/art gallery was papered with pages from the popular illustrated magazines of the time. One member, Gaskin, could not tolerate the vegetarian fare and, after consultation with Frey, was allowed a special diet of pork. The smell of roasting meat offended the vegetarians and provoked an appetite in the others, who abstained from meat only for the sake of harmony within the commune.

The stormy meetings of the commune awakened in Mandelkorn a latent ability to draw caricatures of Frey and the others. Through an intermediary, Mandelkorn was ordered to stop making these drawings. He soon left the commune to pursue a career in photography in San Francisco and New York.

After the demise of New Odessa, Frey returned to Russia as a Wild West–style communal adventurer and is reputed to have single-handedly converted Tolstoy to vegetarianism during a visit in the autumn of 1885. [Sergei Tolstoy's memoirs]

Buffet des Alexander Park

Tolstoy and the Dairy Restaurant

In the popular press of New York City Tolstoy's vegetarianism and radical sympathies were fused into an irresistible figure of the ideal intellectual. Jewish radicals never forgot that it was Tolstoy who had called upon Alexander III to pardon the members of the People's Will in order to end a cycle of violence in Russia. "As wax before the fire, all Revolutionary struggles will melt away before the man-Tsar who fulfills the law of Christ." The deeply Christian asceticism behind his vegetarian beliefs was largely overlooked by his Jewish admirers; the Tolstoyaner Vegetarian Restaurant on Second Avenue was named in his honor.

In 1897, Tolstoy was also involved in raising funds for the mass immigration to Canada of the Doukhobors, a Christian sect in Russia persecuted for their beliefs in pacifism, the abolition of social hierarchies, and abstinence from alcohol. In some cases, they adopted a vegetarian diet or version of the kosher dietary laws. The strong Judaizing tendencies of the Doukhobors and another sect, the Molokans (or Milk Drinkers, who dared drink milk during the Great Fast), were intended to throw off the influences of Western culture on Christianity. Some of these sects were banished to the "Milky Waters" district of Southern Ukraine, where they may have had an influence upon the founders of Hasidism in their own dissent against normative Judaism. [Yaffa Eliach, "The Russian Dissenting Sects and Their Influence on Israel Baal Shem Tov, Founder of Hasidism"]

Socialist theorists looked toward the cooperative dairies of Switzerland and to early Russian peasant life for models of collective living. Tolstoy's tract *The First Step* helped launch a vegetarian movement in Russia in the 1890s with societies, restaurants, and cafeterias in Moscow, St. Petersburg, and Kiev, although the word "vegetarian" on a storefront was officially forbidden.

The socialist and communistic theorists favored the creation of centralized eating systems that would free women from housework, bring the cost of eating down, and deemphasize the family unit. The cafeteria was the modern feeding mechanism that did away with the social hierarchy of restaurants: waiters and eaters. After the 1917 Revolution, vegetarianism was supposedly scorned by the Soviet state as a pseudoscientific theory that reflected bourgeois ideology, and the word was removed from the dictionaries of Russia. Science, they believed, was on the verge of synthesizing the protein, albumin, from inorganic matter. This breakthrough would end the ethical and supply problems surrounding food.

August Bebel, founder of the Social Democratic Workers' Party of Germany in 1869, expressed his opinion of vegetarianism:

"People who believe in the so-called 'natural manner of living' frequently ask why Socialists remain indifferent to vegetarianism. Everyone lives as best he may. Vegetarianism, that is, the doctrine of an exclusive vegetable diet, found its chief supporters among the persons who are so comfortably situated that they are able to choose between a vegetable and an animal diet. But the great majority of persons have no choice. They must live according to their means, and the scantiness of their means compels them to live on a vegetable diet almost exclusively and often on one of the poorest quality. For the German laboring population in Silesia, Saxony, Thuringia, etc., the potato is the principal article of food; even bread comes only second. Meat only rarely appears on their tables and then it is meat of the poorest quality. The greater part of the rural population, although they raise cattle, also rarely eat meat; for they must sell the cattle and, with the money obtained, must satisfy other needs. To these numerous people who are obliged to live as vegetarians, a solid beefsteak or a good leg of mutton would mean a decided improvement in their nourishment. If vegetarianism opposes the overeating of an animal diet, it is right. If it combats the partaking of meat as harmful and detrimental, mainly for sentimental reasons, it is wrong: when it is claimed, for instance, that natural feelings forbid to kill an animal and to partake of a 'corpse.' The desire to live in peace compels us to wage war upon and destroy a great many living creatures, such as vermin, and, in order not to be devoured ourselves, we must kill and exterminate wild beasts. If we could allow 'the good friends of man,' the domestic animals, to live undisturbed, these 'good friends' would multiply to such a degree that they would 'eat' us by robbing us of nourishment. The assertion that a vegetable diet creates a gentle disposition is false, too. Even in the gentle, vegetarian Hindus the 'beast' was aroused when the severity of the English drove them to rebellion."

Bebel establishes a connection between the facts of the physiology of nutrition and social conditions.

"The modern residents of large cities, especially the masses of the working class, live under social conditions that are bound to destroy their normal appetite. Work in the squalid factory, the constant worry over their daily bread, absence of mental repose and pleasant impressions, complete physical exhaustion, all these are factors that are destructive of appetite. In this psychological condition we are unable to furnish the appetite juice required for the digestion of vegetable food. But in meat we possess an article of food that — if we may thus express it — provides for its own digestion. A considerable quantity of meat can be digested without appetite; it also acts as a stimulant and a creator of appetite. So meat aids the digestion of vegetables consumed at the same time, and thereby insures a better assimilation of the consumed matter. This appears to be the great advantage of an animal diet to modern man."

According to Bebel, the preparation of food should be approached scientifically. Proper equipment and knowledge should free women from the drudgery and wasted time of kitchen work.

"The abolition of the private kitchen will come as a liberation to countless women. The private kitchen is as antiquated an institution as the workshop of the small mechanic. Both represent a useless and needless waste of time, labor, and material.

"The centralization and mechanization of domestic life — from kitchen to laundry to house cleaning — is transforming the lives of the wealthiest of society. It is only a matter of time when all society will partake of this transformation."
[August Bebel, *Woman and Socialism,* (1879), Chap. 27]

During his brief two and a half months in New York City (January 13–March 27, 1917), Leon Trotsky, his wife, and two sons, lived in a rented apartment at 1522 Vyse Avenue, or possibly East 164th Street and Stebbins Avenue (since 1943 Rev. James A. Polite Avenue) in the Bronx. A confirmed vegetarian who considered meat eating immoral, he had most of his meals in the city's many Jewish dairy restaurants — his favorite being the Triangle Dairy on Wilkins Avenue in the East Bronx. He refused to tip, considering it an insult to the dignity of the waiters, and the waiters retaliated with poor service, accidental spillings of hot soup, and insults.

The self-service cafeteria — considered America's one contribution to restaurant culture — did away with waiter service and the need for reading menus. The steam table and tray-track system for feeding large numbers

Friedmann's Milchhalle in Czernowitz, a City in Bukovina

The existence of Jewish dairy restaurants in the Old World must be largely established from a few sparse mentions and vague interpolations from surrounding restaurant culture. Kotik's mleczarnia, and others like it, were no doubt a popular type of dairy-oriented eating-and-drinking place. From Mandelkorn's favorite dairy restaurant in Odessa to a makeshift stand erected on market day in the smallest shtetl to sell clabbered milk or a bakery with one or two tables, we can imagine a world of dairy-eating places that have largely eluded documentation.

The Jüdisches Adressbuch for Greater Berlin for 1931 lists 443 ritual, or kosher, eating houses in Germany and the rest of the world. Only two are specifically named as dairy restaurants: a **Milchspeisehalle** (milk-based food pavilion) at Franz Hochlingerhasse1 in Vienna, **run by Johanna Deutsch,** and a **Milchhalle operated by Lorenz Schonfeld** in Zlaté Moravce in Slovakia. The rest are unspecified.

Henry Mayhew in his *London Labour and the London Poor* describes the lively business in street foods among the Jews: "At the corner of Duke's-street was a stall kept by a Jew, who sold things that are eaten only by the Hebrews. Here in a yellow pie-dish were pieces of stewed apples floating in a of people without unnecessary labor and fuss made it the dining choice for cooperative groups and industrial workers. The self-service dairy cafeteria w the perfect expression of an anti-bourgeois restaurant culture.

After visiting the full range of eating houses in New York City, one reporter came to the conclusion that not one was run according to "the true principle." "By the application of a proper system of cooperation and distribution of labor and profits, all of the advantages of Delmonico's could be easily furnished at the minimum sixpence of the others. This will some day be understood by capitalists as well as consumers; and then it will be accomplished at once — while all the world will wonder why they had not thought of it long ago."

The automated dining systems developed in Germany in the late nineteenth century were imported to America by Horn and Hardart, stripped of their ornate decorations and transformed into streamlined Art Deco feeding machines.

When people who grew up in Eastern Europe were asked about their restaurant memories, the common reply was "Who ate in restaurants? We were lucky to have anything to eat." Since the staple diet for most people included meat only once a week, if at all, well-to-do Jews, if they chose to eat in a restaurant, ate meat delicacies. In descriptions of European Jewish public eating, the smell of roast goose, stuffed veal, and meat borscht hangs heavy on the page.

According to Christ (Mark 7:14–15), it did not matter what went into a person, only what came out in the way of behavior and speech. "There is nothing from without a man, that entering into him can defile him: but the things which come out of him, those are they that defile the man." This idea coincided perfectly with the extravagant eating and drinking that came to be associated with the ruling Christian majority in Europe.

thick puce-coloured sauce." The Jews were renowned for their street pastries — butter cakes and tarts — that all emanated from a dozen pastry shops in Whitechapel. Also in great demand were Jewish puddings (baked plum, boiled plum, batter-pudding studded with raisins) that for a halfpenny could make a meal.

A form of non-meat restaurant arose in nineteenth-century London around the Jewish vendors of fried fish (a specialty long associated with the Jews of Spanish and Portuguese origin). There exists a contemporary illustration in an article on the Jews of East London showing a Jewish fish shop/restaurant complete with Yiddish signage. It has been theorized that from these Jewish fish shops there developed the popular fish-and-chips shop of England.

Of all the restaurants in Europe offering Eastern European–style dairy cuisine only one has been well documented. Variously referred to as Friedmann's Dairy Restaurant, Vegetarian Restaurant, or Milchhalle, it stood at 4 Russichegasse, just around the corner from the Ringplatz or central square of Czernowitz, a city in Bukovina, an administrative division of the Habsburg Monarchy located over the years in Romania or Ukraine. It has been documented and preserved through the collective memory of a surviving group of Czernowitzers. Their recollections can be found in the virtual pages of the Internet.

On a map from 1870, the lot is marked with trees and formal gardens. Both 1898 and 1909 directories of Czernowitz list a restaurant at 4 Russichegasse owned by a Josef Katz. The directory includes another seven restaurants, but the full spectrum of public eating options are rarely covered by such directories. Herman Sternberg, in his "On the History of the Jews in Czernowitz," mentions a pleasure garden occupying that same space.

A Jew in Romanian costume

"On summer evenings around the turn of the century, families liked to visit Katz'schen Garden on Russischen Gasse. Music was provided by the lively musician Schlomele Hirsch and his brother Leib, who played at all the weddings."

In 1898, Meschulam Freidmann is listed as a feed handler and in 1909 he is listed as operating a Milchmeirerei (milk dairy) at Franzensgasse 12.

Czernowitz was founded as a resting place on the route of trade caravans crossing the Pruth River. The land rose steeply at that point and the caravans stopped to "gather their strength." Jewish merchants worked on this trade route and from that time the transportation business was in Jewish hands. There were no ghettos for Jews, but they settled in an area east of the railroad station.

This part of Moldavia was annexed by the Habsburg Empire in 1175. An influx of Jews from neighboring countries following the revolutions of 1848 and proclamation of their emancipation in 1867 led to the cultural and commercial growth of Czernowitz. Goldfaden's Yiddish theatrical enterprises found success in this particular mix of Jewish entrepreneurs who had moved to the cities of Iaşi, Czernowitz, and Bucharest to supply the Russo-Turkish War. A cosmopolitan population of children and grandchildren of the Polish, Russian, and German Sudits, or foreign guest workers brought to the Romanian principalities in the mid-eighteenth century, a concert-cafe and wine-cellar culture of Eastern and Western influences added to the cultural mix. The temperate climate and agricultural economy fostered the pastoral mood. Before the failed Moldavian Revolution of 1848, Prince Sturdza rescinded the law that forced Jews to wear identifiable Polish clothing of kaftan and shtreiml; forty years later, young Jewish actors adopted the flowing blouse, leather boots, and freewheeling behavior of the Romanian peasant.

Another influx of Jews followed the Kishinev pogrom of 1905. By 1904, 42 percent of the students at the German University of Czernowitz were Jews. It was the regional capital of Bukovina with a population of 68,000—21,587 Jews. The first Yiddish language conference, at which the centrality of that language to Jewish national identity was formally proposed, took place there in 1908.

CZERNOWITZ, BUKOVINA

FRIEDMANN'S MILCHHALLE

NO. 156

Imaginary postcard from Friedmann's Milchhalle

In this pro-Habsburg, assimilationist atmosphere, bourgeois restaurant culture blossomed. The loyal subjects of the Habsburg monarchy, who accounted for a large portion of the regional tax revenues, expressed their freedom of choice and comfort through the countless restaurants, cafes, and other public eating places. Their children were educated in Christian schools and spoke both German and Yiddish. To them, it was a "Little Vienna."

To the Hasidim, whose wonder rabbis held court in nearby Sadagura, Wiznitz, and Bojan, to an Orthodox faction struggling to uphold Talmudic traditions in the modern world, and to a Zionist faction who promoted the "return to Judaism before the return to a Jewish land," it was a "Jerusalem on the Pruth (the river running through the town)." The tension between these groups and the other nationalities residing in the city — Ukrainians, Romanians, Poles, Rutherians, Roma, and Germans — gave Czernowitz its dynamic and cosmopolitan flavor.

Today, a lively business in antique postcards from Czernowitz takes place on eBay. Most feature the large hotels — Zum Schwarzen Adler (To the Black Eagle), the Hotel Central, Palace Hotel, Hotel Bristol — all featuring fashionable restaurants and the Kaffehaus culture of Vienna transplanted in miniature in the Cafe de l'Europe, Cafe Habsburg, Cafe Astoria, and the Cafe Bellevue along with the usual landmarks of the civic glory. Postcard views of lush garden restaurants with music pavilions exist: Friedwalde, Göbelshöhe (1899), Habsburghöhe (1898), and Horeczer Wäldchen (1907). The awning covered Kaiserkafe Kiosk, the entrance gate to Steiner'sche Bierbruerei, and the Volksgarten cafe were all desired images to send to friends. Images of modest Gasthäuser and unremarkable cukiernie and suburban Meiereien can be found. Even an image of the awninged Milch Palais erected in front of the Jewish National House can be found. One dealer assured me that he had two postcards of Friedmann's restaurant. He refused to show me scans of the cards

Cafe Habsburg in Czernowitz

and asked for payment in advance, and I refused. I believe that he was preying on my desperate need to find images of that lost world.

In an era when the picture-postcards celebrated the lowliest business, why are there no postcards of Friedmann's to be found — and why so few postcards of Jewish dairy restaurants at all? It seems that the subtle boast implied by sending a picture-postcard is at odds with the milekhdike personality and the entire atmosphere of a dairy restaurant.

In the fictionalized post–World War I Czernowitz of Gregor von Rezzori's *An Ermine in Czernopol* (1958), "Laughter . . . had been elevated to an art form, a folk art of unparalleled authenticity . . . understood and appreciated by all. . . . Laughter was everywhere, part of the air we breathed. . . ." "We did not roar, bellow, whinny, bleat, or bat, but rather performed a kind of smirk or sneer for which our language has, sadly, no expression: a quick exhale dispatched through the nose, with scarcely sound or grimace. Because while Czernopol may not have been a good or beautiful city, it was, without doubt, an extraordinarily intelligent one." Czernopolers "had a soft spot for stupidity, since they placed a certain value on anything exotic, which they viewed with a tender, heartfelt irony." It was a city of true cosmopolitans who accepted everything that came their way.

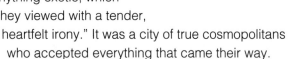

The plaza before the town hall was sprinkled with spat husks of sunflower seeds. There were "three kosher eating houses, as well as Kucharczyk's Cafe and Confectionery, where as soon as the weather turned warm, tables and chairs were set up on the sidewalk outside the mirrored window display." The golden youth congregated at the White Eagle Hotel (the Schwartzer Adler) or Lucullus sandwich shop.

"The city was famous far beyond the provinces for its knife-wielding

matchyorniks — a particularly strong-willed type of amateur procurer — as well as for its unusually resistant strain of gonococcus, and for being the setting for most Jewish jokes circulating between Riga and the Levant."

Friedmann's would come to occupy a prominent place in the food business of the city. A wholesale bakery was run by the Weissmann family. Eggs, vegetables, and poultry were supplied by women from the surrounding countryside. Around the marketplace there were numerous inns, taverns, and canteens for drink and "fish prepared in the traditional manner."

With goods imported from Vienna and Paris on sale in local shops, Czernowitz was a model of consumer sophistication. The city's industries centered on steam-powered mills, three breweries, a tile manufacturer, and six mineral-oil refineries — all operated by Jews. The production of alcohol was almost entirely in Jewish hands. Jews ran taverns, but Christians held the concession for brandy inns, which were leased to Jews.

Mr. Friedmann was captured in a few snapshots taken in Czernowitz in 1928.

The following memories of surviving Czernowitzers date from the 1930s until the Second World War. In each account, the atmosphere and physical arrangement of Freidmann's are reconstructed from memory. The reader is left with a composite view marred by blank sections, conflicting details, and no aromas.

A bit of banter from Friedmann's was recalled by Gaby Rinzler: An impatient customer addresses the waiter who has been ignoring him for some time. "Herr Ober, wen sie mir nicht sofort den Tee bringen hebe ich mih auf un gehe zum Geller" (Waiter, If you don't bring my tea I'll get up and go to Geller's [another dairy restaurant in town].) To that the waiter answered, "Bin ich mit a fuss im Prut?" (Am I with a foot in the Pruth River?), meaning, "Well, worse things could happen."

Miriam Taylor remembers this institution "famous for the borscht and for the impudence of its waiters. Whenever someone wanted to express an offhand attitude, they would repeat the words of a Friedmann's waiter: 'natzech a borsht' meaning: There is your borscht."

Husbands, left by their vacationing wives in the summer, went there for dinner. Erica Glynn recalled sitting outside of Friedmann's in the summer eating strawberries and sour cream.

Beyle Gottesman, a native of Czernowitz, recalled mounting a few steps to a small garden with tables and chairs. The restaurant building was at the back of this garden and had a central staircase separating the establishment into two rooms. She did not recall there being any signage. Everyone ate there, not just Jews. Her family ate meat every day at home; her father, a doctor, had chicken soup every night. As for vegetarians in Czernowitz, she recalled only the name of a Mr. Rosenblatt, an ophthalmologist and well-known vegetarian. The people of Czernowitz, she recalled, were considered the most conceited of all people. It was a full day's trip from Czernowitz to Vienna.

Stuart Winter, who spent his childhood in Czernowitz, recalled at least a dozen other dairy restaurants in the city. These were small mom-and-pop operations: a few tables and a counter. One was owned by a Mr. Picker, who appeared to be an unassimilated Polish Jew. Another restaurant was run by two widows on Hauptstrasse, next door to an agricultural supply store. He also recalled Geller's dairy restaurant.

He recalled entering through a gate; the building was set back eighteen feet on a plaza; no trees, some shrubbery. A new wing was built on the left side (facing building) that took up half of the "garden."

Winter does not recall stairs up from the sidewalk and says the building was one or two stories in height. There were no tablecloths, at least not in

the old wing. The big moneymaker was coffee and pastry. They served large portions at a fair price. No alcohol was served. Mr. Friedmann had a Vandyke beard. For Czernowitz, it was a big operation: maybe ten tables. On the menu he remembers pierogi, vegetable soup, beet borscht, baked cornmeal and vegetables. As a child he did not know of vegetarians. In Czernowitz, there were some non-kosher restaurants run by Jews. He mainly ate dairy at home, but did eat at meat restaurants such as Gross or Steinmetz, a manufacturer of cured meats.

Through a series of e-mail exchanges, Lucca Ginsburg was able to recall a wealth of childhood memories of Friedmann's restaurant.

"It was a rather low and unadorned building from the outside, however you immediately sensed its special atmosphere when you entered. The ceiling was not particularly high, floors were made of wood. Each table seated four, if I remember right, which were put together in case of larger parties. White tablecloths . . . I don't think that the restaurant could accommodate more than 100 guests, even not that many.

"There were no pictures on the wall. There was a very long buffet with salads, herring, pickles, and Friedmann's famous stuffed eggs — stuffed with a mixture of the yolks, mustard, mayonnaise, herbs. There were endless varieties of this dish, I don't know what made the eggs there special, but they were!

"In the main hall, right opposite the entrance, Mr. Friedmann sat at the cash register. I don't remember any Mrs. Friedmann at all, I don't think she was active. Although Mr. Friedmann never helped with taking orders or serving food, he seemed to have his (kind) eyes everywhere.

"The place was noisy but not unpleasantly so. The waiters were nice and most of them had a sense of humor. Knowing this kept us from getting offended when for instance we reproached a waiter saying: 'What's the matter, have you forgotten our order?' And he replied smilingly, 'And if so, what do you want me to do, commit suicide?'

"Once my father ordered a borscht and the waiter brought him a vegetable soup. When my father pointed out that he had ordered a borscht, the waiter said, 'And what's wrong with the vegetable soup? Isn't it good?'

"The prevailing language was German of course, with Yiddish here and there.

"The restaurant had a very pleasant outdoor space. There was a large building somewhat like a barn, open in front. Tables were placed there as well; guests ran there for shelter in case of sudden rainfalls, or when the sun was too hot. I remember this garden as a very pleasant place; there was a bit of grass at the side and I liked the crunchy noise my shoes made on the gravel.

"Friedmann's was strictly dairy (no, Mr. Friedmann himself was not a vegetarian!). My family and myself ate there at the rate of about twice a week, especially in summer when my mother tried to cook as little as possible.

"Among the many specialties of the restaurant — and there were so many I can't begin to count them — there was the typical Bucovinian 'Totsch,' which was like potato pancakes, but much thicker with added yeast and flour, baked in the oven. The second dish was a 'Malai' (mamaliga) made of cornmeal, also baked in the oven, then cut in the middle like cake, and filled with sweetened white cheese. These two specialties were often taken home, especially for weekends. I hardly remember one weekend without Totsch or Malai brought in from Friedmann's. His food was not eaten on the street . . . Totsch and Malai were strictly for the weekend and takeaway. . . . Somehow, I believe that the restaurant was closed for Pessach — but I am not sure.

Mămăligă

"Portions were generous, but by far not 'full plates' as presented today. The atmosphere was pleasant and peaceful; I can't remember any unpleasant incidents while eating there.

"There was gefilte fish (carp) and carp served in a sour cream sauce with dill. It was very good. Eggplant, blintzes, omelettes, wonderful pirogen, knishes, wild (small) strawberries with cream. The sour cream was very thick. Another specialty was the 'halushken' (filled cabbage). They were filled with rice of course. No meat. On biggest demand was his vegetable soup and his borscht. Cold borscht with sour cream was a real delight on a hot summer day. The borscht was made with sour cream and occasionally with beaten egg."

Schmettentorte

As for beverages, Lucca remembers "coffee (excellent), tea, water, soda water. I don't remember wine." She does not recall vegetable cutlets or vegetarian chopped liver being on the menu.

Two memorable desserts — "pure heaven" — were Schmettentorte and a chocolate cake. The recipes for these cakes were given to Lucca by Mr. Freidmann and are cherished by her to this day.

There were no printed menus. "Guests at Friedmann's knew exactly what they wanted and ordered from the waiter. . . . There was a fixed variation of food available and waiters recited the dishes available.

"The restaurant was kosher but I don't remember them being extremely strict about it. My grandfather who was a bearded and very religious Jew (twice a day in the synagogue) often ate there. The restaurant did not cater to the orthodox exclusively, although they too were frequent guests. I don't remember anyone praying before a meal, and hand-washing was optional, according to every guest's idea of hygiene.

"Josef Schmidt (1904–1942), the world-famous tenor, was a very frequent guest at Friedmann's. He became so much part of the scenery that we stopped regarding him as a celebrity."

Lucca could not recall other vegetarian restaurants or Milchhallen in Czernowitz. She was only ten years old in 1940, when the first Russian invasion of Bukovina occurred. This event, she recalled, also marked the end of Friedmann's.

On the second day of Hanukkah in 1959, Lucca Ginsburg's father noticed an old man sitting alone on a bench in front of the Haifa Municipality. He looked familiar, and on closer inspection they realized that this was Meshulam Friedmann of the famous restaurant in Czernowitz.

The elderly Friedmann was forced to share a small apartment with his son and daughter-in-law. She was disturbed by his presence and they often fought, so Mr. Friedmann spent as much time as possible outside. The Ginsburgs invited him to their house for lunch and ended up finding him a room to rent in their building. "He became a member of our family." Although he never worked in the kitchen, he was able to re-create some of the cake recipes. In time he grew ill and passed away.

The Dairy Restaurant in the New World

The European visitors to the New World were confronted with a second earthly paradise in which they were compelled to reenact an expulsion of the native population — this time playing both the roles of Satan and Jehovah.

In 1830, Mordecai Noah, the sheriff of New York and a contemporary of the renowned Indian-killer Andrew Jackson, was more than willing to embrace the native people as members of a lost Jewish tribe if they'd agree to populate his newly proposed Jewish nation-state of Ararat on Grand Island in the Niagara River. The local tribes did not take him up on his generous offer — nor did the Jews of the Old World.

Seventy years later, in 1900, 1,527,535 Jews had migrated to North America. 672,776 settled in New York City to form a de facto Jewish city-state, almost 20 percent of the city's total population. 8,977,581 Jews still remained in

Europe and Russia, with 262,015 in Warsaw (41 percent), 168,985 in Budapest (23 percent), and approximately 150,000 each in Odessa (12.5 percent), Vienna (8.95 percent), and London (2.27 percent).

In transit, Jews often resorted to a milkhiker diet of black bread, herring, tea, and occasionally cheese and butter, to avoid the non-kosher and unpalatable food supplied in steerage. [Deborah Dwork, "Health Conditions of Immigrant Jews on the Lower East Side, 1880–1914," *Medical History* (1981)]

Sholem Aleichem, traveling in a higher class in 1906, remarked on the delicious ice cream being served.

Although escape from the constraints of Jewish communal life must be included among the motives for immigration, Jewish culinary tastes and fears were not easily thrown off. America, referred to as Di Goldene Medina (The Golden Land), not only referred to a land of unlimited economic possibilities but also to a place of Arcadian pleasures that had been denied them in Europe.

In a crowded tenement apartment, the typical diet, often eaten from shared plates, seemed Arcadian when compared to near starvation. "Rolls, coffee or tea for breakfast; a hunk of bread and a few cents' worth of herring for lunch; and for dinner, soup, bread, potatoes, and a bit of baked fish or roasted or boiled (in the soup) meat or poultry." "Herring . . . the single most common food eaten by immigrant Jews . . . in 1898 cost between two and four cents a pound."

Writers in the popular press typically attributed the low disease rates among Jews to alcoholic temperance, ritual hand-washing, housecleaning for the Sabbath, sweat baths, full meals on the Sabbath, and the observance of dietary laws, particularly the inspection of kosher meat. The physical anthropologist Maurice Fishberg refuted this idea. "In Eastern Europe, where the Jews follow the dietary laws, strictly adhering both to the letter and spirit of the sacred ordinance, there is more consumption among them than among their coreligionists in Western countries who disregard the dietary laws in part or completely. . . . The Jews in the Lower East Side are more orthodox, more strictly adhering to their faith and traditions, and still have proportionately a higher rate of morbidity from tuberculosis than their coreligionists in Harlem who, as is characteristic of Jews all over, with their prosperity have more or less

discarded many of their religious practices. . . . The incidence of tuberculosis among Jews depends more on their economic and social environment." We see few cases of tuberculosis among the prosperous Jews of Berlin. It is a disease of people who live indoors and in the overcrowded conditions of the ghetto. "The Jews have only the advantage of having passed through a process of infection during the past centuries. Hence their [comparatively] lower mortality from tuberculosis" [*The Sun,* January 3, 1909]. On the other hand, Jews suffered from a disproportionately high incidence of mental and emotional disorders, attributable to inbreeding.

To appreciate the appearance of the Eastern European dairy restaurant in New York City in the early years of the twentieth century, one needs a sense of what the public dining options were before the influx of Jews after 1881. But trying to get a visceral sense of that culture is not easy. The restaurant experience is a fleeting one even for contemporary diners. Out of the corner of your eye you see a waiter rushing past your table with a plate of glistening hot food and catch the faint, yet tantalizing, aroma of some braised meat. You struggle to connect the fleeting image with a text entry on the menu. It's being brought to a table like yours — possibly a "better" table — to be eaten by a contemporary man or woman, possibly on a diet. It's a dish you'll never taste under those exact circumstances. Five minutes later, you ask the waiter what it was, and even he can't remember. Meanwhile, your own dinner has grown cold.

Trying to imagine the restaurant culture of New York as it existed at the turn of the last century is like that, only removed by 120 years of radical changes in food production and handling, public sanitation, and the human capacity for suffering. Instead of the faint aroma of food, the search is accompanied by the smell of moldy newsprint and microfilm readers (the machines and the users).

Was everything tinged by the smell of horse manure, as today it is by car fumes? Was all food somewhat adulterated, or slightly spoiled because of imperfect refrigeration? Did the men and women once have more vitality?

The danger of projecting our own understanding of the eating experience onto the early-twentieth-century scene, much less earlier dates, is to reduce the past to a stage set inhabited by contemporary players in period costumes, eating a stage version of period food. The idea that culinary traditions form a visceral link between us and our ancestors is just bad theater.

The grazing and gnawing instinct is all that remains: even the most disturbed twenty-first-century man assumes a momentary bovine calm when he bows to eat his food — it saves him from choking. You can see it at any truck-stop diner. But the human animal itself has changed over that short period of time.

An observer of the situation in 1827 explained that "most of the cooking was done by Negroes; and good cooks, too, some of them were — particularly the Creoles and East Indians." These were cooks working by instinct, he goes on to explain, unacquainted with the art and science of Old World French cooking. He described the gustatory and health benefits of French cooking as compared to the primitive cooking of America. "The Americans are a nation of dyspeptics" suffering from a diet of salt pork, pies, and puddings. [*Christian Union,* April 16, 1879]

An 1849 guide to New York City counted no less than 100 eating houses within a half-mile of the Stock Exchange in lower Manhattan [*New York in Slices,* 1849]. To save the time of a trip home, businessmen required fast and ready

lunches near their place of work. In the summer, with their families at country resorts, they needed a place to have their supper. The economic engine of the city depended upon their existence. An estimated 30,000 businesspeople had their lunch at eating houses every day.

Based on a travel account of 1849, there were four classes of eating house. The most expensive and aristocratic form of eating house in New York was the "restaurant," of which Delmonico's was a rare example: a French-style restaurant transplanted to New York in which eating was an art form. The decor of carved wooden buffets, upholstered seating, heavy curtains, gaudy paper decoration, mirrored walls, and white sand–covered floors set a tone of refinement. Diners were presented with a printed bill of fare with prices indicated in the margins. "To dine at Delmonico's . . . two things are requisite — money and French." The majority of customers came from the French and other

continental import houses of the city; the rest were well-traveled Americans who wanted to join in the spirit of culinary art. The highly trained waiters seemed to read one's mind. Upstairs were numerous private suites that were constantly busy. The menu included stewed oysters, stewed terrapin, lobster salad, and cold wild geese and ducks, but also delicate little entrées appearing under their French names: sardines grillées, petits vol-au-vent, des huitres, ris de veau piqué, and omelette aux champignons.

At the mid-priced lunch house, businessmen of refined taste and habits at home put such considerations aside to gather at these places between the hours of noon and 3 pm and "to gorge disgusting masses of stringy meat and tepid vegetables." To endure these large portions of mediocre food and then rush back to work was the sign of a successful and driven businessman.

The din of orders being shouted and calls for the waiter combined with the "clattering plates and clashing knives and forks, perfumed with the steam from a mammoth kitchen, roasting, boiling, baking, frying, beneath the floor — crowds of animals with a pair of jaws apiece, wagging in emulation of the one wielded with such terrific effect by Samson — and the thermometer which has become ashamed of itself and hides away behind a mountain of hats in the corner, melting up by degrees to boiling heat — and you will have some notion of a New York eating-house."

Images of New York lunch counters of the period show men eating in a standing position. The speed of activity set the New York eating house apart from its continental equivalent. "A regular down-town diner surveys the kitchen with his nose as he comes up-stairs —

selects his dish by intuition, and swallows it by steam and the galvanic battery. As to digesting it, that is none of his business."

At the lower-priced lunch house, "the room is laid out like the floor of a church, with tables and benches for four, in place of pews. Along the aisles are ranged at 'stated' intervals, the attentive waiters who received the dishes . . . and distribute them on either side with surprising dexterity and precision" as they're ordered from a bill of fare with all of the prices for extras marked and priced in the margins. A small plate is 6 cents, a large plate 12 cents. The bill of fare is announced at the door. Bread, pickles, etc., are charged separately at the discretion of the waiter. The simple dinner: a small plate of roast beef mixed [a mashed mixture of turnips and potatoes] with a glass of Croton (42nd Street Reservoir) water can be had for as little as 6 cents.

A fourth class of eating house is the cake-and-coffee shop that's open all night and serves a plate of biscuits with a lump of butter for 3 cents and a cup of coffee for 3 cents. Pumpkin pie is 4 cents with free Croton water. Seated at wooden benches, firemen join Bowery b'hoys in discussion of the latest catastrophes — should the fire bell ring, they all immediately leave.

Sea captains, the celebrities of the schooner trade, were directly responsible for the physical transfer of foreign dining culture to NYC on a weekly basis. John Delmonico, originally from Ticino, an Italian-speaking canton of Switzerland, was working as a sea captain on the Cuba–New York route, became acquainted with the city, and in 1827 brought his brother, a Swiss confectioner, to New York for the purpose of opening a boarding house with restaurant on the

2nd Class
dining room
RMS Olympic

European model. The exchange of European eating culture was linked and grew with the commercial shipping interests of the Port of New York. This constant exchange continued through the steamship era, with the shuttling of large dining rooms in full operation back and forth across the Atlantic Ocean.

The restaurants that offered cultivated European cuisine boasted a French or Austrian kitchen staff and waiters regardless of where they actually came from. Becoming connoisseurs of a consciously refined European culinary style appealed to many nineteenth-century New Yorkers bored with simple home cooking. The Eastern European dairy restaurant, in its humble way, was to become one of those styles. Slumming uptowners in the city's ethnic enclaves — an adventure tinged with danger and indigestion — helped support many a small restaurant. Where one chose to eat was a momentary barometer of one's social, economic, gustatory, and political standing in the world.

The ice-cream saloons of Broadway and the confectionery shops on the Bowery, then a theatrical district, were "fitted up in a style of exaggerated finery, which has a grand effect from the street, but is a little too glaring and crushing when you are within. At night, when the gaudy curtains, silver paper, and gilded mirrors are highly illuminated by gas-light, the scene rises almost to splendor itself, or at any rate to that which most people are willing to accept for it, and never know the difference." [*New York in Slices*]

The sizable German emigration following the 1848 revolutions in Europe created a Bowery dominated by German food culture in the form of saloons serving lager beer and wurst, cafes, restaurants with "dark wood furnishings and quaintly carved wooden chairs," and indoor beer gardens such as the Atlantic Gardens. The American literary types who affected a European bohemianism frequented these cafes and beer Stuben. In the cellar rooms of Pfaff's cafe at 647 Broadway near Houston, Walt Whitman found himself surrounded by overly clever, fast-talking men with literary and journalistic aspirations and a taste for turtle soup and wild game. He would have preferred the not yet existent atmosphere of a dairy lunchroom. Nearly all the bakeries in New York were run by Germans.

Walt Whitman at Pfaff's NYC

The German beer garden involved the planting of a grove of linden trees to provide shade to keep the stored beer barrels cool. The introduction of tables into this grove made for a pleasant place to drink and eat. This man-made realization of the pastoral environment spread throughout Europe and came to America with the German immigrants of the early nineteenth century. The city was dotted with pleasure gardens of the English and German styles: Niblo's Gardens, Willow Grove Pavilion (Williamsburg, Brooklyn), Castle Garden, Atlantic Gardens, the Chinese Assembly Rooms, Schwartz's Swiss Cottage of Hoboken (Louis Schwartz, prop.), and Vauxhall Gardens, named after the London original. Newspaper clippings from the 1850s describe these places being hired by Jews for Purim balls and Benevolent Society banquets with food supplied by a Jewish caterer. The menus included some Eastern European–styled dishes, by way of France: roast meats and goose, smoked and pickled tongues, tongues à la Polonaise, fricaseed chickens, and calf's-foot jelly (included under desserts). All patrons enjoyed the pastoral atmosphere maintained in these urban establishments. The German-American beer hall and beer garden is credited with having increased the tempo of restaurant service to a speed unknown in America at that time. The food that accompanied the beer was anything but dairy: sausages, ham, and pig's knuckles.

If there was no room for an actual outdoor garden in a dense urban setting, the form could be reinterpreted as a rooftop garden restaurant or an interior palm court — some furnished with living plants, some with elaborately painted backdrops. The Paradise Roof Garden on Oscar Hammerstein, Sr.'s New York Victoria Theater offered Manhattanites a full-scale replica of a Dutch-style dairy farm complete with cow, barnyard animals, a burbling waterfall, and costumed dairymaids — all as a backdrop for dinner, dancing, and summer entertainment. Years later, Eddie Foy, Jr., would recall the glass of warm fresh milk given to him and his brothers by the dairymaid after their performance. Hammerstein was a German-speaking Pomeranian Jew, whose early success in the cigar industry financed his theater-building spree at the turn of the nineteenth century.

For the twenty-first-century reader curious about this world, the quantity and quality of historical evidence depends upon the restaurant's place in the economic ladder. The elegant Delmonico's Restaurant in the Hoffman House (and its later locations) is preserved in fine engravings, accounts in architectural journals, and menus for banquets commemorating members of the upper classes. The mid-priced restaurant-cafe (Mouquin's on Fulton Street or the Vienna Bakery at Broadway and 10th Street) are recorded in lithographic postcards, trade cards, printed menus, and accounts of their owners' charitable activities. The lower-priced

The Paradise Roof Garden

Italian table d'hôte restaurants (Martinelli's at 136 Fifth Avenue, Colombo at Third Avenue and 10th Street), the French restaurants around Washington Square (Giffou and Vattel's), and the English chop houses (Old Tom's on Thames Street behind Trinity Church with its mock air of British antiquity) survive as mentions in guidebooks and memoirs of the early twentieth century and printed ephemera (postcards, trade cards, menus, and commemorative paper napkins). Among the Eastern European restaurants documentation shrinks to their description by journalists covering the bohemian downtown scene (Cafe Boulevard on 2nd Avenue), mentions in newspaper accounts of crimes that happened on the premises, rare postcards, and menus and advertisements. To find a good photograph of one of the oyster saloons, found everywhere in the city of that period, is not easy. The Jewish eating houses fall into that category and survive in the historical record through small ads in the Yiddish press, mentions in travel guides, essays on social pathology, postcards (if they survived to become second-generation shrines for eating), and battered matchbooks — a tribute to the tenacity of matchbook advertisement salesmen of that era. If not for these customized matchbooks, there'd be no physical evidence of certain restaurants.

Under the scrutiny of an optical loop, the deluded historian sees below the surface of the printed objects. The stain on a menu reveals the ingredients of a soup, the climatic conditions of the evening, etc.

The Chinese restaurants around Mulberry Street are the subject of

picturesque engravings and dramatic accounts because of their exotic nature. At the lowest end of the socioeconomic ladder — the poorest basement eating houses of the Lower East Side and the Irish hash houses along the East River — there exist a surprising number of attempts at documentation. The utter degradation encountered by upper-class visitors from the various philanthropic societies was described with the goal of raising funds for the financial support or eradication of these places.

Of all these eating places, it's the twentieth-century Jewish dairy restaurant, possibly due to its utilitarian design and lack of picturesque ethnic qualities, that's least memorialized and preserved. They did not attract boastful tourists or self-promoters in need of postcards to send home. An eminent collector of Yiddish food memorabilia commented on the scarcity of dairy restaurant material.

A growing literature on Jewish-American restaurant culture concentrates on the delicatessen and fleyshik restaurants because of their prominence in popular imagination: the big eater, the upwardly mobile immigrant, the wisecracking waiter, etc.

Matchbook from The Original Moskowitz Roumanian Restaurant, c. 1930. (See page 267.)

The coverage of restaurant culture is enlarged with the rise of the popular press and a middle-class audience interested in reading about their own lives. Among the many English-language accounts of the exotic atmosphere of downtown Jewish cafe-restaurants, dairy restaurants are rarely mentioned as they fail to fit the bill. These East Side adventures ("In New York's Midway of Exotic Eating Places," etc.) involve both the allure of the unknown and the fear of foreign invasion, all depicted in a sensational tone that would not satisfy the social scientist. The urban anthropologists often reduced the restaurant-cafe to a generic space in which specific quantities of certain foods were eaten by certain ethnic groups. In even the most artful novels set on the Lower East Side, descriptions of the restaurant-cafe are incidental and limited by the inability of language to deal with spatial relationships. The mental image formed in the reader's mind, regardless of its vivacity, is a rehash of other half-baked images. Therefore, the most valuable guides to understanding the restaurant culture of the early twentieth century are the existing cabinet photographs of interiors and exteriors. By carefully studying these reflections upon collodion emulsions we can vicariously experience the spatial drama of walking into and being seated in a long-vanished restaurant: the disposition of sawdust on a wooden floor, the sheen of chicken fat on a bentwood chair, the broken shoes of a dying waiter. For the most part, the details of working-class immigrant eating places, like the bulk of Yiddish spoken culture, have been lost. As the meal was consumed, its physical remains were brought to the kitchen to be discarded and washed away. But again, in the case of dairy restaurants, for the reasons mentioned, such valuable evidence is very slim.

For the most part, restaurants only appear in the Yiddish press when something newsworthy happened in them: a holdup, a riot, etc. Restaurant advertisements in the American Yiddish press of the 1880s feature engraved images of the owners — their personalities were a major attraction. Until the 1900s, most eating places were identified simply by the owner's name. After 1900, most ads are pure text, often for grand openings or modernizations. Ads for dairy restaurants specify their "milkhiker" menu to set them apart from meat restaurants and delicatessens. The rare restaurant ad in the Yiddish press mentioned the serving of both dairy and meat (see pages 324 and 327), the norm in most later Jewish-run restaurants.

A search of the newspaper archives might lead one to believe that restaurants were primarily a site of murders, knifings, and the planning of crimes. The daily business of a dairy restaurant — the pleasure of a blintz eater — is not considered news. A cursory study of the history of Western art shows that after Giovanni Bellini and Poussin, painters turned away from the contemplation of paradise to depict the more dramatic scenes of Baroque struggle and the Romantic sublime in all of its fearful variations.

An 1899 magazine article ranked the numbers of ethnic restaurants in descending order: "Irish-American, German and Austrian, French, Italian, Jewish (kosher), Russian and Polish, Scandinavian, Mexican-Spanish, Chinese, Greek, Syrian and British chop houses." [*Outlook,* May 20, 1899]

The Philadelphia Centennial Exhibition of 1876 did much to popularize the various cuisines of the world, in palatable form, to the American public. Visitors could sample each cuisine along with its associated national dress and architecture, transplanted in miniature to the fairgrounds. Featured were: A Great American Restaurant; Trois Frères Provençaux, a French restaurant operated by Léon Goyard, who oversaw the dining arrangements for the Emperor of Austria during the Vienna Exhibition of 1873; the Restaurant of the South, offering plantation-style dining with a "Darky Band" and plantation scenes; a German restaurant operated by P. J. Laubers, a garden setting seating 1,500 people with musical entertainment; a French restaurant, La Fayette; and a Hungarian Wine Pavilion.

George's Hill Restaurant, operated by Charles Calmann (rabbi of Adath Israel, 1873–76) and Kohn of Philadelphia, was situated on the slope of George's Hill and served meals prepared "according to the dietary laws of the Israelites." Known as the Hebrew Restaurant, it was a one-story wooden structure of a vaguely Oriental style for lack of something more ethnically recognizable. "From its verandas a fine view of the whole grounds can be had. It contains a large Dining-Hall, Smoking-Room and Ladies' Dressing-Room. All modern languages are spoken. Meals will be furnished at a general table (table d'hôte), or from a bill of fare (à la carte). Meals prepared in this Restaurant according to the dietary laws of the Israelites." "Here are served delicious wines and liquors of Hungary, which are served by attendants in the national dress of that country." To go along with the colorful ethnic stylings of the other pavilions and maybe because of Calmann and Kohn's background, a Hungarian/Oriental style was adopted. In fact, Jewish culture lacked a single visually identifiable aspect. Those costumes imposed upon European Jews by law were not something they'd choose to wear voluntarily in their own restaurants. Here a rabbi worked in partnership with a businessman to guarantee his personal level of kosher observance. Passersby may have associated the smell of garlic and onions with their Jewish neighbors. A menu for this restaurant, if discovered, would be revealing.

The Dairy was a rustic building with a garden in which "girls dressed as Swiss peasants" served milk, cream, buttermilk, cheese, ice cream, pastries, fruit, and berries. The Vienna Bakery and Coffee-House, operated by Graff, Fleischman and Co. of New York and Cincinnati, was a coffeehouse and bakery "designed to show the Vienna method of baking with compressed yeast." And finally, there was the New England Farmer's Home of 100 Years Ago and Modern Kitchen, comparing the two and offering "meals cooked and served in old-fashioned style" by ladies in authentic colonial dress. [*Visitor's Guide to the Centennial Exhibition and Philadelphia* (1876)]

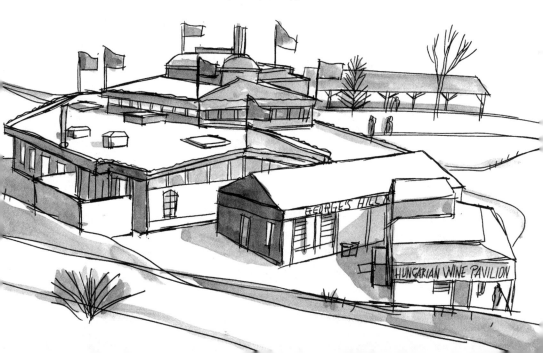

The Dairy Lunchroom as an American Institution

A species of dairy restaurant, in name at least, had existed in America since the 1870s. Its origins — usually attributed to the businessmen who went on to build large restaurant chains: Ward, Whitcomb, Dennett, and Childs — should be taken with a grain of salt.

In 1887 Frank Ward, a Washington, D.C., milkman, hung a small sign offering "Buttermilk by the Glass" outside of his cellar storage depot on E Street NW. The menu was expanded to milk, buttermilk, and half-and-half by the glass along with a basket of Maryland biscuits to which customers could help themselves for 1 cent each. The operation was moved to a half-basement across the street with a crude counter offering biscuits, pie, and coffee. The milk depot was propelled in this way into an eating establishment. A more elegant room was found nearby and sandwiches were added to the menu. Customers were obliged to stand while they ate, until Ward got the idea of fastening round disks to the arms of wooden chairs so that patrons could rest their mug or glass while eating. Two employees of Ward's opened a similar place near the U.S. Treasury.

J. A. Whitcomb, a shorthand reporter and customer of the lunchroom, patented the idea for the chair and opened his own version of this lunchroom: the Baltimore Dairy Lunch. A local pottery produced sturdy coffee mugs modeled after shaving mugs with his logo. By 1916, there were 140 branches in operation.

Alfred W. Dennett was already in the quick-lunch business in Boston in 1883. By 1897, he had a chain of fourteen restaurants from New York to California. An ardent supporter of the temperance movement, he decorated his Park Row branch with religious mottoes ("What doth it profit a man if he gains the whole world and loses his own soul") and required waitresses to attend religious sermons at a stated time every day in an on-site chapel. A sparse menu of 1892 features griddle cakes with maple syrup, a choice of breads, graham crackers, Zepher crackers or rice in milk, 10 cents each, milk toast, corned-beef hash, ham and boiled eggs, coffee, pies, and crullers. The back of the menu boasts: "One quart of the richest cream is added to every can of milk used in this establishment." In 1907, Dennett was found wandering in the Piedmont Hills section of Oakland, California, a pillowcase wound around his head, yelling "Glory! Glory!" A failed mining investment had driven him to insanity.

Samuel Childs (1863–1925), a farm boy from New Jersey with training in civil engineering, went to work with his brother William at Dennett's restaurant on Park Row. In 1887, the brothers were fired for being overly ambitious and with their savings opened their own restaurant at 41 Cortlandt Street. In 1889, with Whitcomb as a partner, they leased an expensive space at Broadway and Cedar Street. William, who formerly worked a milk

Imagined interior of
Columbia Dairy Kitchen
NYC

route in Bernardsville, New Jersey, took the dairy idea literally and had their new restaurant outfitted to evoke the cleanliness and style of a modern, sanitary milking room, with brilliantly lit white tile walls and floors, and washable enamel surfaces. Waitresses (not waiters) neatly dressed in white uniforms attended to patrons seated four to a table at fixed rotating stools. The brilliantly white exterior facades were in a neoclassical or nautically tinged Spanish Colonial revival style. A common sight in lower Manhattan was the cooks "who deftly turn the tawny buckwheat cakes in the windows of dairy restaurants" [*New York Times,* November 18, 1887]. The Childses' business plan was to multiply their small profits on affordable items through scale of operation. By 1916 there were 81 branches. Childs Lunch Rooms flirted briefly with a vegetarian menu, but soon returned to its wide range of foods from oysters, eggs, and omelets to steaks. A menu proclaims: "The Milk used in this establishment is fresh from my own Dairy every morning."

From the sale of buttermilk and other dairy products, the Home Dairy Company of Michigan spawned a large chain of lunchrooms, cafeterias, and restaurants across the country. This chain represented the epitome of wholesome Midwestern family dining. The Mattei Brothers of Denver, Colorado, opened a large and elegant Home Dairy Restaurant in 1890, apparently not connected with the Michigan chain. Pictures of the strangely vacant dining rooms are preserved in postcard views. *The Jewish Outlook*, a Denver newspaper, reported that the annual B'nai B'rith Day celebration was scheduled to take place at the Home Dairy Restaurant on November 8, 1908.

Business directories and other print sources record the existence of countless dairy lunchrooms. The earliest dates to July 12, 1873. Banker's and Broker's Dairy Lunch Room at 62 Cedar Street, opposite the post office, advertised in the *Brooklyn Eagle* of that date: "Pure Orange County Milk and cream received daily direct from the country and served to our guests. Ice cold berries and all other kinds of fruit in their season received daily direct from the country, arriving before 5 o'clock AM, thus preserving their freshness and beauty . . . Don't be deluded with the idea that you are obliged to flee to the country in order to obtain pure milk and cream, fresh fruits, etc. Come to 62 Cedar Street — satisfy yourselves. . . . Much cheaper and better than medicine. Dyspeptics, come one and all, partake heartily of our oatmeal cakes and cream, and be cured. Hundreds are being cured daily. . . . Look for Banner and sign of Big Cow across the street. Politeness, attentive waitresses, good order, cleanliness, no offensive smell of cooking, cool, airy room, which will be improved within the next few days with patent revolving fans, characterize our Dairy. Note: Gold and Stock Indicator Telegraph printing European financial and all other cable news and important American news as received. N.B. No liquors sold. Bowe & Slater, proprietors."

The origins of the dairy lunchroom lie in the combined aspirations of two interconnected reform movements of the time: temperance and pure food.

Free lunch at a NYC saloon

The American Temperance Society was formed in 1826, but its origins go back to the eighteenth century. Through those years, it was a goal of the movement to provide an alternative to the saloons, then located on nearly every street corner, that attracted customers with an offer of free lunch with the purchase of beer or whiskey.

An 1895 editorial in *The American Jewess* explained that total abstinence was incompatible with Jewish culture as wine was used for rituals and at social gatherings and therefore the Jews could not join the temperance movement. By placing unjust restrictions upon behavior and commercial activities, the movement violated the civil rights guaranteed by the Constitution. The Prohibition Party and the Anti-Saloon League thus came into conflict with the urban Jew involved in business and moderate social drinking.

After the establishment of Prohibition in January 1920, special permits were issued for the sacramental consumption of wine. The number of spurious

congregations requesting these permits led to the Internal Revenue Service calling for a repeal of these exemptions. Reform and Conservative congregations were willing to forgo the exemption and use unfermented grape juice. Orthodox congregations

FRESH
BUTTER
MILK
EVERY
DAY

POT
CHEESE

rejected this idea but offered no reason. The so-called raisin-wine controversy led to the widening rift between Jewish religious denominations.

While the temperance movement held Jews up as models of moderation in drinking (their compulsions were more likely to be directed toward eating), Jews worked as saloonkeepers, in the beer-and-spirits business, and, during Prohibition, were involved in bootlegging.

The physical comfort of a saloon was clear: "the warm, brilliantly lighted cheery barroom" in winter, and in summer, "the ice-cold lager beer and the breezes created by the electric fans." The saloon was the social meeting place that crossed socioeconomic grounds for games, talk, and music.

Attempts at opening temperance hotels, restaurants, and cafes modeled after their alcohol-serving namesakes were never very successful. An ambitious Temperance Coffee House movement in England also came to naught. In the phenomenon of the dairy lunchroom, the temperance leaders saw their dream finally realized.

"The crowded condition of the numerous 'dairy' restaurants of the well-known Dennett, Childs and Bailey type at many hours of the day demonstrates the fact that thousands of men are quite willing to pay more money for their lunch away from the saloon and its associations than the saloonkeeper asks, if only the places and provisions are to be found in convenient and attractable situations." It was proposed "that the city should buy out a certain number of saloons in each ward" for the purpose of converting them into non-alcoholic lunch and meeting places. [*The Independent,* February 6, 1902]

The pure food movement of the 1870s was the culmination of a growing popular discontent with food and its handling, especially in big cities. The special attention directed to the problems of milk purity, in its supply and delivery, had people thinking about reliable sources from the nearby countryside and, by association, the spanking-white, easy-to-clean tiles of model dairy farms and milking rooms.

Clever restaurateurs must have seen the possibility of aligning themselves with this movement by offering an alternative to the spittle-flecked, sawdust-covered floors of the quick lunch counters common in that day. The heavy baronial-styled banquets and drapes could give way to a new scientifically based aesthetic of cleanliness and purity. What better way to attract customers than to appeal to their fear of illness due to unsanitary and unhealthful eating conditions.

These dairy lunchrooms offered the Kellogg's health-food products of the day along with a large selection of farinaceous foods, milk, and eggs. To appeal to the heavier eater they also included a substantial meat-and-fish menu. These popular establishments, like the Christian Meierei and Milchhallen of Europe, were dairy restaurants in name, decor, and spirit, but were not limited to a dairy-based menu.

In 1873, a branch of the Holly Tree Inn was opened in Brooklyn, New York, by the Woman's Christian Temperance Association. It was a cheap eating house in which a meal and coffee could be purchased for 15 cents on a clean tablecloth in a neat, warm room. [*New York Observer,* January 2, 1873]

Two well-known dairy lunchrooms were located near the Jewish East Side: The Centennial Dairy Lunch

& Dining Room at 106 Fourth Avenue, between 11th and 12th Streets, run by Hollingsworth & Grum [*Important Events of the Century*, 1876] and the Columbia Dairy Kitchen at 48 East 14th Street on Union Square. The Columbia Dairy Kitchen's menu announced that it was open from 5 am to 1 am and featured "Pure milk and butter from our Shrub Oak Dairy Farm." The service was summed up in a poem on the menu. "The Columbia Lunch so tempting, so neat, with jolly good company and comfortable seat. No five-minute lunch at some way station, No elbows to hunch, no quarter-ration." It featured "Genuine Old-fashioned Griddle-cakes with pure Vermont Maple Syrup" for 10 cents. "These are the cakes men have long sought, and wondered where they could be bought." On its vast menu of roasted and broiled meats, oysters, and vegetables there's a sizable list of dairy dishes: variations on a bowl of milk or cream with various cereals or breads. "The Columbia Orchestra will play popular selections every afternoon and evening. Ask the Leader to play your favorite selection while you dine. Table d'hôte dinner with wine served from 11:30 to 8 pm for 75¢." The Columbia Dairy Kitchen was described as being "something of a curiosity for its size, its music and its methods." [Ernest Ingersoll, *A Week in New York* (1891)]

For an immigrant Jew, deciphering the English-language menus and eating in one of these American-style dairy lunchrooms would be a major step toward assimilation. For the familiar dairy dishes of home, they'd have to patronize an Eastern European Jewish-style dairy restaurant, if one existed.

The Reason: A Journal of Prohibition from February 1886 carried ads for "DAIRY LUNCHES! PURE MILK CO." at four locations in Chicago. "Our specialty: A glass of pure milk or butter milk, with one biscuit or bun, 5 Cents. Cheap, Cleanly Lunches. No alcohol surroundings."

In 1881, the visiting secretary of the National Temperance League of Great Britain, Robert Rae, described the proliferation of dairy lunchrooms in many American cities. "One large establishment of the kind I saw at Washington, and there they were giving milk luncheons to the people who were flocking in to get them. A charge was made of five cents for a pint of milk. In New York, I found there were a great many of these Dairy Lunch Rooms opening up in various parts of the city. . . . These Dairy Refreshment Rooms appear to be on the increase in our own country. We are acquainted with several in the City of London, and they seem to carry on an extensive business."

"Dr. David Blaustein, superintendent of the Educational Alliance [1898–1907] declared that the Hebrews of the East Side had no liquor problem." This fact was attributed to the moderation of drink in the cafes of the East Side. "In the district south of Houston St. and east of the Bowery there dwell sixty-five thousand families, who support two hundred cafes. . . . The East Side cafe is an eating house by day and a drinking place by night." The single men and women make up the daytime business. They work until 9 pm and then devote two hours to their intellectual development through lectures, concerts, and political meetings. "At the

Gibbs's Alderney Dairy and Restaurant ad in *The Life Struggle, Fall, and Reformation of T. N. Doutney,* 1880

From the menu of Geyer's Dairy Restaurant and Lunch Room, 176 Fulton Street, 1901

EGGS AND OMELETS.

Fried Eggs (two) 15		Scrambled Eggs on Toast . . 20	
Boiled Eggs (two) 15		Egg Omelet, Plain 15	
Poached Eggs on Toast . . 20		Ham Omelet 25	
Scrambled Eggs 15		Hash Omelet 25	

Oyster Omelet 25
Each additional Egg 5

All the above are to order, and require about 5 minutes for preparation.

GRIDDLE CAKES.

Buckwheat Cakes }
Rice   "   } With Pure Maple Syrup . 10
Wheat   "   }

DAIRY DISHES,

SERVED WITH BOWL OF MILK.

Oat Meal, hot or cold & Milk 10	Snow Flake Crackers & Milk 10
Boiled Rice and Milk . . . 10	Oat Meal Crackers and Milk 10
Graham Bread and Milk . . 10	Milk Biscuits and Milk . . 10
Corn Cakes and Milk . . . 10	Brown Bread and Milk . . . 10
Graham Crackers and Milk . 10	White Bread and Milk . . . 10
Zwieback and Milk 10	Vienna Bread and Milk . . 10

Shredded Wheat Biscuits and Milk . 10

The above served with half Cream, 15.   All Cream, 20.

COFFEE, &c.

Coffee, per cup 5	Tea 5
Chocolate 5	Milk, per glass 5

Cream, per glass 10

CAKES, TOASTS, &c.

Chocolate Eclairs 5	White Bread Milk Toast . . 10
Corn Cakes 5	Graham Bread Milk Toast . 10
Corn Cakes, with Butter . . . 8	Muffins Milk Toast 15
Lunch Cakes 5	Hot Rolls 5
Wine Cakes 5	Dry Toast 5
Home-Made Crullers 5	Buttered Toast 10
Charlotte de Russe 5	Zwieback 5
Cream Toast 15	Vienna Rolls, with Butter . . 5

SEE SPECIAL BILL OF FARE.

Not Responsible for Hats, Overcoats, Etc.

stroke of 11, however, the places begin to fill up for hard as his day's work the East Sider must end it with an hour or two of social enjoyment. Tea prepared in the Russian fashion is the drink most in demand. If a man wants whiskey or beer the waiter goes out to the nearest saloon for it. There is no custom of treating. Each man pays for what he orders. Discussion of a wide range of subjects gives the necessary entertainment, and no fiery liquor is need to give it zest. There is little or no music, as it would interfere with the discussion. . . . There are three kinds of cafes in this district — Russian, Rumanian and Galician. One finds intellectual life at its height about the tables of the Russian cafes. Tea is the drink, almost exclusively, and the discussion is most spirited.

"At the Rumanian cafes the light grape wine of the country is much in demand, but there is no drinking to excess. . . . The discussions in the Rumanian places are not so lively, and card playing without gambling is indulged in.

"Most of the patrons of the Galician cafes are older people. They write letters at the little tables, they bring their own books and read away the hours, sipping tea or coffee. The dietary laws are more strictly adhered to than at the cafes of the other two classes.

"The tone of the cafe depends upon the proprietor almost entirely. . . . His is a respected businessman and his opinions have weight. Where the musicians gather, one will find, usually, that the proprietor of the cafe is a musician. And so with the other professions, Socialists gather about a man who advocates socialism. . . . Does anyone need a more extended explanation why the Jews have no drink problem?" [*New York Daily Tribune,* Sunday, April 14, 1904]

An 1891 report notes: "A few years ago a class of restaurant called dairies sprang up in the region below the Post Office [bottom of City Hall Park] which met with great success. They make milk and bread in a great variety of forms the standard nourishment, adding some simple desserts and pastries, and always berries and fruit in season. They are nearly all located between Broadway and the East River, below Newspaper Square." They charged 5 cents for coffee. [Ernest Ingersoll, *A Week in New York* (1891)]

A reporter for *The Sun* in 1893 noted that "a surprising number of new restaurants of the cheaper sort are painted white. Probably their proprietors are following a fashion set by a New Yorker, whose bill of fare consisted largely of milk, who intended to imply as much by the cream-colored front of his place. The so-called 'dairy' restaurants and coffee houses that are scattered about the land and that are painted white are numbered by hundreds."

A chain of fifty dairy restaurants in New York City gave its patrons a printed brochure containing a "dietetic code." It included instructions on "How to Eat," modeled after the rules of the famous mastication advocate Horace Fletcher (1849–1919): "Chew all solid food until it is liquid and practically swallows itself," "Never take food while hungry or worried and only when calm," and "Do not eat anything that disagrees with you." Patrons were warned that following these rules might "require self-denial, but sometimes in your life you must definitely decide whether you are to be master over your body or be its slave." [*The Friend,* May 19, 1906]

Quaker groups favored dairy restaurants for their wholesome grains and vegetarian possibilities. Early dairy lunchrooms were often referred to as Quaker Lunch Rooms.

It was not beyond W. C. Barraclough, owner of a chain of dairy restaurants in Los Angeles, to sell impure milk in 1911 [*Los Angeles Times,* July 15, 1911].

An observer in 1873 noted that "the prevailing colors in signs for the dairy restaurants are blue and white. These are also the prevailing colors in their milk." [*The Independent,* August 21, 1873]

The menu for July 19, 1900, of the Royal Dairy and Quick Lunch Restaurant Co. at 194 Broadway and 276 Sixth Avenue boasted "only the best and purest food of all kinds used." "Perfect cleanliness and Prompt Service." Horace L. Harriman the general manager offered a small selection of "Dairy Dishes" — Milk or Dipped Toast for 15 cents and Cream Toast for 20 cents. Beef stew was priced at 10 cents. The dairy dishes were not necessarily less expensive than the meat dishes.

The printed bill of fare for Geyer's Dairy Restaurant and Lunch Room at 176 Fulton Street, opposite St. Paul's Churchyard, in 1901 offered a full menu of clam chowders, fish, lamb chops, chicken, prime rib of beef, turkey, veal, and

hot roast-beef sandwiches. A small section of its five-page menu (see page 245) listed eggs and omelets, griddle cakes, and, under "Dairy Dishes," an assortment of cereals, boiled rice, graham bread, corn cakes, zwieback, snow flake crackers, Vienna bread, shredded wheat biscuits all served in a bowl of milk. All in the range of 10 cents, with half-cream 15 cents, with all cream 20 cents.

The front of the menu for Arnold's Restaurant and Dairy at 107 and 100 Water Street, in 1901, features a drawing of a Jersey cow flanked by the slogans: "Sign of the Golden Cow," "Pure Milk and Cream," and "As to Quality None Better." The vast menu, rivaling a modern diner, features fish, hot roasts, steaks and chops, oysters, a section of farinaceous food (cereals, rice, and grits), ice creams, and many desserts of French style. "Fresh Eggs Received Daily from our Poultry Farm Rockville Centre, L.I." "Pure water: Our Drinking Water is filtered and purified by an improved system, stored in Block-Tin Cylinders and packed in ice, free from contamination." Pure milk, rich cream, and fresh buttermilk were sold by the glass, as was Vichy water (naturally sparkling) and Vichy water with milk. A wood engraving on the back shows a peaceful gathering of farm animals alongside the text "We strive to please our customers in every way and to make this Restaurant as home-like as possible.

We do not claim that our Milk and Cream come from our own dairy, but do claim them to be unexcelled. Meats used are the best obtainable, and while Philadelphia Poultry, Boston Ducks and Long Island Eggs cost us more, you will find nothing else on our tables. Everything used is absolutely fresh and the best in the market, but special mention is made of our coffee. Try it!"

The Day Light Luncheon at Sixth Avenue and 18th Street in 1900 featured "Fresh Buttermilk made every morning in our Creamery, and served to our patrons just as it is when taken out of the churn."

In 1906, the Siegel Cooper Department Store at Sixth Avenue and 18th Street boasted of a pure food restaurant in their basement whose menu had a small section of "Dairy Dishes": Milk Toast, Shredded Wheat with Cream, Boiled Rice with Milk, and other cereals. The menu was otherwise a wide selection of foods including "Chicken Croquettes with Peas, Ox-Tongue with Potato Salad, Oyster Cream Stew, and Broiled Lamb Kidneys with Ham, Henry IV." They used ". . . only absolutely Pure Rich Cream and guarantee to serve you with Strictly Fresh Cream made Fresh Every Morning."

Milk toast — bits of toast soaking in a bowl of warm milk — found on the menu of most dairy restaurants, was the inspiration for the name of a popular comic-strip character, Caspar Milquetoast, in the series *The Timid Soul* by H. T. Webster that ran in newspapers from 1924 to 1952. Milquetoast was the embodiment of a mild, ineffectual male. The habitué of the dairy lunch counter

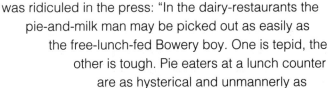

was ridiculed in the press: "In the dairy-restaurants the pie-and-milk man may be picked out as easily as the free-lunch-fed Bowery boy. One is tepid, the other is tough. Pie eaters at a lunch counter are as hysterical and unmannerly as women at a bargain sale. . . . The effects of pie are, like those of every other injurious food, insidious. The hardened pie eater becomes art blind. Nothing makes him glow or warms him to any enthusiasms but his chosen food. No great man was ever fond of pie. No important work was ever consummated on a pie diet. Pie is a clog on the spirit and a ball and chain on the imagination." [*New York Times,* August 10, 1902]

In January 1897, a delegate from the Central Labor Union

proposed organizing female waiters. "More than half the waiters down town were females, and in the dairy restaurants they were paid $3.50 to $4 a week. Male waiters could not afford to work for such low wages." [*New York Times,* January 25, 1897]

The notorious Variety Theatre Saloon and dancing hall owned by Harry Hill at 26 East Houston and Crosby Streets was suddenly being advertised as a "'Dairy' Restaurant and billiard parlor." In 1874, in an astonishing change of heart, Mr. Hill offered to open his hall free of charge to the Union Temperance Society meetings on Sunday. After a life of fighting and drinking, he announced his conversion to the temperance movement. At the conclusion of these meetings, dissenting views were aired: "The Bible from which the temperance speakers had just quoted was employed to prove not only that the use of wine was not prohibited by the Scriptures, but that there was even a positive command in certain portions of the Old Testament to use it." [*New York Times,* March 9, 1874]

A Supreme Court judge smiled when Harry Hill explained that he kept his place on East Houston Street open for the "education of the people who line up for the pure milk, fresh from Mr. Hill's three farms on Long Island, where nothing but Jerseys with long pedigrees are kept, and where the milk is never skimmed of its cream." His variety hall was eventually closed for giving performances without a license and serving beer [*New York Times,* March 29, 1887]. Over the years, Hill paid a fortune in protection money to the police to allow him to run his various businesses. The dairy restaurant was a last-ditch humorous ploy to continue operation.

As early as 1909, the slang expressions of dairy lunch-counter men shouted to the kitchen were common knowledge. "Poached eggs" became

"Adam and Eve on a raft"; "scrambled eggs" became "three eggs wreck 'em!" The countermen and customers enjoyed these inventions. ["Boosting Their Game," *Washington Herald,* February 21, 1909]

The innocuous quality of the best-selling books of 1902 was attributed to a class of people attracted to "the sweet and clean," "the mental cleanliness of the bulk of our people — a cleanliness that is finding physical expression in bathing facilities and dairy restaurants, with plain cooking and electrical contrivances for shooing off flies. The great public do not like the high flavors that your epicures affect." [John Paul, *New York Times,* May 11, 1901]

Cooking for Profit: A New American Cook Book, "adapted for the use of all who serve meals for a price," by Jessup Whitehead, an 1893 compendium of tricks of the restaurant trade, includes a section on the "Quaker Dairy Lunch." "Farinaceous and milk food; such dishes as mush and milk, bread and butter and fruit and buttermilk are the specialties of some lunch houses. These are all cheap and healthful dishes and many customers avail themselves of the opportunity to avoid meat eating altogether. A large variety of pastry, puddings and cakes, however, gets into the bill of fare of most of the 'dairies' eventually, such as have been enumerated already under the head of fine bakery lunch, and a few more will be found following these simpler dishes." Recipes for Oatmeal Mush and Milk, Soda Crackers and Milk, Doughnuts and Milk, Boston Brown Bread, Sour Milk Cheese or Smearkase, Boiled Rice and Milk, and Batter Cakes with Syrup are given in detail. The dairy lunchroom was already a codified form of restaurant business.

By 1929, William Childs, deposed as head of the Childs chain, undertook a new restaurant venue. In contrast to the standardized and sanitized Childs chain, which seemed to have exhausted its appeal, this was to be a small chain of unique 1,000-seat eateries — each one modeled after a location in the Old World: an Algerian Village, Old Normandy, Old Paris, Old London. The plans were never realized.

As a Christian-based temperance institution, the dairy lunch can be seen as a last public stand against drink and the influx of foreign culinary taste. It was the epitome of a "goyisher" restaurant with its meager, insubstantial portions of insipid food — dietary control as a tool of assimilation and conversion.

The antagonism between labor and capital is unwarranted, the temperance societies argued. The plight of the working classes will improve through the increased mechanization of labor. "Few serious difficulties would arise between classes where all revere God and observe the golden rule," and reform of the drink habit is essential as one-third of every workday of ten hours goes to pay for intoxicating drinks. The saloon was condemned as a center of political agitation.

The scientific approach to restaurant design, however, did have an impact on the Jews. The neutral, stainless-steel and enamel (later Formica) dairy lunchroom interior was the perfect choice of decor for a cuisine that did not have a national style. It went on to serve as the model for countless luncheonettes and coffee shops. Furthermore, the quick dairy lunchroom was so omnipresent in large cities of America that many items from its vast Anglo-American cuisine — sandwiches, certain salads, etc. — found their way onto the menu of many Jewish dairy restaurants. In fact, many Jewish dairy restaurateurs simply used the words "dairy lunch" to identify what was a substantially different type of establishment.

The goals of the temperance movement were finally realized on January 17, 1920, with the ratification of the Eighteenth Amendment to the U.S. Constitution. There followed thirteen dry years filled with more crime and more surreptitious drinking than ever before. It was estimated that 60 percent of bootleggers were Jews.

Jewish Restaurant Culture in Lower Manhattan

We read of Dr. Lilienthal, M. M. Noah, and other luminaries of early American Jewish life of the 1840s and '50s participating in banquets celebrating the Jewish charitable institutions of New York City: the New York Jews' Hospital, the New York Hebrew Assistance Society, etc. These public dinners were held at popular concert- and banquet-hall venues such as the Apollo Saloon, the City Assembly Rooms, or Niblo's Saloon on Broadway, rented for the evening. The banquets, for as many as 600 people, were supplied by caterers, or the kitchen staff of the specific institution sponsoring the event and, according to a contemporary report, were "prepared with great skill and particular regard to our religious rules." The menus ranged from cold meats to "every thing that the season afforded, together with a rich display of all kinds of fruit and choice wines." In honor of Joseph Jacobs, a visiting Jewish lawyer from London in the 1890s, a kosher caterer was engaged to serve a meal at Delmonico's in the style of rarefied pan-European cuisine (Palmettes Varsovienne, Filets de Boeuf aux Olives, etc.).

By the 1860s elaborate Purim costume balls at the 14th Street Academy of Music were an annual fixture among the New York Jewish elite. Nine hundred or so invited guests streamed into the concert hall, which was transformed for the evening into elaborate tableaux vivants from ancient Jewish history. Among the wide range of fanciful costumes could be seen a caricature of a Polish Jew complete with tefillin. The extensive thematic decorations were accompanied by music, "wines and choice edibles." The proceeds went to various Jewish charities.

The Jewish Times of New York, a bilingual German-English newspaper of the 1870s, carried advertisements for a variety of restaurants. Some, such as Blaut & Minsesheimer, described as "The most elegant Jewish Restaurant in America," with its main branch at 100 Duane Street off Broadway, were explicitly Jewish while others, such as Adam Kiefer's Restaurant Frascate at 52 University Place, Denis Donovan's Restaurant at 5 East 12th Street, and Maison Richelieu, a "First class French restaurant" at 61 Lexington Avenue, make no mention of Kashruth or Jewish cuisine, simply their hours and offerings.

One of the earliest restaurants geared toward the needs of the observant Jew was the Felix Kosher Dining Saloon at 256 Broadway, opposite City Hall. Felix Marx, in partnership with Isaac Ederheimer, started operation in 1857 and by 1866 expanded to a branch at 45–47 Lispenard Street.

Born in the Alsace region of France in 1825, Felix Marx arrived in New York c.1854 at the age of twenty-nine with some adult knowledge of Alsatian restaurant culture and worked as a caterer and cook. Mr. Ederheimer, of German Jewish origin, arrived in New York in 1840, moved from the fancy goods business to wine and liquor, and by 1860 was operating a saloon at 45 Lispenard Street.

At the first location, on Broadway between Warren and Murray Streets, it attracted an affluent clientele of Jewish businessmen and merchants.

Imagined scene in Felix Marx restaurant

Ad in *The Occident, Jewish-American Advocate,* 1866

In July 1867 the partnership was dissolved and Marx's restaurant, following the growth of a Jewish quarter, moved from 11 Thomas Street to 185 Church Street to 438 Broome Street (1884) to 79 Mercer Street (1886), and by 1889 was at 193 Mercer Street.

The New York Evening Sun of 1887 describes the Felix Marx restaurant as the only true kosher restaurant in New York City. Their business card bore the phrase "The Kosher Delmonico's." Situated in the dry-goods district just off Houston Street, it had a German chef and attracted wealthy German Jews at lunchtime for a 40-cent meal of several courses: "barley or chicken soup, boiled beef or Hamburger steak, with fried potatoes and sauerkraut, veal cutlets, roast duck or broiled chicken with salad, and a compote of prunes and raisins or some delicate pastry. A dish of the choicest fruit and a jar of celery stands always on the table. A small cup of black coffee completes the meal." In compliance with Jewish dietary law, no dairy products were served.

"A spirit of jollity pervades the place, and for a time all thought of business is cast aside." The reporter explains that the many other kosher restaurants in the area are kosher only in name, "as the service is filthy and the food scarcely fit to eat. . . . They are mostly small rooms in the cellars or upon the ground floors of tenements, furnished with a few wooden tables and chairs, with a bill of fare, printed in Hebrew characters, hanging outside the door. In the windows the shrunken carcasses of geese are allowed to hang until blackened with exposure." A meal can be purchased for from 8 to 15 cents, but "a strictly orthodox Hebrew would turn in horror from such restaurants. . . ."

A 1903 account describes it as "a big and comfortable appearing restaurant, with nothing about its equipment to indicate its distinctive character . . . but as it is the cooking, and not the manner of the killing, that determines the taste of the food eaten, the food served here looks and tastes precisely as similar food would look and taste in any other restaurant."

The large space ran almost through the block. One reporter thought that the many long wooden tables on the south side were reserved for table d'hôte lunch, the only meal served, from 11:30 to 3 pm, and so had no bill of fare. The menu was changed each day, with "a choice of the entrées, the roasts, the salads, the fruits and the desserts." There was one uniform price and so no

checks were needed; "every person eating pays at the desk upon his departure the same amount. . . ." Another reporter believed that the tables on the north side of the restaurant were occupied by wealthier clientele who wanted à la carte service.

Three-fourths to seven-eighths of the patrons were well-dressed "Hebrew" businessmen of middle age or younger and their customers visiting town. Among observant Jews, it was known around the country as "The Felix."

A reporter from *The Sun* in 1887 notes that "there are some wealthy Jewish merchants in New York who still adhere to the strict letter of the dietary laws and the most prominent of these meet every noon in a Jewish restaurant in Mercer street. . . . All at the tables wore their hats. . . . The rear end of the room was divided off, by means of curtains, from the space reserved for tables. Just inside of these curtains was a washstand, with running water, hidden behind a screen. As each customer came in he would take off his overcoat, hang it up, and then go to the washstand and wash his hands, looking very devout in the meantime, and moving his lips in rapid muttering. Having thus performed his first duty, he took his seat and ordered dinner. He began this by cutting off

a little piece of bread, which he dipped in salt. Before touching it he repeated this prayer: 'Blessed be Thou, O Lord our God, King of the Universe who bringest forth bread from the earth.' Then he bit off a piece of the salt bread and swallowed it before touching anything else. . . . All the dishes were of the German-Jewish type; that is, they were German dishes prepared in the Jewish way. There was goose breast, and stuffed goose neck, and calves' tongue and sour-sweet sauce and almond cake. Excepting the abundant grease, the never-failing accompaniment of Low German dishes, everything was well cooked. The portions were very large; still, with nearly every course the diner was asked by the waiter whether he did not want more. . . . This is the only Jewish restaurant in New York that is sanctioned by Chief Rabbi Joseph. It closes every Saturday, but is open on Sunday. . . . It is evidently not the custom to give tips in this restaurant." [*New York Evening Sun,* 1887, in *Current Literature,* March 1891]

According to another report, "The Jewish dishes are prepared by a French [Alsatian] chef. Being a meat restaurant, no milk, butter or cream is served, being Kosher, no game of the kind that has been shot is served . . . otherwise, it has the usual appearance of a quiet, refined place, where men of means and leisure gather for unhurried repasts." [*New York Daily Tribune,* August 11, 1907]

When offered the position of Chief Rabbi of New York by the Association of American Orthodox Hebrew Congregations in 1888, Jacob Joseph (1840–1902) was hesitant to accept because he feared that religious observance in the city was in decline. If, in fact, the Felix was the only restaurant up to his standards, or willing to bear the costs of certification, then his fears were well founded.

In 1893, the restaurant, then under the direction of Felix's son Ernest, had its kosher reputation shaken by an unfortunate experience with a mashgiyekh from Kiev. The man, Yuddel Mannecker, came with high recommendations from Rabbi Joseph and a long lineage in the Orthodox community. Business among the Orthodox picked up with Yuddel's hiring at $40 a week. Within a few days, Yuddel was fired for

Queen Esther meets a Polish Jew at a Purim ball

259

incompetence — Marx did not want to pay this exorbitant salary to an employee who was no better at handling food than the old chef — and a lawsuit ensued. Upon his firing, Yuddel claimed that Marx said his presence was worthless as his customers "didn't know the difference between kosher and traefa meat any how. . . ." Also, Yuddel wouldn't work on Saturday. "Why, I work on Saturday myself. Is he any better than I am?"

Felix Marx retired in 1897, sold the restaurant, traveled to France, and then returned to the U.S., where he died in 1903. The restaurant closed by 1906.

Through restaurant culture, the regional, linguistic, political, culinary, religious, and class distinctions among the Jews of New York City in these years were brought into relief. There existed as many types of Jewish restaurants as there were types of Jews. English-language reports highlighted the obvious divisions between kosher and non-kosher, affluent and poor restaurants, but among Jews themselves public eating choices were propelled by a smell in the air, a momentary assimilationist impulse, or a pang of homesickness.

A report in the New York Observer and Chronicle of Thursday, March 19, 1868, entitled "Jews in the United States" offered a sober statistical picture: "120,000 Jews live in New York and Brooklyn. . . . Those of German origin are most numerous. . . . Till 1850 no Jew was ever convicted or tried, in this

State, for a capital offense." A section on "Jewish Restaurants" notes that Jews "preserve their national peculiarities with jealous care . . . Gentile meat and cookery are still an abomination among them. It will surprise many to know that there are more than fifty Jewish restaurants in this city, cosher [sic] eating-houses, as they are called. These are particularly numerous in the neighborhood of East Broadway, five of them being located on a single block of that thoroughfare."

An account of a visit to a Jewish restaurant in the *New York Times* of 1872 entitled "A New Cuisine" is a model of exotic adventure within an otherwise familiar city. A neighborhood pawnbroker explains, "You will hear all lanquinches spoken there: Bolish and Russian and Hungarian and Dutch and German and French. You will meet people there from all parts of the United States. . . . You can buy or sell most anything you like there, from a pair of breeches to a house." It's recommended that the adventurer eat the "vried fish."

"It was a good-sized establishment, well filled with people who seemed to be doing full justice to the fare placed on small tables around the room. The kitchen was evidently in the cellar below from whence arose a steam of cooking food. The master of the house would rush to the trap-door, yell down something in an impossible language, which was speedily followed by the appearance of a dish or so, placed on the floor which a waiter would pick up and bring to the guests. On a slightly raised platform was a rather stout woman, with a tremendous quantity of jewelry about her fat person, who was the accountant of the establishment. Around her was arranged a pile of what we made out to be smoked geese, and long, amber-colored cucumbers, prepared in some peculiar way. All were Israelites. . . . A waiter cleared a place for us and presented to us the most fearful catalogue of dishes imaginable."

In French restaurant style, the waiter and customer negotiate the most suitable dish through trial and error: Polish beet soup ("the idea of vinegar . . . set our teeth on edge"), Moldavian beef with raisins floating in a sea of gravy ("beef and raisins were incompatibilities"), and finally fish, not in yellow or red stew, but, as recommended, fried Portuguese-style in sweet oil.

All around diners were discussing business enterprises on a local and international scale. The waiter, a recently arrived Cockney, expressed the futility of the experiment: "I've seen many gents, Americans, trying this kind of thing, but it wasn't of no use. Wariety is the spice of life, except in the eating line, and never . . . never, Sir, do you eat nothing again as wasn't used to be cooked in your mother's house. . . ." The fried fish, however, was a success, calling for a celebration of the Jewish people and the perfection of their fish preparation.

Abraham Cahan (1860–1951), editor of the *Jewish Daily Forward,* noted in his memoir that upon arriving in NYC in 1882 he found no Jewish restaurants or cafes on Grand Street, the center of the Jewish quarter, so he began to eat in what he thought of as American restaurants. Within a few years, he describes the onset of a nostalgia for the food and culture of Russia. Would Felix Marx's restaurant, had he known of it, have been repugnant to the young socialist Cahan because of its affluent clientele and overt religious tone? Perhaps the Alsatian-style cuisine would not have appealed to his Lithuanian palate.

Of the 230,257 Jews in America in 1880, only 130,496 were affiliated with a synagogue. Orthodox Jewish organizations with 122 synagogues claimed 51,597 members. The 179 Reform Judaism temples counted 217,899 members. From these statistics, we can see that the majority of Jews in America at that time were not necessarily constrained by dietary laws.

The term "restaurant" can also add a layer of confusion to this study. *Der Strahl,* an illustrated Warsaw magazine, reported the opening of the first Jewish restaurant-cafe in that city in 1910, based on the fact that this new Jewish-owned and kosher establishment was the first to conform to the popular French-style restaurant-cafes of Warsaw. The numerous Jewish eating houses and mleczarnie of Warsaw did not fit this definition of restaurant. Early New York

City directories do not even include the category of "restaurant," but use "eating-house," "house of refreshment," "refectory," "dining room," and "dining saloon."

The Byron Restaurant of New York City, named after the famous Parisian restaurant on the Place de l'Opéra Comique, opened in 1845 by William Dinneford, a Jewish actor from London, would hardly be identified as a Jewish restaurant. And what of Cafe Sachs at 86 Canal Street (near Eldridge Street), established 1887 by Isidore Sachs, who was director of the Consolidated Music Publisher's Association of NYC. It was open day and night, offering an assortment of European specialties: pâté de foie gras, steak à la Tartare, Russian caviar, herring, French and German cheeses, German pancakes, Vichy seltzer, imported and domestic cigars.

Or Fleischmann's Vienna Cafe and Restaurant on Fourth Avenue, corner of 10th Street, next to Grace Church. Louis Fleischmann, a Jew born in Olmütz, Moravia, followed his brothers to America. In 1874, his distaste for American bread and his brothers' successful compressed-yeast factory led him into commercial baking. To publicize his business and incidentally introduce Americans to Viennese-style coffee, he opened a Vienna Model Bakery and Cafe at the 1876 Philadelphia Exhibition. When the fair closed, he transferred the elegant cafe-bakery and its reputation to New York City and several other cities. During business hours, it was a meeting place for prominent Germans in business and the arts, but at midnight Fleischmann had bread and coffee given to hundreds of indigent men who lined up along 10th Street.

Moses Rischin, in *The Promised City: New York's Jews: 1870–1914,* summarized the eating possibilities in the late 1880s: ". . . wine cellars, cafes, restaurants sprang up, popularized by Jacob J. Kampus, the blintz-maker of Delancey Street and other Rumanians, accustomed to them at home. In the evenings lunchrooms became frugal 'Kibitzarnias.'" There, over steaming Russian tea and lemon, think slices of cake and Russian cigarettes, "confused minds, disturbed by life's complexities, found respite and tonic in talk. On Rutgers Street and East Broadway, cafes entertained through the night as journalists of Yiddish Newspaper Row defended their signed columns against the sallies of their challengers. Even Talmudists with untrimmed breads and long black coats drank honey cider, chewed lima beans and disputed the finer points of the Law in their favorite cafes. By 1905 some 250 to 300 coffee houses, each with its Tendenz and special clientele, congregated on the Lower East Side. By then a dozen fashionable restaurants had sprung up as relative affluence encouraged more luxurious tastes and less overflowing, if more precise, talk."

Advertisements for the following Jewish restaurants and cafes appeared in the Yiddish-language *The Worker's Newspaper* of 1890. Some are illustrated by woodcuts of the proud owners, who set the tone of conviviality with the hope of attracting customers.

Victor Steiner's Restaurant, at 105 Delancey Street, offered "regular dinners for 20 cents" and was "known by every worker. Everything tasteful and elegant. Drink and food at moderate prices."

"Ch. Goodelman Diner Restaurant at 84 Spring Street near Broadway, in which each guest is politely dealt with and receives the finest foods. I hope that for my good prices and well-known wares you'll visit my new restaurant."

"I. Ginzberg's Restaurant 116 Canal St."

"M. Licht Restaurant, 1 Canal St."

"B[ernard] Silberman's Jewish Restaurant, 44 Canal St."

"Adolf Grosman first class restaurant, Jewish and tasty food. Regular dinner 15 and 20 cents. 22 Orchard Street."

"H[enry]. Presler. 27 Broome St. between Allen and Orchard. Restaurant and Kafe Salon. Regular dinner with two meats 20 cents."

"B. Smukler's Kafe and Restaurant, 167 East Broadway."

Restaurants were often the scene of religious conflict. On Yom Kippur, September 27, 1898, Herrick Brothers' Restaurant at 141 Division Street stayed open to accommodate its socialist and atheist customers. A crowd of Orthodox Jews from a nearby shul gathered in front and brutally attacked diners as they left, despite police protection. At one point, the Orthodox Jews rushed into the restaurant, "overturned tables, smashed dishes and threw crockery at the proprietors." One customer had scalding-hot tea poured down his neck. In time, non-believing Jews made a point of flaunting their non-observance of this high holiday by patronizing open restaurants and organizing Yom Kippur fêtes. [*New York Sun,* September 27, 1898]

Walter E. Lagerquist, a young economics professor at Cornell, mentioned studying a map of synagogues on the Lower East Side compiled in 1905 by David Blaustein, the superintendent of the Education Alliance. "This map," he claimed, "shows that the Jews settled in the same relative geographical places [positions] they occupied in Europe, so that this map presented a map of Europe in miniature." [*New York Times,* April 2, 1910]

By 1910, New York was the third-largest Hungarian city in the world with 60,000 living between Houston and 12th Street and Second Avenue and the East River. They were equally divided between Slavs and Magyars — most were Jews. In 1900, Second Avenue between Houston and East 10th Street was known as the Hungarian Broadway and "every second house presents the sign 'Hungarian Restaurant.' The wide sidewalks were worked by more hurdy-gurdy men than any other in the city and used for elaborate community Maypole dances" [*New York Times,* August 5, 1900]. The numerous souvenir postcards and trade cards advertising the Cafe Boulevard at Second Avenue between 9th and 10th Streets attest to its exotic appeal to the uptown crowd. The first three stories were garden balconies with ornate ironwork. Its business was irrevocably hurt by Prohibition laws of the 1920s.

The Hungarians constituted a "Little Hungary" on East Houston Street, known as "Goulash Row" in the early 1900s. Bohemians situated themselves on First and Second Avenues between 70th and 80th Streets.

Romanian Jews had a unique impact on Jewish eating in New York City through the introduction of a specific Jewish-Romanian cuisine and a lively restaurant culture. Romanian immigration to America began in large numbers in 1877, and by 1901 there were almost 40,000 Romanians in America and 24,000 in New York

City. In 1884, two Romanians opened a basement wine cellar on Hester Street complete with a kitchen offering a full range of wine and food after the style of their homeland. Their popular and lucrative carciuma (wine house) and brutaria (bakery) were copied by other Romanians and soon patronized by the wider Jewish community. Also, in Romanian style, some introduced musical performance. The famous cimbalon virtuoso Joseph Moskowitz played in a Houston Street wine cellar before opening his own restaurants on Second Avenue. (See matchbook on page 233.)

The few Romanian synagogues that were opened in New York City

Joseph Moskowitz in a Romanian wine cellar

were not successful, and so, for single Romanian young men, the cafes functioned as social meeting places, where they could smoke and linger over a cup of black Oriental-style coffee. For outsiders, eating and drinking was central to the experience.

A number of Romanian benevolent and cultural societies were formed, but as persecution of Jews continued in Romania, the interest in their old cultural identity withered. They quickly and patriotically adopted their American citizenship and were quicker than most immigrants to speak and read English. The entrepreneurial spirit of the Romanian Jew supported the Yiddish press and literature. Modern Yiddish theater was born in the entrepreneurial climate of Bucharest and Iasi. In 1886 a company of Romanian Jewish actors came to New York and soon opened their own Romanian Opera House on the Bowery.

By 1901, there were "150 restaurants, 200 wine-cellars with lunch rooms attached and about 30 coffee-houses kept by Romanian Jews." They were popular with all Jews and attracted a non-Jewish clientele as well. [D. M. Hermalin, "The Roumanian Jew in America," in *American Jewish Year Book 5662* (1901)]

Rivington Street was known for several Romanian-run delicatessens featuring goose pastrami, ripe olives, salted vine leaves, "the moon shaped cashcaval cheese made of sheep's milk, the figure of an American version of a Roumanian shepherd in holiday costume with flute at his waxen lips, standing erect in the window." [Marcus Eli Ravage, "My Plunge into the Slums," in *Harper's,* April 1917]

A 1910 ad in *Der Gazlen* claims, "You can find the cream of the New York Intelligentsia eating their meals at L. Satz' cafe at 182 Henry Street, first floor." Ludwig Satz was a star of the Yiddish theater.

A 1905 account of two popular Russian cafes on the Lower East Side, one catering to socialists and one to anarchists, stresses the fact that the main attraction was socializing, conversation, and tea served in glasses with lemon and sugar — food was of secondary interest. For 25 cents one had a meal of sour cabbage soup, dark bread, a Hungarian-style goulash, squares of apple cake, and other hard seeded pastries. The conversations, on topics of politics, science, the arts, and economics, were conducted in every language but English, began at 10 or 11 pm and continued until 3 am. The anarchist cafe featured classical music played on a phonograph; the socialist cafe had tables for chess and dominoes. "There is nothing of the personal self-absorption and culinary concerns of a European bourgeois restaurant." [*The Sun,* March 26, 1905]

"The materialistic school of the drama hold forth on Canal Street near Chrystie, where, when the theater is out Jacob Gordin, the great Jewish playwright, leads the discussion. 'Herrick's' on Division Street near Seward Park, is perhaps the best known of the Socialist strongholds. . . . Music hall performers gather at the 'Cafe Marcus,' opposite the Grand Theater. To the more elegant of the Grand Street cafes the young men take their sweethearts after the play. Businessmen frequent places such as 'Burger's' on Avenue C. Laborer's cafes are on every block. To such an extent is natural selection carried that on Second Avenue is a cafe where pickpockets and small crooks gather on one side and prostitutes on the other." [Louis H. Pink, *The Independent,* March 1, 1906]

The *New York Tribune* of August 1907 reports on the opening of a Russian teahouse and cafe on the East Side. "The entrance hall appears as though an untrained impressionist had passed through it with his brush. It is bright and many colored. Upstairs garlands of flowers wave from the ceilings and palms stand around the spacious floor." It's decorated in Russian style, "at night with electric lights glimmering through artificial flowers and leaves." Called Komimepyeckar Locinnhniia, the headwaiter "has been imported from the Cafe Corcercheaky, in Odessa, after which the New York chie [teahouse] is patterned."

At the Russian cafe tea and talk dominate — "a bit of fried herring, stuffed fish, soup meat — anything will do as long as the tea is good and strong, and the lemon that goes with it is sliced thick." [*New York Daily Tribune*, July 24, 1910]

By 1899 the Russian and Polish Jewish restaurants of the East Side were popular among the sightseeing public eager for a taste of authentic European cuisine beyond the French and Italian. Tour buses cruised the streets by day and night.

In 1899 a Polish-Jewish restaurateur complained of the Americanization of the ghetto restaurants. The young men "go to high-toned places on the Bowery and Grand Street and fancy things, and then they come here and want the same. Whoever heard of a man eating butter with his dinner, and how can one keep a kosher place and give people milk with their after-dinner coffee? But that is all done in the restaurants now, and some of the boys go so far as to stick up their noses at the Yiddish bill of fare and want it printed in English. I suppose before long we'll have boiled Welsh rabbits and pickled pigs' feet.

"At [Adolf] Lorbers a 'kosher' on Lower East Side [295 Grand St.] in 1905, a table d'hote dinner could be had for 35¢, poultry 40¢. Ham, pork and rabbit were not on the menu. 'White or black coffee,' inquired the waiter at the end of the meal, and the Spectator found that cafe au lait was 'white coffee' here. Some diners were drinking beer and light wines, but the majority seemed to order only coffee or tea." [*The Outlook,* March 4, 1905]

A 1910 newspaper reports of the dissatisfaction of first-generation European Jews with the quality of American food. "To them it's 'tasteless and unhealthy.' A traveling salesman, Americanized in every other way, takes his meals on Grand Street. New York's foreign newspapers are filled with advertisements for 'Meals that taste exactly like the Old World' and 'Strictly European kitchen.'

"The Viennese restaurants are known for their coffee, the Russian cafes for their tea, and the Romanian, Hungarian, and Italian restaurants for their wine. American bread sickens the first-generation European — it has no life in it. Married men are reported to leave their American wives and homes uptown once a week to seek some familiar food on the East Side. And he eats his chopped liver or chopped herring, served on a little wooden tray, instead of a plate; consumes his 'cheese blintzes,' and takes his wine from a jug instead of a bottle, all with a relish he never knows for the roast, the delicate puddings, the hot light breads and perfect coffee served in his uptown home."

Several socially minded restaurateurs established so-called penny restaurants on the East Side, to provide meals for less than they could be made at home. In September 1905, Julius Pallay, a successful Russian Jewish accountant, opened a philanthropic basement restaurant at 47 Stanton Street. In the remodeled, brightly illuminated basement room with light-green walls and electric fans for ventilation (with warning signs for bearded patrons) one could purchase a full meal of soup, meat, bread, tea, and unlimited seltzer water for 7 cents.

It attracted Polish and Russian Jews from the sweatshops in the neighborhood: many devotees of a wide range of reformist ideologies. It was also patronized by Italians and Irish Bowery types. A notorious bigamist and fake doctor, George Witzhoff, was reportedly a regular, as was Chaim Zhitlowsky on his fund-raising tour of America for the Socialist Revolutionary Party. In accordance with Jewish dietary law, no milk or butter was served.

By 1868, the Bowery was already a center of Jewish shops for cheap jewelry, clothes, apothecaries, and furniture. The Bowery was the western boundary of the so-called Jewish ghetto located to the east. Interspersed among these shops were Irish, Italian, and German saloons and large German lager-beer gardens. The Atlantic Gardens accommodated up to 1500 people in an indoor simulation of a German beer garden — live music and long tables to accommodate drinking. Families brought with them baskets of food, picnic-style. Profits came from the sale of great quantities of lager beer. "They play dominos, cards, dice; they sing, they shout, they dance; in some places billiards and bowling are added, with rifle shooting. The room and entertainment are free to all" [Matthew Hale Smith, *Sunshine and Shadow in New York,* 1868]. The beer was served by twelve-to-sixteen-year-old girls wearing "short dresses, red-topped boots with bells attached; they are frowzy, have an unwholesome look."

In 1899 stalls along the Bowery and Third Avenue sold oysters, clams, and fried soft-shell crabs and were operated mostly by Italians. [*New York Times,* November 12, 1899]

In 1903 a price war was reported among three Jewish restaurant keepers on Essex Street on the Lower East Side. The going rate of 15 cents for a meal including seltzer and a cigarette had dropped to 9 cents. "These restaurants do not cater to the overly particular observant Jew — only two on Broome Street are strictly kosher and charge 25¢. The strictly kosher

restaurant is no longer as profitable as the up-to-date East Side Hebrew is less particular than formerly. He wants milk with his coffee or tea, and butter with his bread and meat." While some may observe dietary laws at home, "when they are away from home they eat what they like." Ten years earlier there were only six "good" Jewish restaurants on the East Side charging 40 cents for a three-course meal; now there were at least thirty. The bill of fare had been reduced and the prevailing price was 30 to 35 cents.

"The patrons of the better class of restaurant are businessmen, clerks, professional men and the occasional Yiddish actor. The cheaper restaurants, patronized by pushcart peddlers and clothing operators who earn $10 a week, offer a full meal (soup, meat, vegetables, dessert, coffee and cake) for 20 cents. With a profit of 3 cents on each meal the restaurateur can earn $10 a day. Liquor of a homemade variety is available at some restaurants under the table." [*The Sun,* February 1, 1903]

By 1904, Austrians gathered around lower Second Avenue, known as "Little Vienna." "The best and least expensive coffee in New York is to be had for 5¢ at the dozen, or so, German and Viennese cafes on the east side between Second and Avenue B, First Street and Tenth Street. These cafes, serving a strong black coffee with hot milk, are busy from morning until midnight" [*New York Times,* 1892]. "The skin of milk is skimmed from the many quarts of boiling milk and kept warm. It is collected in a glass when ordered and counts as one of the great luxuries of the menu." [*Washington Post,* July 16, 1905]

"South of East Broadway to the River, from Catherine to Jackson Streets, live immigrants from Western Russia, the Pale — mostly Lithuanian Jews. North of East Broadway to Houston, between Bowery and Mangin St. lived immigrants from Poland, Galicia, Bessarabia, Bukovina, and a scattering of Sephardic Jews from Turkey and Greece." [S. L. Bluemenson, "Culture on Rutgers Sq.," *Commentary,* July 10, 1950, describing the East Side around 1902]

The New York Sun on June 1, 1905, reported on the lack of religious observance among the three-quarters of a million Jews residing in the city: ". . . in the fifteenth Assembly District 63 per cent of Jewish families were without synagogue connection; in Twenty-first he found that of 1,018 Jewish families 78 per cent reported themselves not to possess a pew in any synagogue; of the remainder 13 per cent claimed affiliation with downtown synagogues. . . . Among the 1,748 Jewish families in the Fourteenth Assembly District in 1899 over 93 per cent were without regular synagogue connection and there was not one synagogue in the district. In the Greenpoint section of Brooklyn over 76 per cent of the Jewish families were churchless. This percentage rises to over 80 per cent in the Twenty-second and 90 per cent in the Eleventh and Thirteenth Assembly districts of Manhattan. Thus, if we except the so-called Ghetto proper, over 81 per cent of the Jews of New York" were churchless. The 10,000 well-to-do Orthodox families in New York City failed to support the only conservative rabbinical seminary in America.

"The most fashionable Jewish restaurants, those kept by Jews and

Vegetarian Boarding House NYC 1857

almost exclusively patronized by Jews, have long ago thrown away the last religious fig leaf. I mean the kosher sign." [Isidor Singer, "Is Judaism Passing?" (letter), *New York Sun,* June 1, 1905]

Private boardinghouses and tenement flats with rooms for rent were home to many of the single men who arrived in New York City. In 1856, it was estimated that seven out of ten New York dwellings sublet rooms to lodgers and that nearly three-quarters of the population lived in those rented rooms. Most provided some meals, but many boarders were the customers of public eating places on nights off. Some boardinghouses catered to particular clientele: vegetarian, political affiliation, or landsmen from particular towns in Europe.

The culinary tone of the house was set by the owner. Near Bowling

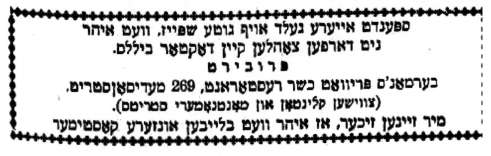
Green in the 1850s there existed a vegetarian boardinghouse run by a
gentleman who practiced transcendentalism, Quakerism, spiritualism, various
water cures, and other new systems of living. His hobbies were ventilation and
sunlight. The meals were composed of herbaceous or farinaceous foodstuffs.
Tea, coffee, wine, and spirits were not allowed. This diet produced a certain
character in the six boarders: "A strong disinclination to do any thing; an
unnatural meekness of disposition; a tendency to boils; and a generally-
sublimated and windy estimation of their own importance and destiny . . ."
They expressed "a sort of tranquil dissatisfaction with the world in general, and
a desire to set it to rights through the medium of writing letters to the *Spiritual
Telegraph, Water-Cure* and *Phrenological Journals* . . ." [Thomas Gunn, *The
Physiology of New York Boarding-Houses,* 1857]. Some boardinghouse kitchens
turned into retail restaurants and were opened to non-boarders.

The "private restaurant," a type of establishment seen in the
background of East Side photographs, was private in that it catered exclusively
to the culinary tastes of a certain immigrant group: Pinskers, Dwinskers,
Minskers, Saraslovers, Bialystokers, etc. The front parlor of a tenement was
converted into a small dining room whose window bore the words PRIVATE
RESTAURANT. "Here aliens meet their friends from the Old Country and lose
their homesickness in the midst of familiar faces and dialects and in the odors
from the kitchen, which evoke for them images of their home and surroundings."
[*New York Tribune,* August 31, 1919]

Turning the necessity of eating into a business — whether boarders
in one's own apartment, or customers in a private or public restaurant — was
an obvious source of income for a recent immigrant who wanted to avoid the
long hours and exploitive and unsanitary conditions of the garment industry.
A restaurant or cafe owner attracted customers by the quality of food and
conversation they offered. Working as a waiter suited those individuals who had
a general disdain for manual labor or dish washing and wanted a job that relied
upon their wit and charm.

In 1892, three-quarters of all New York Jews lived in lower Manhattan; in 1903, 50 percent; and in 1916, only 23 percent. With this shift of population to Harlem and Brooklyn, the majority of New York Jews looked back upon the Lower East Side with a double-layered sense of nostalgia for their Jewish origins. A trip to a downtown restaurant could revive the food memories of their youth. It was reported that the hundred thousand Jews living in Harlem in 1904 had shaken off the habits of the Old World and had adopted the customs and clothing of America. In these years of assimilation, the Jewish restaurateur had an opportunity to make a living based on the divergent culinary tastes of this large Jewish population.

The Politics of Eating Out

Through the pages of Emma Goldman's autobiography, we can chart her sociopolitical movements by the cafes and restaurants she visits. Upon arrival in New York City, she's "taken to Sachs' Cafe [on Suffolk Street] by a young anarchist. . . . It was the headquarters of the East Side radicals, socialists and anarchists as well as the young Yiddish writers and poets." There she meets Alexander Berkman, who admonishes her for ordering coffee and cake when

the movement is in dire need of money. He takes her to a German saloon (Joseph Knirim's on North William Street and at 60 Gold Street) to hear Johann Most, editor of *Die Freiheit,* speak. The fiery socialist makes her acquaintance and invites her to the Terrace Garden, a pleasure garden complex at the Lexington Opera House on East 59th Street, to eat and listen to light opera over food and Liebfrauenmilch. So as not to be seen by his radical followers, Most next suggests they meet at a theatrical cafe at Sixth Avenue and 42nd Street. In 1891, she leaves New York for Worcester, Massachusetts, where she opens an ice-cream parlor to earn enough money to return to Russia. "It was spring and not yet warm enough for an ice-cream rush, but the coffee I brewed, our sandwiches and dainty dishes, were beginning to be appreciated and soon we were kept busy till early morning hours." "We continued our daily work, waiting on customers, frying pancakes, serving tea and ice-cream; but our thoughts were in Homestead, with the brave steel workers."

Back in New York City, she visits the Group Autonomie at their weekly gatherings held at Zum Groben Michel (5th Street near Bowery), a rough German saloon. Evenings are spent back at Sachs' Cafe. On Saturdays, she'd visit the saloon of Justus Schwab at 50 1st Street, a center for radical activity in New York. "The rear room of his little place on First Street was a Mecca for French Communards, Spanish and Italian refugees, Russian politicals, and German socialists and anarchists who had escaped the iron heel of Bismarck."

To support her political activities in New York, she opened an ice-cream parlor in Brownsville, Brooklyn, chosen because of its location near the racetracks. The crowds passed the shop by for one closer to the track, and it quickly failed.

Max Baginski, a somewhat disillusioned old friend and writer on the

Arbeiter Zeitung, offers to take Emma for lunch: "Let's get out of this prison. We'll go to lunch at the Blue Ribbon Restaurant." In the slums of Whitechapel, London, she was nauseated by the smell of fried fish. In Paris, she's quick to accept an invitation from an unknown admirer at the Cafe du Châtelet. An old American friend who has come into an inheritance treats her to an evening of food, wine, and merriment.

Back in New York, after Berkman's imprisonment for the attempted assassination of Henry Clay Frick, Emma finds herself at the fashionable Hofbrauhaus (Broadway and 30th Street). A friend "asked whether I had married a Rockefeller or struck a gold-mine. I was entirely too swell for a proletarian like himself."

The reverse phenomenon, of an uptowner "slumming" in the cafes and restaurants of the Lower East Side in search of a bit of authentic cafe life, helped bolster the income of many Jewish restaurants and accounted for their survival after the bulk of the Jewish population moved away.

Consider the public eating trajectory of the young Emmanuel Goldenberg (actor Edward G. Robinson). Born in Bucharest, he arrived in New York City in 1903. As a young man he ate the cheap clams and oysters sold from pushcarts; frequented the Automat (opened 1912), where he enjoyed raisin pie and pork and beans; and Thompson's lunchrooms where the tables were built into the arms of the wood chairs. He could not afford Guffanti's (Seventh Avenue and 26th Street) even when it was a modest Italian restaurant. His acting success brought him to the Cafe Royal, a social center of the Second Avenue Jewish theater world; he followed Lorber's (established 1893 on Grand Street) as it moved uptown to 1420 Broadway at 40th Street; Rector's (a lavish Times Square restaurant with a floor show); Shanley's (an Irish bar and restaurant in the Times Square area), Reisenweber's (established 1856, a large German restaurant at Columbus Circle with cabaret featuring Sophie Tucker); Mouquin (established 1898, French restaurant on Sixth Avenue at 28th Street); and the Brevoort (basement French cafe at Fifth Avenue between 8th and 9th Streets). [Edward G. Robinson, *All My Yesterdays: An Autobiography* (1974)]

A 1920 issue of *The Jewish Forum* contains a small ad for the Zion Restaurant at 197 Lenox Avenue in Harlem. Along with "Real Home Cooking, Sanitary kitchen, superb food, moderate prices," it claims to be a "Rendezvous for Zionists." Restaurant ads in the communist *Morgn Frayhayt* assure potential customers of their "proletarian prices." Although some restaurants would tailor their ad copy to the political or religious tendencies of various newspapers and journals, for the most part they seem to have placed ads wherever and whenever they could afford to, in the hope of attracting more customers.

The Dairy,
Central Park 1875

The Sour Milk Craze

The pastoral impulse manifested itself in New York City not only through the establishment of pleasure- and beer-gardens, but the milk-drinking culture of the Old World transplanted to the parks and streets of the city.

In both Manhattan's Central Park and Brooklyn's Prospect Park, "dairies" in the Swiss-cottage style were established. "A restaurant where milk and ice-cream and a few simple things are for sale, and it furnishes a nice place for children's lunches" is how they're described in a guidebook of the time.

Photos of the Lower East Side show the lively business in corner soda-water and malted-milk stands. The enrichment of milk through use of nutritional additives, or malt powder, was also a practice in the Milchhallen of Europe. The egg cream, that fabled East Side drink, very likely had its origin in the milk-cure spas of Europe, where, deep into the rigorous regime, seltzer water would be added to the milk to make it more palatable.

But the urban milk drinker in nineteenth-century America was no better off than his European equal. Major cities were beset by the "milk problem" — the effects of diseased and adulterated milk on public health. To increase profits, urban milkers stretched their salable product by adding water of questionable purity, masked spoilage with various chemical whiteners, refrigerated their adulterated product with dirty ice, and handled it with dirty ladles, sieves, and cans.

The pure food movement of the 1870s resulted in the Pure Food Act of 1906 and an ongoing series of National Commissions on Milk Standards (1912–1920) defining "milk" as cow's milk and deciding other labeling questions.

In the summer of 1908, a sour-milk (buttermilk) craze was noted in New York City. Soda fountains, drugstores, and lunchrooms sold an estimated half-million quarts per week. Instead of sweet carbonated drinks, sour milk became the fashionable thing to order. [*New York Tribune,* August 2, 1908]

The craze was linked to both temperance campaigns and the findings of the Russian microbiologist Elie Metchnikoff (1845–1916) of the Pasteur Clinic in Paris that clabbered milk could extend human longevity. According to a news report, "a microscopic organism — bacterium lactis — which his great predecessor, Pasteur, had discovered to be the cause of milk souring, is inimical to another microscopic organism which is abundant in the intestines, and to which the professor attributes the inauguration of some of the degenerative processes occurring in old age."

Dr. Isaac Carasso (1874–1939), a young Sephardic Jew from Selanik (Thessaloniki), was inspired by Metchnikoff's work and began importing yogurt cultures from the Balkans to Barcelona, where he was practicing medicine. In 1919, he perfected the first industrial yogurt-making process and founded a factory named after his son Daniel's nickname in Catalan, "Danone."

Simon Baruch, a local physician who advocated the drink, reminded the public that the milk must be soured by a particular micro-organism — *Bacterium lactis* — in order to have the beneficial effect of counteracting other, inimical micro-organisms found in the intestines. Milk is properly clabbered by placing it in a warm place for six to ten hours. In that time the *Bacterium lactis* will multiply, turning the milk into a "smooth gelatinous

Metchnikoff at work

mass upon which the cream has risen. It should not be curdled into lumps, but in a form which may be cut with a spoon and thus eaten. It has a slightly agreeable acidulous taste which may be improved by sprinkling granulated sugar thickly over it. A pint or more of this clabber forms, if eaten with bread and butter, an ample luncheon. . . . The peasantry of Europe thrives upon this diet. . . . It forms a good substitute for meat. . . . It is inexpensive, clean and wholesome and readily obtainable in many restaurants. . . . One German restaurant in the financial district . . . makes a specialty of the preparation of clabber and sells large quantities of it. . . . I have no doubt that the increased consumption of clabber would limit the consumption of beer and other alcoholics. . . . Degeneration of the arteries, which sour milk bacterium is intended to limit, is enormously furthered by alcoholic drinks and by meats." [*New York Times,* Aug. 16, 1908]

Before the advent of the supermarket, an unspoken guild mentality — a combination of economic protectionism and decorum — separated the sale of various foodstuffs. The city was filled with specialty dairy stores selling eggs, milk, cheese, and butter, with names like, Serv-U Well Dairies (111 Avenue N), Neuman's Economy Dairy (816 Franklin Avenue) and Zucker's Dairy (3005 Avenue L). They were eternal fixtures in all the neighborhoods of New York — miracles of specialization utterly taken for granted. Around 1909, the Yiddish-reading grocer had his own periodical, *Der Groseriman: A Weekly Paper for Business and Literature.* Its pages were filled with illustrated ads for dairy, bread, and grocery supplies. In 1938 there were still 768 retail dairy stores in Brooklyn, and, as late as 1941, 472 retail dairy stores in Manhattan.

As cities grew, dairy farms were moved to the outskirts and sellers brought their milk to the city, twice a day in the summer months, either carried in horse-drawn carts or on the shoulders of milkmaids bearing yokes. Milk, because of its fragility, had traditionally been consumed locally.

In 1893, a pipeline, similar to that used by the Standard Oil Company to convey petroleum from Pennsylvania to the Atlantic coast, was proposed, but

Straus Milk Bar
CITY HALL PARK
1910

proportion of the buttermilk sold in dairy restaurants is made right on the premises, and as much of it from milk that has been allowed to become a little acid as from milk that has been churned." [*New York Times,* July 19, 1903]

A joke "On the Milk Question," from a 1909 issue of *Der Groyser Kundes,* a Yiddish-language humor journal: "Why so expensive? — The fault lies with the Fire Department — they use too much water on the fires."

In 1893, Bavarian Jew and civic philanthropist Nathan Straus applied Louis Pasteur's technique for reducing microbial contamination in wine and beer to milk. The "Pasteurized" milk was sold at below cost or distributed for free at eighteen milk depots around New York City and was instrumental in reducing the city's infant-mortality rate. The milk stands, located in parks and on piers, were utilitarian in design, but offered an echo of the health-giving pastoral aura of the milk pavilions found in European parks and spas. For the poorest Jews of the Lower East Side, healthful affordable milk was a taste of paradise. On the East Side, Straus was affectionately known as "Nathan der Milkhiger."

The last city-based dairies in London and New York were involved in the specialized production of kosher milk. A 1905 report, complete with photographs, of the unsanitary conditions in dairy operating just a few miles from Hoboken was published in the *New York Tribune* of January 15, 1905. Alongside the cramped cow stalls, manure was dumped within twenty feet of the well supplying water to cool the milk. "About thirty cans of milk are made a day, which is sealed by a rabbi as being pure, or 'kosher.'"

A Curious Jew

1891
The London Vegetarian Society

The Vegetarian Jew in America

"A ki git bloyz milkh; oyb men vil fleysh muz men es derhargenen."
[A cow gives only milk; if you want meat you must kill it.]

A brief history of the vegetarian impulse leads from Pythagoras to Plutarch, to certain early Fathers of the Church (Clement of Alexandria, Chrysostom, Tertullian), to the fifteenth-century writings of Luigi Cornaro, to Voltaire, Shelley, and Alexander Pope. In the eighteenth century, Dr. George Cheyne's *Book of Health and Long Life* (1724) advocated a Pythagorean diet of porridge, vegetables, beans, lentils, and onions.

A Headbath

The modern vegetarian movement that started in England in the mid-nineteenth century seems to have been largely undertaken by middle-class freethinkers, spiritualists, and people who could afford to eat meat but declined for ethical reasons. Many suffered from digestive problems and a vegetarian diet seemed to alleviate their discomfort. Their ideas were promulgated through lectures and journals. The place of Jews in this earthly paradise is rarely touched upon, other than to note that Jewish dietary laws were a modified form of vegetarianism as they put strictures upon the killing of animals.

The so-called pilgrim fathers of vegetarianism responsible for its exportation to America were Rev. William Metcalfe and Rev. James Clark — disciples of Rev. William Cowherd. Cowherd was the founder of a Bible Christian sect, a dissenting church whose congregants were committed vegetarians. He was a disciple of Dr. Cheyne and Swendenborg. He died before his plans to emigrate to America could be realized. Metcalfe and Clark managed to emigrate to America with a group of congregants in 1817. They established a church in Philadelphia from which Mr. Metcalfe preached abstinence from all intoxicating drinks and from the flesh of animals. Vegetarianism was good for both reasons and promoted less aggressive behavior in men. Sylvester Graham, of cracker fame, became acquainted with Metcalfe's church and examined their ideas from a scientific point of view.

Around 1868, a Shaker community in Mount Lebanon, New York, practiced equality of the sexes, a communistic sharing of wealth, and a vegetarian diet. Three kinds of bread were served at their table, as they felt that "no one can well abstain from a meat diet unless he has good bread."

Dr. John Harvey Kellogg's *Shall We Slay to Eat?* of 1899, published by his Good Health Publishing Company of Battle Creek, Michigan, helped popularize the ethical and moral questions of diet. He went on to manage and eventually take over the Western Health Reform Institute founded by the Seventh-day Adventist Church. He developed a number of meat analogues, including Protose — a staple of health-food restaurants. At the turn of the century, his sanitarium, renamed Battle Creek Sanitarium, attracted a host of celebrity health-seekers and further popularized his low-protein, grain-based diet. [Charles W. Forward, *Fifty Years of Food Reform, A History of the Vegetarian Movement in England* (1898)]

Sylvester Graham (1794–1851) was educated for the ministry and served in connection with the Presbyterian Church. He did not believe that a system beneficial to human health could be contrary to the teachings of the word of God. He worked to "discover the philosophy of sacred history in relation to human ailment." Graham offered an analysis of the Hebrews living under the Mosaic dispensation. The only means possible to have them adhere to national unity was by appealing to their love of roasted meat and wine drinking. To justify flesh eating, wine drinking, polygamy, usury, and capital punishment in the nineteenth century of the Christian Era is a throwback to the behavior of the ancient Hebrews. "But while the Hebrew nation as a whole was crumbling to decay . . . God was carrying forward His great plan of benevolence, and preparing the moral world for the introduction of a better dispensation. . . . Christ wept over them [the Hebrews], and with all the moral energy of the Godhead desired their salvation — they would not believe in Him — they would not receive Him; but they rejected Him — they hated Him — they crucified Him!"

Through this argument, vegetarianism and moral behavior were set against the stubbornness of the Jews still living under the Mosaic dispensation. [Sylvester Graham, *The Philosophy of Sacred History Considered in Relation to Human Ailment and the Wines of Scripture* (1859)]

Examples of earthly paradise were described in the pages of *The American Socialist* (1876–79), published in Oneida, New York. Swiss dairy farming was held up as an example of organic communal activity. The cows were gathered to graze collectively in the higher meadows, while the owners worked the fields below. Articles and letters discussed alternative health therapies — from water to milk cures. New ideas for communal apartment-house living and centralized dining systems would free women and men from housework, lower the cost of eating, and minimize the importance of the conjugal family. Experiments in vegetarianism were seen as an alternative to the appetitive nature of capitalism. Limited

Alpha Restaurant,
London

meat eating was seen as a form of solidarity with the poor who could rarely afford meat. The organization of Russian peasant life demonstrated natural models for collective living.

Many of the early vegetarians were also advocates of other forms of social and moral reform: abstinence from alcohol and tobacco, hydropathy and homoeopathy, dress reform, anti-shaving, spiritualism, anti-inoculation, anti-vivisection, abolishing cruel sports, and antiwar. The slaughter of animals is connected directly, and indirectly, to other evils of the human race. Recipes for a variety of mock meats were introduced in *Mrs. Rorer's Vegetable Cookery and Meat Substitutes,* published in Philadelphia in 1909.

The earliest vegetarian restaurant, a so-called vegetarian ordinary, was established at Mrs. Matthews' Restaurant on Princess Street in Manchester, England — that city being a center of vegetarian organizing. In 1879, the first vegetarian restaurant to open in London was the Alpha Restaurant at 23 Oxford Street. It was the creation of the American free-love hydropaths and the prolific authors Dr. Thomas Low Nichols [*How to Live on Sixpence a-Day* (1871) and *Penny Vegetarian Cookery* (1883)] and his wife, Mary Gove Nichols. The Nicholses were students of Sylvester Graham who had left America to settle in England. The Alpha's menu featured lentil cutlets, porridges, an assortment of vegetables, savory pie with parsley sauce, stewed fruits, and beverages.

The spirit of
Leo Tolstoy
on 2nd Avenue

A contemporary map of London shows thirteen vegetarian restaurants including the Ideal, the Garden, and the Apple Tree and two vegetarian hotels. Although some were highly successful, others, through inexperience and mismanagement, did much to prejudice the public against the movement.

As early-twentieth-century Jewish dairy restaurants offered a wide range of vegetable-based dishes, many vegetarians patronized them. A number of dairy restaurants added the word "vegetarian" to their names to attract that clientele.

The majority of modern Jews were happy to be able to afford meat and would be hesitant to align themselves with a movement ridiculed in the mainstream press for its fanaticism; fewer considered its obscure anti-Hebrew sentiments rooted in the asceticism of the early Christian Church. Nevertheless, a Yiddish-language, Jewish vegetarian movement came into existence.

For the radical Jews around the world, Leo Tolstoy's vegetarianism and radical sympathies were fused into an irresistible figure of the ideal ethical intellectual. Who could forget (see page 206) that it was Tolstoy who had called upon Alexander III to pardon the members of the People's Will in order to end a cycle of violence in Russia.

In an article in *The New Review* of 1892 Tolstoy wrote: "The Vegetarian movement ought to fill with gladness the souls of those who have at heart the realization of God's kingdom upon earth, not because Vegetarianism itself is such an important step towards the realization of this kingdom (all real steps are equally important or unimportant), but because it serves as a criterion by which he know that the pursuit of moral perfection on the part of man is genuine and sincere. . . ."

Tolstoy's tract *The First Step* helped launch a vegetarian movement in Russia in the 1890s with societies, restaurants, and cafeterias in Moscow, St. Petersburg, and Kiev. His work on behalf of the vegetarian Doukhobors in 1897 was widely publicized (see page 206) and not forgotten.

In his *Ten Days That Shook the World,* John Reed mentions eating in a Moscow vegetarian restaurant "with the enticing name, 'I Eat Nobody'"; Tolstoy's picture was prominently displayed on

the wall. The planners of early Soviet Russia favored the creation of centralized eating systems. In that sense, they held common ground with the capitalist editors of *The Restaurant Man,* a New York trade magazine, who extolled the economic advantages and convenience of restaurant and cafeteria eating in 1920s America.

The Philadelphia Vegetarian Society published a philosophical tract, *Der Vegetaryaner Gedank,* on the subject in Yiddish, by H. Goldblum in the early 1900s. A Yiddish-language vegetarian cookbook by N. Y. Kvitner, *Vos Zol Men Esen?,* was published in 1907.

A **Vegetarian Cafeteria** at 3rd and Hill Streets in Los Angeles was a regular advertiser in the *B'nai B'rith Messenger* between 1919 and 1920. "Maintain Your Health. Regain Your Health. Patronize your State. Economize, Hooverize."

The Progressive or Pythagorean Vegetarian Eating Place, operated by a Meyer Litheron on the second floor at 42 Norfolk Street. Signage proclaimed "For Humane Beings Try the Humane Diet."

Several restaurants advertised in the *Vegetarian World,* a Yiddish-language journal from 1921: **Paradise Vegetarian Restaurant** of 1627 Pitkin Avenue and 239 South 4th Street in Brooklyn; **Miss Rogin's Vegetarian Restaurant and Tea-House** at 31 St. Mark's Place in Manhattan; **M. Gruber's Venus Vegetarian and Milkhiger Restaurant** of 26 Delancey Street; and **Ideal Vegetarian Restaurant** ("A center for the vegetarian intelligentsia of Brooklyn—ask us about our vegetarian summer place") of 1805 Pitkin Avenue, Brooklyn. To demonstrate their advanced position in society, most vegetarian restaurants, even those, like Schildkraut's (see page 327), run by Yiddish speakers, dispensed with most Eastern European dishes and adopted a menu based upon the latest dietetic research. In the same issue, A. Konviser and F. Shaffer advertised a summer place for vegetarians in the Catskill Mountains.

The 1929 Yiddish Vegetarian Hymn by I. Pirozshnikov goes "Blessed wilt thou be, blessed wilt thou be, when you look into life with pity! Blessed wilt you be, who feels stranger's misfortune, who feels stranger's pain! Not eating any meat, not spilling any blood! When you find in all spirit and pure living humankind."

Dr. Benzion Liber, editor of *Unzer Gezunt,* a Yiddish-language health journal (1910–1917), "hated the mixture of an ethical principle with health matters, accompanied as it would have to be by quackery and opposition to scientific medicine. Besides, the individuals attracted to vegetarianism were not always pleasant. Their only preoccupation was food. . . . Some of them were so

Benzion Liber—the People's doctor

eccentric that except for nutrition, no conversation was possible with them. As a rule, from the social viewpoint, they were not progressive — only some were." [Dr. Benzion Liber, *A Doctor's Apprenticeship* (1957)]

The reaction of a mid-twentieth-century Yiddish meat-eating New Yorker to the vegetarian's ethical argument is played out to comical purpose in Moishe Nadir's story "Nuttose and Protose," concerning Kellogg's Sanitas Nut Food Company's canned meat substitutes.

A long-haired, bearded vegetarian in canvas pants accuses a passerby of cannibalism and making his stomach into a graveyard for innocent chickens. He sells the passerby a vegetarian tract that recommends eating at Verimkroit's Vegetarian Restaurant. At this restaurant, the new customer is served a four-course meal by a pale, congestive waiter. For each course he's offered a choice of Nuttose or Protose — two vegetarian meat substitutes, one for veal, the other beef. To his disappointment, each course consists of a tiny portion of an unidentifiable substance. Toward the end of his meal, the waiter's deliberations between Nuttose and Protose — "I wouldn't advise you to take nuttose,

but protose, because protose is a lot healthier than nuttose, although nuttose is also a health dish, but how can it compare to protose! Because protose contains more fat than nuttose. Besides that, we're all out of nuttose tea" — drives the customer to murder the waiter.

As in the English-language press, vegetarianism was an object of ridicule and curiosity in the Yiddish press:

"What one sees and hears in a New York Jewish restaurant." [*Forverts*, February 15, 1928, translated by Eddy Portnoy]

A herring in a vegetarian restaurant: "Years ago, there weren't many vegetarian restaurants. But nowadays, sworn vegetarians have really become true vegetarians who refuse to eat any food that comes from animals, no eggs, milk, butter, fish, herring, only things that grow in the plant world.

"It was this kind of vegetarian that we got as a customer in our vegetarian restaurant. He drove everyone crazy with the things he did. One time this vegetarian came in — seems he was a Hebrew teacher — and said to the waiter: 'Waiter, you already know what I want to eat.'

" 'Of course,' answered the waiter with a smile.

" 'Very good. And don't be cheap with carrots, spinach or big string beans, the things I love. And not cooked, or I'll send the whole meal back.'

"The waiter went to bring him everything, even peanut butter, since he won't eat milk butter. The vegetarian made himself comfortable and waited for his dinner.

"What does God go and do? He sends a herring vendor who has a craving for some vegetables into the very same restaurant and sits him down right next to the vegetarian teacher.

"The teacher, as usual, stuck his nose close to the plate to take a whiff of his meal. He sticks his nose down once, then again, and it smells like herring.

" 'Since when do you sell carcasses here? I'm going to write a letter to the Board of Health.'

"With that, the Hebrew teacher turned a number of different colors, grabbed his hat and ran out. Meanwhile, the herring vendor finished off the Hebrew teacher's dinner and promised to come every day to eat a vegetarian meal. And so, the restaurant didn't actually lose a customer."

Although Carl Rasmussen, a Danish immigrant, was serving a full vegetarian menu of mock meats at the Tabloid Restaurant at 170 Fulton Street in 1901, the earliest "Jewish" vegetarian restaurant in Brooklyn was apparently opened by

Louis Epner (Eleizer Epner). Epner was born in Volhyn, a town in the western Ukraine, in 1882. He moved to Warsaw in 1908, married, became a confirmed vegetarian, and moved in the vegetarian circles of that city.

A grandfather in the umbrella business in Borough Park, Brooklyn, brought him to the United States in 1910, where he opened a vegetarian restaurant on the corner of Pitkin and Stone Avenues in Brownsville, Brooklyn, in 1912. It was named **Emese Essen** (True Eating). His wife, Gretta Epner, worked in the kitchen.

Some of their customers were Jews who had left Palestine and had apparently adopted a vegetarian diet. In the 1920s, Louis Epner was involved in a poultry-and-egg colony founded in Plainfield, New Jersey. During the summers, men worked in the garment industry and women raised chickens. A 1921 ad for the Ideal Vegetarian Restaurant in the *Vegetarian World,* a Yiddish journal, mentions Epner as running a vegetarian summer place: "a hotel with modern conveniences, a river alongside the hotel, EPNER, R.D. No. 2, Middletown, New York."

The couple were friends with Herman Schildkraut, the popular vegetarian promoter and restaurateur in Manhattan. The restaurant was sold in 1926 and became a Devega sporting goods store.

In addition to his restaurant career, Mr. Epner was a founder of the

A vegetarian on Pitkin Ave.

Farband Houses
Bronx, N.Y.

Yidish Natsionaler Arbeter Farband or Jewish National Workers Alliance, a Yiddish-language, Labor Zionist landsmanshaft that organized cooperative insurance along with Yiddish and Hebrew educational schools. In November of 1928, the family moved into the Farband Houses that had opened in the Bronx. He sold eggs on Tuesdays and Fridays.

Being a member of the American Vegetarian Association, Louis was a pacifist and so did not enter the army in World War I. In World War II, he was given the choice of jail or armed forces and joined the air force in 1943.

Louis remained a vegetarian all of his life. According to his son Daniel, this was not a popular practice among Jews. Growing up in the Bronx, Daniel did not know another vegetarian family. At summer camp, Kindervelt, his parents had to arrange to get vegetarian meals for him and his sister. Louis Epner died in 1950.

Simon Gerson, a carpenter, and S. K. Cohn, a capmaker, the prime movers behind the United Workers Cooperative Colony Association and its 1926 plan to build a large-scale housing development in the Bronx for wage earners, were both confirmed vegetarians. Their insistence on separating the smells of meat from vegetables and dairy played a part in the failure of both their cooperative supermarket on Allerton Avenue and their summer resort, Nitgedeiget, near Beacon, New York.

Mention should also be made of Menke Katz (1906–1991), Yiddish poet of the leftist writers' group Proletpen, who was a lifelong vegetarian. He's seen in photos wearing sneakers to avoid having leather shoes. "Absentmindedly thinking about a poem during the Furriers' Union strike of 1934, he blundered into an alleyway concealing the back entrance to a Lower East Side fur factory. Union leaders mistook him in the dark for a scab and beat him up, laughing at

300

his protests about ethical vegetarians having nothing to do with the fur business in principle." [Dovid Katz, *Menke: The Complete Yiddish Poems* (2005)]

Another notable vegetarian was Nissim Behar (1848–1931), a modern-Hebrew language educator in Jerusalem and later in New York City, who lobbied against anti-immigration legislation. He was described in the press as an Oriental man of mystery who subsisted on chocolate and nuts.

Around 1927, Mordecai Tobias's vegetarian restaurant, known as the **Splendid Health and Perfect Eating Academy of New York,** also operated summer and winter resorts. They published a Yiddish book entitled *Health, Wealth and Prosperity* by Dr. C. D. Samuelson.

Franz Kafka wrote: "The sound of the taut sausage skin being cut has rung in my ears since childhood." Kafka's turn toward teetotal vegetarianism may have been a reaction to a family history of heavy meat eating (his grandfather was a shoykhet) but can also be explained by his digestive problems.

In Berlin, he'd feel most at home in a vegetarian restaurant where he "rhapsodizes about the semolina pudding, raspberry syrup, lettuce with cream, gooseberry wine, and strawberry-leaf tea."

In *The Metamorphosis,* Gregor's sister offers the insect what she thought was her brother's favorite food:

"By the door he first noticed what had really lured him there: it was the smell of something to eat. A bowl stood there, filled with sweetened milk, in which swam tiny pieces of white bread. He almost laughed with joy, for he now had a much greater hunger than in the morning, and he immediately dipped his head almost up to and over his eyes down into the milk. But he soon drew it back again in disappointment, not just because it was difficult for him to eat on account of his delicate left side — he could eat only if his entire panting body worked in a coordinated way — but also because the milk, which otherwise was his favourite drink and which his sister had certainly placed there for that reason, did not appeal to him at all. He turned away from the bowl almost with aversion and crept back into the middle of the room." [Translated by Ian Johnston]

This bowl of milk toast — the epitome of wholesome dairy fare — is nauseating to the insect.

His sister experiments with a variety of foods and finds that only decayed cheese and vegetables appeal to the insect: ". . . all set out on an old newspaper. There were old, half decayed vegetables, bones from last night's supper covered with a white sauce that had congealed, some raisins and almonds; a piece of cheese that Gregor would have pronounced inedible two days ago. . . ."

Kafka played with the idea of emigrating to Palestine with his dear friend Dora Dymant and opening a restaurant in Tel Aviv. Dymant would be the cook and Kafka the waiter. The restaurant would undoubtedly have been vegetarian. In Kafka's mind the Zionist dream of returning to the land was circumscribed by the four walls of a restaurant. He died in Dymant's arms in Dr. Hoffman's sanatorium just outside Vienna in 1924.

For the reasons discussed in this chapter, Jews often organized their own vegetarian associations and restaurants between the two world wars. By

302

1920, the existing German vegetarian league agitated against Jews and held anti-Semitic views. In February of that year, a separate Jewish vegetarian organization called Danielbund was founded in Munich for "the physical and moral uplift of the Jews." It also wanted to assist in "the foundation of Jewish farming colonies and maintains that the establishment of a Jewish Palestine will make possible a more satisfactory and friendlier feeling between the Jews and other nations."

Fania Lewando

Alter Kacyzne

Yudl Mark

harney

Imaginary dinner at Lewando's Vegetarian-Dietetic Restaurant, Vilna

It's not surprising that a Jewish-run vegetarian restaurant operated in Vilna during those years. The city was a hotbed of Jewish intellectual and organizational activity. **Fania and Lazar Lewando's Vegetarian-Dietetic Restaurant** (14 Niemiecka Ulica) was in business from the 1920s until sometime before the Nazis entered Vilna in 1941.

It may have been through visits to her family, Polish Jews who immigrated to England around 1889, that Fania was introduced to the long vegetarian tradition in that country.

This enterprising woman not only ran the restaurant, but also a cooking school, briefly oversaw a vegetarian dining room on the Polish ocean liner *Batory,* and compiled an exhaustive vegetarian cookbook in Yiddish.

She was a confirmed but pragmatic vegetarian, and urged the readers of her cookbook to avoid meat at least three days a week. Many of her recipes are directed toward the non-vegetarian who needs mock-meat concoctions to make vegetable dishes palatable. Besides the standard vegetarian cutlets and roasts, she offers an entire section devoted to mock schnitzels and, going to extremes, a Stuffed Imitation Kishke (or stuffed intestinal casing) made of mushrooms, onions, bread crumbs, and herbs, minced and wrapped in a potato dough rolled up to resemble a kishke, and even Imitation Caviar made of sago. The recipes otherwise span the entire Polish/French/Russian culinary spectrum, including a range of traditional Jewish dishes, including a few medicinal concoctions such as "Vitamin Salad" and "Special Bread for a Stomachache." The Passover section includes "Milkhik Matzo Balls." Lewando suggests adding them to Beet Soup, Prune Soup, or milk in lieu of chicken broth.

A photo of the establishment shows an attentive Fania Lewando, dressed in a floral jacket, overseeing an uncomfortably posed group of diners about to have their meal administered by two waitresses dressed in white nurselike uniforms. A high curtained bookcase holds hundreds of slim volumes of dietetic tracts, or vegetarian literature, along with framed photographs of

notable clients. The photo gives no sense of what was described as a lively art-and-literary salon atmosphere. Yudl Mark, an important scholar of the Yiddish language and linguistics, wrote in the restaurant's guest book: "Everyone can be a vegetarian once in a while."

A 1930 ad for "a Homey Mid-day meal in a Special-Dietetic and Milchige style is offered at Kolozshanske 22" in Grodno (now in Belarus) by a Chana Kokov (sp?). Before 1939, Jews made up half the population of Grodno.

"In a Vegetarian Restaurant," Zuni Maud's comic strip, was published on August 3, 1919, in the *Forverts* (below and facing page).

1. Waiter: Believe me, mister, I'll give you a little piece of vegetarian fish. You'll really enjoy it. I'm telling you, you'll think it's a regular fish.
Customer: Anyway, gimme. [Sign on the wall: Vegetarian diner 50¢.]
2. Customer: From the looks of it, it's like a real fish. Seems like he was right, this waiter. It's impossible to tell that it's not fish. [Picture of Tolstoy on the wall.]
3. Customer: Dat's right! Mister waiter, it's too bad for the real fish. The vegetarian fish is even better than a real fish. Now bring me a, whadja call it? "A cement steak." [Humorous variant of the then-popular "mushk steak."]
4. Waiter: So, how do you like the steak?
Customer: Fine, fine, mister waiter. Your vegetarian food is simply a joy. Even the bones seem real.

5. The story comes to an end. We will now show you what is going on in the other room of the very same vegetarian restaurant so you can convince yourself that their fish and meat are like real fish and meat.

A 1927 headline in *The Restaurant Man* states, "Shoe prices soaring; vegetarians blamed. The public is eating less meat today, which means that fewer cattle are being killed."

The Meat Strikes of 1902–16

From 1902 to 1916, a series of strikes against the kosher meat industry altered the eating habits of New York Jews. "The kosher butchers of the East Side, numbering about 1,600, had abandoned their fight against the wholesale meat dealers and had raised their prices even higher than the retailers of uptown New York. The consumers of the East of the Bowery district were up in arms. They had shown their rage all day by minor outbreaks against individual butchers." Five hundred policemen were called out to control an angry mob of five to six thousand women. [*Chicago Daily,* May 16, 1902]

The price increases were the result of a struggle that arose among rabbinical groups representing the various immigrant communities, their approved inspectors, kosher slaughterers, plombirers (workers who tagged approved carcasses with lead seals), and meat wholesalers to gain control over what had become a lucrative industry — the Beef Trust. The retail kosher butcher was forced to pass any price increase on to his customers. This history of kosher supervision in New York City has been well documented [Harold P. Gastwirt, *Fraud, Corruption, and Holiness* (1974)]. In Europe, taxes on kosher meat were levied by each community as a means of covering their

operational expenses. With the vast resettlement of Jews from various Eastern European communities in New York City after 1881, the handling and selling of kosher meat was fraught with abuse and outright corruption.

While most meat consumed in New York came from Chicago and points west, in 1913 meat was still slaughtered in New York City for the kosher market in two districts, First Avenue from 43rd to 47th Streets and Tenth and Eleventh Avenues between 38th and 41st Streets. As kosher meat must be kashered (the blood removed by salting) within seventy-two hours after slaughter, this "rule bars outside meat from New York and will probably keep New York's slaughtering industry alive forever." [*New York Times,* Sept. 29, 1913]

The meat riots were centered on the East Side and Williamsburg, where Jewish housewives still chose to shop at what were identified as kosher retail butchers. These butchers offered the cuts of meat they were familiar with and a congenial culinary atmosphere. Whether or not the women observed dietary laws in general, they patronized kosher butchers. The cuts and varieties of meats on display at a non-kosher butcher would be bewildering and unappetizing. The low level of religious observance and synagogue attendance in those years (see page 276) points to the culinary reasons for patronizing kosher butchers.

The attempt in 1887 of eighteen congregations to organize a citywide Association of American Orthodox Hebrew Congregations with the importation of a Chief Rabbi, Jacob Joseph, was decried by the overwhelming majority of local Hasidic and Orthodox rabbis as an outright protectionary business deal to cover his exorbitant salary and would force more butchers than ever to sell treyf meat as kosher in order to cover the cost of supervision. The idea of a korobka, or tax on kosher meat, evoked memories of the corrupt Crown Rabbis of Russia and the tsar's method of extorting money from the Jewish community. The kosher poultry business was rife with racketeering and violations of the anti-trust laws. In response to their customers' outrage, 1,200 kosher butchers closed their shops in protest against wholesalers in 1902, again in 1910 and 1916: "Because of the high prices on kosher-killed products, this shop will be closed until further notice." Inspectors for the commissioner of weights and measures reported that the public was not buying kosher meat at all. [*New York Times,* December 27, 1916]

The *New York Daily Tribune* of April 19, 1902, reported: "East Siders Protest. The high price of beef hits them hard. The 350,000 tenement dwellers living between Houston St., Bowery and the East River join in an outcry against prices that mean not starvation, but a diet that can only result in a weakening of the physical constitution of thousands." Kosher meat prices rose from 14 to 20 cents a pound. "The factory workman who has had meat for one meal in the day will be obliged to subsist without it. . . . Canned goods to some extent supply the place. Vegetables are introduced into the meagre bill of fare, but East Side vegetables are neither very fresh, since they come from pushcarts, nor likely in the long run to be very healthful. Other than bread, all food prices have risen."

And in another article on the same page:

"President of Vegetarian Society, at dinner in Brooklyn, says it is a good thing." At a dinner held at Parker's Restaurant in Brooklyn, two hundred members of the Vegetarian Society of New York rejoiced over the fact that the Beef Trust "had placed the price of meat so high that many persons had been forced to become vegetarians."

Ernest H. Crosby, president of the society, wanted to commend the action of the Beef Trust.

As a final outrage, Rabbi Joseph extended his supervision to cover Passover brandy and matzo. Opponents of the association witnessed "this sacred soil of America . . . defiled by money making à la Russia" [Letter to the *Jewish Messenger,* September 28, 1898]. The socialist press called Rabbi Joseph the "Chief Charlatan" of an association of "robbers who live off swindle, and who make the poor penniless through hekhsherim and korobkas" [*Der Volksadvokat,* April 1889]. A satirical editorial in the May 24, 1889, issue of *Der Volksadvokat* accused Rabbi Joseph and the association of planning to place a korobka on ice cream and snuff.

Several rival organizations for the supervision of Kashruth were founded — each accusing the other of certifying treyf meat. Upon Rabbi Joseph's sudden death in 1902, no "kosher" butcher shop could be trusted. An attempt in 1909 at placing kosher supervision under the Kehillah of New York also failed, because of the reluctance of Orthodox Jews to cooperate with non-Orthodox Jews in the complex questions of ritual observance. Hayyim Ball, a professional shoykhet, refused to eat meat after 1912. An attempt in the 1920s to have the State of New York oversee kosher supervision also failed, as it proved impossible to define any reasonable standards by which a company could claim that its products were kosher.

"Vegetarianism has a great boom, thanks to the Beef Trust," proclaimed the *Brooklyn Eagle* of May 4, 1902. All of the efforts of organized vegetarians to gain adherents to a meatless diet were in vain. The ethical and health arguments were useless, "but when it comes to getting back at the beef trust, why that is another affair. And to the one who is a vegetarian from conviction there are springing up ten who are vegetarians through the necessity for economy and a hundred who are vegetarians (pro. tem) as an expression of their righteous indignation." Carl Rasmussen's vegetarian restaurant at Fulton and Cranberry Streets in Brooklyn was, for the first time in its sixteen years, doing a "rushing business." [*Brooklyn Eagle,* May 4, 1902]

The dairy restaurateur was not obliged to become ensnared in the business of kosher certification. In the early years of the twentieth century, dairy restaurant fare stood outside the concerns of official certification. The market for rabbinically certified milk was small; most observant Jews and Jewish restaurateurs were satisfied with U.S. government approval of milk.

In the midst and aftermath of the meat riots, the *Brooklyn Eagle* reported a popular turn on the part of the public toward vegetarian and dairy foods — foods outside of rabbinical and Beef Trust control. It was in these years that the Jewish dairy restaurant proliferated in New York City.

The Rise of the
Dairy Restaurant in New York City

The proliferation of restaurants serving an Ashkenazic-style dairy cuisine in New York City after 1881 can be attributed to the unique historical confluence of events and ideas.

The historically unprecedented growth and concentration of a Jewish population provided a ready base of customers with a knowledge of, and taste for, Eastern European dairy dishes. Within a few years of their arrival, some of the immigrants and their children had amassed enough capital to go into business for themselves. The restaurant business was booming in New York and as everyone ate and cooked at home they felt they had the skills to enter this field. Their clientele, in the aftermath of the meat strikes of 1902, were happy to avoid meat altogether and trusted that their landsmen would handle the dairy and parve foodstuffs according to their commonsense understanding of Jewish dietary law — professional certification was unnecessary. The clientele was also spurred by an awareness of the vegetarian and pure-food movements. The health giving and ethical benefits of a dairy and vegetable-based diet were popularized in the Yiddish and American press. The model for their new dairy restaurant was readily found in the omnipresent American dairy lunchrooms. Here was a decor devoid of Old World associations and organized on the scientific principles of sanitation and food handling. Finally, between June and August of 1906, the *Forverts* serialized a Yiddish-language translation by Abraham Cahan of Upton Sinclair's *The Jungle* — an exposé of the brutal and unsanitary conditions in the slaughter- and meat-packing houses of Chicago. Sinclair noted that his celebrity came about "not because the public cared anything about the workers [depicted in the book], but simply because the public did not want to eat tubercular beef."

According to Marcus Eli Ravage it was the Romanians "who, out of a complex desire to serve his stomach and his faith, brought forth an institution which has now become universal in America — the dairy lunch-room — which, owing to the exigencies of religion, was originally just what it is called, a place where nothing but the most palatable dishes built out of milk and milk products were to be had, and where no morsel that had been in the vicinity of meat could be obtained for love or money." ["My Plunge into the Slums," in *Harper's*, April 1917]

When we look back at the history of eating places in Europe, it's clear that the model for a dairy-based restaurant already existed in Christian and Jewish cultures. This simple direction of influence, from Romanian dairy restaurant to American dairy lunchroom seems to involve both a historical and chronological error. It may be true that Romanian immigrants, such as Jacob Kampus (see page 320), were the first in New York City to have the entrepreneurial energy to revive the idea of an eating place dedicated to dairy dishes for an audience of Jews. But, as we've seen, the early American dairy restaurants predated and did not follow the Romanians' dairy menu. There's no evidence of any of the numerous early-twentieth-century American dairy restaurants adopting Eastern European dairy dishes, yet there is ample evidence of early-twentieth-century Jewish restaurateurs adopting the American quick-lunch staples, sandwiches and salads, to their milkhiker menus.

Surrounded, in New York City, by the readily available cuisines of the world, these nascent Jewish restaurateurs recognized that the Eastern European dairy dishes they grew up eating at home constituted a cuisine of their own and could serve as the basis for a specialty restaurant — a New World version of the

Sinclair Cahan

bakery or dairy-eating place they knew in Europe, or a Judaized version of the American quick dairy lunchroom.

From a historical point of view, it was the unwitting combination of the French idea of the restaurant, with all of its Enlightenment connotations, paired with a pre-Noahic cuisine derived over centuries of eating under Jewish dietary law that resulted in a unique cultural institution.

One could argue that all restaurant menus are structured around ancient taboos (cannibalism, etc.) and social decorum, but the Jewish dairy restaurant offers a unique restaging, on a daily basis, of a historical/mythological incident. Within the walls of a Jewish dairy restaurant, there was no possibility of eating meat — the theoretically unfettered desires of the diner were willingly limited to those of a wanderer in Arcadia: fruits, vegetables, grains, milk, cheese, and fish. It was, in effect, a four-walled paradise "garden." The business structure of the "restaurant" allowed diners to order the dishes of their choice from a large menu with clearly marked prices. At the end of the meal the diner paid for what he'd eaten and was encouraged to return — a far cry from the shame and angry expulsion from Eden. Through the structure of the dairy restaurant, paradise is de-Hellenized; the extensive precincts of Arcadia are returned to the modest scale of a Persian walled garden (recast in stainless steel and Formica) where the vegetables, fish, and milk are delivered fresh each morning. Paradise is de-Christianized; the Fall of Man is replaced with a satisfied customer and a "Come Again" sign. Most important, from a mythological point of view, YHVH is replaced by an Enlightened restaurateur, a figure of limitless commercial generosity, who's open for business 24 hours a day, 7 days a week. Satan is demoted to the position of a union waiter, who tempts customers via a borscht-stained menu.

Some Jews never made the mistake of equating the Garden of Eden with a Golden Age of man. Even before the invention of money, the Garden of Eden remained a circumscribed business arrangement. The Jewish dairy restaurants of New York were subject to the brutalities and vagaries of the restaurant business — holdups, profit margins, union struggles, embezzlement, temper tantrums, etc.— yet offered their customers a culinary and atmospheric respite from the larger meat-eating world.

The typical dairy restaurant customer may not have been consciously aware of this remarkable situation, but surely felt a sense of relief. The heavy oppressive aromas of meat and poultry were replaced by the fragrance of sizzling butter and sweet boiled fish. The mood and agenda of the dairy restaurant was one of relative passivity. By contrast, the vegetarian restaurant was filled with an air of proselytizing — actively trying to readjust the course of the world through eating.

The menu would, in time, be expanded to included popular American dishes that fit within the pre-Noahic guidelines: tuna fish salad, scrambled eggs, etc. These dishes were available elsewhere but the early Jewish dairy restaurants attracted a Jewish clientele by their congenial atmosphere and the availability of both Eastern European dairy dishes and American-style dishes, prepared under the supervision of a Jewish cook. For later generations of American Jews it was the only place to eat those dishes that were nostalgically associated with their mother and grandmothers. For vegetarians, it offered a largely non-meat menu.

According to a 1903 report in the *Sun,* "One [Jewish] restaurant [on the East Side] has a separate table devoted to 'milicha' or dishes which are devoid

of meat of any kind. The favorite milicha dishes are nudels and milk, gefülte fish (stuffed fish), mammeliga (corn meal with a layer of baked potcheese); vorenikess (baked corn meal dough, oval shaped and filled with barley), and Kraploch mit kase (a dough of eggs and flour filled with baked potcheese). Sometimes Russian caviare, rice or barley soup, or herring, are included."

Although mixing meat and milk was the norm in the larger American restaurant culture, some Jewish restaurateurs advertising in the Yiddish press were careful to note that they served both fleyshige and milkhige dishes, if they did. The idea of separate tables for milk and meat did not catch on. The offering of an exclusive dairy experience seemed to make better business sense. The dairy restaurant patron was not looking for rabbinic certification (for dairy and parve foods were left to commonsense appraisal), they were not even looking for Sabbath observance (the most popular dairy restaurants were open seven days a week), nor were they looking for political camaraderie — they were looking for a chance to return to paradise.

The owners of successful dairy restaurants were not necessarily themselves milekhdike personalities and almost none were vegetarians.

A degree of ambition and business acumen was needed for the day-to-day operation of a restaurant. Only a handful of dairy restaurants became known beyond their neighborhood; there seems to have been a ceiling built into the success of a dairy restaurant, as they were rarely destination

restaurants. What they did provide was an environment in which customers could surrender to the milekhdike aspect of their personality.

Unlike the other ethnic restaurants of New York, the dairy restaurant offered a dining experience that was not based upon nationalist decor, but upon its absence. The Jewish restaurateur in America was faced with a dilemma when it came to questions of decor and service style. Some wholeheartedly adopted the cultural trappings of their native city: Viennese cafes and grapevine-festooned Romanian wine cellars, German Rathskellers with wooden rafters and fake wine casks built into the wall. Others adopted the decor of the culture they thought their customers would be attracted to: French brasserie, English chophouse, etc.

The Jewish dairy restaurateur had an obvious alternative to any sort of Old World ethnic decor. He most often opted for the style of the modern American dairy lunchroom with its emphasis on cleanliness and efficiency — a style, in turn, derived from the washable tile-walled milking room. This industrial aesthetic for food handling included a bar, or buffet, fitted with stools along with baked-enamel or marble counters and tabletops.

Through the addition of a single baked-enamel table, a bakery or appetizing store could be transformed into a dairy restaurant of sorts. Yonah Shimmel's knish bakery on Houston Street is an example of a limited dairy menu: knishes, coffee, tea, and buttermilk. Mrs. Stahl's knish bakery of Brighton Beach attracted a crowd of après-beach eaters to their Formica-covered

Imagined
dairy restaurant
interior, c. 1910

tables. Gertel's Bakery on the East Side had one or two tables and chairs to accommodate a customer who couldn't wait to get home to eat their eyer-kikhl. In later years, appetizing stores, selling a selection of milekhdike products — smoked fish, cheese, dried fruit, and candy — might also install a few tables and chairs.

The use of the words "dairy," "lunch," and "restaurant" that we see on the storefront windows of some early dairy restaurants, in English or transliterated into Yiddish, was a major assimilationist move, as was the adoption of the sandwich, that unfamiliar quick lunchroom Anglo method of placing cheese or whitefish salad between "two little walls of bread."

As we've seen, the American dairy lunchrooms of the early twentieth century were known for their low prices—in fact, stigmatized as the dining option of the cheapskate. A look at menus from non-Jewish dairy lunchrooms of the early twentieth century shows that dairy dishes were priced only marginally lower than meat. In Geyer's Dairy Restaurant at 176 Fulton Street in 1901: beef stew at 15 cents, two boiled eggs at 15 cents, buckwheat cakes at 10 cents. Through an economy of scale, it was possible to prepare and sell a limited menu of dishes at a very low price. The cost of ingredients was negligible. In general, prices in the small dairy restaurants of the East Side were geared to what a working-class person could afford.

Early tooth loss in the 1900s may help account for the popularity of dairy dishes — less strenuous chewing was needed than for meat. The tortured and often ulcerated digestive system of the Jew of that era, used to eating smoked meats, pickles, and rendered chicken fat, was occasionally in need of soothing milk-based dishes with antacid properties.

The majority of Jewish restaurant customers, making up for generations of deprivation, frequented the meat restaurants and delicatessens of German/Romanian/Hungarian style: Zum Essen, in a basement off Rutgers Square, to Moskowitz' Roumanian Restaurant on Second Avenue (featuring broiled meats and karnatzlach), to The Little Hungary Wine Cellars and Cafe Liberty on East Houston Street, to the more upscale Lorbers "Art Nouveau Restaurant" on Grand Street. The decision to eat in a dairy restaurant was not made lightly.

Dairy Restaurants on the East Side

The documentation of Jewish dairy restaurants in America, scant as it is, far outweighs that of the Old World. The earliest Jewish dairy restaurants appeared in that dense business and residential concentration of Jewish immigrants below Houston Street and east of the Bowery. A 1919 newspaper account of Second Avenue reports that the dairy restaurants all bore "a striking sameness, with their stained woodwork, marble-topped tables crowned with little baskets of rolls, and exhibiting window displays of a great and seasonable variety of fruits and vegetables" [*New York Tribune,* Aug. 31, 1919].

The known histories presented here give us an idea of how and why Jewish immigrants entered the restaurant business. Each story is different —

דער וועלט בעריהמטער בוקארעסטער
בלינטשעס, קרעפפלאך אונד מאמא-
ליגא מאכער
דער איינצעלנער אין דער גאנצער וועלט
.... איז ....

יאקאב י. קאמפאס,
64 דעלענסי סטריט, ניו יארק.
סטריקטלי כשר.

Jacob J. Kampus ad, *Der Teglikher Herald,* January 1900

working one's way up as a low-level employee; being born, or marrying, into the business; borrowing money to start out; or subsidizing the business through work in another field while a wife and child operated the restaurant — but the details of most remain unknown.

Morris Rosenfeld (1862–1923), the Yiddish poet, describes a walk toward Rivington Street: "On both sides . . . there were many restaurants, most of them dairy. In the window of one of these 'dairy restaurants' lay so many dead flies on a little hunk of cheese that the question came up as to whether the cheese was dairy or meat. . . . Up the way from this pareve restaurant was a little store, also a 'dairy.' A Gibson cow stood in the window on which hung a sign, on which was written in this kind of language: 'Frise piter un tsverekh fun undz aleyn gemakht. Tey unzere melkhekes fun bor uv hel unterzukht.' (Fresh homemade butter and cottage cheese. Try our dairy products, inspected by the Board of Health.)

"Pretty good Yiddish! Not so? Only through prophecy did I understand that 'bor uv hel' meant Board of Health. . . ."

Trying to identify the earliest dairy restaurant in New York is like trying to find the site of the original Garden of Eden. Hopefully, in time, more information will come to light about these places.

Although advertisements are self-promotional by nature, it seems that the first popular dairy restaurant was that owned by Jacob Kampus. A listing appears in an 1889 New York directory. An advertisement for this restaurant appeared in the Yiddish-language *The Worker's Newspaper* of 1890. The illustrated ad shows, in four images, a man gaining weight over four months.

The text reads: "Where are you going? To **Jacob J. Kampus.** For What? To find their good blintzes, kreplakh or mamaliga with cheese and butter. When you want to convince yourself that it's good and tasty come to the world famous Romanian blintz-maker. 64 Delancey Street (bet. Eldridge and Allen)."

In 1900, the signing of a three-year lease at 64 Delancey Street for $840 is reported in the *New York Times.* An ad featuring the likeness of Mr. Kompas (another spelling of his name) appeared that same year in the Yiddish *Daily Herald.* He's called "the world famous Buckarester blintzes, kreplakh and mamaliga maker. . . . the only in the whole world . . . strictly kosher."

Jacob J. Campus (the spelling on most government documents) was born in Bucharest, Romania, in 1862 and arrived in New York in 1892 at the age of thirty. He was a short, dark-haired man with a handlebar mustache, if we can believe the drawing in that ad and his draft registration card. In a 1901 ad in the *Jewish Daily Herald,* Campus proclaims himself "the famous Placintar [piemaker, see below] Romanian Spaniard (or Sephardi) from Bucharest decorated at the Paris, Chicago and Antwerp exhibitions." Placinta is a traditional Romanian, Moldovian, and Ukranian thin leaf of dough (square or round) filled with fruit, cheese, or potato. Campus may have adjusted this sweet or savory

LA MAMALIGA DE LUX
JACOB I. CAMPUS
Renumitul PLACINTAR roman spaniol din Bucuresci.
Decorat la expositia din ;
Paris. Chicago si Anvers,
64 DELANCEY ST.

רומעגישע בליגצעס, פריש געשטאָק,
געפיגט איהר א פייגעם סטאָק ;
קרעפּלאָך, בײ נעלאָך ערשט פֿן אויווין,
עסקען מען זײַא דער גרעסטער סבין ;
מײַן מאמאליגע איז ווערטה גענוסען,
מיט קעז אונד פּוטער צוזאמען מישען ;
דער נאמען קאספּוס איז בעקאנט איבעראל,
פֿיר טײַנע שפּײַזע קריג איך א מעראל,
קומט איבערצײַנט זיך בעקאנטע ברעגגסטע ט
אין פיער אונד זעכצינ דעלאנסי סטריט,
איהר מוט אויך געהמען גוט אין אבט,
אז שבת האַלם איך צוגעמטכט,
זײַן בין א איר מיט אללע גליידך,
אונד יאָן מיך גיט צו ווערען רײַך ;
אונד עס טהוט מיר אויך גיט באנק,
איך מאך א לעבען, נאט זײַא דאנק.

וואו געהט איהר ?
— צו יאָקאָב י. קאמפּוס.
— צו וואס ?
— צו פערזוכען זײַע גוטע בליגצעס, קרעפּלאך אדער מאמאליגע מיט קעז און פּוטער. ווען איהר וולט זיך אײַ בערצײַגען ארב עם אזו איז גום נעשמאק קומט צום וועלטבעֿ ריהמטעז רומעגישען בליגצענמאכער, 64 דעלאנסי סטריט.

pastry to more closely conform to his New York customers' idea of a blintz.

The text of the ad is in the form of a poem boasting of his products, the medals he's won and his Shabbos observance. Although Campus may have had a career as a baker in Bucharest, there's no record of awards in his name at any of those international exhibitions.

His overblown claims were likely in jest, parodying the sort of claims made by better-known firms and of a piece with his pseudo-French "La Mamaliga De Luxe" and other humorous copy in his numerous ads in the Yiddish press. In any case, he arrived in New York City old enough to have had a sense of restaurant culture in Bucharest and to trade upon his Romanian Jewish-Sephardic identity and skill as a baker.

A New York business directory of 1889 lists two Campus (spelled with a "C") eating houses, one at 64 Delancey and another, diagonally across the street, at 47, under the name of Leon Campus, his brother (?). To avoid direct competition, Leon's eating house may not have been a dairy.

A 1909 ad continues to boast of La Mamaliga De Lux. A 1910 ad in the *Di Yidishe Bine* (*The Yiddish Stage*) asks, "Do you want to drink a good glass of Rumanian wine? Go to Kampus, 64 Delancey Street. The world famous Bukarester blintzes, kreplakh and mamaliga maker."

An advertisement in the form of a humorous article in the June 16, 1911, issue of *Der Kibetser* "reports" having received many letters from doctors and pharmacists complaining that the magazine was publishing ads for Mr. Kampus's restaurant. Some offered to pay the editors not to run the ads. Mystified, *Der Kibetser* sent a reporter to find out why such anger was directed at Mr. Kampus. It was discovered that since the ads began to appear, the doctors and pharmacists were losing a lot of business. After eating at Kampus's restaurant, it was "Goodbye stomach sickness, goodbye doctors." That was the reason they wanted to do away with the Kampus advertisements. *Der Kibetser* refused to comply with these requests and continued to recommend Kampus's food to their readers.

"The blintze-fabricator Mr. Campus of Broome Street" was incidentally immortalized in Moishe Nadir's 1932 *Rivington Street,* a poetic account of Yiddish and American culture c. 1903 as "the largest industrialist on the East Side." Broome Street may have been the bakery/restaurant's original location.

Jacob J. Campus died in 1913 at the age of fifty-one; his wife and brother seem to have continued the business for several years. A May 1916 advertisement in the *Forverts* for **Kampus's Milkhiger Restorant** (see facing page) boasts of being in the same place for twenty-four years (thus established in 1892, the year of his arrival in New York). The text reads: "Eat Blintzes and become Fat!" "For the last 24 years we had the only Rumanian Milkhiger restaurant, now we're back on 64 Delancey Street."

A drawing of a fat and a thin man with corresponding captions reads: "Fat man: Come quick, don't wait. Look at me, I was thin like you. I listened to the advice of a friend and began eating steady in the famous milkhiger Kampus Restaurant. Now you can look good and healthy if you listen to me.
Thin man: I don't know what I'm doing that's making me so 'refined.' I heard of the famous Kampus and that from their food one can become fat. I'll go try.

Rumanian blintzes, tasty fresh,
You'll find here a nice smell,
Kreplekh, beygelekh right from the oven,
May the greatest connoisseur eat them.
One gets by us all milkhige foods to eat.
Mrs. J. Kampus, 64 Delancey Street.
You shouldn't forget!"

Sometime in 1916, Leon seems to have taken over the restaurant at number 64 in his own name and run it for one more year. In 1922, Samuel Campus, a probable relation to Jacob, was running the **Placintaria Romana Le Mamaliga De Luxe** at 153 Forsyth Street.

Feyvish Katz Premiere Kosher Milkhiger Restaurant, 210 Stanton Street near Pitt Street. "Hello, hello! Are you hungry? Do you want to have a delicious and nutritious bite to eat? Go into Feyvish Katz. The best milkhige foods made as tasty as in your own home." [Ad in *Der Yidisher Gazlen,* 1910]

מאָקאָבייער
ערשטער קלאַס
מילכיגער
רעסטאָראַנט
און לאָנטש רום
אין דעם פאַסענדסטען און בעסטען פלאַץ
אויף דער איסט סייד.
L. SCHOENFELD
30 Rivington Street
Near Forsyth St.,   New York

From 1909 to 1913, **L. Schoenfeld Milkhiger Restaurant and Lunch Room,** 30 Rivington Street near Forsyth Street, was advertised as a "first class Milkhiger restorant and lunch room in the most convenient and best location on the East Side."

In 1913 **S[imon L.] Scho[e]nfeld and Bacher** opened another "milkhiger lontsh rum" at 6 Second Avenue near Houston Street. "When a businessman treats the customer good, the customer treats the businessman good." By October of 1914, Schoenfeld was the sole proprietor of both restaurants.

Simon Yonkel at 134 Prince Street, between Wooster and West Broadway, announced in 1911 that they had added the separate handling of dairy foods in their well-known, strictly kosher restaurant. "Regular dinners of meat, or dairy, 50 cents. Guaranteed best treatment and freshest foods." The exact method of separation is not described.

Ads in *Der Kibetser* from 1910 and 1911 proclaim "The pride of East Broadway is only, only and only, **I[saac] Fayfer's Milkhiger Restaurant.** You must try it! 183 E Bway, A. Fayfer, proprietor." In a 1910 ad in *Der Yidisher Gazlen,* Fayfer calls his place "The best and most beautiful in the east side. The freshest foods and the best prices." Eva Feifer, his wife (?), was listed as the proprietor in 1903

פייפער'ס
מילכיגער רעסטאָראַנט
183   א. בראָדוויי,
דער בעסטער און שעהנסטער אין
דער איסט סייד.
די פרישסטע שפּייזען,
און די בעסטע בעהאַנדלונג.

and may have actually run the place. Feifer's was to occupy that basement space until 1912, when it moved to 22 Rutgers Street. Between 1913 and 1916 **Feifer's Dairy Restaurant** moved to, or opened a branch at, 139 East Houston Street.

A 1911 ad for **Izidor Klepak's Vegetarian Restaurant** at 237 East Broadway, New York, asks, "Have you already been there?

If not — why not? Come in. It won't disappoint you. All foods made from substantial fruits and vegetables. Everything sparkling, white and clean. Open from 8 in the morning til 1 at night." A 1910 ad from *Der Yidisher Gazlen* features a small photo of Izidor posed as an aesthete with rustled hair and hand to head in bemused contemplation of the world. Israel (Isadore) Klepak (born 1888, Chomsk, Russia–died 1940, Texas) was involved in vegetarian activities and then moved to Texas, where he operated a cafe.

A 1910 ad in *Der Yidisher Gazlen* for **M[ax] Kirshner's Cafe, Dairy Restaurant,** 22 Avenue A, New York, cries, "Help! Robbers! Don't steal from yourself. Do you want to eat a good, substantial meal? Come in Max Kirshner's cafe and dairy [transliterated "dairy"] restaurant. A beautifully fixed up place and, the main thing, clean not adulterated food. Open day and night."

By 1917, Kirshner adds the word "kosher" to his restaurant's ad and beseeches "Men, Boys and Girls to demand to come for breakfast, dinner and supper, good and quickly served."

שפּייזע צעטעל פֿאַר איין טאָג

— פֿאַרשפּייז :

שוואָמען מיט פֿאַטשאַמס	רעטים און קרים
בהומענקאָהל	פּאטאַטאַ סאַלאַד
געהאַקטע נאָטאַס	וועדזשעטעבעל און קרים
געדעמפּטע אַרבעס	קרויט סאַלאַד
אַמעריקאַן **סאַלאַד**	אייער סאַלאַד
וועדזשיטעבעל סאַלאַד	געדעמפּטע שוואָמען
גריכישער **סאַלאַד**	פּרינסעס נוס סאַלאַד
שפּינאָטש	מעהרען

— קאָטלעטען :

מאַקאַראָני מיט קעז	עגג פֿרענט
פֿרענטש פֿרייד פּאטאַטאָס,	וועדזשעטעבל
פּראָטאָס און נאָטאָס	ראָסט (בראָטען)
נוס בראָטען	פּראָטאָס אָדער נאָטאָס פּענ-קייקס
געדעמפּטע אָדער געפֿרייט	ברוינע רייז מיט פּוטער

— זופּען :

בוליאָן דע פֿראַנס	רייז פֿלייקס מיט מילך
בומס	גראַנאָלא מיט מילך
רייזינס אָדער בוימלען	רייז מיט מילך
וועדזשעטעבל	פֿאַרס מיט מילך
	נוס מיט רייזינס אָדער פֿייגען

— צושפּייז :

רייז פּודינג	קעראָמס (מערן)
פּיינאַפּעל	קאַמפּאָס
פּרונס (געטריקענטע פּלוימען)	געבאַקטע עפּעל
פּרובט סאַלאַד	

Dr. Kellogg's Battle Creek foods served in our daily menu and on sale.

Schildkraut's menu for one day, from *Unzer Gezunt,* 1915

Appetizers
Mushrooms with sour cream
Cauliflower
Chopped nuts
Steamed beans
American salad
Vegetarian salad
Greek salad
Spinach
Lettuce and cream
Tasty salad
Vegetables and cream
Cabbage salad
Princess nut salad
Carrots

Kotleten (cutlets)
Macaroni and cheese
French fried potatoes
Protose and Nuttose
Nut roast (steamed or fried)
Eggplant
Vegetarian roast
Protose or Nuttose pancake
Brown rice with butter

Soups
Bouillon de France
Raisin or dates
Vegetable
Rice flakes with milk
Granola with milk
Rice with milk
Bran with milk
Nuts with raisins or figs

Dessert
Rice pudding
Pineapple
Prunes (dried plums)
Carrots
Kompot
Baked apple

Ike Krakovski's Cafe and Lunch Room,

173 East Broadway. In 1904, eight years before the construction of the *Forverts*'s building at this address, Krakovski's lunchroom made "fresh, homestyle milchige foods to order." It was advertised as "a home for everyone." By 1906, this address was occupied by Wolf Kozlowsky's restaurant.

Between 1909 and 1913, the **Houston Hippodrome** at 141–143 East Houston (more recently the Sunshine Movie Theater), an early moving-picture theater and then Yiddish theater, had a dairy restaurant in its basement run by Harry Brown and Morris Perlmutter.

In 1911 the newly opened **Moishe Levin's Milkhiger Restaurant** at 146 East Broadway is advertised in *Naye Leben*. This is likely the Levin who went on to operate a number of dairy restaurants on the East Side. Ads in *Der Kibetser* from 1912 mark a series of partnerships: a milkhiger restaurant at 183 East Broadway, **Kolodny & Levin's** (June 1912); **Levin & Greenberg's** (August 1912); the restaurant that finally became **Levin & Goodman** by 1915 (see page 368).

N. Berkovitz's Milkhiger Restaurant, 66 Suffolk Street, claims, "One gets the best and freshest eating for the cheapest prices." [Ad in *Di Arbeter Tsaytung,* 1906]

In open defiance of Jewish dietary law, **Maks Bekenshteyn** of 185 Clinton Street, in a 1908 ad in *Der Kibetser,* promises that the best milkhiger and fleyshige foods can only be had at his restaurant.

An ad in *Der Kibetser* from 1913 reads: "True experts are invited to eat in **N. Berenknopf's Milkhiger Restaurant,** 169 East Broadway, N.Y. When you eat by us, you won't worry about getting married and will avoid taking on trouble. We mean the best for you."

Schildkraut's Vegetarian Restaurant at 198 East Broadway, New York (later 200 East Broadway). By 1926 there were restaurants at: 400 Fourth Avenue (corner 28th Street), 37 West 32nd Street, 221 West 36th Street, 4 West 28th Street, 53 West 28th Street, 171 East Broadway, 1363 Fifth Avenue (between 113th and 114th Streets), 191 Joralemon Street, Brooklyn, 1769 Pitkin Avenue, Brooklyn, 46 Graham Avenue, Brooklyn, and resorts at these locations: Pine Terrace Hotel, Highland Falls, New York; Schildkraut's Hotel, Lakewood, New Jersey; Beach 35th Street, Edgemere, Long Island; Surf Avenue and 130th Street, Coney Island; Saratoga Springs, New York.

Herman Schildkraut (1879–1956) of Tarnow, then Austrian Galicia, was the foremost advocate of the meatless diet within the New York Jewish community. He arrived in New York in 1910 and eventually built a chain of fifteen restaurants and three health resorts with a publishing arm,

"All those who travel to Lakewood to recover, those seeking to be healthy and to stay healthy visit Schildkraut's Vegetarian Hotel. There your wishes will be fulfilled in every respect." *Forverts*, January 1922

the Better Health & Correct Eating Institute. He strove to make vegetarianism delicious and popular. "No one decries the slaughterhouse with more vigor than he. He is against eating of dead carcasses, devitalized white bread, refined sugar, stimulants of coffee, tea and alcohol and canned goods."

His first store, a small restaurant at 198 East Broadway, opposite the Educational Alliance, had a flashy electric sign. A previous vegetarian restaurant was located at the same address in 1912 run by a **Benjamin Sazer** (see page 367). Schildkraut attributed his success to "three factors: vegetarian dishes that tickle the palate; tastefully decorated restaurants; and his wife."

It was Mrs. Sadie (Sarah) Schildkraut (1886–1937) who supervised all of the restaurants and was responsible for revolutionizing the preparation of vegetarian fare. To appeal to those diners addicted to the taste of meat, she worked in her experimental kitchen in Highland Falls, New York, to perfect the preparation of "vegetable meats: chopped liver, chopped herring, Protose cutlets rolled in eggs, with fresh stewed vegetables or Protose steak with creamed spinach and carrots, fried onions, and potatoes. Mrs. Schildkraut became known as an authority on vegetarian cooking and lectured and taught widely.

Did those same meat addicts ever consider preparing meat in the form of mock vegetables?

A profile in *The Restaurant Man* of June 1927 explained that Mr. Schildkraut did all he could to avoid having his restaurants smack of Bohemianism and "queer folk." His establishments were attractive and modern in appearance. "The largest at 400 Fifth Avenue occupies two floors, the second being devoted to banquets and parties. Mr. Schildkraut has established himself as an authority in his field — composes verse in praise of vegetarianism and offers dietary advice to patrons. The walls of the restaurants are filled with placards presenting health facts and names of famous vegetarians. The patrons of his health resorts return to the city as converts to the meatless diet and frequent the restaurants."

From 1915 to 1917, Schildkraut was a principal advertiser in Benzion

Liber's *Unzer Gezunt,* a digest-sized Yiddish periodical, printed in almost microscopic type, advocating sexual reform and healthful eating.

Schildkraut also operated two vegetarian hotels: one in Lakewood, New Jersey, and another, Schildkraut's Pine Terrace Park and Vegetarian Hotel, in Highland Falls, New York. A postcard for the New York hotel featured a view of an open-air sleeping room with a dozen beds covered with floral spreads.

Vegetarishe Kokh Bukh: Ratsyonale Nahrung (Vegetarian Cook Book: Rational Eating) by Abraham B. and Shifra Mishulow was published in 1926 by Schildkraut's Better Health & Correct Eating Institute of 6 West 28th Street in New York. It offered menus and recipes for a vegetarian-based diet. The cookbook featured mock-meat dishes: nut roasts, mushroom cutlets, vegetable croquettes, Hungarian goulash, hamburgers (lima beans, tomatoes, pine nuts, celery, whipped butter, bread crumbs, eggs, sweet cream, peanut butter, water), vegetable wurst — most using fresh vegetables, some using the nutmeat concoctions such as Protose (nuts and wheat gluten) and Nuttose, manufactured by John Harvey Kellogg's Battle Creek Food Company. Some recipes were outright inventions such as the Yidisher Apetizer (lentils, peanut butter, egg, American cheese, oil, and sautéed onions). Many of the recipes consist of American-style sandwiches and toasts, chop suey, macaroni, and spaghetti. When they happened to fit into the dietary scheme, traditional Eastern European dishes included blintzes, mamaliga, kreplekh, various latkes, kasha, and vegetarian stuffed peppers and cabbage.

The milk section included spaghetti Italian (using American cheese), macaroni with cheese, noodles with cheese, blintzes, kreplekh, potato latkes, omelets, and kasha dishes.

In November of 1944, the Vegetarian Society of New York celebrated its thirteenth annual Thanksgiving Day dinner at Schildkraut's restaurant at 4 West 28th Street.

Ads for Herman Schildkraut's first restaurant feature a photograph of the proprietor: a swath of black hair plastered across his forehead, determined black eyebrows, strong nose, and drooping black

Ad for Schildkraut's Vegetarian Restaurant, *Der Morgn Zhurnal,* March 1919

mustache above an open mouth with heavy lower lip as though caught between proclamations — not the stereotypical vegetarian.

An ad from 1915 explains: "Our vegetarian selection of food consists of over 150 meat free dishes from which we put together our daily bill of fare. A combination of 3 or 4 of our dishes will satisfy the strictest physician-worker." There follows a letter in English from the artist S. Goldberg, who has offered to supply the restaurant with a portrait of Dr. Kellogg of Battle Creek to add to the gallery of famous vegetarians. "As an esthetical vegetarian I am delighted to find so hygienic and splendid an eating place; as an old patron of your place I have no hesitancy in saying that I have found your foods are not only hygienic but also very nutritious and properly combined. The instruction and advice you give to your customers as to the proper selection of food is productive of good results, and most praiseworthy."

Surprisingly, a February 1916 menu contains not a single Eastern European dairy dish, just soups (Bouillon de France), vegetables (steamed or with cream), salads ("American salad, Princess nut salad"), fruit, and artificial meat roasts of Protose or Nuttose. Schildkraut's menu with the names of the dishes transliterated and/or translated into Yiddish was presented as part of an advertisement in *Unzer Gezunt*. We can imagine the dishes being ordered by customers in his East Broadway restaurant, the names shifted into a Yiddish pronunciation and thus transformed in their mouths into a part of Jewish dairy cuisine.

In the 1920s, Schildkraut's was on an expansionary campaign, opening two restaurants on West 28th Street. An ad from the 1920s is surrounded by rhyming aphorisms: "Nemt nit avek dos leben, vos Got hot geben!" [Don't take away the life, that God has given!] By 1948 only one location remained: 4 West 28th Street.

The New Modern Vegetarian Restaurant of 26 Delancey Street, between Christie and Forsyth Streets, invited the readers of *Unzer Gezunt* in July of 1915 to its opening: "No tips — 25 cents regular meal — no tips. For *Our Health* readers is now open." See **M. Gruber's Venus Vegetarian and Milkhiger Restaurant,** pages 296, 336, and 355.

Sam Mancher's Dairy Restaurant, 132 Ludlow Street, New York.
In 1910, one item in the *Forverts*'s Gallery of Missing Husbands read as follows:

"Sarah Solomon is searching for her husband who is now uptown, 38–40 years old, solid built, medium height, black eyes, black mustache, left me 2½ years ago. I offer $25 to anyone who will notify me of his whereabouts. He doesn't have to be afraid of divorcing me. Notify me at 132 Ludlow Street, in the restaurant."

Sixty-six years later, Gertrude M. Frankel came across that item reprinted in Irving Howe's *World of Our Fathers* and recognized that address. It was the location of her father's dairy restaurant. She knew it as a girl in the late 1920s but understood that it had been an existing dairy restaurant when her father, Sam Mancher, took it over from its Polish owner, Isaac Miller, in 1921. As for Sarah Solomon, whether she worked in the kitchen of the earlier restaurant, lived in the building above, or simply pined for her missing husband over a plate of cold borscht every day is unclear.

From Mrs. Frankel's recollections, prompted by an exhaustive list of questions, we can reconstruct a sense of the restaurant as it operated under her father's ownership (1921–1943).

The name "Sam Mancher" (pronounced "Mencher") was painted on the front window along with the words "Dairy Restaurant. Ladies Welcome" and a Star of David. "As you walked in, the steam table was on the right with the cash register at the end nearest the door. Then a glass-covered counter, filled with ice, to protect the baked fish and other dishes. I am sure there was

a glass partition over the food. Behind the counter were cutting boards to make sandwiches. On your left were four tables, marble tops with four wooden chairs, black bentwood — they were not too comfortable. On the table you had a napkin dispenser, salt and pepper shakers, a glass container with granulated sugar. My job was to see to it that everything was filled. As you walked further into the store, it opened up like a 'T,' there were two tables on each side and you had the door to the kitchen. First into the kitchen you had a zinc washtub full of dirty dishes, to the right you had two washtubs to wash and rinse the dishes. By the way, I think they were made of wood. The Department of Health would come by to check the water temperature of the tubs. Proceeding further you had a large icebox and on the right side a large surface where they made pastry and cut and sliced, etc. On the left was a large commercial oven. Also, some cupboards . . . I remember mirrors on the walls, no pictures."

There were tin ceilings with overhead electrical fans and hanging strips of flypaper. The floor was covered with sawdust that was swept up each evening.

Her father never served tuna fish, as he suspected that it wasn't kosher. He did serve salmon, sardines, and tomato herring. Peanut butter was also suspect. They used only butter and sweet cream and milk. She never saw Protose being used. Her father once tried making vegetarian chopped liver, but it didn't go over. The customers were not vegetarians.

Her family was not religiously observant but they did not eat "treyf." The store was open seven days a week from 6 am to midnight. Her grandmother was observant and the store was closed for Passover and Yom Kippur. At home they ate a meat meal once or twice a week, but otherwise fish and dairy.

The restaurant served lox, whitefish, and carp. As a girl she was sent to a fish market on Orchard Street to buy the needed supplies. Tomatoes were kept in the basement to ripen. They served baked goods with onions, some smoked fish, gefilte fish (formed in flat patties) made from pike, whitefish, and carp, kippered salmon, whitefish salad, and chopped herring. Both hot and cold borscht (with a hot boiled potato) as well as wide noodles and cheese, and noodle pudding with cheese. The pushcart men came in to eat mamaliga (baked cornmeal mush topped with goat cheese). Five cents for coffee; 10–25 cents for a sandwich; baked fish, 50 cents. Tea was served in a glass with a metal holder; coffee in heavy white china.

As for other restaurants in the neighborhood, Gertrude recalled Ratner's, two blocks away, and Koch's, another dairy (see page 336), on Essex Street. On Orchard Street, she knew of a woman who operated a restaurant out of her apartment.

Sam Mancher considered his restaurant to be strictly kosher but had no official kosher supervision or certification and did not serve kosher milk. Eggs were cracked into a glass to look for blood spots before cooking. Very Orthodox people came in to eat and trusted the owner. She first saw Hasidim in 1947. If someone came in collecting for charity, her father would give them a nickel. "The sin is on him if he keeps it."

As a girl and young woman, she washed dishes. Her father was afraid of black people but had a Chinese dishwasher. The cook was a Jewish woman who remained with them for many years. Her father's specialty was soup. After the Crash of 1929, her mother worked in the restaurant as a cook and baker. They did all their own cake baking but ordered rolls and bread from a commercial bakery. Milk was delivered daily in a large milk can and served with a ladle. Next door was a barbershop. The Mancher family lived on the fourth and then second floor of the building. "It was a nice building with a dumbwaiter for garbage. . . . We lived from hand to mouth.

"The customers were mostly people who owned other businesses or pushcart peddlers or people who had no family and came every day to eat their main meal. These people had a great many opinions about everything and were very expressive but none that I know of were poets. Some had inventive ideas that struck me as ingenious. Tempers ran hot and curses were frequent about politics and the government. English and Yiddish were spoken interchangeably. The people who lived in the neighborhood very rarely ate there. Tourists sometimes came in; people who were looking for bargains on Orchard Street. Also, the gangsters from Brooklyn who used the limos [a rental business] from across the street and Nyberg's funeral parlor. The name of Dutch Schultz was once mentioned." She recalls more talking than eating. They'd remain open until midnight if there were customers. They sometimes catered affairs. Gertrude recalled carrying pirogen or gefilte fish across the street to regular customers.

Her mother played the numbers game for 5 cents a day. A woman bookie kept the slips of paper with bets in her hair. A pasty-faced fellow named Schemker was a regular customer. He was a heroin user. The police once discovered a little packet of drugs in the toilet tank. Her father would occasionally point out homosexual customers: "Er's a feygele." The restaurant was a refuge for married middle-aged men: a painter who invented a safety harness for exterior work, a plumber, a truck driver.

"Breakfast would be either hot cereal or scrambled eggs with something like hash browns (made from cold cooked potatoes that had not been used). Sometimes we had customers who wanted boiled eggs (three minutes). Cornflakes were also popular. Coffee and a roll with butter. I don't remember whether orange juice was served but I think so.

"A new customer would sit down and my father would go over to him and take his order. An old customer would come up to the counter to tell my father what he wanted if he knew and then sit down. My mother would help out at lunchtime. When I was older, I also helped out.

"The coffee urn sat at the other end of the counter with the pitcher of hot milk, forming a scum on top, on the single gas burner beside it. Also, the can of milk with the dipper hanging beside it."

The sink was located outside of the toilet closet for Orthodox, who wouldn't eat before washing hands and saying blessings. There was a basin and a roll-a-towel machine next to it.

"Sour milk was served, no yogurt, though sour cream was eaten a lot. Portions were generous, but I don't think they ate as much as people do today because they could not afford it. The restaurant was brightly lit at night, and the lights were left on after closing. Garbage pickup cost $1."

Sam Mancher was born in Horodenka, then part of the Habsburg Monarchy, in Western Ukraine. He gave up the restaurant in 1943, when his wife had a stroke. Through the Democratic Party, he got a job as fire watchman at the Navy Yard.

At sixty, her father went back into the food business, buying a little luncheonette at 71 Fourth Avenue and 7th Street, opposite Wanamaker's

Department Store. The place had no name and served treyf meat and dairy. It was a more "bohemian" clientele who frequented the secondhand book stores of Fourth Avenue. For three years, Gertrude worked the counter, or stood outside to attract customers with her good looks.

Geffner's Dairy Restaurant, 143 Second Avenue, corner of 9th Street. A surviving matchbook proclaims: "Never

closed, catering to parties. Where we all meet. Baking on our own premises."
In 1920, Abraham Geffner and his partner, a Mr. Koch, announced to their many friends and patrons that they had "taken back" ownership of a **Milkhiger Restaurant** at 122 Rivington Street as well as opened a second restaurant, **Reyven's Restaurant** at 510 Sixth Avenue between 30th and 31st Streets. The word "dairy" is not mentioned in connection with this restaurant. They described themselves as well-known restaurateurs. In 1921, Abraham Geffner appears as the manager of **Gruber's Dairy Lunch Room** at 143 Second Avenue. In 1923, Geffner, doing business under the name of Gruber's, goes bankrupt, and by 1927, a restaurant with his own name is established here with an ornate facade and a large electric sign. In that year, Geffner, as proprietor, offered New Year's greetings to his customers through a large ad in the *Forverts*. The event is marked by an article in *The Restaurant Man* of the same year: "After extensive alteration of the building and premises, necessitated by a fire some months ago, Geffner's new dairy restaurant at 143 Second Ave., corner Ninth St. was formally opened to the public on June 14, and catered to a record patronage. The new restaurant is one of the finest examples of the modern dairy restaurant that is to be found on the East Side and A. Geffner, president of the company which operates the restaurant, has been the recipient of many congratulations from his patrons and friends for his confidence in the neighborhood to justify such a large expenditure in creating such a fine establishment." By 1941, Geffner's moves to 123 Second Avenue and has a second branch at 37 West 37th Street in the Garment District. By 1948, it's gone. (See Farmfood Vegetarian & Dairy Restaurants, page 380.)

Rapoport's Dairy Restaurant, 91–93 Second Avenue.
Opened 1918–19 by Harry Rapoport (born 1893, Radom, Poland–died 1967).

On a crowded block of Second Avenue in 1934, the still-thriving home of Yiddish theater in New York, competing with a dozen electric signs ("Beauty Salon," "Chop Suey"), Rapoport's awning announced, "We have increased our seating capacity — cooling system. Lunch 35¢, Dinner 45¢." A few steps up the avenue was **Thau's Dairy Restaurant** and **Ratner's** — the choice must have been difficult for contemporary diners. According to several informants Rapoport's was the more upscale of the two large dairy restaurants on Second Avenue with five hundred tables; a 1946 newspaper account describes its atmosphere as resembling "nothing so much as a large and noisy cafeteria."

Harry Rapoport worked as an army mess sergeant in France during World War I and upon his return to New York City in 1918 worked for one year as a waiter in the **Avenue Dairy Restaurant** on Second Avenue. At some point he became part-owner with a Mr. Gotlieb, and in 1924, they opened a second branch at 21 Second Avenue. Sometime after, Rapoport purchased the restaurant and changed its name to Rapoport's.

Rapoport's

DAIRY RESTAURANT

Catering
For All Occasions

91-93 SECOND AVENUE
NEW YORK

Tel. GRamercy 7-9338
7-9344

Appetizers and Entrees

Chopped Vegetable Liver	85	Chopped Sturgeon	85
Chopped Salmon	85	Imported Kippered Herring	95
Chopped Eggs (Onions or Celery)	85	Fried or Baked Herring	95
Chopped Herring	85	Imported Anchovies Salad	1.15
Chopped Egg Plant	85	Imported Sardines Salad	
Spring Salad	85	(Boneless & Skinless)	1.15
Greek Salad	85	Imported Antipasto Salad	1.15
Maatjes Herring	85	Tomato Herring Salad	1.00
Filet of Pickled Herring	85	Tuna Fish Salad	1.10
Pickled Lox	1.05	Chopped Spinach & Eggs	85

Soups and Cereals

Noodles with Milk	45	Tomato and Rice	45
Rice with Milk	45	Mushroom Barley	45
Brown Kasha with Milk	45	Potato Soup	45
Corn Flakes with Milk	45	Vegetable Soup	45
Grape Nuts with Milk	45	Cold Borsht or Chav with Cream	55
Rice Krispies with Milk	45	Split Pea Soup	45
Puffed Rice with Milk	45	Cold Fruit Soup	55
All Bran with Milk	45	Cold Borsht or Chav Improved	80
Yankee Bean	45	Lima Bean	45
Brown Cabbage	45	Liver Kreplach	65

Consomme Boullion with Veg.

(Cereals with Sweet Cream 10c Extra)

Salads

Lake Sturgeon Salad	1.95	Cream Cheese Salad	80
Cold Cuts Salad	1.65	Cream Cheese and Jam	90
Salad a la Rapoport	1.65	Lettuce and Tomato Salad	80
Smoked Whitefish Salad	1.20	Chopped (Entree) Salad	1.00
Smoked Chicken Carp	1.20	Ind. Canned Salmon Salad	1.20
Combination Salad with Herring	1.00	Ind. Canned Tuna Fish Salad	1.20
Lake Sturgeon and Nova Scotia		Tropical Health Salad	1.35
Salmon Salad	1.95	Imported Russian Caviar Salad	2.10
Nova Scotia Salmon Salad	1.35	Smoked Salmon Salad	1.25
with Cream Cheese	1.50	with Cream Cheese	1.35

Dairy Dishes

Fresh Huckleberry or Cherry Pirogen		Cauliflower a la France	95
(in Season)	95	Stuffed Green Pepper	95
Huckleberry, Cherry, Strawberry,		French Pancakes (to order 5 min.)	95
Pineapple or Lekvar Blintzes	95	Potato Pancakes (Latkes)	85
Boiled or Fried Pirogen	85	Matzoh Pancakes	90
Boiled or Fried Kreplach	85	Matzoh Brei	90
Fried Cheese Blintzes	85	Noodles with Cheese and Butter	90
Fried Potato Blintzes	85	Cheese Pancakes	1.00
Fried Kashe Blintzes	85	Brown Kasha with Onions	80
Fried Jelly Blintzes	85	Mameliga with Cheese and Butter	85
Kashe Varnishkes	85	Stuffed Cabbage	95
Spaghetti with Sauce	80	Mushroom Chow Mein	95
Vegetable Goulash	1.00	Mushroom Roast	1.00
Protose Steak	1.10	Mushrooms, Fried or Stewed	1.25
Egg Plant Steak	1.00	Vegetable Dinner	1.00
Boiled or Fried Cauliflower	95	Corn Pancakes	1.00

(Any Order Served with Sour Cream or Applesauce 10c Extra)

Sour Cream Dishes

Bowl	60	Bananas with Cream	85
Pot Cheese with Cream	85	Strawberries with Cream	90
Vegetables and Cream	85	Peaches and Cream	85
Boiled Potatoes and Cream	85	Huckleberries with Cream	90
Fruit Salad with Cream	95	Sliced Egg with Cream	85

Cheese

Camembert	80	Liederkranz	80,
Imported Swiss	80	Swiss Gruyere	80
Roquefort	80	Pimento	50
Philadelphia Cream	50	1/2 Cream Cheese with Jam	60
American	65	Bleu	65

Per Portion—Served with Lettuce and Tomatoes

Toasts

Dry Toast	15	Milk Toast	30
French Toast	75	Buttered Toast	20
Cinnamon Toast	50	Creamed Toast	30

Coffee, Rolls and Butter Without Entree or Roast 35

Try Our Delicious Griddle Cakes with Butter & Maple Syrup ——— 85

Eggs and Omelettes

Boiled Eggs	55	Vegetable Omlette	90
Fried Eggs	60	Onion Omlette	75
Scrambled Eggs	60	Lox Omlette	95
Poached Eggs on Toast	65	Spanish Omlette	90
Poached Egg on Spinach	90	Jelly Omlette	80
Mushroom Omlette	1.10	Cheese Omlette	90
Tomato Omlette	75	Sturgeon Omlette	1.25
Plain Omlette	60	Nova Scotia Lox Omlette	1.10
Side Order Smoked Salmon	40	Side Order Nova Scotia Salmon	45

(Eggs Served with Sliced Tomatoes 15c Extra)

Side Orders of Vegetables

Carrots and Green Peas	45	Spinach with Mashed Potatoes	65
Creamed Spinach	45	Asparagus Tips	85
Mushrooms with Kashe	1.00	Asparagus Tips on Toast	95
French Fried Potatoes	35	Mushrooms on Toast	1.25
Boiled Potatoes	35	Corn Niblets	35
Tomato or Lettuce or Cucumbers or		French Fried Onions	35
Peppers or Onions or Olives	25	Mashed Potatoes	35
Boiled Cauliflower	45	Corn on Cob (in season)	25

Cutlets

Mushroom Cutlet	1.00	Salmon Cutlet	1.00
Vegetable Cutlet	1.00	Salmon Croquettes	1.00
Cauliflower Cutlet	1.00	Mushroom Goulash	1.00

Fish

Cold Fried Flounder	1.30	Stuffed (Gefilte) Fish	1.30
Fried Filet of Sole	1.30	Broiled Mackerel	1.40
Boiled Yellow Pike	1.30	Broiled Salmon Steak	1.40
Boiled Whitefish	1.30	Broiled Whitefish	1.40
Fried Veg. Scallops	1.35	Broiled Halibut Steak	1.40
Boiled Winter Carp	1.30	Broiled Baby Flounder	1.40
Baked Whitefish	1.30	Broiled Filet of Sole	1.40
		Marinated Fish	1.40

Fish Broiled to Order in Butter (20 min.)

Sandwiches

No. 1—Lake Sturgeon and Swiss Cheese,		Roquefort	85
Cole Slaw, Sliced Tomatoes	1.85	Swiss Gruyere	65
No. 2—Cream Cheese with Walnuts		Cream Cheese and Lox (Combination)	85
and Jam	75	Chopped Veg. Liver	70
No. 3—Russian Caviar, Chopped Egg,		Chopped Eggs and Unions	70
Sliced Tomatoes, Queen Olives	1.95	Imported Swiss Cheese	75
No. 4—Club Sandwich (3 Layers) on		Hard Boiled Egg with Mayonnaise	55
Toast, Sturgeon, Swiss Cheese, Smoked		American Cheese	55
Salmon, Cole Slaw	1.95	Ind. Canned Salmon	85
Lettuce and Tomato with Mayonnaise	55	Tomato Herring	80
Fried Egg	55	Combination Vegetable	55
Smoked Whitefish	1.00	Tuna Fish	80
Imported Boneless & Skinless Sardines	90	Lake Sturgeon	1.60
Cream Cheese and Lox on Bagel	75	Smoked Chicken Carp or Butterfish	1.00
Lake Sturgeon on Bagel	1.45	Nova Scotia Salmon	90
Cream Cheese	55	With Cream Cheese	1.00
Smoked Salmon	80	Sturgeon on Biayolistoker	1.45

Fruits and Desserts

Grapefruit, Half	30	Ice Cream	30
Orange Juice, Small	20	Sliced Pineapple	35
Orange Juice, Large	35	Sliced Orange	25
Stewed Prunes	35	Stewed Figs	55
with Cream	45	with Cream	65
Baked Apple	35	Apple Sauce	30
with Cream	45	Stewed Cherries	35
Our Own Danish Pastry	30	Cheese Cake	50
Homemade Pies	35	Strawberry Short Cake	55
Fruit Jello or Chocolate Pudding	25	Fresh Fruit Salad Deluxe	55
Rice Pudding with Fruit Sauce	35	Farina Pudding with Fruit Sauce	35
Melon in Season	45	Fresh Fruit Cocktail	45
Fruit Strudel	45	French Pastry	45
Strawberry Cheese Cake	60	Noodle Charlotte with Fruit Sauce	35

Coffee, Tea and Beverages

Coffee	15	Iced Tea or Coffee	25
Tea	10	Glass of Sour Milk	20
Cocoa	15	Hot Chocolate	15
Milk	15	with Whipped Cream	20
Buttermilk	20	Dr. Brown's Celery Tonic	15
Glass of Sweet Cream	45	Saratoga Geyser	25
Glass of Cream and Milk	35	Postum	15
Canada Dry (All Flavors)	15	Sanka	15

Coffee, Rolls and Butter Without Entree or Roast ——— 35

---

ner

9:00 P. M.

5

P.M. —
R PERSON

Entree
15¢ EXTRA)
S

Cocktail	Chopped Sturgeon Salad
Juice	Chopped Eggs and Celery
uice	Pickled Herring Filet
nes	Schmaltz Herring
	Chopped Egg Plant
ce	Chopped Herring
	Honey Dew (in Season)

Soup

Cream	Cold Fruit Soup

Lima Bean (Monday and Friday)
Tomato and Rice (Thursday)
Cold Chav with Cream (in season)
Green Split Pea (Tuesday, Wednesday
Saturday and Sunday)
Kreplach (Saturday & Sunday)

Roast

Vegetable Cutlet
Baked Herring
Noodles with Cheese
Fried Herring
Potato Pirogen
Cheese Kreplach
Kashe Pirogen
Vegetables with Cream
Pot Cheese with Cream
Kashe Varnishkes
Vegetable Dinner
Huckleberry Pirogen (in Season)
Applesauce 10¢ Extra
OAST IS EXTRA •

	30¢
	30¢
Fish	40¢

Dessert

Watermelon (in season)
Apple Pie
Huckleberry Pie
Chocolate Pudding
Coffee Cake
Danish Pastry
Fruit Strudel
Ice Cream

Beverage

Milk	— —	Buttermilk

Cream 5¢ Extra)
CHILD 25¢ EXTRA
Property Unless Checked

Largest Seating Capacity
in New York City

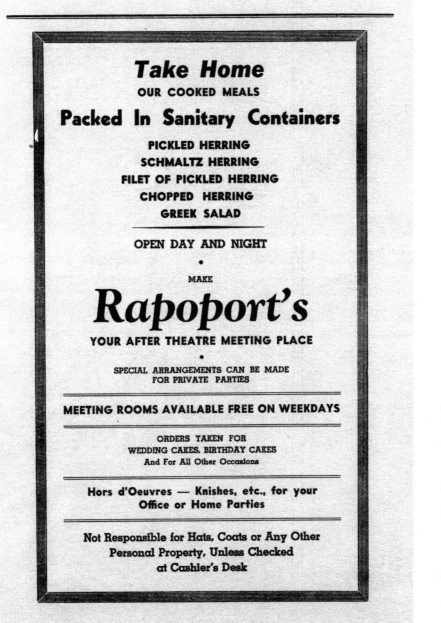

During the Depression, Harry was known as the "Mayor of Second Avenue." He was celebrated for his charity — never turning away a hungry man — and fed three hundred cap makers during a seven-week strike. For a nickel cup of coffee, patrons could eat all the rolls they desired from baskets on each table. According to Rapoport, "the customers were entitled." His wife, Anna, was also active in the management of the restaurant.

A matchbook survives, decorated with drawings of the management: Marv, Harry, Ray, Jack, and Jerry, along with the assurance that they're "Always on hand to serve you." "Never closed. Open day and night. Catering for all occasions. Seating capacity 500." An earlier matchbook exists with a simple goyisher escutcheon design. "Meeting rooms available. Free on Weekdays. Orders taken for wedding cakes, birthday cakes and all other occasions. Private dining rooms available."

The menu offers a set dinner until 9 pm for $1.75 with a choice of entrée, soup, choice of roast (everything from stuffed cabbage to mamaliga with cheese, fish 30 cents extra), choice of dessert, and choice of beverage. A child sharing your plate would cost an extra 25 cents. The tables were set with seeded rolls, chickpeas, radishes, and pickles. The pastry chef produced a famous cheesecake. Notable dishes: Vegetarian Liver Kreplach, 65 cents; Lekvar

Blintzes, 95 cents; Corn pancakes, $1; Sliced Egg with Cream [sour], 85 cents; Kasha Blintzes; Cauliflower cutlet, $1; Noodle Charlotte with Fruit Sauce, 35 cents.

In 1954, Danny Lewis, father of the comedian Jerry Lewis, was dining in Rapoport's "when he overheard a woman say to her husband: 'Sam, I had a dream last night in which you bought me a beautiful new mink coat.' 'When you go to sleep tonight,' replied Sam, 'wear it in good health!'"

Ray, a son of Harry's, worked his way up as a waiter. After a falling-out with his father, Ray and his family moved to Los Angeles. For five weeks he lived with Lenny Bruce — an old customer and friend of his father's — and then he ended up working in a delicatessen and then running his own kosher catering business. A phone call from his ill father brought Ray back to New York City to manage Rapoport's. As the East Village changed, Ray closed the restaurant and opened a new Rapoport's in Forest Hills, Queens. This restaurant found few customers and closed in 1970. At that point, Ray ended up working for his brother Marvin Van Rapoport, who ran the Spindletop Restaurant, a steakhouse in the Broadway area. Van moved in elite social circles, became a noted breeder of show horses, and was briefly married to Meyer Lansky's daughter. Ray finally retired in 1974.

Ratner's Dairy Restaurant, 111 Second Avenue, between 6th and 7th Streets, and earlier locations. This restaurant, and the Ratner's Dairy Restaurant at 138 Delancey Street (see page 448), were the last in a long line of restaurants, owned and operated under various names and at various locations by the Harmatz brothers and their partners in the first half of the twentieth century.

Jacob (Gedale) Harmatz (1884–1966) arrived in New York 1903; his brother Harry L. (Harris) (1871–1945), thirteen years his senior, arrived three years later. They were both born in Galicia, then part of Austria. Census reports them all as Yiddish speakers.

By 1905, Harris. L. Harmatz is listed as operating a small kosher milkhiker restaurant at 165 Stanton Street, near Suffolk Street, with a second branch at 87 Pitt Street near Rivington Street. In 1907 he's operating an eating house at 25 Jefferson Street. In the same year, a Joseph Harmatz (1859–1937), their father(?), is recorded as having an eating house at 147 East Houston.

In 1908, Jacob is operating his own eating house at 41 University Place. It was in business for about two years.

In these early endeavors Jacob's wife, Fannie, and Harry's wife, Rebecca, were involved as bakers and cooks.

An ad in the fall 1910 issue of *Der Yidisher Gazlen:*

"H. L. Harmatz kosher milkhiger restaurant, at 165 Stenton St. near Sofolk Street and at 87 Pitt Street near Rivington Street.

"Our grandfathers tell us that in New York there once existed good restaurants. The usual sort of restaurants are no more and no less than fattening institutes which propose to recruit from the big army of dyspeptics. A good fresh meal one gets only at H. L. Harmatz." A 1909 ad for H. L. Harmatz's restaurant quotes Professor Metchnikoff and Tolstoy's recommendation of a dairy diet.

Alex (Abraham) Ratner was the brother-in-law of Jacob and Harry, having married their half-sister Annie (1880–1954). He was born in Poland (Russia) in 1878 and arrived in New York City in 1889. His family had their own history in the restaurant business. In 1905, Isaac Ratner (a brother) ran an eating house at 26 Bond Street. In 1906 Alex has a restaurant at 80 Chrystie Street. A Harris Ratner has one at 25 Jefferson.

By 1910 Alex has an eating house at 147 East Houston, and moved over the years to 137 and 170 and then by 1917 to 111 Second Avenue.

There's an ad in a 1911 issue of *Naye Leben* for a Ratner's Dairy (the word "dairy" transliterated into Yiddish) Restaurant at 179 East Broadway. Up until 1913, the Harmatz brothers were still operating restaurants under their own names.

In April 1917 the two Harmatz brothers, Jacob and Harry, along with Alex Ratner formed a corporation with $5,000. The Harmatz brothers' restaurant business is henceforth conducted under the name of Ratner's, the name chosen, according to legend, by the toss of a coin. In fact, Ratner's may have already been the more established name. The Harmatz Brothers Bakery opens at 107 Second Avenue (Jacob and Harry are listed

as living upstairs) and Ratner's Dairy Restaurant is next door, at 111. By 1918, Harry L. is the president of Ratner's Dairy Restaurant.

Isidore Harmatz (born 1898, Galicia, Austria–died 1969, New York), a son of Harry L., is also involved in the restaurant business. In 1918, he's the treasurer of the **Avenue Dairy Restaurant** at 93 Second Avenue (the future site of Rapoport's Dairy), and by 1920 he's involved with the Grand Boulevard Bakery and Restaurant at 15 Avenue B.

By 1920, the 111 Second Avenue operation is closed, and the restaurant moved to 107 Second Avenue with apparent branches at 263 Grand Street (formerly Philip Sachs' Bakery and Lunchroom, c. 1910) and 14 Astor Place.

By 1921, H. L. Harmatz is listed as the proprietor of Ratner's Dairy Restaurant. He makes news in the restaurant business. "H. L. Harmatz, proprietor of Ratner's Restaurant, 107 Second Ave., has built and equipped a beautiful new dairy restaurant with a seating capacity of 150 in his own building at 101 Second Ave. on the corner of Sixth St. which was scheduled to be opened about June 1. Mr. Harmatz is a veteran East

103 2nd Avenue 1936

Side restaurateur who has made substantial success in the restaurant business. His genial disposition, unfailing courtesy and sustained reputation for providing good, clean, wholesome food at reasonable prices has endeared him to many permanent friends in the neighborhood. His new restaurant is a fitting testimonial to an unblemished career in the restaurant profession" [*The Restaurant Man*, July 1927]. As there's no record of a Ratner's at 101 Second Avenue, it may have been a typographical error, or an aborted deal.

In 1922, Jacob Harmatz (treasurer) forms a corporation with Max (president) and Louis Zankel (secretary) to pursue a real-estate business and operate a separate Ratner's

Dairy Restaurant, Inc., at 107 Second Avenue (location of the Harmatz Brothers Bakery), with a second branch (headquarters) at 138 Delancey Street (see page 448).

Harry L. and Alex Ratner are not principals in this new partnership. Alex continues to operate a restaurant with Louise Eisenstein at 147 East Houston (a location that figures in the history of Yonah Schimmel's restaurants (see page 463) and then leaves the business to move to Roscoe, California, in 1913, to live there until his death in October of 1935.

In May of 1924, Harry L. Harmatz, now operating on his own, opened a **Self-Service Dairy Cafeteria** at 115 Second Avenue near 7th Street. "A new phenomenon on the East Side! A self-service dairy cafeteria is something never before seen anywhere!" (See ad, page 349.) Harmatz is trading upon the reputation of Ratner's yet not using its name for this new enterprise. It seems to have been a short-lived experiment, and soon returned to being a bakery connected with the restaurant.

Around 1925, Harry L., now under the registered trade name "Ratner's Restaurant" (not Dairy Restaurant), has taken over the 107 Second Avenue space. The Delancey Street Ratner's, Jacob's operation, is not yet listed as a restaurant. That street is being torn up for water and sewer lines and sidewalk vaults. From 1926 through 1928, no Ratner's or Harmatz restaurant appears in public directories.

In 1928, numbers 107 to 113 Second Avenue were demolished to make way for Saul Birn's new six-story building displacing the 107 Ratner operation. By 1930, Ratner's on Delancey is opened (see page 448).

By 1931, Harry L., with the participation of his sons Isidore and Abraham (1908–74), have moved Ratner's Restaurant to 103 Second Avenue at the corner of East 6th Street. They have a ten-year lease and a 6 percent mortgage for $2,000. This was the former site of George Balaznek's restaurant (1915). It was an ornate corner restaurant with illuminated signage and a decorative non-kosher clamshell motif, both inside and out, probably a

remnant of the earlier restaurant. A 1934 menu confirms its exclusive dairy menu, but a purported interior photograph from a later date (unswept floor, large team of uniformed waitresses, and bow-tied countermen) shows a sandwich menu on the wall whose first item appears to be "ham sandwich." The Harmatz and Zankel brothers were involved with non-dairy restaurants: Paramount Cafeteria on Delancey Street by 1930 and, in 1949, Gilmore Cafeteria on Second Avenue, and so it's possible that the "Ratner's" at 103 Second Avenue was at some point a general luncheonette.

By 1935, the 115 Second Avenue space, lately Ratner's Self-Service Dairy Cafeteria, becomes **Ratner's Daylight** [as opposed to the less sanitary cellar-based] **Bake Shop** run by Isidore's wife, Eva. (The space later housed Moishe's Kosher Bake Shop.) A 1935 ad in the *Morgn Frayhayt* offers New Year's wishes and lists the baked goods offered for sale: sponge cake, honey cake, bread, rolls, challah, cookies, and Danish pastries. "When you try our products, you'll first begin to understand what's called truly tasty baked goods."

Abraham becomes a lawyer and the day-to-day operation of the restaurant is handled by his brother Isidore (Irving). Ownership of the Second Avenue Ratner's is shared between Harry L., his sons (Isidore) Irving and Abraham, and his four daughters, Celia, Sadie, Esther, and Rose.

Harry L. dies in 1945. A family death notice mentions his "dear brother Jacob," possibly belying the rumors of animosity between the two branches of the Harmatz family.

Around 1949, the company took over the Stratford Cafeteria at 111 Second Avenue, rechristened it Gilmore Cafeteria, and operated that as well. It was not until May of 1955 that Ratner's Restaurant leased the ground floor of the Saul Birn Building at 111 Second Avenue and left the 103 Second Avenue location. The new restaurant was planned to seat 250 diners and specialize in dairy foods.

In fact, it was smaller (175 seats) than the Delancey Street Ratner's; this restaurant served about 1,000 meals a day. Also open 24 hours, it closed only on Rosh Hashanah, Yom Kippur, and the first two days of Passover. It offered a similar menu to the Delancey Street Ratner's. In the summer it sold 80–100 portions of cold beet borscht and cold schav (sorrel soup). In an average day, 300 cups of coffee and 40 glasses of sour milk were sold. It featured a take-home department and offered catering for all occasions.

Central Plaza, a large ballroom, catering hall, and rehearsal space, was located four floors above Ratner's, and so well-known actors, playwrights, and directors were a common sight. Theodore Bikel recalls rehearsing *There Shall Be No Night,* a TV movie, there. Through the 1950s, the rehearsal spaces were used for TV programs: the *Goodyear-Alcoa Hour, Producer's Showcase, Hall of Fame, Kraft Television Theatre,* and *Frontiers of Faith.* "In one hour, we counted off Nanette Fabray, Edward Mulhare, Charles Boyer, Katharine Cornell . . . lunching on blintzes and borscht." One afternoon, the photographer Saul Leiter, who lived in the neighborhood, looked up from his bowl of mushroom-barley soup to see Laurence Olivier having lunch. In 1962, S. J. Perelman's *The Beauty Part,* starring Bert Lahr, held its rehearsals there. Also in 1962, Harry Kurnitz dined in Ratner's while upstairs José Ferrer and Florence Henderson rehearsed his musical collaboration with Noël Coward, *The Girl Who Came to Supper.* In 1963, the first rehearsal readings of Arthur Miller's *After the Fall, or The Survivor* took place at the Central Plaza. "A tall, ascetic-looking man with horn-rimmed glasses began a first reading of his play to a group of 25 actors as television and radio crews recorded the event" [*New York Times,* October 25, 1963].

When Isidore (Irving) died in 1965, his brother Abraham (1910–74) took over day-to-day operations. During the 1960s, because of its location at the epicenter of alternative youth culture, the Second Avenue Ratner's was the busier of the two "Ratner's."

Ratner's on Second Avenue was an occasional meeting place for lunch of the *Partisan Review* writers. At one lunch in 1946, at the 6th Street corner location, Clement Greenberg, Delmore Schwartz, Will Barrett, and William Phillips confronted Philip Rahv over his "tearing down and playing off" of the contributing writers. Was the dairy restaurant the non-adversarial location at which to have the

"A new phenomenon on the east side! Today! Today! Grand opening of the Self-service Dairy Cafeteria, 115 2nd Ave. near 7th Street. Under the direction of the well-known restaurateur, Henry Harmatz. Henry Harmatz has become virtually the first to bring dairy restaurants on the east side. A self-service dairy cafeteria is wholly new! Never seen before anywhere! One gets there ONLY MILKHIGE FOODS and several times in the day — our fresh home-baked CAKES AND PASTRIES. Don't lose any time! Serve yourself! Such a place was wished for by the neighborhood and will be received with great happiness by most customers who are well acquainted with 'Ratner's Dairy Foods' at 107 2nd Ave. (This is the same manager.) You go in and right away start eating. You take everything you desire, as much as you want and everything is the very best. If you don't want to lose too much time and need a good meal come to SELF-SERVICE DAIRY CAFETERIA. Sample souvenirs at the opening." Ad in the *Forverts,* May 11, 1924

349

confrontation? "Rahv stiffened, turned white, and his hands began to tremble." Their office was at 41 Union Square West. [William Phillips, *A Partisan View* (2004), published posthumously]

Daniel Berrigan recalled that the idea for a faith-based group to resist the Vietnam War, the Catholic Peace Fellowship, was first discussed over borscht and blintzes in Ratner's Dairy Restaurant on the Lower East Side in 1961.

By a historical coincidence, a Loew's movie theater (built in 1926 as the Commodore Theatre for the Meyer & Schneider vaudeville circuit) located next door to their restaurant was converted in 1968 into the Fillmore East concert hall, a New York branch of Bill Graham's San Francisco concert venue and a musical locus of that rare twentieth-century resurgence of the pastoral impulse. The Fillmore's concession stand was stocked with baked goods from Ratner's arranged by the night manager, Sam Jaffee. The 24-hour dairy restaurant was an after-concert breakfast destination.

Long-haired ballad singers and women in peasant skirts enjoyed a largely vegetarian and dairy-based cuisine amid the sanitary stainless-steel and Formica room fixtures of the restaurant. Here 1960s romantics dined in a modern air-conditioned pleasure garden. The baker from the 1950s through the 1970s was Robert Dominick, an African-American.

The musician Frank Zappa recalled having dinner with Leonard Bernstein and some of the members of the band Chicago at Ratner's one evening, possibly June 13 or 14 of 1969, when the two groups shared the bill. Bernstein launched into a rapturous lecture on the origins of gefilte fish and its preparation. His discourse was accompanied by expressive hand gestures worthy of the famous conductor. Zappa confessed that he had been in the dark concerning gefilte fish, but upon tasting it, thought that it was "pretty good."

Abraham Harmatz, who managed the restaurant for forty-five years, was also active in civic affairs (East Side Chamber of Commerce, Stuyvesant Polyclinc, Sons and Daughters of Israel's Institute for the Aged) and served as a trustee for the welfare funds of the Cake Bakers Union and the Countermans Union. He died on May 29, 1974, at the age of sixty-six — one day after the restaurant closed for business.

New York Times ad, June 20, 1955

Schickler's Dairy Luncheonette, 207 East Broadway.

An August 11, 1959, newspaper account of the robbery and murder of Philip Schickler, aged sixty-five: "Mr. Schickler, who lived above his restaurant, got up at 3 am to prepare coffee and bagels. At 4:30 am holdup men entered and demanded cash from the register. The amount was not enough and they followed him to the rear of the store where they kicked, cut and shot him. Witnesses say attackers were Puerto Ricans. Puerto Ricans began to move into the neighborhood six years ago." In the 1940s this space was occupied by **Borden's Dairy Luncheonette.**

Seward Kosher Dairy Restaurant, 11 Essex Street.

Visible in several photos from 1935–40. One of four small stores flanking a central entrance stairway, the restaurant was entered by descending several steps below the grade of the sidewalk. A barbershop operated just above the restaurant. A sign hung from the facade of the building and three well-fed people stood outside the restaurant. Its namesake, Seward Park, is across the street.

M. Gordon's Bakery and Vegetarian Restaurant, 145 Clinton Street between Broome and Grand Streets.

An ad in the *Forverts* from 1928 announced the opening of this new "modern and up-to-date" restaurant.

Wolsk and Priluk, proprietors of the **Plaza Bakery and Dairy Restaurant,** at 149 Delancey Street, corner of Suffolk, took an ad in the *Forverts* on January 12, 1922, to thank their customers for supporting their new restaurant and guarantee to continue their reputation for good food at reasonable prices.

Jacob Miller's Vegetarian Eating Place, 80 Attorney Street, in 1927 operated out of a second-story space just off Delancey. Extensive signage beckoned English-language readers. We can imagine the place infused with tobacco smoke from the cigar store below.

Thau's Brothers Dairy Restaurant was in 1925 situated at 43 Second Avenue and by 1934 moved to a location between Rapoport's and Ratner's, still on Second Avenue, between 5th and 6th Streets. By 1948, it's now called Thau's Restaurant and Bakery at 59 Second Avenue between 3rd and 4th Streets. A September 1951 ad announced its renovation into a modern, air-conditioned restaurant, now located at 59 Second Avenue between 3rd and 4th Street opposite the Public Theatre (later the Anderson Theatre), and mentioned that its fame was, in part, due to its onion rolls. The restaurant was managed by brothers Sam, Max, and Dave Thau. In December of 1955, Sam, age fifty-four, mysteriously disappeared. Waiter Max Riner "said he had seen Thau talking to 'hoodlums' shortly before he vanished." They visited his bachelor apartment but found nothing amiss. It was assumed that this reputedly wealthy restaurateur had been kidnapped, and the brothers offered a $1,000 reward. A few weeks later, his dead body was discovered at the Bellevue Hospital morgue, where it had been brought several weeks earlier without

80
Attorney St.
off Delancey

identifying papers. Thau had died of natural causes while attending a show at the Lyric Theatre at 213 West 42nd Street.

A 1929 photograph by Percy Loomis Sperr shows a disproportionately large electric sign for **Vogel's Vegetarian & Dairy Restaurant** on Grand Street near Forsyth Street — a small storefront wedged between Zinn's Fur Shop and the Grand Street Theater (255 Grand Street). In 1929, Abraham Vogel (born 1905, Poland-Austria – died?) lost his restaurant through debt. In 1930, the Grand Street Theater and the entire block upon which it stood was demolished.

"**Bakery and Kosher Milkhiger Restaurant** (formerly Yonah Shimel's), 44 Avenue B. Bet. 3rd and 4th Streets. Famous with their tasty milkhiger foods, be it known that its opening will be Sat. 18 December 1920. Upon universal public demand we will bake — the tasty knishes which are baked — with the best butter fresh every 5 minutes. **Kohen and Harmatz,** proprietors" [ad in *Forverts,* December 18, 1920]. (See Yonah Shim(m)el, page 463, and Harris L. Harmatz, page 342.)

L & W Vegetarian and Dairy Restaurant,
300 Grand Street.
A 1931 ad in the *Forverts* announces "large Hall to Rent, also pretty meeting room."

Adler and Barondes Dairy Restaurant, 216 East Houston Street. The two well-known restaurateurs announced their grand opening on a Saturday morning in July of 1919. This "first-class" restaurant featured its own bakery and "the finest tastiest dairy dishes like your mama used to make for you."

The opening of the **Cooperative Restaurant** at 201 Second Avenue was announced in August of 1921. It took over the space of the popular Strunski's Cafe-Restaurant — expanded and beautified. Besides their regular menu, they added a "lavish choices of milchige foods, lunches and a la carte, etc."

This was a restaurant that also offered meat from the own cooperative butcher with no mention of separation from dairy dishes. "Our prices are moderate while this is a restaurant for

Ad for Thau's Dairy Restaurant,
Forverts, September 1, 1951

the worker — not for profit! Our place is open from 7 in the morning until after one at night." By 1935 this became the **Second Avenue Bakery, Vegetarian Dairy and Lunch Bar,** managed by Brekher and Liev.

Malich's Dairy Restaurant,

338 Grand at Suffolk Street and 124 Delancey, opened 1932.

Julius Malich, a nattily attired portly fellow, was a prominent restaurateur on the East Side. In 1901 his name was associated with Meylach and Marcus' Cafe and Restaurant at 28 Grand Street, and 1915 with Malich & Reines, a restaurant at 151 Canal. He was the vice president of the East Side Chamber of Commerce in the late 1920s while operating a restaurant at 388 Grand Street. Mottoes for Malich's Dairy included "Where Every Dish Serves a Wish," "Where Hundreds Eat," and "Where Fastidious People Dine Inexpensively."

In 1933, unemployed waiters were defrauded of payments made under the pretense of securing them jobs at, among other places, Malich's Delancey Street establishment. "It was charged that the business . . . afforded work for only six or seven waiters, but that as many as thirty had been employed. The earnings of none of them amounted to more than $8.50 weekly, out of which, they said, they had to pay $5 to some of those in the conspiracy. . . . Malich, 42 . . . accused of having worked with union officials in the job racket through go-betweens, was arraigned on a charge of extortion." One of the defrauded waiters, Benny Glast, arrived at a meeting of the Waiters' Local 1 and shot two of the business agents. According to Glast's lawyer, Malich took on about twenty men who were "absolutely down and out" demanding the fee "with the understanding that they would pay the rest in installments [*New York Times,* January 20, 1933]. (See Big 3 Vegetarian & Dairy Restaurant, page 382.) Malich was eventually acquitted and set free after most of the witnesses changed their stories or disappeared. Glast served a term in Sing Sing.

Vegetarian Restaurant, 99 Second Avenue, between 5th and 6th Streets. An announcement for its opening in October of 1921 in *Der Morgn Zhurnal* proclaims, "A new home for Vegetarians!"

In February of 1920, "the famous Gruber, the expert dairy and lunchroom man," announced the opening of a branch of Ratner's of 263 Grand Street, in a "large beautiful store" at 41 Canal Street near Ludlow, simply called **Dairy and Restaurant.** Three experts in the "line," Mr. Gruber and his partners Mr. Blum and Mr. Sam Lider, all of whom had lunchrooms on the East Side, are now managers in this new enterprise. "They need no introduction, they have already convinced the public in New York. . . . They are certain that in their new lunch room . . . will the public find all that's best in cleanliness, good, punctual service, modern sanitary improvements and also strictly kosher." Their motto: "The largest guarantee of milchige, pareve and vegetarian dishes, tasty and cleanly served, best coffee and cake, popular prices." Their "sanitary day-light: bakery" under the direction of the "eminent expert Mr. Blum, formerly of the **G & G Lunch Room** [see page 358], uses the best butter and eggs." Curiously, no mention is made of Mr. Harmatz, the owner of Ratner's, even though this is described as a branch of Ratner's. The famous "Gruber" was most likely Max, owner of several eating houses in partnership with the Gruber brothers, Joseph and Samuel, on Grand Street and other locations on the East Side.

In 1927, Eddie Silverberg took over Sobel's Restaurant at 701 Broadway near West 4th Street and renamed it the **Mayfair Vegetarian and Dining Restaurant.**

Melrose Dairy & Vegetarian Restaurant, 316 Grand Street, corner of Allen, in operation from the 1920s to 1939, exists now only as a matchbook ("Try our delicious sandwiches") and a listing in various telephone directories. Another branch existed at 111 Avenue C in the 1940s.

Meybakh's Dairy Restaurant,

751 Broadway, near 8th Street. An ad in *Der Morgn Zhurnal,* February 1919: "Is now open for business. The best fresh foods served at moderate prices. All that we bake, cook, and fry is with the best fresh butter. Careful observers of dietary laws and cleanliness will by us be satisfied. Closed shabbos and holidays." (See ad at left.)

"Meybakh's magnificent strictly kosher milkhiger restaurant, 751 Broadway." Ad in *Der Morgn Zhurnal,* 1919

On Grand Street, near the Bowery, in 1932, two dairy restaurants stood on a single block. **The G & R Dairy Lunch,** a narrow storefront with hanging sign, bedecked with red, white, and blue bunting, and two stores away (Goldberger Trusses and then an unidentifiable industrial supply company) **Supreme Health Food Lunch Dairy Restaurant** also bedecked with red, white, and blue bunting. A double grand opening or a patriotic holiday? The same block also houses a small coffee shop (the Coffee Pot) and a malted-milk stand. The rich variety of eating places on this one block is a sad reminder of the homogenization, and corporatization, of businesses on New York's streets and the deadly boredom it creates.

Louis Driks Milkhiger Restaurant at 175 Rivington Street. A 1921 ad asks: "Friend where do you eat? This is a very important question. The answer is simple. Eat at Driks Milkhiger Restaurant. Which is now under the personal management of your old, well-known friend Louis Driks. A branch at 147 East Houston St." (This was the early location of Alex Ratner's restaurant and S[c]himel's Milkhiger Restaurant; see page 463.) Driks (born 1889, Austria-Hungary–died 1964, Brooklyn, New York) was a longtime New York waiter and then restaurateur with an eating house at 185 Rivington Street as far back as 1912.

Hyman Kotlitzki and his partners fell prey to the craze among restaurateurs in the 1920s for oversized hanging signage. Alongside their bakery, Kotlitzki's Champagne Biscuit Co., hung a large illuminated sign. The business was also listed as **Kotlitzki's Warschauer Conditorei, Inc.,** of 122 Essex Street — a combination bakery and dairy restaurant. In 1916, Mr. Kotlitzki, self-described as a subject of the tsar of Russia, patented a "new, original" pastry form. It was a mold for a slender, tapering rectangular wine biscuit that would impress the image of a champagne

DESIGN.

H. KOTLITZKI.

PASTRY FORM.

APPLICATION FILED JAN. 12, 1916.

48,903.

Patented Apr. 18, 1916.

Hyman Kotlitzki
Inventor

By his Attorney

flute on each biscuit. The bakery originated in Warsaw in 1898 and by 1928 had a branch in Berlin, six in New York, and one at 3534 Lawrence Avenue in Chicago. "Their cheese cakes are justly famous and the delicious wine biscuits defy description. . . . They specialize in catering for birthdays, bar mitzvahs, weddings and all social functions." The Chicago branch offered table service all day and remained open until 1 am.

Mrs. Rogin Vegetarian Restaurant in 1927 operated at 249 East 13th Street and advertised and offered May Day greetings in the *Daily Worker.* Proprietors, Mrs. Rogin and Markoff.

The Public Art Dairy Restaurant, 75 Second Avenue, opposite the Public Theatre advertised in the *Daily Worker* of the late 1920s. Later, the **Eatwell Vegetarian & Dairy Restaurant,** 78 (75?) Second Avenue in 1925.

An ad in the *Der Morgn Zhurnal* on February 4, 1919, announces the opening of a new **Bakery and Milkhiger Restaurant** by Goodman and Goldman at 138 Delancey Street, owners of **G & G** at 300 Grand Street. "Souvenirs will be given the whole day from 11 in the morning til 10 at night." What the souvenirs were can only be imagined. See Goldman's Dairy Restaurant, Bronx (page 404).

Sometime around 1906 until 1910, **Harris Rosenzweig's Kosher Milkhiger Restaurant** operated at 186 Delancey Street. An ornately painted window announced prices.

Rational Vegetarian Restaurant,

199 Second Avenue, near 13th Street, offering "strictly vegetarian dishes," was a steady advertiser in the Yiddish-language Communist daily the *Morgn Frayhayt* in the late 1920s.

Avenue Dairy Restaurant,

93 Second Avenue, opened in 1918 by David Gottlieb. A second branch, at 21 Second Avenue, opened in 1924 in partnership between Gottlieb and Rapoport "with one policy: Best and freshest foods, friendly treatment, satisfying prices and a homey atmosphere." In 1925 the name changes to **Gottlieb & Rapoport.** Both restaurateurs went on to run their own restaurants.

Gottlieb's Avenue Dairy

Restaurant, 21 Second Avenue, above First Street. Sometime after 1925, partnership with Rapoport ends and David Gottlieb continues under his own name. A matchbook proclaims, "All Baking Done by Daylight on Premises."

Pell's Bakery and Dairy

Restaurant, 11 East Broadway. In operation 1927–31. Max Pell (born 1893, Lomza, Poland– died ?) arrived in New York in 1911 with his wife, Clara. This bakery-restaurant is in operation by 1925; by 1948 it moves to 19 East Broadway.

Ad for the Rational Vegetarian Restaurant in the *Morgn Frayhayt,* 1929

Stuyvesant Dairy Lunch Bar c. 1915

Grove Dairy and Vegetarian Restaurant, 294 Grand Street. Ads in the *Forverts* from 1930: "Meet with your friends in Grove Vegetarian Restaurant. You'll have pleasure from our foods all year."

Weiner's Private Kosher Restaurant & Dairy Lunch Room, 27 St. Marks Place. Between 1915 and 1917, Max Weiner's restaurant operated in a still-standing small storefront that once flanked a central stairway entrance to number 27. The window lettering, all in English except for the tiny word "kosher," beckons a wide range of customers: those attracted to the city's popular "dairy lunchrooms," Jews concerned with dietary observance, and, with the phrase "Tables for Ladies," women seeking a basic level of refinement and cleanliness. A basement store, just below, deals in ice, coal, and wood.

Stuyvesant Dairy Lunch Bar, 156 Second Avenue. Despite its prominent corner location in the Yiddish theater district from at least 1915, there's little information about this restaurant. A photo from 1934 shows a dark enamel facade and a flashy hanging electric sign. Awnings shade the front window filled with baked goods. By 1939, the space is occupied by **Katz's Dairy Restaurant.** In 1928 a **Stuyvesant Dairy Lunch** is operating at 246 Grand Street, former location of Joseph and Max Gruber's eating house around 1912.

Vegetarian & Dairy Restaurant at 436 Broome Street. Operated in the 1930s by Nathan Stark, later participant in the Big 3 Vegetarian & Dairy Restaurant (see page 382).

In the 1940s **Hirsch's Dairy & Vegetarian Restaurant** operated two branches: 76 Clinton, corner of Rivington, and 14 Avenue B, corner of East 2nd Street. From photographic evidence both seem to have been lively enterprises.

"Astonishing news! A new milkhiger restaurant, under the name **Eatmor Dairy Restaurant.** 84 Nassau St. bet. Fulton and John St. For the convenience of those who have their business or work in the neighborhood" [ad in *Yidishes Tageblat,* June 25, 1919]. And a year later: "Today will open a new milkhiger restaurant in 4 Bond Street near Broadway. Under the supervision of the well-known restaurateurs **Parnes and Fayfer**" [ad in *Yidishes Tageblat,* October 7, 1920]. Their motto: "If you prefer to NOURISH your stomach rather than FEED it." The same partners opened another branch at 139 East Houston Street in 1921,

Ad for Eatmor Dairy Restaurant, *Yidishes Tageblat,* June 25, 1919

emphasizing its "kosher" food. In 1925, another Eatmor Dairy Lunch, operated by Lillian Feifer, existed at 84 Nassau Street. (For its possible connection with Feifer's Dairy, see page 324.)

Max Parnes ran a number of restaurants under his name: at 343 East Houston in 1912; at 116 Rivington from 1913 to 1918; at 4 Bond and 26 Clinton in 1922. It's not clear if any before the Bond Street location were dairies. After working as a waiter, **Morris Parnes** opened a restaurant at 161 Stanton in 1922. By 1928 its name became the **Stanton Dairy Restaurant.** (Also see Parnes Dairy Restaurant, page 377.) An Osias (Oscar) Parnes ran an eating house at 1919 Third Avenue in Harlem as early as 1910. A fuller history of the Parnes family remains to be written.

In a series of ads in *Der Tog* in 1916, the restaurateur Max Green, of **Max Green's Knishery** (est. c. 1903) of 150 Rivington Street, announced the commencement of a "knish war" on Rivington Street. The text of one illustrated ad (reproduced on the facing page) describes the cause of the war and his tactical response.

A War in Rivington Street
But instead of howitzers the weapons are knishes.

For the last 13 years Max Green has been known as the Master Baker not only at 50 Rivington Street but also in all of New York. The older he gets the more experiments he has made in his industry. Four years ago he introduced the latest favorite dish, "knishes." Since then many others have imitated him, and because he didn't apply for any patents on them in Washington, he couldn't stop them from also selling knishes. Therefore, he exerted much energy and spent much money preparing his knishes to make sure that the customer that eats them once will always remember the taste. This method works better than all the patents.

And so his business at 150 Rivington Street began to grow ever larger. This attracted the attention of others who were very envious of Max Green of 150 Rivington Street and the competition began, even on the same block. To steal customers from Max Green, the rivals moved in next door.

Max Green was already deeply invested in his business and is also known by everyone outside his business as a true friend and good neighbor. And just as no one can beat him in his dairy dishes, neither in their tastiness, nor in cleanliness, and also not in price and in business dealings, no one will be able to beat him in the field of entertainment, either.

Max Green recently hired an orchestra and every evening they play the finest music and latest hits. And his architect is currently drawing up plans to prepare a regular stage and as quickly as the carpenters can finish with the work, there will be a regular concert every evening.

362

Max Green says that it won't take long before other celebrities from up-town will begin arriving in their automobiles to his store on Rivington Street to eat his knishes. A sign that he is right appears in the columns of the "New York World," "The Morning Times," and other English newspapers, who wrote early Thursday about the business of Max Green of 150 Rivington Street.

Green, a Yiddish-speaking Austrian Jew, was born in 1878 and arrived in New York in 1899. By 1917 he was operating two restaurants: the knishery at 150 Rivington and another restaurant at 96 Forsyth Street. His wife, Mary, two daughters, and a "servant," Rosie Korn, may have helped him in these businesses.

News of the "knish war" was humorously reported in the *New York Times* of January 27, 1916. Green may have popularized an improved version of the knish ("mashed potatoes with onions and a sprinkling of cheese, all wrapped up in baked dough, like an apple dumpling"), but he was hardly its inventor. The competitor M. London (the famous matzo king and uncle of the famous socialist congressman of the same name, who had died in November of 1915, but the business was apparently carried on in his name) had opened up a rival **United Knish Factory** across the street from Max Green, at 155 Rivington Street. A price war followed: Green lowered his price from 5¢ to 3¢. London matched him and introduced a cabaret show. Green retaliated by hiring a German band to provide entertainment and then began giving out gift coupons. One customer ate twenty knishes to collect enough coupons for a pocket knife and had to be carried from the premises. As of January 1916, the war raged on.

By 1920, these restaurants had disappeared and Green, as president,

along with Oscar Arnold, vice president, had moved out of the war zone and opened two branches of the Central Lunch Co. Inc., at 543 and 833 Broadway, toward Union Square — apparently a regular luncheonette. By 1927, these businesses are gone.

Abraham and Gussie Schwebel operated **Schwebel's Kosher Dairy Restaurant** at 191 East Houston from at least 1910, possibly earlier.

A 1945 article carried by the United Press described the career of Gussie Schwebel and marked the closing of her restaurant. Forgetting the East Side knish wars of the early 1900s, she maintained that food, and knishes in particular, was the way to international peace. Her potato-onion knishes were made in the form of a tube, wrapped in a coil for baking.

A native of Borislav, then in the Austrian Empire, she claimed to have opened her restaurant at 191 East Houston Street in 1900 and over the years had Eleanor Roosevelt, Leon Trotsky, Enrico Caruso, and Theodore Roosevelt as steady customers. Abraham, her husband, was written out of this history. Her future plans were to manufacture knishes, "baked in jars," on an industrial scale.

A *New York Tribune* article from August 1919 describes the architecture of the knish as "flat and round, about six inches in diameter and one inch in thickness. It is made of common dough and its interior is composed of buckwheat, cheese or potatoes. When ready for the oven it is baked in oil or butter."

155 Rivington St.
1940

191 East Houston St.
1940

In these same years Yonah Shimel was involved in a knish war of his own (see page 463).

A 1934 photo reveals a bit of the sign and facade of **Sadie Hyman's Kosher Dairy Restaurant** at 212 Broome Street. She was born in Poland in 1887 and was the widow of Sam Hyman, who operated an earlier restaurant at 145 West 30th Street.

A 1915 ad in *Unzer Gezunt* reads, "H[arriet] Littauer, proprietor, **The Tolstoyaner Vegetarian Restaurant** of 28 Second Avenue and now 55 Second Avenue. The best vegetarian food in the state of New York." A reporter for the *New York Tribune* counted four vegetarian restaurants on the East Side in August 1919, and claimed that they were all started by Russian

86 Willet St.
off Delancey.
1928

365

163 East Broadway; c.1930
before widening of Rutgers St.

refugees who were disciples of Tolstoy. In 1900, Tolstoy's name was also attached to a brand of cigarette.

In *Rational Living,* a successor to *Unzer Gezunt,* in January 1917, we learn that: **"Zilberfarb and Topilovski's Vegetarian Restaurant,** 68 Second Ave. is one of the cleanest and most comfortable eating places. Clean and healthy foods of our time."

Fischer's Dairy Lunch, 165 East Broadway. Operated by brothers Alex, Louis, and Rubin Fischer and Rubin Himmelstein from 1919 to 1930 when the building was demolished for the widening of Rutgers Street. The new corner location was eventually occupied by the Garden Cafeteria Dairy Restaurant (see page 439). In the early 1900s, the Fischer brothers (Louis and Alex) operated a bakery at 34 Canal Street, a space previously occupied, c.1889, by S & P Shinkmann Cafe and Ice-Cream Salon.

G & G (Z?) Bakery and Dairy Restaurant, 86 Willett Street. Another bakery expanded into an eating place appears in a 1928 photo.

Ad for Benjamin Sazer's Vegetarian Restaurant, *Unzer Gezunt*, 1915

A small ad in *Unzer Gezunt* of 1915 reads: "Ask anyone. Which is the best and cleanest Vegetarian Restaurant? The answer will be: **B[enjamin] Sazer's,** at 67 Second Avenue, corner 4th St. The first vegetarian restaurant in the East Side. Filtered water to drink with food." Benjamin Sazer (born in Russia, 1888) was a seminal figure in the Jewish vegetarian restaurant business. In 1911 his **Vegetarian and Milkhiger Restaurant** was at 273 East Broadway. A small ad in *Dos Naye Land* offers "An intellectual fellowship to play chess" as well as healthy food at modest prices. (See H. Sazar's Health Inn, page 395.)

A sign for **Strulovich's Kosher Dairy Restaurant and Knish Bakery** at 80 Rivington Street appears in a 1912 photo by Lewis W. Hine of the Lower East Side. It's an example of the transformation of a bakery into a dairy eating place.

M. Nimetz, 189 East Broadway, corner of Jefferson Street. "The well-known restaurant of 232 East Broadway which provided students of Yeshiva Rabbi Yitskhok Elchanan with fine kosher foods, has opened yet a new larger milkhiger restaurant with its own bakery" [opening announcement June 3, 1920, in *Der Morgn Zhurnal*]. By 1925 it became a partnership, Nimetz & Kaplansky, and, in that year, placed a congratulatory announcement in the Teachers Institute for Men yearbook.

Orange Dairy Luncheonette, at 65 Canal Street, appears in a 1931 photo. The narrow storefront offers a glimpse of old-style wooden fixtures. The front window reads "Best Dairy Luncheonette." Signs on the adjoining stores announce: "Final Sale! Building coming down!" to make room for the widening of Allen Street. The name goes back to a 1925 directory listing.

65 Canal St.
1931

Di Yunge

Jews did not readily fit into the so-called bohemian culture of 1850s New York.
In the mind of the American bohemians who drank at Pfaff's saloon on lower
Broadway, the Jews were too interested in money and material things. By the
1880s the Lower East Side cafes were not part of that bohemian scene because
"[Jews] were too passionate and belligerent about the gentle problems of
politics, literature and life. 'They lack the repose and balance which is an
essential of the true Bohemian.'" [Albert Parry, *Garrets and Pretenders: A
History of Bohemianism in America*]

     Through the first decades of the twentieth century, shared passions and the physical proximity of neighborhoods allowed for first- and second-generation Jews to participate in the radical culture of Greenwich Village. Names in Yiddish avant-garde theater, publishing, lectures, cartooning, and socializing turn up on both sides of the language divide. For writers and poets who were dedicated to working in Yiddish the crossover to the larger English-language audience was difficult, if not impossible.

A group of European-born poets and writers — Zishe Landau, Mani Leib, Moyshe-Leyb Halpern, Lamed Shapiro, David Ignatoff, David Kazanski, and others — for some time, during the early years of the twentieth century, had their center of artistic operations in a basement dairy restaurant at 183 East Broadway called Levin & Goodman Milkhiger Restaurant. Known as "Di Yunge" (The Youngsters), they espoused and practiced a form of literary aestheticism. They are considered the first Yiddish-language poetic movement in America.

In her study of this group, Ruth R. Wisse explains that for them "aestheticism, the acceptance of artistic beauty as a fundamental, self-referring standard independent of social, ethical, or national value, was a challenge, not so much to traditional Judaism which opposed all secular art, but to the expectations of newly emancipated Jews who turned to literature for an elucidation of ethical and social problems, for a new kind of guide to the perplexed. By insisting on sensibility rather than social conscience as the ultimate arbiter of value, the Yiddish aesthete appeared to be defying his culture entirely, opposing not merely halakhic Judaisim, but even the secular transposition of Jewish values, as in 'Yiddishkayt.'" [Ruth R. Wisse, "Di Yunge and the Problem of Jewish Aestheticism," *Jewish Social Studies,* 38, nos. 3-4 (Summer/Fall 1976)]

In his reminiscence "With Zishe Landau," Reuben Iceland sums up their aesthetic position: "When we arrived, Yiddish poetry was in the service of ideas and movements, social and national. The poets stood tall, took an honored place. But the poetry was, as always in such circumstances, dead and buried. We proclaimed its freedom and its right to an independent life. We maintained that poetry should not exist by reason of whatever idea it promotes, but because it lives for its own sake. It has its own place and its own function in life. . . . In order to properly express intimate, lyrical feelings, we realized we must do two things: on the one hand search within ourselves for understanding so that we could better comprehend the world, and on the other hand clean out all the garbage, all the absurd words that immature little poets and half-baked newspaper writers had gathered in various alien places, and from which had spread that florid gushing that passed for poetry." [Reuben Iceland, "With Zishe Landau," trans. Gerald Marcus, *Pakn Treger,* no. 62, 2010]

They felt they had no Yiddish literary traditions to build on. Instead of employing a "poetic" Germanized Yiddish, they sought an intimate, authentic Yiddish in satirical writing, in the humorous speech of low characters

in popular trashy novels, and in folk songs and Hasidic legends. They made a fetish of stillness, softness, silence, and patience. Their poems are suffused with a gentle melancholy.

> A poem is such, when you
> First touch it with your finger,
> If something strange is there,
> You prick your finger.

[Excerpt from "A Lid" by Zishe Landau, trans. Hyala Laundau Bass]

Di Yunge poets came from the working class: "Mani Leib, a shoemaker; Reuben Iceland and David Ignatoff, occasional frame-makers in small millinery factories; Zishe Landau, a house painter; Joseph Rolnick, a newsvendor; H. Leivick, a paperhanger; Isaac Raboy, a worker in fur pelts; Moyshe-Leyb Halpern, a sometime waiter and presser." Landau was a chef, a gourmet, and, although often poor, a great frequenter of Japanese and Chinese restaurants. Many fled to America between 1902 and 1913 as young men because of their involvement in revolutionary activity. They read in other languages and translated widely from German, Russian, and French. They were influenced by late-nineteenth-century Russian poets and early symbolists. Yet it's unlikely that they'd have felt at home in the Polish literary mleczanie of Warsaw.

"Probably in no artistic group did aestheticism seem as anomalous as among the Yiddish poets in New York. . . . They were neither aristocrats nor bohemians, the two categories at either end of the social scale equally distant from the 'common man' and equally receptive to exclusivist ideals." [Wisse, "Di Yunge and the Problem of Jewish Aestheticism"]

Reuben Iceland's story "At Goodman and Levine's," of 1954, describes an evening in that basement dairy restaurant at 183 East Broadway. The basement location housed a previous dairy restaurant, Fayfer's Milkhiger Restaurant, in 1910. During 1912, A. Feifer moved to 22 Rutgers Street and the space was taken by Kolodny & Levin's Milkhiger Restaurant; by August of 1912 the partnership became Levin and Greenberg's Milkhiger Restaurant. Only by the fall of 1913 does the Levin & Goodman partnership take over the space, inadvertently memorialized through small display ads in the Yiddish press, but no longer specifically identifed as a dairy restaurant. In the story, the order of the names may have been switched due to an unconscious right-to-left reading of the English-language signage, or to establish a fictional distance; the space's long-standing dairy associations were retained.

There, one was met with "a smell of roast herring and cooked fish, sour borscht, fried pancakes, bad coffee and scalded milk." The young poets of New York passed through this restaurant to discuss literary ideas or recite a new poem. Iceland claims it was "not because, God forbid, they had such a fondness for dairy dishes, but because it was the center of Di Yunge."

According to the story, the relatively more successful Yiddish writers congregated at Herrick's Cafe on Division Street, later known as Sholom's. This was the literary world known to the general reading public.

According to Iceland, the poets of Di Yunge congregated at Goodman & Levin's for two reasons:

The popular Division Street coffee house was too expensive for them. At the basement dairy restaurant, one could sit over a cup of coffee, a cookie or roll for five cents.

"The other reason was snobbishness." The young poets did not want to pass time in the company of their elders. Establishing Goodman & Levin's as their own center was a way of separating themselves aesthetically and socially from the old guard. They published in their own journals and drank coffee in their own cafe.

In the winter of 1915, Goodman & Levin's days were numbered. *Der Tog* (*The Day*), a Yiddish newspaper, was about to move from Pearl Street to the building on East Broadway housing Goodman & Levin's, forcing it to close.

One evening that winter, the disciple of a famous Yiddish poet came down the stairs and announced to the gathered poets that a banquet was being held at Lamed Shapiro's Restaurant on East Broadway near Rutgers Street and all were invited. The famous poet was throwing a banquet in his own honor.

The group refused to leave their basement cafe and honor the famous poet with their presence.

A number of other emissaries of the famous poet came to invite them, and in time, only one of Di Yunge dared to leave. Their stubbornness verged on foolishness but of a heroic nature.

Their devotion to Goodman & Levin's was not repaid by the owners. They took up four or five tables and bought little food. These poor poets should relinquish their tables to more respectable customers.

"Hours flew. Night fell: no one noticed. Half the crowd had vanished; yet we sat — talking. Goodman, at the buffet, sent sharp and contemptuous glances. Not seeing him or his eyes
we continued the

די צאהל פון חתנות איז בעדייטענד
פערקלענערט געװארען, זײט

לעװין און גודמאן

האָבען געעפענט זײער
ר ע ס ט א ר א נ ט

אױף 183 איסט בראָדװײ, נ. י.

װײל דאָרט קריגט איהר אַזעלכע פרישע,
הײמיש־געשמאַקע שפּײיזען — און דער־
צו פאַר אַזאַ בילינע פּרײז, װעלכע איז
אומעגליך בײ זיך אין דערײם צו האָבען

discussion. Finally, Goodman exclaimed, 'Even in Hell there is a time when they rest. Go in good health!' But it sounded like — Go to the devil!"

Smells of frying from the kitchen door assaulted them. In summer it was unbearably hot. In winter, cold. "The food — as in most East Side eating places of the time — was barely endurable. The coffee simply horrible."

Yet, the poets of Di Yunge clung to this gathering place, often missing days of work. "It drew us like a magnet."

The story describes the deep social and aesthetic meanings with which eating places on the East Side were imbued. Iceland maintains that the poets were not based at Goodman & Levin's for its dairy cuisine. But to believe that Di Yunge chose a dairy restaurant for their "center" just because of the price of its coffee, in a neighborhood filled with hundreds of cheap cafes and restaurants, is to underestimate the lure of this particular dairy restaurant. The milekhdike quality of place put it on the edge of bourgeois cultural importance; its basement location further removed it from the path of the upwardly mobile. It was the fitting locale for ruminations on introspective poetry and authentic life. Their aesthetic program was a reflection of the milekhdike personality. These young men were barely able to operate in the workaday world; they chose to remain on the proverbial "milekhdiker bank." The history of Lamed Shapiro's failed efforts in the restaurant business in Chicago and NYC reflect the conflict of a committed communist trying to run a business. And what was a likelihood that even a "successful" Yiddish poet would be able to pay the bill for his own banquet?

Iceland: "The prophet is a monotheist, the artist is a polytheist. They are alike in that both seek ultimate realization in life — the prophet in a single truth, the artist in various truths, one of which may happen to be the prophet's."

Wisse explains Iceland's feelings: "When the Jews became monotheists they became the enemies of all art. They have profaned the creativity of their forefathers by failing to recognize Shir Hashirim for the perfect poem it is, and by reducing it to mere allegorical pretext. Until Jews learn that a word of a poem is no more than itself, they will never have any understanding of poetry."

Iceland describes Jews wandering through the natural splendor of

Yaddo Park in Saratoga Springs after having taken the cure. They see the splendor but feel that something is lacking. What useful purpose does it serve — to house an orphanage or TB sanatorium? "The beautiful has no value unless it brings some use, not to themselves, but to society at large, to all humanity, or at the very least, to the Jews." He calls this "a reyn yidishlekher kuk, a purely Jewish point of view, and bemoans the fact that since the war the whole world has been Judaized!" The bourgeois philistines and the proletarian ideologues are in agreement that beauty is valueless unless is it made to serve some material function. Iceland pleads for "the poet who does not want to change the world, only to express his vision of it."

As long as they worked in Yiddish, they felt they were enriching Jewish literature. "The power of language over content, the degree to which linguistic resonance dominates and shapes all aesthetic considerations, raises serious doubts about the possibilities of Jewish literature in a non-Jewish language. . . ." [Wisse, "Di Yunge and the Problem of Jewish Aestheticism"]

As already observed, saying the name of a dairy dish in Yiddish changes its taste. Did the dairy restaurant offer them a kind of food-for-food's-sake, as opposed to a meat menu to fuel appetitive action in the world? A diet of coffee and scant dairy fare to provide just enough energy to accomplish its own consumption?

According to Landau, "The prophet, the preacher, the politician have distant goals; distant and often obscure. . . . Only we, the aesthetes, have no goals and no purposes. . . . The tree blooms — the tree is beautiful. . . . Everything that is here is beautiful; and because it is here. This is the truth known to all who live with their senses." He strove to liberate poetry from what he called "the rhyme department of the labor movement."

Unzer Shrift, a 1912 Latinized Yiddish journal of literature and art featuring several members of Di Yunge, carried a small ad for **Faifer's Milxigen Restoran** — "Those who want to have a good healthy stomach, should come to eat in Faifer's Milxigen Restoran. The best, freshest dairy food. A. Faifer, 183 East Broadway, New York."

In 1922, after World War I and the victory of communism in Russia, several former Yunge turned to the *Morgn Frayhayt,* the Yiddish-language communist newspaper, as an outlet for their return to realism and a public art.

Dairy Restaurants Around Union Square

This second historical locus of dairy restaurants was developed in a burst of activity by Polish and Russian building contractors in the early years of the twentieth century. It was home to the first department stores, a Millinery Row, theaters, a used-book district, and the site of radical political activity. By 1930, the cultural life of the East Side shifted toward 14th Street.

Hammer's Dairy Restaurant at 243 East 14th Street, near Second Avenue, was an unpretentious storefront that operated for almost seventy years. Max Hammer, the owner, was from Rohatyn, a small town in Galicia; Jenny, his wife, was from Lemberg (Lviv), the capital of Galicia. They arrived in America in 1907, met, and married. Max had a pushcart, worked as a waiter, and then opened a dairy restaurant at 261 Stanton Street and Attorney and moved to 14th Street in 1913 (1914 according to their own ad). The restaurant had just six or seven tables. The family lived above the restaurant, and their son recalls being given his Thursday night bath by his mother, when there suddenly came a knocking on the pipe and his father's voice, "Jenny, we're busy! I need you in the kitchen!" She left him in the bathtub. In 1932 Hammer's moved from 205 East

14th Street to its final location, a considerably larger space. It was open seven days a week for breakfast, lunch, and dinner. Max died in 1957 and Jenny continued to operate the restaurant even after she was confined to a wheelchair. She taught her kitchen help how to cook and several of them went on to work at Ratner's. After her death, her children ran the place for a few years. As the neighborhood had changed, they were not able to sell the business and closed in 1980. Their son remarked that he hasn't had a good meal since. The Steinberg's Dairy scenes in *The Front* were shot here.

A 1914 New York Telephone Directory also lists a Hammer's Dairy Lunch at 886 Prospect Avenue in the Bronx.

Palm Tree Dairy Restaurant, 864 Broadway (near 17th Street), final location. The name evokes a Sumerian pleasure garden. A two-color matchbook proclaims, "It takes quality to build a reputation — we have both." In the 1970s, the Palm Tree Dairy was just up the street from the offices of *Screw* magazine, where some of its regular customers worked. Earlier incarnations of the Palm Tree Bakery and Dairy Restaurant were at 130 West 26th Street (1928) and 263 West 37th (1931). Unusual items on a 1960s menu are Fried Kashe with Onions (75 cents), the unknown Columbia Roast with Potatoes and Vegetable (90 cents), and Jelly Polachinken (90 cents).

Melgreen Dairy & Vegetarian Restaurant, 828 Broadway, between 12th and 13th Streets (also 825 Broadway in 1939). A surviving matchbook announces: "Special dinner 7 course — 50¢."

Ben Sol Vegetarian and Dairy Restaurant, 146 Fifth Avenue, near 19th Street. Only an imprinted paper-wrapped sugar cube survives. In 1928, the **S & S Vegetarian and Dairy Restaurant** was located at this same address.

Royal Cafeteria, 470 Sixth Avenue at 11th Street was reported in 1926 in *The Restaurant Man* to have reopened as a vegetarian and dairy lunchroom.

The Royal Bakery and Dairy Restaurant, 49 West 19th Street sold February 14, 1922. The only mention of this restaurant is found in the Bankruptcy and Business Transaction column of a daily newspaper.

In 1937, the **Parnes Dairy Restaurant,** now owned by O. Geffner, at 830 Broadway, ran a congratulatory ad in the *Tenth Anniversary Almanac of the Yiddish Arbeter Univerzitet*. By 1939 the restaurant had moved to 1180 Broadway.

F & M Foods, Broadway at 7th Street (see page 404).

Dairy Restaurants of the Garment Center and Midtown Manhattan

The third historical locus of dairy restaurants was in lower midtown Manhattan, the Garment and Fur District. Here, homesick Jewish businessmen with peptic ulcers were the perfect customers for a mid-twentieth-century dairy restaurant.

Rabbi Lehrman and K. Kohn Milkhiger Restaurant, 400 Sixth Avenue, between 24th and 25th Streets. An ad in *Yidishes Tageblat* for May 6, 1919, announces the opening of this most beautiful and true kosher milkhiger restaurant. "To manufacturers, workers, business people — radicals and religious — if you want to have pleasure from your mealtime, come in to us and you will be convinced, as here is the right place to come at mealtime for the healthiest, tastiest, cleanest, freshest and strictly kosherest vegetarian foods. . . ."

J. Meibach Milkhiger Restaurant, 240 Fifth Avenue at 28th Street, open September 1919, strictly kosher, closed Shabbos. "Pay us a visit. You won't have any regrets" [ad in *Der Morgn Zhurnal,* September 28, 1919]. Also later locations at 597 Broadway (placed a congratulatory message in the Teacher's Institute for Men yearbook for 1934) and 751 Broadway.

Around Passover 1919, Meibach ran an ad in the *Yidishes Tageblat* reaffirming his principal to stay closed on Shabbos. Other dairy restaurants, he says, are open every Shabbos and then close for Passover as though they're doing a great favor to the Jewish people. "No! A Thousand times no! I don't want to be a rich man! Money is not everything!" His restaurant will remain closed every Shabbos, all year round. By 1928 Meibach is located at 454 Broadway, the future location of Dayton's (see page 461).

R. Gross Vegetarian & Dairy Restaurant, 1372 Broadway, between 37th and 38th Streets. An elegant menu from Thursday, July 28, 1949, includes such homey dishes as Baked Spinach

Rabbi Lehrman and K. Kohn Milkhiger Restaurant, 400 Sixth Avenue. Ad in *Yidishes Tageblat* for May 6, 1919

with Hard-Boiled Egg and Potatoes, 90¢, the Yankee Pot Roast with Vegetable, Potato Pancake for 90¢ and Wiener Schnitzel à la Holstein with Poached Egg for $1.00. It's understood that these are all mock-meat dishes. To the milekhdike personality, words are open ciphers to be interpreted by those in the know. Only farther down the menu does the Fried Vegetarian Calf's Liver with Vegetables, 90¢ reassure the alarmed reader that he's not in a *regular* restaurant. Unusual dairy dishes include: Polachinkes [Hungarian crêpes] with Jelly, 75¢, Half Cream Cheese with Lettuce, 45¢, Glass of Half and Half, 25¢, and that turn-of-the-century dairy lunch standard, Crackers with Milk, 35¢. An exasperated manager insisted that the line "Children's Service - 25¢ EXTRA" be placed at the top of the menu. A long-running operation still in business in the 1960s.

שבעת ימים מצות תאכלו

איזהו גבור הכובש את יצרו

פריינדע!

זייט 15 יאהר אין די דעפּטאראנט ביזנעס, בין איך בערייט צו מיינע פריינצוזען. איך האלם געשלאסען שבת און יום טוב, וי איך געניז גאנין פּסח. עס קומם מיר קיין מעדאל דאפיר, אנשטעוענדיג מיל'כינע דעפּטאראמארם, וועלכע האלמען זאנאר אפען שבת א גאנין יאהר, שליסען צו גאנין פּסח. איבער די אונמענד'ליכקיים פון בשרות.

דענקם איהר, אז עם וואלם געוועזן ראמזאם פון מיר, שטעענדיג יעטם אין א גרויסע סמאר צו קוימען נייע דישעס? מונטערין זיין וואם זעלבע מיל'כינע וואם אם א גאנין יאהר? משארדושעו דאפיר פסח'דיגע פריינען? מאכען שועער'עם נעלד פראפים? און דערבי טאאן א גרויסע טובה דעם גאנען כלל ישראל?

נין, טרייענד מאל נייו! איך וויל נים זיין עטישין פיקלו! שבר כפנחם, נעלד אין נים אלעם!

האפטענדיג, וועם איהר, מיינ לייבע קאסטאמער, מיין אדרעס אי בער די פסח וואך נים פערגעסען, ווינש איך אייך א גיזונטען ושמחה בחגך.

אייער פריינד,

J. MEIBACH
751 BROADWAY

לא תאכלו כל מחמצת

שבעת ימים שאר לא ימצא בבתיכם

Garment Vegetarian & Dairy Restaurant,
270 West 39th Street. A purple matchbook states: "Vegetarian & Dairy for Health" and "Air conditioned."

Melgreen Dairy Restaurant, 316 Seventh Avenue at 28th Street. A sugar cube
with a printed wrapper has somehow survived. A second branch or earlier incarnation existed on Broadway at 12th Street (see page 377).

Hygrade Dairy Restaurant, 140 West 28th Street near Seventh Avenue.
A vaguely Deco-style matchbook for this now forgotten restaurant boasts "Famous for Good Food." Their eccentric waiter, Mr. Katz, was profiled in newspapers and on TV. To Fred Allen's question, in Yiddish, "Vos iz a blintz?" Mr. Katz explained, "A blintz iz pot cheese — in an envelope." In 1939 there was a second branch at 138 Fifth Avenue.

Rialto Vegetarian & Dairy Restaurant, 141 West 41st Street. The back of
their matchbook lists a full menu with hours, including "Club Luncheon 40¢," "Famous 5 course dinner 60¢."

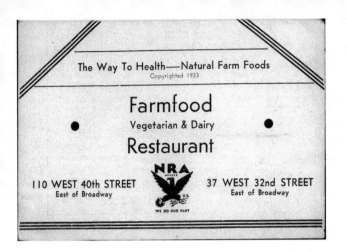

The Way To Health—Natural Farm Foods
Copyrighted 1933

Farmfood
Vegetarian & Dairy
Restaurant

NRA MEMBER
WE DO OUR PART

110 WEST 40th STREET
East of Broadway

37 WEST 32nd STREET
East of Broadway

Promenade Dairy Restaurant, 846 Seventh Avenue. All that remains is a battered green-and-blue matchbook depicting a couple about to enter the doorway of a generic restaurant. The back proclaims "Waffles & Sandwiches A Specialty."

Farmfood Vegetarian & Dairy Restaurants (established 1921) at 37 West 32nd Street. (Original location of **Geffner's Farm Food Restaurant**). The chain of four restaurants managed by Charles Schatz, a charter member of the Progressive Restaurant Owners Association, shifted location within the midtown area (142 West 49th Street, 104 West 40th Street, and 37 West 32nd Street in the 1940s) to the Garment District (261 West 35th in the 1960s). Their 1940s menu bore the image of a contented man casually tending his vegetable garden. "The Way to Health — Natural Farm Foods." A dozen Eastern European dishes — stuffed fish, blintzes, potato pancakes, and various "Jewish-style" fish dishes — are buried in a large menu of vegetarian fare: breaded cauliflower, Vigorost steak (a meat substitute), the unique Mock Lamb Chops, a special salad à la Max Warmbrand (the then famous nutritionist/vegetarian), along with salads and sandwiches. The healthful intentions of the restaurant are announced throughout the menu: "We Do Not Serve Fried Fish." "NO ANIMAL FATS USED." "All Vegetables Prepared Salt Free." In the 1940s, the West 40th and 49th Street branches were opened at 8 am for breakfast and, on weekdays, closed at 11 pm, weekends at 1 am. This menu, like most of the period, was dated and printed daily to include specials.

A 1933 brochure issued by the restaurant diagrams the six food groups for correct food combinations. "What a relief to dine and be courteously served in a clean, quiet atmosphere, partaking of natural wholesome foods as nature intended. Our foods, featuring the Battle Creek and Farmfood Systems, are scientifically prepared of fresh fruits, vegetables, dairy and 100% whole wheat products. Pies, rolls and cakes are baked in our own personally supervised bakery. And you'll find our prices are NO HIGHER than the ordinary eating place. Lunch 40¢. Vegetarian dinner 65¢ and 55¢." Its motto was "How you feel to-morrow, depends upon what and where you eat today."

An NRA (National Recovery Administration) logo attests to the restaurant's participation in the New Deal fair labor practices. They advertised in the 1935 ten-year jubilee book of the communist workers' theater group, Artef. Members of the Vegetarian Society of New York had their Thanksgiving dinners at the 40th Street branch from 1932 to 1948 ("Greens, nut meat roast, cranberries, potatoes, and pies"), and in 1952, the Vegetarian World League held a lecture series in the West 49th Street branch. Schatz died of a heart attack in 1954 at the age of fifty-four, but the restaurants remained in business through 1980. The last location, at 49th Street, advertised itself as "A Tradition for Jewish Dining for 50 Years. Strictly Kosher and Shomer Shabbos."

Centre Dairy Restaurant, 150 West 36th Street. This ornate facade appears in a 1940 tax photo of a densely packed street in the Garment District, below a billiard hall.

Best Food Vegetarian & Dairy Restaurant, 225 West 36th Street. A single sugar cube from the 1930s wrapped in paper is all that remains. In 1937, this restaurant was under the management of V. Tofilovski. It operated at another location as **Bestfood Self-service Restaurant** or **Vegetarian Cafeteria,** 147 West 36th Street, between Broadway and Seventh Avenue. A matchbook proclaims: "Wholesome Vegetarian Food for Good Health. Special full course Health dinner 50¢. A La Carte at our Regular Moderate Prices." A steady advertiser in the *Morgn Frayhayt* during the mid-1930s, managed by V. Tofilovski. "Healthy tasty food and a hemishen [homey] atmosphere."

Trufood Vegetarian Restaurant, 158 West 44th Street. Another early-1930s operation of V. Tofilovski. A few Eastern European dairy dishes (matzo pancakes, blintzes, pirogen, and kreplekh) survive on the menu of this largely Americanized restaurant. Mock-meat dishes included a "Braised Beef a la Jardinere." Operated by Vita-Ray Health Shops, Inc., along with the Vita-Ray House, or Tofilovski's Vegetarian Hotel, a resort in Freehold, New Jersey. Ads in the Yiddish press describe it as a "new modern house with all comforts. Special ultra-violet room for sunbathing in winter. Open all year."

"Stay Healthy — Eat at **Big 3 Vegetarian & Dairy Restaurant,** 260 West 38th Street and other locations." An ad in the *Forverts,* October 1930, announces that three prominent East Side restaurateurs have joined forces to open two new restaurants in the Garment District: 11 West 37th Street and 243–245 West 38th Street (later 260 West 38th).

The ad includes photos of the Big 3 men: Julius Malich of the Vegetarian & Dairy Restaurant of 288 Grand Street, David Gottlieb of the Vegetarian & Dairy Restaurant at 21 Second Avenue, and Nathan Stark of the Vegetarian & Dairy Restaurant at 436 Broome Street. It boasts of having served 10,000 meals daily and that baking is done on premises.

Original Pine Tree Vegetarian & Dairy Restaurant, 104 West 38th Street. A matchbook adorned with clip-art trees reminds us of this once popular restaurant. In 1969, the Vegetarian Society of New York hosted their thirty-eighth annual Thanksgiving Day banquet in this restaurant. Sam Beer, the restaurant's owner, had been in the vegetarian restaurant business since 1927 but was not a vegetarian himself. The dinner consisted of celery and fruit cocktails, a fresh salad, and for the main course, a vegetable roast made of beans, spinach, and cauliflower accompanied by string beans and baked potato. A reporter described the roast as "highly seasoned but practically tasteless." The Pine Tree hosted the event for almost four decades. [*Los Angeles Times,* November 28, 1969]

The "Big 3" Vegetarian & Dairy Restaurant ad, *Forverts*, October 1930

Midtown Dairy and Vegetarian Cafeteria, 552 Seventh Avenue, between 39th and 40th Streets. A bright-red matchbook promises "Good Food Reasonable Prices." A September 1951 ad announces an up-to-date remodeling with air conditioning. "The current manager, Mr. Lem, has run restaurants and cafeterias in the finest Jewish neighborhoods and is therefore accustomed to adjusting all dishes to every taste."

"Tasty Foods at **Madison Dairy Cafeteria,**" 176 Fifth Avenue, between 22nd and 23rd Streets. A generic matchbook making the modest claim of "Good food, well served."

Modern Vegetarian & Dairy Restaurant, 261 West 35th Street. "Vegetarian & Dairy for Health." A matchbook and a battered paper-wrapped sugar cube remain. In 1939 there were two branches: 15 East 17th and 27 West 35th Streets. It was still in business in 1948 at the final address.

Schildkraut's Vegetarian and Dairy Restaurant at various locations in midtown through the 1920s: 37 West 32nd Street, 221 East 36th Street, 53 West 28th Street, and 4 West 28th Street. By the 1930s, only the last two of the entire chain remained in business. The 4 West 28th Street location survived until 1948. (See page 327 for Schildkraut's Lower East Side locations.)

The S & H Vegetarian Kosher Dairy Restaurant, 1–3 West 31st Street, near Fifth Avenue, and 751 Broadway near 8th Street. (Shotr and Horowitz,

proprietors.) A 1928 ad for Maxwell House Coffee from the *Forverts* shows an ornate illuminated window display with baked goods, "kosher" in Hebrew characters, and two signs: "We serve Maxwell House Coffee, Good to the Last Drop." A scalloped curtain hangs above four sunbursts engraved into the glass. Beyond that we can see long tables, seating six, but not much else.

A March 1922 ad in *Der Morgn Zhurnal* announces that "M. Miller and dietician experts have opened a modern vegetarian restaurant: **The 'Vitamine' Vegetarian and Dairy Restaurant,** 256 Fifth Avenue at 28th Street." The ad goes on to explain the meaning of the word "vitamine" and guarantees that dieticians are always present to help with the correct combination of foods. By 1941 a restaurant with this name had relocated to 92 Fifth Avenue.

The opening of a **Dairy Restaurant** at 148 West 49th Street was announced in *Der Morgn Zhurnal* on July 11, 1919. "Workers and business people from 7th Avenue and 49th Street, come eat in a new, large milkhiger restaurant. We serve courteously and for a moderate price the finest milkhiger and pareve delicacies which will refresh and strengthen you every time."

Geffner's Dairy Restaurant operated a branch of their Second Avenue restaurant at 37 West 37th Street around 1941 (see page 335).

A. and S. Ashkenazi's Strictly Kosher Milkhiger Restaurant, Bakery and Dairy Lunch at 416 Sixth Avenue near 25th Street. "Come and enjoy a meal of tasty, healthy and strictly kosher dairy and vegetable foods and our own bakery, cakes and pastry which are made fresh every day. Wonderful service to the customer is our motto. Also, we guarantee that the customer will get the best foods for the value of money — no kidding. Closed Shabbos." [Advertisement in *Der Morgn Zhurnal,* May 29, 1919]

A family in the restaurant business since at least 1915, when H. and J. Harfenist operated a restaurant at 52 East 4th Street: **H [arry] Harfenist Restaurant,** 29 West 15th Street, in operation in 1920. Moving to 167 West 29th in 1948, the future location of Hershey's Dairy Restaurant (see page 478). Harry was born in Poland in 1880 and died in NYC in 1962.

D [avid] & J [oseph] Harfenist Vegetarian and Dairy Restaurant, 126 West 25th Street, in operation since 1915. David was born in Kosatowa, Austria, in 1878; date of death unknown. Joseph was born in Poland in 1887 and died in 1987.

Another, younger Harry Harfenist (born 1920, NYC–died 2004, Miami), whose father, Jacob, was in the restaurant business in NYC, had a more upscale career as food-and-beverage director for a number of country clubs, the catering manager of The Fontainebleau Hotel in Miami, the Trocadaro Restaurant, and finally, in 1944, his own **Harfenist Dairy Restaurant** in Miami Beach.

Unique Dairy Restaurant, 58 West 25th Street, in operation from approximately 1925 through 1931.

Reeff's Dairy Restaurant, 36 West 17th Street, in operation between 1928 and 1931.

Upon the founding of the Joint Board of the Furriers Union in July of 1935, the **Dairy Cafeteria** at 13 West 31st Street ran a congratulatory ad in the *Morgn Frayhayt.* "Honored to make the acquaintance of all furrier workers! We invite everyone to try our beautifully renovated dairy restaurant. You'll eat by us the freshest dairy and vegetable dishes at popular prices. Come in before or after your meetings. Eat in comfort. . . ." A steady advertiser in the *Morgn Frayhayt* during the mid-1930s, this cafeteria offered a break from the odious work of handling and sewing dead animal pelts. Operators in the needle trade joked that a furrier's work was akin to sewing up the ass of a cat.

Halpern's Dairy-Vegetarian Restaurant, 297 Seventh Avenue between 26th and 27th Streets. All that survives is a paper-wrapped sugar cube with pale-blue lettering. This restaurant, in operation from 1939 to 1953, may have been Samuel Halpern's last restaurant. It was sold by his wife to Salek and Pola Gefen (see page 466). Halpern and his wife were in the business since 1915 with restaurants at 146 Forsyth Street and 233 Sixth Avenue at Houston.

A **Garden Dairy Restaurant** (1941) is recorded at 324 Seventh Avenue. Its connection, if any, to Metzger's Garden Cafeteria Dairy Restaurant (see page 439) restaurant is unknown.

Dairy Restaurants of the Upper West Side

Jonas Steinberg (born 1878, Austria–died 1941, USA) arrived in New York City in 1906. In 1916, he and his wife, Sadie, opened a dairy lunchroom at 4 Lenox Avenue at 110th Street that continued in business until about 1925.

Aaron Reuben, originator of the Reuben sandwich, announced on March 20, 1931, that he would sell the Upper West Side branch of his restaurant, **Reuben's — That's All,** to Steinberg's restaurant. At Jonas's death in 1941 he was still president of the corporation. Over the years, his two sons would assume management of the restaurant: Ben would be in charge of the kitchen while William dealt with personnel and acted as a front-of-house host. Harry Josefsberg (born 1879, Boyslaw, Ukraine–died 1953, Miami Beach, Florida), Sadie's brother and a baker, arrived in America in 1891 and was a longtime associate of the Steinbergs.

The remains of **Steinberg's Dairy** at 2270 Broadway, near 81st Street, are few: the architectural photos documenting its renovation in 1934 to a modernist interior designed by the architect Morris Lapidus of Fontainebleau Hotel fame and a few specimens of streamlined paper matchboxes emblazoned with its name in a Moderne style of lettering. The photos show an empty and yet-to-be-used interior of glistening stainless steel and glass. The matchboxes contain delicate, thinner-than-normal wooden matchsticks with lavender heads.

Before taking an order, the waiter would bring a basket of

four kinds of bread, plus onion rolls, sweet rolls, biscuits, corn muffins, whole-wheat muffins, and club rolls. A sample of the 1959 menu included matzo brei, scrambled or pancake style ($1.45), kasha varnishkes with mushrooms ($1.35), potato pancakes with applesauce ($1.30), boiled or fried pirogen or kreplekh ($1.30), blintzes with sour cream, maatjes herring, pickled lox, chopped eggplant, borscht or schav with boiled potato, egg barley and onions with mushroom sauce ($1.35), along with salads, a variety of boiled, broiled, or pickled fish, sour cream with chopped vegetables or fruits or pot cheese, omelets, strudels, hearty sandwiches of salmon, tuna, sturgeon on bagels or rolls. A lunch special for $1.45 included appetizer, soup, dessert, and coffee.

ENDICOTT 2-2030

Steinberg's

DAIRY RESTAURANT

2270 BROADWAY
at 81st STREET
N.Y.C.

CLOSE COVER
BEFORE STRIKING

Walter Bernstein met regularly at Steinberg's for lunch with two other blacklisted screenwriters during the McCarthy era. "We look like bums but throw around big numbers. We are discussing prices for scripts, how to pay our various fronts, how to make sure the proper taxes are paid." The same waiter, Max, always serves them. He's suspicious, but finally thinks he understands what these men are talking about: they're in the wholesale fruit business. "He stands over us in triumph, balancing plates of herring, bowls of mushroom and barley soup." These scenes in the film *The Front* (1976) were shot at Hammer's Dairy on 14th Street as Steinberg's no longer existed. [Walter Bernstein, *Inside Out: A Memoir of the Blacklist* (1996)]

Steinberg's annually sold off all of their dishware before closing for Passover. This was their way of ridding the restaurant of chometz, or the remains of leavened bread.

Irving Howe's first meeting with I. B. Singer was at Steinberg's Dairy. "Singer, full of jokes, anecdotes, quotations, and opinions that rolled out between bites of blintzes, left Howe 'dizzy with amusement and dismay.' He could not decide whether he had met a comedian or a genius." This meeting led to the inclusion of two of Singer's stories in Howe's *A Treasury of Yiddish Stories* and to Singer's wider recognition [Gerald Sorin, *Irving Howe, A Life of Passionate Dissent*]. In the 1960s, Steinberg's was open from 7 am to 2 am daily.

Nathan Levinton was the headwaiter at Steinberg's from 1956 to 1969. He was born around 1893 in a small town in Western Ukraine and followed his father and older brother to America in 1910. He apprenticed as a silversmith during a craze for silver walking-stick handles, worked a newsstand, and finally found a job in a large bakery/restaurant in the then Jewish neighborhood of East Harlem run by the Mossman family. There, he met his future wife, the owner's daughter, and married into the restaurant business. Upon the death of her husband, Becky

Mossman remarried a Mr. Stark, who convinced her to relocate the restaurant to the Kingsbridge section of the Bronx, where it soon failed.

Nathan may have worked at other restaurants but ended up at Steinberg's by the late 1940s and worked his way up to being the headwaiter, handling the best tables at the front of the restaurant during the lunch and dinner shifts. Nathan and his young family settled in the West Farms section of the Bronx. He left each morning at 9 am to take the IRT subway to the Upper West Side of Manhattan. His son Jeffrey recalled waiting for the sound of his father's footsteps when he returned from work at 9 pm.

For his regular customers, including an assortment of the Upper West Side show business luminaries — Walter Matthau (two or three times a week), Zero Mostel, and Harry Belafonte — Nathan would prepare salads at their table. Mostel, blacklisted by the Hollywood studios during the 1950s, was a constant presence at the restaurant. He would blow straw wrappers at other diners and, during the run of Ionesco's *Rhinoceros*, bellow at curious onlookers.

Nathan acted as the union shop steward (Local 1 Hotel and Restaurant Workers) and was a member of the Workmen's Circle. He was troubled by the IRS ruling requiring waiters to report a preestablished amount of tips.

Although he was not a vegetarian, he was concerned with eating healthy food and had an aversion to processed and canned foods; he would never eat a tuna fish sandwich. He would sometimes bring home food from the restaurant: fish or salads. The family rarely ate out.

As he got older, Nathan was troubled by the changing demographic of New York City and expressed some disdain for the Puerto Rican kitchen workers at Steinberg's; he was worried about their cleanliness. He read newspapers — the NY *Daily News* and *Post* — but rarely books, yet, thanks to his sister, had a knowledge of and sympathy for Soviet authors and Russian culture. He would spend every Saturday with his son at the Bronx Zoo, Metropolitan Museum of Art (where his brother-in-law worked as a restorer of sculpture), or Museum of Natural History. He voted Democratic.

Up until the birth of his son, he was a pronounced atheist, but then saw to it that his son had a Jewish education and a bar mitzvah. He attended synagogue on High Holy Days yet enjoyed cooking bacon so that his Jewish neighbors would smell it and be horrified.

He mainly spoke English, without a trace of an accent, but was fluent in Russian and Yiddish. The job provided a comfortable, yet solidly working-class life: swimming at the beach with friends, attending baseball games — once a year from Steinberg's box at Yankee Stadium — and free theater tickets courtesy of his regular customers in show business. He was once offered a job at an upscale restaurant but chose to remain at Steinberg's. He respected the owners, Benny and Willy, but had no deep love for them.

Steinberg's
DAIRY RESTAURANT

2270 Broadway
at 81st and 82nd Sts.

Telephone:
ENdicott 2-2030

SPECIALS FOR TO-DAY
SERVED UNTIL 9.30 P. M.

Beer on Draught 10c.

APPETIZERS
CHOPPED FRESH MUSHROOMS AND EGGS 25
FRIED HERRING. FRIED ONIONS, FRENCH FRIED POTATOES 35
VEGETARIAN CHOPPED LIVER 25
BROILED ENGLISH KIPPERED HERRING, FRIED ONIONS. FRENCH FRIED 40
CHOPPED HERRING (SALAD) 20   CHOPPED ROUMANIAN EGG PLANT 25
INDIVIDUAL BOX of SPANISH SPICED SARDINES 40
FILET OF MAATJES HERRING 20   HOME MADE FILET OF PICKLED HERRING 20
BOX OF INDIVIDUAL TUNAFISH, TOMATO SAUCE 45   BISMARCK HERRING 25
TOMATO HERRING 25   PICKLED SMOKED SALMON (LOX) 30
BOX IMP. RUSSIAN (RIGA) SPROTS 40   HOME MADE SPRING SALAD 25
TABLE CELERY 25   FRIED HERRING WITH FRENCH FRIED POTATOES 35
TOMATO JUICE COCKTAIL 15   NOVA SCOTIA SALMON (LOX) 35

SOUPS
YANKEE BEANS, FARFEL 20   BROWN CABBAGE, BOILED POTATO 20
COLD SCHAVE AND CREAM .25   WITH HARD BOILED EGG ..35
COLD BORSCHT, CREAM, BOILED POTATO OR HOT BORSCHT, BOILED POTATO 25
COLD BORSCHT WITH CREAM AND HARD BOILED EGG 35

FISH
BAKED WHITEFISH. EGG BARLEY, STRING BEANS, BAKED
    BROWN POTATOES 50
BROILED INDIVIDUAL BABY FLOUNDER, (SIZZLING PLATTER).
    CARROTS, ASPARAGUS, HASHED BROWN POTATOES 50
SMOKED WHITEFISH AND POTATO SALAD 50
COLD FRIED FLOUNDER AND POTATO SALAD 45
BOILED YELLOW PIKE AND BOILED POTATO 45
COLD BOILED CARP AND BOILED POTATO 45
SMOKED WHITEFISH AND POTATO SALAD 50
MARINATED FISH (PICKLED) AND FROZEN GRAVY 50

SIDE DISHES OF VEGETABLES
FRESH GREEN PEAS 15   BUTTERED BEETS 15   BRUSSELS SPROUTS 15
FRESH STRING BEANS 15 STEWED CORN 15 FRESH SPINACH OR CARROTS 15
Above Orders Do Not Include Bread and Butter

SALADS   (Dressing Served with Salads on Request)
ANCHOVY OR ANTIPASTO SALAD 50   NOVA SCOTIA SALAD 80
SALMON OR TUNAFISH SALAD 50   EGG SALAD (2 EGGS). DRESSING 50
LAKE STURGEON SALAD 80 SALAD STEINBERG 65   COMBINATION SALAD 40
SMOKED WHITEFISH SALAD 65

HOT SPECIALS
STUFFED FRESH TOMATOES, MUSHROOM SAUCE, KIDNEY BEANS
    AND POTATO PANCAKE 40
BOILED AND FRIED KASHE PIROGEN 30
FRESH SALMON CUTLET, FRIED ONIONS, HASHED BROWN
    POTATOES AND ASPARAGUS 40
MUSHROOM LOAF. MUSHROOM SAUCE, KIDNEY BEANS.
    SPANISH RICE 40
NOODLE AND MUSHROOM CHOP SUEY EN CASSEROLE 40
BAKED SPANISH RICE, VEGETABLE AND MUSHROOMS 40
EGG BARLEY, FRIED ONIONS 35
    WITH MUSHROOMS 40
KIDNEY BEANS, FRIED EGG AND POTATO PANCAKE 40
HASHED BROWN POTATOES, BUTTER BEETS, ASPARAGUS 40
BOILED OR FRIED CHEESE KREPLACH 30
BOILED OR FRIED POTATO PIROGEN 30
BROILED ENGLISH KIPPERED HERRING, FRENCH FRIED ONIONS, FRIED POT. 40
NOODLES WITH CHEESE AND BUTTER 35
GARDEN VEGETABLE DINNER WITH POACHED EGG 50
BROWN KASHE (BUCKWHEAT) AND STEWED MUSHROOMS 40
CHEESE, JELLY, POTATO OR KASHE BLINTZES 30
FRIED EGG PLANT STEAK, FRIED ONIONS, GREEN PEAS, FRENCH FRIED .45
POTATO PANCAKES 35   WITH APPLE SAUCE 40
FRIED FRESH MUSHROOMS, FRIED ONIONS, FRENCH FRIED POTATOES ...50
PROTOSE STEAK, FRIED ONIONS, FRENCH FRIED POTATOES ...45
FRESH SPINACH WITH POACHED EGG AND MASHED POTATOES 40

COMBINATION VEGETABLES No. 1
BROCCOLI, KIDNEY BEANS, SPINACH. GREEN PEAS, SPANISH
    RICE 40

COMBINATION VEGETABLES No. 2
BOILED CAULIFLOWER, STRING BEANS, CARROTS, MUSHROOMS
    AND ASPARAGUS 40
FRESH VEGETABLE OMELETTE, FRENCH FRIED POTATOES 40
BROWN KASHE, FRIED ONIONS AND LIMA BEANS 40
LECKVAR BLINTZES 30   CHEESE BLINTZES 30 WITH SOUR CREAM 35
BOILED CAULIFLOWER WITH BUTTER SAUCE AND BROCCOLI 40
BOILED BROCCOLI, BUTTER SAUCE, MASHED POTATOES 40
MATZOTH BREI, APPLE SAUCE, JELLY 35
APPLE FRITTERS OR BANANA FRITTERS WITH JAM 35
FRESH STEWED MUSHROOMS EN CASSEROLE 45
SPANISH OMELETTE, FRENCH FRIED POTATOES 45
FRESH MUSHROOM OMELETTE, FRENCH FRIED POTATOES 50
FRIED CAULIFLOWER WITH GREEN PEAS AND MASHED POTATOES 40

DAIRY DISHES
STRAWBERRIES AND SOUR CREAM 45
BANANAS, POT CHEESE, VEGETABLE OR BOILED POTATO AND SOUR CREAM 40

DESSERTS
NUT FRUIT PUDDING WITH FRUIT SAUCE 15
INDIVIDUAL JAR SOUR MILK (CURDLED) 10
STRAWBERRIES AND SWEET CREAM (DESSERT) 25   STRAWBERRY SHORTCAKE 25
CHEESE STRUDEL 10   FRESH STEWED PEARS 15
PINEAPPLE CHEESE CAKE 15
JELL-O, WHIPPED CREAM 15   CHOCOLATE ECLAIR 10   FRESH PINEAPPLE 15
MOCHA TART CREAM CAKE 20 LEMON MERINGUE PIE 15 APPLE STRUDEL 15
DANISH BUTTER CAKE 15 BAKED APPLE 15 CREAM 20 FRUIT COMPOTE 20
FRESH STEWED PEAR 15 CHOCOLATE LAYER CAKE 15 PIE A LA MODE 20
FRESH APPLE, PINEAPPLE OR COCOANUT CUSTARD PIE 15
CHOCOLATE OR BUTTERSCOTCH PUDDING WITH WHIPPED CREAM 15
FRENCH APPLE CAKE 15   STEWED PRUNES 10   HORLICK'S MALTED MILK 15

Beer on Draught 10c

WINES and LIQUORS

APPETIZERS
Chopped Herring 20
Maatjes Herring 20   Bis
Imported Russian Caviar (Per
Chopped Eggs with Onions 25
Kippered Herring (Imported)
Anchovies (Imported) Box 40
Imported Antipasto (Box) 40
Columbia River Salmon Steak
Maatjes Herring, Filet 20   Pie
                        Veget

CEREALS
Rice with Milk 20   No
Bran with milk 15   Pep w
Grape Nuts 15   Corr
    Above Orders
    Above Orders

EGGS and OMELETTES
(2) Boiled Eggs 30   (2,
(2) Poached Eggs (Plain) 30
(2) Scrambled Eggs with Oni
Jelly Omelette 40   Spar
Spinach Omelette 40   As
Egg Omelette 30   Tom
Sturgeon Omelette 50   Ve
Green Pepper Omelette 40
    Above Or

CREAM DISHES
Sour Cream (Per Plate) 35
Potatoes with Sour Cream 45
Strawberries with Sour Cream
Hard Boiled Egg with Sour Cr
Bananas with Sour Cream 40
Vegetables with Cream 40 Pla
    Fruits wi

DAIRY DISHES (To Ord
Banana Fritters 35   Appl
Jelly Blintzes 35   C
Fried Kreplich 30
Fried Pirogen 30   Kashe
Potato Latkes or Pancakes 35
Brown Kashe with Onions 35

MUSHROOMS
Stewed Fresh Mushrooms 45
Fried Fresh Mushrooms 50
Mushrooms with Eggs 50
Fried Mushrooms on Toast 50

POTATOES and VEGET
Boiled Potatoes 10   Fre
Mashed Potatoes with Fried
Spinach, Plain 25   Spinach
Carrots, Peas and Spinach 35
Mashed Potatoes with Spinach
Fried Cauliflower 45
Asparagus with Butter Sauce
Corn on Cob 15   Stewed Co
Carrots and Peas 25   Julien
Vegetable Dinner, Special 55

COFFEE WITH RO

Baked Potato

Homemade Filet of Pickled Herring 20
erring 25   Appetizing Herring 25
00   Tomato Herring 25
reek Salad 20   Portion Olives 15
          Lake Sturgeon (Per Plate) 80
                   Smoked Whitefish 50
afish (Box) 50   Smoked Salmon 40
          Imported Sardines (Plate) 40
mon (Lox) 30 Chopped Egg Plant 25
pped Liver 25

h Milk 20   Kashe with Milk 20
15   Shredded Wheat with Milk 15
15   Sweet Corn with Milk 20
reet Cream 10c. Extra
clude Bread and Butter

Eggs 30   (2) Scrambled Eggs 30
          (2) Poached Eggs on Toast 35
          Smoked Salmon with Eggs 45
lette 45   Green Pea Omelette 40
Omelette 45   Cheese Omelette 40
lette 40   Mushroom Omelette 50
Omelette 40   Western Omelette 45
     Scrambled Eggs with Mushrooms 50
ved with Potatoes

ASON
     Pot Cheese with Sour Cream 40
     Raspberries with Sour Cream 40
     Huckleberries with Sour Cream 40
     Peaches with Sour Cream 40
     Blackberries with Sour Cream 40
Cream 45 Lettuce with Sour Cream 40
Cream 10c. Extra

s 35   Fried Noodles and Cheese 35
ntzes 30   Boiled Kreplich 30
rogen 30   Potato Blintzes 30
30   Noodles, Cheese and Butter 35
     Matzoth Latkes or Pancakes 35
ese Laktes 40   Kashe Blintzes 30
ancake 50

     Fried Mushrooms and Noodles 45
     Mushrooms with Kashe 40
Mushrooms with Mashed Potatoes 45
     Broiled Mushrooms on Toast 55

Potatoes 20   Mashed Potatoes 10
     Mashed Potatoes with Butter 15
ched Egg 35   Lyonnaise Potatoes 25
     Carrots, Peas and Asparagus 35
     Hashed Browned Potatoes 25
     Stewed Creamed Tomatoes 20
     Cauliflower with Butter Sauce 40
Dish) 15   Green Peas (Side-Dish) 15
es 20   Carrots, Peas, String Beans 35
Peas, Spinach 35 Brussels Sprouts 20

BREAD AND BUTTER 20c.

d From 6 to 8.30 P. M.

Thursday, May 9, 1935

To-Day's Special

DOMESTIC WINE 10c. Glass

SALADS
Tomato Surprise 50   Sardine Salad 50
Lettuce and Tomatoes 35   Cream Cheese Salad 45
Sliced Tomatoes 15   Sliced Cucumbers 15   Table Celery 25
Stuffed Eggs with Caviar 1 00   Hearts of Lettuce 25
Asparagus Salad 45   Smoked Whitefish Salad 65   Anchovies Salad 50
Imported Italian Antipasto Salad 50   Cole Slaw 15
     Mayonnaise or Russian Dressing Served with Above Orders

TOAST
Cinnamon Toast 15   Dry Toast 10   Marmalade and Toast 25
Milk Toast 20   Butter Toast 10   French Toast with Jam 35
                   Asparagus on Toast 35

CHEESE
Cream Cheese with Bar le Duc 45   American Cheese (Per Plate) 35
Imported Swiss Cheese (Per Plate) 40   Whole Cream Cheese 35
Half Cream Cheese 25   Roquefort Cheese, Individual Portion 30
Camembert Cheese 25   Swiss Gruyere Cheese 25   Pimento Cheese 30
          Liederkranz Cheese and Crackers 35
               (Crackers Served on Request)

SANDWICHES
No. 1—SPECIAL—Cream Cheese, Smoked Salmon, Sardine, Tomatoes 35
No. 2—Lake Sturgeon, Swiss Cheese, Cole Slaw, Sliced Tomatoes 55
No. 3—Cream Cheese, Walnuts, Jam 30
No. 4—Russian Caviar, Chopped Eggs, Sliced Tomatoes, Queen Olives ...65
No. 5—Club Sandwich 3 Layers on Toast, Sturgeon, Swiss Cheese, Sliced
     Tomatoes, Smoked Salmon and Cole Slaw 55
No. 6—SPECIAL—Nova Scotia Salmon and Cream Cheese 45
Canned Salmon 20   Imported French Sardine 20   Egg 20
American Cheese 20   Cream Cheese 20   Western 30
Imported Swiss Cheese 20   Tomato Lettuce 20   Smoked Salmon 20
Imported Russian Caviar 55   Cream Cheese and Jelly 25
Sturgeon Sandwich 45   Swiss Cheese and Smoked Salmon 25
Cream Cheese and Smoked Salmon 25   Nova Scotia Salmon 35
     (Mayonnaise or Russian Dressing Served on Request)

FRUITS IN SEASON and DESSERT
Orange Juice 15   Fruit Salad 20   Stewed Prunes 10
Baked Apples 15   Grapefruit 15   Sliced Oranges 15
Cantaloupe 20   Chocolate Pudding, Cream 15   Individual Jar Figs 20
Honey Dew Melon 20   Preserved Pineapple 15   Preserved Pears 15
Preserved Peaches 15   Watermelon 20   Fruit Jello, Cream 15
Persian Melon 20   Bar-le-Duc Jam 25   Blackberries with Cream 25
Raspberries with Cream 25   Strawberries with Cream 25
Huckleberries with Cream 25   Ice Cream 15   Pie a la Mode 25
     (Above Orders do not Include Bread and Butter)

CAKES
Buttered Danish Horns 10   Nut Horns 10   Cheese Strudel 10
Cheese Deckels 10   Chocolate Cake 15   Macaroon Tart 10
Lacquer Deckerls 10   Apple Strudel 15   Sponge Cake 15
Pie in Season 15   Nut Cake 15   Almond Zwieback 10
Buttered Sugar Cake 10   Apple Pie 15   Mocha Tart 15
Fruit Cake 20   Strawberry Short Cake 25   French Cheese Cake 15

COCOA, TEA and COFFEE
Coffee with Cream 10   Cocoa 10   Milk (Bottle) 10
Milk and Cream 25   Iced Tea 10   Pot of Tea 10
Instant Postum 10   Sheffield's Fer-mil-lac 15   Ruppert's Beer 15
Grape Juice 15   Saratoga Geyser 25   Budweiser Beer 20
Malted Milk 15   White Rock 20   Hoffman's Ginger Ale 20
Canada Pale Dry Ginger Ale 20 Dr. Brown's Celery Tonic 15 Buttermilk 10
Iced Coffee with Cream 15   Iced Coffee 15   Acidophilus Milk 25

PORTIONS SERVED FOR TWO 10c. EXTRA
TRU-BLU PILSENER BEER 15c.

Nathan was proud of his skill as a waiter. As a customer at other restaurants, he disparaged waiters who could not memorize a table full of orders but needed to write them down, or had to use a tray to carry dishes rather than their hands and arms. Nathan did not expect his son to enter the restaurant business and, in fact, never took him to eat at Steinberg's. Outside of his work at one of New York's premiere Jewish dairy restaurants, he was not consciously engaged in the transmission or preservation of Yiddish culture.

Friday evening, at home, the week's tips in quarters would be arranged in stacks, ten to fifteen high, to fill the entire width of the bedroom dresser. Tips accounted for close to two-thirds of his income. He died in 1969, still the headwaiter at Steinberg's.

The poet Irving Feldman worked his way through college at a number of New York City restaurants. In 1949, and again in 1952, he worked as a captain at Steinberg's Dairy. This was a part-time job, four hours a day on weekends or during the busy lunch and dinner shifts when two captains — Tommy, the head captain who spoke Yiddish with an Irish accent and Irving, acting as the second captain, stationed in the rear of the restaurant — were needed to usher customers to their tables. The two captains communicated with the use of small metal frog-shaped clickers. Regular customers wanted to sit at their regular tables where they enjoyed being bullied into ordering by their regular waiters. Waiters wore white jackets, emblazoned with the Steinberg's logo, and dark pants; captains wore suit jackets and a clip-on bow tie.

Feldman explained, "I avoided any job that would lead to a career or had to do with writing." It was an ideal job. He enjoyed being a man of leisure — off while most people were at work. From those few hours of work, he earned enough to live modestly like a poor poet.

He recalled Steinberg's busy, warm, and friendly atmosphere; the male waiters were all old friends. The only woman was the cashier. The employees were fed after their shift — he ordered halibut or one of the more expensive items on the menu. The blintzes and potato pancakes were very good. The smell of the bakery upstairs was heavenly. The customers being mainly assimilated second- and third-generation intellectuals, businesspeople, and the occasional celebrity — in his memory, Arnold Stang. He first visited Steinberg's as a customer in the company of Paul Goodman and a group of celebrants after a public event.

A 1941 menu features a drawing of a herd of dairy cows in a pastoral setting beneath incongruous Art Moderne lettering. The menu lists a vast range of Eastern European dairy dishes, from matzo pancakes, blintzes, and pierogi to a wide assortment of fish (gefilte, pickled, baked, broiled, marinated, and cold) to vegetarian dishes such as Vegetarian Chicken à la King and Protose Steak, certified milk by the glass from the Walker-Gordon farm of Plainsboro, New Jersey, the proverbial milk toast, beer, and mixed drinks. There is no mention of being kosher or having kosher certification. Small newspaper ads in the 1960s announce the restaurant being open every day of the week. The closing of Steinberg's Dairy Restaurant was not reported as a milestone in New York cultural history — only a notice of the assignment of its assets appeared in the bankruptcy column of the *New York Times* on December 10, 1969. By 1971 the space was occupied by Hunam (*sic*) Taste, a Chinese restaurant.

The New Lenox Dairy Restaurant and Bakery, 211 West 79th Street. An exhaustive menu, printed on yellow paper, features the standard Eastern European dairy dishes. A special section of "cream dishes" includes every variation on vegetables and fruit with sour cream. "All above orders with sweet cream 10¢ extra." A pitcher of sweet cream costs 5¢. There are fourteen types of potatoes, plus twenty types of stewed vegetable including "carrots and lima beans."

Large type across the top of the center spread boasts: "All our products are made up to take out in sanitary boxes or containers." The clip art on the front depicts an elegant couple being served by a tall, thin waitress in cap, apron, and high heels — a combination of wishful thinking on the part of the management and a lazy printer. The non-ethnic-sounding name would appeal to an assimilationist crowd on the Upper West Side.

Mayfield's Dairy Restaurant, 2150 Broadway at 75th Street. An advertisement in the *New York Times*, in May of 1948, calls it "New York's foremost dairy restaurant offering Breakfast, Luncheon, Dinner, and Supper."

There exists a rare black-and-white photo postcard of the interior space. An elegant bi-level dining room with linen tablecloths and recessed lighting. Their oversized menu for January 21, 1949, offers a cocktail of the day and a complete liquor list — something not common in dairy restaurants. Notable items: Welsh Rarebit, 85¢; Borscht (Beet Soup) with Sour Cream, 40¢; Broiled

A busy afternoon at Steinberg's c. 1961

Weakfish, $1.15 ("Broiled to order. This requires both Artistry and Patience. We'll supply the Artistry. Will you supply the Patience?"); Soup du Jour, 30¢.

Two hundred members of the Vegetarian Society of New York had a meatless Thanksgiving dinner at Mayfield's Dairy Restaurant on November 24, 1949. President Neil L. Ehmke said no meat or animal products, including eggs, fish, and milk were served, just Fresh Vegetable Roast, with traditional side dishes. Rabbi Max Felshin of the Radio City Synagogue gave the invocation. Mr. Ehmke announced the merging of a half-dozen vegetarian groups in the city on December 4 to bring the total to about 1,500. [*New York Times*, November 25, 1949]

Health Inn, 2870 Broadway (between 111th and 112th Streets). Health and vegetarian menu, seats 100. H. Sazar and S. Goldberg join in this new venture according to a brief mention in the July 1926 issue of *The Restaurant Man.*

"Comrades eat in Scientific Vegetarian Restaurant." Ad
from the *Morgn Frayhayt*, March 1929

Dairy Restaurants of Harlem

The wide, tree-lined avenues attracted an immigrant population wanting to escape the congestion of lower Manhattan. By 1900, when The Pabst Harlem Music Hall and Restaurant opened, Harlem was already an upper-class residential address for German Jews. The influx of less affluent Eastern European Jews in the years leading up to World War I threatened real-estate values. By 1918, it was the second-largest Jewish community in America. Several well-known dairy restaurants had their origins in Harlem; others had branches there.

Jonas Steinberg Dairy Lunchroom had been operating at 4 Lenox Avenue, at 110th Street, since 1916. See page 386 for later history of Steinberg's.

Jonah S[c]himel operated a branch of his bakery and dairy restaurant at 1363 Fifth Avenue, near 112th Street. (See page 463.)

Harlem Dairy Restaurant, 1409 Fifth Avenue. A 1927 directory listing, but no other information.

Lust's Health Food Bakery, southeast corner of 105th and Park Avenue. Advertised their Real Gluten Bread in *Der Morgn Zhurnal* of January 1911 as "the healthy food for diabetics (sugar sickness) recommended by all doctors. Available everywhere in New York City. Ask for a loaf."

Scientific Vegetarian Restaurant, 87 East 107th Street. Opened in 1921 by D. Mogilevsky, advertised in both the *Forverts* and *The Daily Worker*. "We serve homey vegetarian foods." Later at 75 East 107th Street and 1604 Madison Avenue. By 1925 the owners are listed as Jonas Tannenbaum and Nettie Frinkmann.

Health Food Vegetarian Restaurant, 1600 Madison Avenue at 107th Street. Ad in the *Morgn Frayhayt*, March 1929

Also regular advertisers in *The Daily Worker* between 1925 and 1927: **Health Food Vegetarian Restaurant,** 1600 Madison Avenue, and **Rational Vegetarian & Dairy Restaurant,** located at 1590 Madison Avenue and 107th Street. "For Health, Satisfaction and Comradeship." Possible connection with the Rational Vegetarian Restaurant on Second Avenue (see page 359).

"For a Home-Cooked Vegetarian Meal served in a home-like atmosphere come to **Esther's Dining Room,** 26 East 109th Street."

עס האָט זיך געעפענט א

וועגעטאַריאַנער

רעסטאָראַנט

מיר סערווירען היימישע, וועגעטאַ-
ריאַנישע שפּייזען.

SCIENTIFIC VEGETARIAN RESTAURANT

D. MOGILEVSKY,

87 E. 107th St.,   New York.

"There has opened a vegetarian restaurant. We serve homey vegetarian foods." Scientific Vegetarian Restaurant ad, *Forverts,* 1921

Schildkraut's Vegetarian Restaurant, 1363 Fifth Avenue, at 115th Street. An uptown branch of this popular restaurant in 1928.

Dairy Restaurants of Brooklyn

Famous Dairy of Brooklyn, 1131 Eastern Parkway, near Utica Avenue, Brooklyn.

Paul Bluth, the founder of the Famous Dairy Restaurant in Brooklyn, came to America in 1912 from a town near Kraków, Poland, where his father worked as a land agent for a Polish royal family. His mother ran a tavern and farm. Paul worked as a busboy at a dairy restaurant on the East Side of Manhattan, where he met his first wife, who worked as the cashier. According to family legend, she would not marry him until he had his own business. Around 1920, he and Isidore Abenstein opened the first Famous Dairy Restaurant in Bensonhurst, Brooklyn, at 20th Street and Bay Parkway. In the mid-1920s, with Bluth's brothers Jack and Sydney and a friend, a second branch was opened at Eighteenth Avenue and 86th Street, also in Brooklyn. Paul and Isidore Abenstein were bought out of their share in the restaurant and opened a third Famous Dairy Restaurant at 263 Schenectady Avenue, between Eastern Parkway and Lincoln Place in Crown Heights. *The Restaurant Man* for October 1927 announced: "The Famous Vegetarian and Dairy Restaurant at Schenectady Avenue and Eastern Parkway, Brooklyn, recently completed by Messrs. Bluth and Abenstein at a cost of $50,000, has been opened for business. The place was equipped by H. Friedman & Sons and seats 200."

In 1937, the restaurant moved to its final location at Eastern Parkway and Utica Avenue, diagonally across from Dubrow's Cafeteria. It remained the premiere dairy restaurant in Brooklyn. The restaurant accommodated 250–300 people. They baked their own cakes, Danish, and rolls; rye and pumpernickel bread were supplied by an outside bakery. For 25¢, people could order a bowl of soup and sit with the *New York Times* or the *Forverts* and eat endless onion rolls and salt sticks, and so, eventually, the minimum was raised to 35¢. The owners kept an eye on waiters who would nibble on the sturgeon — the most expensive dish on the menu. The restaurant was open from 4 am until 2:30 am, seven days a week. Although the restaurant was open on Saturday, it closed for Rosh Hashanah and Yom Kippur, and the dishes were changed on the first day of Passover and the tables covered with cloths. Although the brothers were raised in an Orthodox home, as adults they were no longer observant. The brothers spoke Yiddish when playing cards and in conversation, but English for business dealings. They strove to be Americanized and assimilated. When the Hasidim came to Crown Heights after the war, they did not patronize the restaurant. It never had rabbinical supervision, and never served kosher milk or certified kosher products, yet the rabbi of the local Orthodox shul ate there. In an adjoining catering hall, dairy weddings and bar mitzvahs took place with music by Ernie Mann and his one-man band. Another brother, Abe Bluth, came to America in 1924, worked as a waiter, and eventually became a partner in the business. All of the restaurants were opened in growing middle-class Jewish residential areas. According to Lawry Bluth, the family historian, there was never mention of the existence of dairy restaurants in Poland.

On Thursdays, Abe Bluth's family went to eat out — always a meat meal. Abe's favorite restaurant was the Old Homestead, a steakhouse on Ninth Avenue in Manhattan. The owners' children were allowed to work in the restaurant as young men, and only as a lesson as to why they should not go into the difficult and labor-intensive business. All seven children became lawyers and doctors. In the white flight of the 1960s, all but the Hasidic Jews left Crown Heights. Children came from Long Island to take their elderly parents for lunch, but parking was a problem. The restaurant closed in 1976.

Famous Restaurant Vegetarian and Dairy,

4818 Thirteenth Avenue, Borough Park, Brooklyn. Self-described in a November 1929 ad and on matchbooks as "The Rendezvous of Boro Park." Isidore Beitscher, owner with partners.

Famous Sunset Inc. Vegetarian and Dairy Restaurant,

203 Havemeyer Street, Brooklyn. "Wholesome Food Moderately Priced. We do our own baking on premises 3 times daily." A matchbook, a sugar cube, and a menu remain. Reportedly owned by Leo Schimel, a younger brother of Jonah the knish baker (see page 463). In business from the mid-1930s to 1955.

Famous Dairy Cafeteria, 713 Brighton Beach Avenue,

Brooklyn (diagonally across from Mrs. Stahl's Knishes). Under the direction of Abraham Weingast (see Famous Dairy Restaurant of 72nd Street, page 428). In operation from c. 1938 to 1943.

Getreu's Vegetarian and Dairy Restaurant,

793 Flatbush Avenue, Brooklyn. In a 1930s novelty matchbook, each match is the body of a chef, with the head of each match a toque blanche. "Catering to all Functions." A 1940 tax photo shows the store, with its elaborate illuminated marquee, for rent. In 1935, a Max Getreu operated a restaurant at 710 Rockaway Parkway.

Herman's Dairy Cafeteria, 1574 Pitkin Avenue, corner of Herzl Street, Brooklyn. "Finest food. Smartly served and Reasonably Priced. Baking done on premises." A worn and nearly illegible gold-colored matchbook yields no other secrets.

"If you require still the best? Think of **Sutter Vegetarian Dairy Restaurant and Cafeteria,**" 589 Sutter Avenue, corner of Georgia Avenue, Brooklyn. "Serves Grade A products." An occasional advertiser in the *Morgn Frayhayt* during the mid-1930s.

"Watch over your health and eat the best, fresh vegetarian food in the **Premier Vegetarian Cafeteria,**" 521 Sutter Avenue, corner of Hinsdale Street. Another advertiser in the *Morgn Frayhayt* during the mid-1930s.

Hoffman's Vegetarian Restaurant, 1529 Pitkin Avenue, Brooklyn. Isidore Hoffman announced the grand opening on Saturday, July 26, 1924, in the

Forverts. "Men, women, young and old are invited to come to the opening of the new vegetarian gan-eydn [paradise] place. . . . You'll feel a rare pride that Brownsville is worthy of having such a wonderful place." In 1929 the restaurant relocated to 1329 Pitkin Avenue "under the same good management as always: Sam Rutter, Louis Lechner and Julius Hader." A 1939 newspaper account described a labor dispute that resulted in a picket line in front of this restaurant.

The **Paradis Vegetarian Restaurant** (1627 Pitkin Avenue and later 239 South 4th Street, Williamsburg) along with **The Ideal Vegetarian Restaurant** (1805 Pitkin Avenue) advertised in the *Vegetarian World,* a Yiddish-language monthly journal of humanitarian thought in 1921 (see page 296).

"Williamsburg alert! We have already opened our splendid and sanitary health-center." Ad for Paradise Vegetarian Restaurant in *Der Morgn Zhurnal*, July 1921

The story of **Emese Essen** at Pitkin Avenue corner of Stone Avenue can be found on page 299.

Zion Vegetarian and Dairy Restaurant, 4923 Twelfth Avenue, Brooklyn. A surviving matchbook reminds you to "Meet your friends at the Zion."

A 1908 ad in *Der Kibetser* jokes: "Secretary Taft became fat from dreaming that he had eaten a fresh meal in a Brownsville kibetzarnie, in **A. Slonimski's Cafe and Milkhiger Restaurant,**" 103 Thatford Avenue, Brownsville, Brooklyn.

In 1929, **Schildkraut's Vegetarian Restaurant** has a branch at 3001 Surf Avenue in Brooklyn (see page 327).

In February of 1939, **Ratner's of Delancey Street** announced the opening of their first Brooklyn **Bakery and Retail Food Shop,** at 1910 Kings Highway. It offered prepared dairy foods as served in their restaurant.

Square Dairy Cafeteria, 217 Havemeyer Street, Brooklyn, at Williamsburg Bridge Plaza. A matchbook depicts the motto "Dairy food means health" pouring from the mouth of a bottle of milk. Other mottoes include: "Where we all meet," "Truly on the Square," "Milk is the foundation of dairy food. Never closed." A stainless-steel-clad facade on this vast corner cafeteria is festooned with banners reading "Air Cooled."

The knish bakeries of Brooklyn sometimes served an abbreviated dairy menu of soup or sour milk but often introduced varieties of knishes stuffed with meat or pastrami. **Shatzkin's** operated a stand on the Coney Island boardwalk at 33rd Street (and later 22nd Street) and finally Surf Avenue. **Jerry's** and **Hirsch's** also operated popular knish stands on the boardwalk.

Dairy Restaurants of Queens

Steinberg's Dairy Restaurant

Queens Boulevard at 75th Road, Forest Hills. A matchbook lists this branch of the Upper West Side restaurant (see page 386).

Kantor's Dairy Lunch Room on Springfield Boulevard, Laurelton, Long Island. A 1928 photograph shows a wooden house on a potholed country road. Painted in four-foot-high letters on the side is the name of the restaurant in English and Yiddish. "Dairy" is not transliterated but becomes "milkhiger." Its business may have depended upon its proximity to Montefiore Cemetery.

Henry's Dairy Restaurant, Queens Boulevard at 68th Street, Forest Hills. Memorialized by an ad in the March 13, 1956, issue of the *New York Times*.

Dairy Restaurants of the Bronx

Goldman's Dairy Restaurant, 866 Longwood Avenue, near Prospect Avenue subway station. Samuel Goldman (born 1886, Hungary–died 1952?, NYC) was involved in many New York City dairy restaurants. Starting as early as 1916 with locations at 33 Avenue C and 806 Seventh Avenue; in 1920 at 231 Delancey and a dairy lunch in the Bronx at 889 East 180th Street in partnership with Harry Harnick. He was also a partner in the G & G Dairy Restaurant at 138 Delancey. The spacious and elegant Goldman's Dairy Restaurant on Longwood Avenue was incorporated in 1926 by E. M. Lebowitz and S. Nydick; Goldman's involvement is unclear. Physical remains consist of a decorative gold-and-blue matchbook, advertising the large co-owned Goldman's Restaurant and Bar at 65–67 East 161st Street, Bronx, and tax photos from 1940.

Crown Dairy Restaurant, Elder Avenue and Westchester Avenue in the South Bronx, and **F & M Foods,** on Broadway near 7th Street. Albert Ottenheimer (1903–81) left Gemmingen, Germany, in 1928 and arrived in New York City at the age of thirty — the first male in his family since 1640 not to become a rabbi.

Someone put him in touch with Max Hammer, owner of Hammer's Dairy Restaurant on 14th Street, and he worked there as a counterman and waiter. He learned the business and became a good cook and baker. He then worked at the **Hunts Point Dairy** in the Bronx and eventually borrowed money, without interest, to buy fixtures for his own dairy restaurant, the Crown Dairy Restaurant, on Elder Avenue near Westchester Avenue in the South Bronx, third store from the corner. It was open 24 hours a day, 7 days a week, and closed only on Passover, to have the interior painted by non-Jewish painters, and on Rosh Hashanah and Yom Kippur. The restaurant had no hechsher from Vad Hashem — if the local rabbi on Elder Avenue said it was okay, it was okay. No kosher milk was used. Albert was not observant, and had only some Orthodox customers.

In the mid-1950s when Elder Avenue became a Hispanic neighborhood, he moved his business to Manhattan. This was F & M Foods, on

866
Longwood Ave., Bronx
c. 1940

Broadway between 7th and 8th Streets, near Wanamaker's Department Store. He took over an existing luncheonette (not a dairy) and kept the neon signs and fixtures. The luncheonette was open only for breakfast and lunch and closed by 3 pm each day. It was a 30-foot-wide store, with a counter and long tables against the wall that each seated ten people. Albert Ottenheimer spoke German and Yiddish; most of his customers spoke Yiddish.

The business was dependent upon first-generation European Jews who wanted to eat knishes, pierogi, cheese blintzes, vegetable plates, eggs, hot cereals, hot milk with noodles, pumpernickel bread, vegetarian chopped liver

(Protose, whole-wheat bread, and onions), and soups made from the previous day's leftovers.

On Thanksgiving, Albert constructed a vegetarian turkey using Protose for the dark meat and soybean for white meat. Their gefilte fish was stuffed into the carcass and not just patties. They baked their own rolls and pastry.

They did not have to deal with kosher inspectors, just the Department of Health. Mr. Ottenheimer was also involved with a restaurant at 9th Street and First Avenue and Henry's, a dairy on Queen's Boulevard. (See page 403.)

The countermen and waiters were all members of Local 2 — they were lifelong waiters. Although there was a printed menu, they'd recite and push the specials of the day. The cooks were black, Chinese, and Puerto Rican — whoever was available. In a basement room, elderly women prepared the food to be cooked. The decor consisted of gray-veined marble walls and Formica counters. He finally gave up the F & M when factories in the area closed. The sales no longer covered the rent of the store.

Dairy luncheonette interiors were often furnished with an interest-free loan from the Italian Mafia. In exchange for the loan, the restaurant would be used as a front for the numbers game. The runners were local building

superintendents or door-to-door insurance salesmen. Bets were left and picked up at the restaurant. Nothing was put on paper; everything was done by memory. When a winning payoff was made, the winner would give the runner a $10 tip. Winnings were from $100 to thousands of dollars. Cars would pick up the money at the store. The winning number (the handle at the racetrack) was originally telephoned, but after police wiretapping, the number was reported in the right-hand corner of the *Ching Chow* comic panel in the *Daily Mirror*. One insurance man ran away with the bet money and was murdered for doing so. Also, in exchange for allowing the numbers racket, the Health and Fire Department inspections were taken care of. This arrangement all blew up during the Knapp Commission hearings [Interview with Kurt Ottenheimer, 2008]. And what more perfect example of the milekhdike personality than the numbers player who hopes to improve his financial situation by ruminating over dream-book interpretations of lucky numbers instead of engaging in the world.

Triangle Dairy Restaurant, Wilkins Avenue, Bronx. In 1917 this was Leon Trotsky's favorite restaurant during his short stay in New York City. By 1925, it's located at 1379 Intervale Avenue. (See page 208.)

Hunts Point Dairy Restaurant, 942 Southern Boulevard, Bronx. An ad in the *Forverts* from September 1956 offered a separate room for catering, free parking, and fine foods. Remembered for their pea soup and vegetarian Delmonico steak.

College Inn Coffee Shop, 1201 Morris Park Avenue, Bronx. Consisted of a restaurant serving a meat menu and a coffee shop serving milkhiks with separate kitchens and staff. Both, opened in 1956, under the management of Max M. Schechter. Closed on Shabbos, with rabbinical supervision by Rabbi M. Schechter.

Mesinger's Vegetarian Restaurant, 1763 Southern Boulevard, Bronx, was a regular advertiser in the *Morgn Frayhayt* during the late 1920s.

"Comrades patronize for good fresh food" **Ritz Dairy Vegetarian Cafeteria,** 974 Southern Boulevard, near Aldus Street, Bronx, advertised in the *Morgn Frayhayt* in 1935. "Friendly atmosphere." It was situated on a busy commercial strip between a chow-mein parlor and a kiddie shop.

"For healthy foods, comrades find themselves in **Bronstein's Dairy Vegetarian Restaurant,**" 553 Claremont Parkway, between Fulton and Third Avenue. An occasional advertiser in the *Morgn Frayhayt* during the mid-1930s.

Upstate New York

The Vegetarian Hotel of Woodridge, New York, among a host of other left-leaning businesses, bought an ad in the 1935 ten-year Jubilee Book of the communist workers' theater group, Artef.

New Jersey

A 1928 issue of the *Forverts* carried an ad for **Hamburger's Health Farm** of Farmingdale, New Jersey. "Vegetarian house in one of the healthiest and wonderful areas of New Jersey, 50 miles from New York. All activities. Healthy and tasty foods." We can only imagine that those foods included some Eastern European dairy dishes.

Ideal Vegetarian and Dairy Restaurant at 97 Mercer Street, at the intersection of Prince Street and Springfield Avenue in Newark, operated since 1920 under

the direction of Mr. and Mrs. Henry Teitler and later under the management of Oscar Klein and Rosensweig. Under an earlier management, it was known as the **Ratner Dairy Restaurant** (connection, if any, to the Harmatz Ratner's of NYC is unknown). Under the name of the **Palm Tree Dairy and Vegetarian Restaurant,** its opening at this location was announced on Oct. 25, 1930.

The restaurant's high ceiling was pressed tin; the floor was covered in decorative tiles. Diners sat on bentwood chairs at the double row of rectangular wooden tables or at small square tables for two along the wall. A basket of seeded kaiser rolls was placed on each table. The waiters were dressed in white shirts, with rolled sleeves, and black bow ties. The menu featured standard dairy dishes including vegetarian chopped liver (onions, hard boiled egg, string beans, mushrooms, salt, pepper, and ground walnuts). Fish dishes included pickled fish, gefilte fish, salmon croquettes, and baked halibut. The restaurant's specialties were vegetable cutlets (chopped onions, grated carrots, green beans, eggs, salt, pepper, and matzo meal formed into a cutlet, dipped in egg, and fried with Mazola oil), mock kishka (stuffed derma), kugel, cheese blintzes, and matzo brei. Desserts included baked apples with sweet cream and rice pudding. [Nat Bodian, on *Old Newark* Web site]

A 1940s series of matchbooks, featuring "cheesecake" drawings of women, states that the restaurant is "OPEN ALL NIGHT, Friday and Saturday," and that it's "Air Conditioned." In 1945, the manager was Isidore Krigel.

S. & F. Dairy Restaurant, 2122 Pacific Avenue, Atlantic City. A worn, green-and-white matchbook boasts, "Eat here and keep cool," and "Knishes, blintzes, kreplach — our specialty."

"**Vege-Tarry** in Berkeley Heights, New Jersey. An Ideal Healthy Resort for Weekends and Vacation. Opening May 15, 1937, Wholesome, Tasty, Vegetarian Food. Real Workers' Atmosphere." Congratulatory ad in the *Tenth Anniversary Almanac of the Jewish Workers University,* 1937.

Royal Restaurant, 55 Brenford Place, in downtown Newark. Run by the Polikovski brothers and serving vegetarian and milkhiger foods. Advertised in the *Forverts,* March 1953.

Philadelphia, Pennsylvania
Tolstoy Vegetarian Restaurant, 423 South 5th Street. An ad in *Unzer Gezunt,* from July 1915: "The moral purpose of restaurants at this time is not only to know of flesh-eating, but that one can also from tender plants bring tasty and healthy dishes. Also, the restaurant strives to be the center of the vegetarian movement and the center of all radical parties."

Goldberg's, 6505 Castor Avenue. "The only Jewish Dairy Restaurant in the Greater Northeast" handed out a twelve-inch wooden ruler as a promotional item. Operated in the 1970s.

Hartman's Dairy Restaurant, 248 South Broad Street. "Never Closed." A surviving menu, with faux wood-grain cover, includes a full range of dairy dishes including the unusual: Noodle or Kashe Chop Suey (50¢) and Cold Pastrami Fish Platter (70¢).

The Blintza, 301 South Broad Street, self-service kosher dairy restaurant at Broad and Spruce Streets. Operated by Harry Solomon in the late 1950s. He had plans to introduce live folk music. Under the supervision of Rabbi Abraham L. Poupko.

Ambassador Dairy Restaurant, 702 Girard Avenue, opened in 1928 and remained in business until the 1970s. Owners were Sam and Rose Bahr.

A 1974 profile in *The Philadelphia Inquirer* describes it as the last of Philadelphia's great dairy restaurants; its ambience composed of pressed tin ceiling, straight-backed chairs, and plastic tablecloths. Located in the once-Jewish neighborhood of Northern Liberties, the restaurant now catered to black and Puerto Rican customers. It featured a standard dairy menu with several mock-meat dishes: chopped liver, sweet-and-sour meatballs, and cutlets made of mushrooms or eggplant. A specialty was pastrami carp.

In the 1970s, they still employed eight waiters, only one a woman, all dressed in black trousers, black bow ties, and white shirts — all union members. Notable waiters over the years were Jack Holdsman, Wille Hahn, and by 1954, Harry Dichter, a waiter and, in his free time, eminent collector and publisher of old American sheet music.

Lonzee Carr, a black man from North Carolina, served as the busboy and cleaning man from the age of sixteen and over the years managed to learn Yiddish. Sylvia Zellinger was the cook; other kitchen workers were identified only as Fannie, Reba, and Frieda.

The final owners, Jean and Irving Horowitz and Clara and Sam Zmochnick, although holding on to a declining business, felt unable to raise the prices on their elderly clientele.

Quaker Dairy Restaurant and Lunch, 25 Market Street. With a name evoking a pure American-style dairy lunchroom, this restaurant advertised in *Der Tog* in 1921: "Meat and dairy dishes prepared from the freshest food and best products cooked two times a day." Although they don't follow Jewish dietary laws and are open Saturdays and Sundays, they are a "strictly Union house."

More research is needed on the following restaurants: **Shubert Dairy Restaurant; New Capital Dairy Restaurant,** c. 1922; **Garden Dairy Restaurant,** 326 North Broad Street, c. 1952; **Bernice's Greener Pastures Dairy Restaurant,** 1506 Spruce Street, c. 1980s; and **European Dairy Restaurant,** 20th Street and Sansom, c. 1980s.

Boston, Massachusetts

Prime Vegetarian and Dairy Cafeteria, 11 Harrison Avenue. A flashy silver, orange, and green matchbook bearing a discreet Star of David promises "Choice Liquors" and "Music Every Evening."

Ad for Schwartz's Dairy Restaurant, *Forverts,* 1929

Baltimore, Maryland

Kosher New York Dairy Lunch Room, 827 East Baltimore Street. C. Rabinowitz, proprietor. Identified on its matchbook as kosher in Hebrew letters. "Pure Food, Quick Service, Meals At All Hours." With its name, trying to evoke the dairy restaurants of New York City.

The Silverman Dairy Restaurant, 1008 East Baltimore Street, "is now under the management of a New York restaurateur. There you can get the best milchige foods, fresh and tasty like in your own home. L. Shoenfeld, proprietor [ad in the *Forverts,* February 1923]. Shoenfeld later operated the restaurant under his own name.

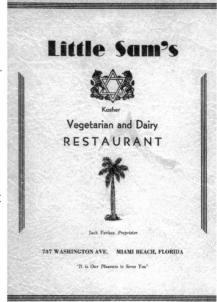

Little Sam's

Kosher

Vegetarian and Dairy

RESTAURANT

Jack Farkas, Proprietor

747 WASHINGTON AVE.   MIAMI BEACH, FLORIDA

"It is Our Pleasure to Serve You"

Schwartz's Dairy Restaurant, 901–903 East Baltimore Street. A 1929 ad in the *Forverts* proclaims, "Baltimore! You can now enjoy a tasty breakfast, dinner or supper in Schwartz's Dairy Lunch which has been much enlarged and beautified. Good food every time at moderate prices."

Miami, Florida

LIttle Sam's Kosher Vegetarian and Dairy Restaurant, 747 Washington Avenue, Miami Beach. A matchbook exists from 841 Washington Avenue. Jack Farkas, proprietor. "Why indulge in heavy indigestible animal food. We recommend our best quality of fish and natural vegetarian and dairy foods which are digestible." Menu includes: Vegetarian Pot Roast with Mushroom or Tomato Sauce. A lunch in November 1938 was priced at 40¢ and a dinner at 65¢. Their daily fish special was priced at 40¢. On the cover, a Magen David floats above a date palm tree.

Palm Vegetarian and Dairy Restaurant, Collins Avenue and 8th Street. Harfenist and Schandler, management. "Always the best in foods."

Harfenist Dairy Vegetarian Sea Food Restaurant, 1381 Washington Avenue, Miami Beach. In the 1960s advertised two Passover Seders, with a 10-course dinner and a prominent cantor. Began operation around 1944. (See page 384 for more on the Harfenist family.)

Sobel's Modern Dairy Restaurant, 701 Collins Avenue, Miami Beach. A hand-drawn 1940s linen postcard depicts a sprawling one-floor structure flying an

American flag, all against an airbrushed blue sky. The street and sidewalk are vast spaces occupied by a few lost-looking figures and a single red car.

Star Dairy, Vegetarian & Fish Restaurant, 841 Washington Avenue, Miami Beach. A 1961 ad in *The Jewish Floridian* claims that this is the "oldest and best-known dairy restaurant," in its eighteenth consecutive year of operation. The ad suggests you "Try our Special Roumanian Cheese Bagels." Likely successor of Little Sam's (see page 411).

Gorklein's, 929 Washington Avenue, Miami Beach. "Largest Vegetarian & Dairy Restaurant in the South," according to their matchbook and postcard.

Blumenfield's Vegetarian Restaurant, 668 Collins Avenue, Miami Beach. A matchbook proclaims: "Eat here Keep Well, Charcoal broiled fish. All vegetables steamed."

Jewish Physical Science ran a strictly kosher dairy restaurant at 820 Lincoln Lane North, c. 1966.

Michigan
Lash Brothers Dairy Restaurant, 381 Hastings Street, Detroit. In operation around 1900.

Miller Road Dairy Restaurant, G-3341 Miller Road, Flint. Matchbook asks you to "Bring the Family for Sunday Dinner."

Chicago, Illinois

Tolstoy Vegetarian Restaurant and Library, 2609 W. Division Street. On January 2/3,1920, this restaurant was the scene of a Palmer Raid. According to an account by B. Slater, an official of the Ladies' Tailors union, who stopped by to attend a lecture on vegetarianism, the place was filled with policemen. "They asked me if I belonged to the Communist Party and I replied that I was not affiliated with any party. That seemed to satisfy them . . . and they let me go. They warned me, however, to keep away from the Tolstoy Restaurant." The library consisted of a few books on the Tolstoyan doctrine of nonresistance.

Many dairy restaurants advertised in the Jewish newspaper *The Sentinel.* **Maxwell's Vegetarian Restaurant** (known as **The Health-ateria**), 365 West Madison, opens on December 8, 1924. "Foods that are biologically correct only will be contained on the menus. No freak meals but good tasty food."

Modern Vegetarian Restaurant, 3120 Roosevelt Road. "Here, indeed, is a place where you never have to worry about what food to eat or not to eat," from a 1927 advertisement.

Lindlahr's Vegetarian Restaurant, 170 North State Street. "Famous for its salads! A profusion of delightful salads and wonderful health pastries freshly baked," from a 1927 advertisement.

Tel Aviv Kosher Restaurant, 70 West Madison Street, announced the opening of a dairy kitchen on March 17, 1933.

Bowl and Blintz Dairy Restaurant, under the management of Alan Ray, was located on the Arcade Level of the Sherman House at Clark and Randolph. Opened April 19, 1971. It was a project of the Chicago Jewish community and featured a full dairy menu including mock hamburgers and mock cheeseburgers.

Chaim's Kosher Pizza and Israel Dairy Restaurant, 6349 North California, near Devon. Run by Chaim and Hanna Ohayon in 1972.

Los Angeles, California

Tanner's Vegetarian Restaurant and Fancy Bakery, 2326 Brooklyn Avenue. In operation in 1931. "There is nothing like steady dairy-vegetarian diet for Southern California climate." A regular advertiser in *B'nai B'rith Messenger.*

Dave Barnholtz's Farm and Dairy Restaurant, 627 South Fairfax, opened on June 21, 1953. Described as the only dairy vegetarian restaurant west of Chicago, it was a large, modern establishment seating 100 with ample parking. It featured a complete dairy menu "as served in the famous Miami Beach resorts . . . and New York restaurants." It was managed by Dan Hartman, formerly of the Shubert Dairy Restaurant (see page 410) and Balfour Kosher Restaurant of Philadelphia. The chef was Rudy Weinstein of New York and Miami.

Wilshire Dairy Vegetarian Restaurant, 5463 Wilshire Boulevard, opened August 1955 under the management of Dan Hartman. Described as a modern restaurant offering homemade gefilte fish, baked goods, and a full dairy menu.

Two Worlds Kosher Health Food Restaurant, 8022 West 3rd Street, "bringing you exciting and nutritious well-balanced vegetarian recipes from the East and West," from a 1973 advertisement.

The Milky Way, opened in June 1977 by the "Shomer Shabbos couple" Bernie and Leah Adler, with Chef Evelyn Zweig Kaufman. Described as a kosher Cholov Yisroel restaurant under the supervision of Rabbi Yehuda Bukspan. (See page 488.)

Unknown U.S. location
A photograph of two girls taken in front of **Miller's Kosher Dairy Lunch** in the 1920s shows a narrow storefront in a tenement building. A drawn sunshade obscures everything but a horizontal stack of grapefruits or very large oranges. The word "kosher" is in Hebrew characters. Two girls (identified on the back as Anna Teitel and Mildred Needle [?]) in knee-length pants outfits are the subject of the photo. They may have had some connection to the lunchroom, but more likely it's just a neighborhood backdrop.

San Juan, Puerto Rico
The Lee Hotel briefly housed a dairy restaurant, **The Shalom Room,** catering to Orthodox tourists from 1964 to 1965. According to the general manager, Sam Rosenberg, one reason for its failure was that each Orthodox group believed only in their own rabbi and would not accept the supervision the hotel offered.

Toronto, Canada
United Bakers Quick Lunch, Agnes Street (now Dundas Street),1912–1920. In 1920 moved to 338 Spadina Avenue.

Aaron and Sarah Ladovsky of Kielce, Poland, were the proprietors.

Between the world wars, the Jewish clothing trade in Toronto was centered on Spadina Avenue and supported at least two dairy restaurants. In 1986 they followed the residential migration of Jews to the suburbs and relocated at 506 Lawrence Avenue West, where it still operates in a busy strip mall.

The decor is that of a contemporary family restaurant. Diners are handed an oversized laminated menu. It's open seven days a week, closed Passover and High Holy Days. They state that they use only dairy and pareve ingredients but have no rabbinic certification. They maintain an online archive of their history.

Bagel King Coffee Shop, 1000 Eglinton Avenue West with a bakery at 3519 Bathurst Street in the Yorkdale Shopping Centre. A surviving c.1970s menu for "Toronto's most modern dairy restaurant and bakeries" operated by the Luntzmann family includes standard breakfast and salad dishes (omelets, waffles, Greek salad, etc.) with a large selection of specifically Eastern European dairy dishes: Baked Spiced Carp Platter (cold) "prepared with that real Hamisha Tam," blintzes, cabbage rolls ("stuffed with rice & mushrooms"), gefilte fish, etc. The so-called "Hamisha [home-style] Favourites" include such cross-cultural dishes as Fresh Mushroom Crêpes (in addition to blintzes), a Latke Pizza, the English-influenced Deep Fried Halibut (Fish & Chips), and Bagel Pizza ("tangy sauce, topped with Mozzarello [*sic*] Cheese, Green

415

Peppers & Mushrooms, $2.85 extra for Imported Anchovies"). A section of the menu features Sour Cream Combinations ("Remember Mama's?") offering a choice of boiled potatoes, assorted vegetables, peaches, or bananas in sour cream and/or cottage cheese. For the diet conscious patrons they offer a "Waist-away Fruit Bowl" served with cottage cheese.

Palestine/Israel

Besides numerous pensions and hotels offering vegetarian food, the following restaurants existed:

Lifschitz Vegetarian Restaurant, 28 Gurzenberg Street, Tel Aviv. Operating in 1936.

Hygienic Dairy, first-class vegetarian lunches and suppers, Jerusalem, 1936.

Farberov's Vegetarian Restaurant and Dairy, Jaffa Road, Jerusalem. Operating in the 1940s. "We serve all kinds of fish dishes: fried, boiled, stuffed, with mayonnaise, fish salad . . .etc." Advertised as the leading vegetarian restaurant in town. Had a pleasant garden.

Goldman's Dairy in Jerusalem offered "a varied assortment of hot and cold vegetarian dishes, deliciously cooked." Operating in 1942.

Dan Vegetarian Cafe-Restaurant, 19 Ben Yehuda Road, Tel Aviv. "Courteous Service, Cosy Place." Operating in 1946.

Glaser's Vegetarian Restaurant, Jaffa Road, Jerusalem. Operating in 1946.

Beit Hashmonaim, Vegetarian Naturist and Dietetic Restaurant, 61 Hashmonaim Street, Tel Aviv. Advertised in November 1949 as a first-class kosher restaurant offering fresh, tasty food . . . in accordance with physician's instructions.

Recreation Home (Vegetarian), Mohrus House Bayit V'Gan, Jerusalem. Offering quiet surroundings, spacious rooms, and large shady gardens in 1949.

Japan

In 1966, **The Jewish Center in Tokyo** was reported to be operating a kosher dairy restaurant.

In Memoriam

For many dairy restaurants, not even a matchbook remains. The following restaurants exist only as listings in various New York City directories. It's not always possible to identify a dairy restaurant from these listings, as before 1920 restaurants were simply known by the name of their proprietor. During the early years of the twentieth century it's often impossible to differentiate by name between an American-style "dairy restaurant" or "dairy lunch" and a Jewish dairy restaurant. Some might differentiate themselves by adding the word "kosher" to their name, but in many cases did not include even the word "dairy" in their name. As the American-style dairy restaurant went out of fashion and as Jewish-style dairy restaurants strove to differentiate themselves from hundreds of other restaurants and luncheonettes, these words were often worked into their names. Restaurants with the word "vegetarian" in their name can only be assumed to include Eastern European dairy cuisine if linked to a Jewish family name and/or operating in a certain time period and location. The countless Jewish bakeries and appetizing stores that installed a few tables for eating are impossible to identify by name alone. A restaurant's actual menu was a complex, unspoken negotiation between proprietor and clientele. Obviously, the vast majority of small eating places could not afford advertising beyond a listing in the phone book. As a memorial for these still undocumented dairy restaurants, we offer the following list.

1921 Directory of Manhattan

J&M Dairy Restaurant, 10 West 21 St.

New York Directory 1925

Alter's Dairy Lunch, 32 West Houston St.

Atlantic Dairy, 52 East 4th St.

Borden's Dairy, 226 East 14th St.

Clarice Dairy Restaurant, 120 Spring St.

D & B Dairy Lunch, 941 Intervale Ave., Bronx

Gold Medal Dairy Restaurant, 356 Canal St.

Gruber & Halpern, 1126 3rd Ave.

Jackson Dairy Restaurant, 726 East 152nd St., Bronx

Jefferson Dairy Lunch, 220 East 14th St.

Ladar's Bakery and Dairy Restaurant, 7 West 19th St.

Liberman's Dairy Restaurant, 245 Stanton St.

Melrose Dairy & Vegetarian Restaurant, 1787 Southern Blvd., Bronx

National Dairy Lunch, 106 Prince St.

New Jersey Dairy, 14 Jefferson St.

Original Vegetarian & Dairy Restaurant, 36 West 26th St.

P & S Dairy Lunch Room & Restaurant, 300 Grand St.

Pelham Health Inn, 1500 Pelham Parkway, Bronx

Puritan All Dairy Lunch, 17 East Houston St.

Regin's Vegetarian Restaurant, 29 St. Marks Place

Rivington Dairy Restaurant, 249 Rivington St.

Ritz Up-to-Date Dairy Lunch & Restaurant, 1946 1st Ave.

Sanitary Dairy Lunch, 127 Rivington St.

Schildkraut & Nagler, 83 Ave. B?

Seventy-Nine Second Avenue Dairy Restaurant, 79 2nd Ave.

Spring Dairy Lunch, 118 Spring St.

Triangle Dairy Restaurant, 196 Broome St.

Turk's Dairy Lunch, 913 Broadway

Victory Dairy Lunch, 62 East 12th Street

Zion Kosher Dairy Restaurant, 217 East Broadway

The Restaurant Man, April 1926

F&P Veg. and Dairy Restaurant, 313 B'way, Brooklyn, near Marcy Ave.

1928 Yellow Pages of Manhattan

Best Health Dairy Luncheonette at 99 Canal St.

H & A Vegetarian and Dairy Restaurant at 131 West 33rd St.

Pure Food, 121 University Pl.

Rockford Dairy, 305 E. 32nd St.

Rosalind Dairy, 332 Broadway

Rosewind Dairy Restaurant, 332 Broadway

S & S Dairy Restaurant, 28 Orchard St.

Terminal Bakery and Dairy Restaurant, 167 W. 29th St.

True-Food Vegetarian Restaurant, 62 E. Mt. Eden Ave., Bronx

Vernon Dairy Restaurant, 988 6th Ave.

Willard's Dairy Lunch, 95 Delancey St.

New York 1929 Yellow Pages

Comel Vegetarian Dairy Restaurant, 289 Washington

Country Dairy Inc. 11 E. B'way

Fulton Vegetarian and Dairy Restaurant, 141 Fulton St.

H & A Vegetarian and Dairy Restaurant, 131 W. 33rd St.

Ivy Dairy Lunch, 61 Warren St.

Lafayette Dairy Restaurant, 34 Great Jones St.

Mayflower Vegetarian Restaurant, 701 B'way

Mansion Vegetarian Restaurant, 145 W. 27th St.

The Original Vegetarian and Dairy Cafeteria, 5 West 21st St.

P & B Dairy Luncheonette, 22 Orchard St.

Rivington Garden, 48 Rivington St.

Swan Dairy Restaurant, 105 West 38th St.

Brooklyn Classified Telephone Directory, Winter 1929–30

Capitol Dairy Restaurant, 184 Tompkins Ave.

Cozy Vegetarian Restaurant, 632 Brighton Beach Ave.

Elsmere Vegetarian & Dairy Restaurant, 4413 New Utrecht Ave.

M & C Vegetarian & Dairy Restaurant, 94 Graham Ave.

Premier Vegetarian & Dairy Restaurant, 521 Sutter Ave.

Russell's Dairy Lunch, 332 Livingston St.

Sun-Ray Vegetarian, 1222 Kings Highway

SWS Vegetarian Restaurant, 4312 13th Ave.

Brooklyn Classified Telephone Directory, Winter 1938–39

Bushwick Dairy Lunch Bar, 396 Bushwick Ave.

Famous Dairy Cafeteria, 1821 Ave. I

Famous Restaurant, 931 3rd Ave.

Farm Food Diner, 1454 Ralph Ave.

1939 Guide to Union Restaurants in Manhattan

Balbary Dairy Lunch, 1149 B'way

Berkowitz's Dairy Restaurant, 29 Ave. B

Blumenthal's Dairy Restaurant, 43 2nd Ave.

Borden's Dairy Restaurant, 123 Rivington St.

Burnside Dairy Restaurant, 25 W. Burnside Ave., Bronx

Capitol Dairy Lunch, 51 Canal St.

Economy Vegetarian Rest. 232 W. 37th St.

Everbest Vegetarian Restaurant, 296 Fifth Ave.

F & H Dairy, 751 B'way

Famous Dairy, 812 West Tremont Ave., Bronx

Famous Dairy Restaurant, 1199 B'way

Goldstein & Zucker Dairy, 232 Delancey St.

Grandal Dairy, 316 Grand St.

Mansion Dairy Restaurant, 145 W. 27th St.

Menshel's Dairy, 8 E. 18th St.

Midtown Dairy Restaurant, 225 W. 37th St.

Milk Bar, 14th St. and 4th Ave.

N & L Dairy Lunch, 109 E. Burnside Ave., Bronx

Natlin's Dairy Restaurant, 270 W. 39th St.

Wainstock's Boston Dairy Rest., 54 Canal St.

Brooklyn Classified Telephone Directory, Summer 1939

Famous Dairy Cafeteria, 2139 86th St.

Famous Dairy Cafeteria, 1122 Ave. J

Fundamental Food, 315 Washington Ave.

Haven Dairy Cafeteria, 217 Havemeyer St.

L & Z Dairy Restaurant, 8 Moore St.

Max's Dairy Cafeteria, 710 Rockaway Ave.

Melrose Dairy Cafeteria, 1907 Kings Highway

S&J Vegetarian & Dairy Restaurant, 121 Sutter Ave.

Union Dairy Cafeteria, 300 Utica Ave.

Vitamore Vegetarian Dairy, 606 Brighton Beach Ave.

Manhattan Red Book for February 1941

Best Dairy Cafeteria, 29 W. 37th St.

Breckman Dairy Restaurant, 316 Grand St.

Clingrand Dairy Restaurant, 401 Grand St.

Gramercy Dairy Lunch, 156 2nd Ave.

Health Food Dairy Restaurant, 1594 Madison St.

Krell's Dairy Cafeteria, 213 W. 35th St.

Mansion Dairy Restaurant, 145 W. 27th St.

Philray Dairy Cafeteria, 542 B'way

Public Dairy Lunch Bar (Melrose Dairy Lunch), 111 Ave. C

Scientific Foods, 128 East 86th St.

Threefold Vegetarian Restaurant, 320 W. 56th St.

Toby's Dairy Cafeteria, 474 B'way

Wainstock's Boston Dairy Restaurant, 54 Canal St.

Other Sources:

Friedman's (formerly Nachman's) Dairy Restaurant congratulations in Stern College for Women yearbook, NY, 1963

Esther's Kosher Dairy Restaurant, 165 Madison Ave. (near 33rd St.) congratulations in Stern College for Women yearbook, NY, 1973

Tov M'od Dairy Cafeteria — Talmudical Academy, NY, 1964 yearbook

[below] Laurel Dairy Restaurant
Based upon unidentified photo of a restaurant exterior, possibly in Brooklyn

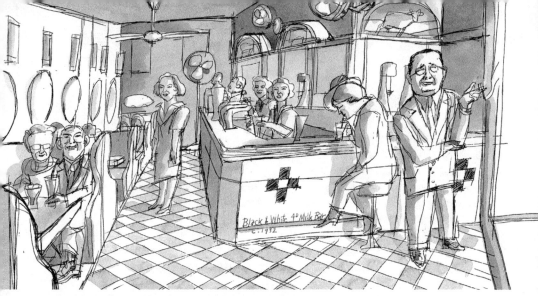

The Milk Bar Phenomenon

The term "milk bar" was already in use in the U.S. as early as 1919, as the temperance movement's repurposing of a saloon bar to sell milk-based drinks instead of alcohol. The table across which the business was transacted could be a wooden board, an ornate carved-wooden counter with brass "bar" for the buyers to rest their feet upon, or fitted with stools to allow for a more leisurely transaction. The National Dairy Show in 1919 in NYC featured a milk bar staffed by "actresses" serving "everything from buttermilk to fancy fizzes" [*New York Times,* April 20, 1919]. Throughout the U.S., the term remains in use for luncheonettes with soda fountains to this day.

In 1930 the term was applied to an ice-cream shop, the Lake View Milk Bar, in Bangalore, India, run by an Englishman, James Meadow Charles. It featured four flavors of ice cream. In 1947 it was sold to Vraj Lal and is still in operation.

In November 1932 the "milk bar" was introduced in Australia as an American/Hollywood import by a Greek immigrant, Mick Adams (Joachim Tavlarides). He had experienced the soda fountain on a trip to the United States. His Black and White 4D Milk Bar was located at 24 Martin Place in Sydney. It was a modern soda-fountain counter with fixed stools serving milk and milk-based drinks: malteds, strawberry shakes, ice cream, and wrapped chocolates. A glass of milk cost fourpence. It was decorated in black-and-white checkerboard tiling; the window featured a model cow, and her calf, that emitted an endless stream of milk into a model bucket. There was nothing like it in Australia and by 1937 other Greek immigrants had opened 4,000 milk bars across the country, each with waitresses/counterwomen in unique uniforms. Some did away with the stools and instead had customers seated at tables or in booths. [Effy Alexakis and Leonard Janiszewski, *Greek Cafes & Milk Bars of Australia*]

Supposedly, it was an Australian, H. D. McIntosh, with a background in mining, dairy farming, journalism, and theater, who, upon having difficulty getting a glass of milk in London restaurants, thought of importing the milk bar concept from Australia to London in 1937. His first bar, on Fleet Street, catered 24 hours a day to the newspaper workers and featured milk, milkshakes, malted milks, and sandwiches. During the cold months, they offered canned soups made with hot milk. After he opened eleven in London and the provinces, competition soon followed: the Sunshine (Charles Forte, proprietor) and the National Milk Bar (R. W. Griffiths, proprietor). By 1939, there were more than a thousand in England.

The trend spread across Europe, back to the U.S., where, after the repeal of the National Prohibition Act in 1933, it became "as smart to drink the cool white liquid as champagne." Over the years, the temperance movements in the U.S. re-adopted the term for "dry" nightclubs and other social-drinking establishments.

Sheffield Milk Bar and Modern Milk Bar were among the popular chains in Manhattan from the 1930s to the 1950s. In 1939, Isaac Levy leased a large store opposite Macy's to expand his milk bar chain.

1935
London

The Demise of the Dairy Restaurant

Through the 1920s and 1930s Jewish immigrants and their children began to own and manage such bastions of middle-class dining as Rector's, Lindy's, and Longchamps. They were responsible for culinary inventions that flouted all Jewish dietary laws as well as the Sabbath. Arnold Reuben's (1883–1970) restaurant in the 1920s featured its eponymous sandwich of hot corned beef, sauerkraut, melted Swiss cheese, and Russian dressing. Ratner's, Rapoport's Dairy, Cafe Royal, and many other Jewish-owned restaurants on the East Side were open twenty-four hours a day, seven days a week to accommodate the late-night after-theater crowd and night-shift workers in the city. The Bowery, once the western border of the East Side Jewish ghetto, became the city's restaurant-supply district.

The number and variety of Jews in the restaurant business by the 1920s is reflected in the pages of the trade magazine *The Restaurant Man*. Although it was not identified as a Jewish periodical, the masthead and contents reflected the large number of Jews in the United Restaurant Owners' Association who managed the low- to middle-class restaurants dealing in "pies instead of caviar" and including 300 lunchrooms and inexpensive restaurants. Higher-class businesses belonged to the Society of Restaurateurs.

Articles celebrate their success, business acumen, and deep connections to the real-estate business of the city. Accounts of trips by association members to visit ailing parents and the scenes of their boyhoods in Russia and Poland in 1926 are revealing. The conditions among the Jews of Poland were "worse than anyone could believe; even the bare necessities of life were lacking." To Moses Levine, the restaurants of Paris seem old-fashioned. "They have good foods," Mr. Levine confessed, "but the American Restaurant man can learn nothing about operation methods from them. We advance more in a minute over here than they do in a month in Europe."

The openings and closings of dairy restaurants are occasionally mentioned, but they are far outweighed by coverage of restaurants that served both meat and dairy. A profile of the highly ambitious Herman Schildkraut and his chain of vegetarian restaurants is an exception to the rule. The small homey dairy restaurants of the East Side or Garment District are rarely mentioned. The pages are devoted to the upwardly mobile restaurateurs of the first and second generations. Issues from the 1920s make it seem as though home cooking is about to become a thing of the past. "The increasing thousands of people who are abandoning the boarding house and home for restaurant service, prefer the surroundings and the atmosphere of a well-conducted restaurant for their evening meal." [*The Restaurant Man,* March 1926]

Sensible people seek "escape from the pervasive aroma of stewing meat and chicken in the streets and hallways of apartment houses." This publication repeatedly proclaimed the inevitable end of people eating at home — they could eat better and for less at restaurants.

The magazine is filled with a cocky optimism. *The Restaurant Man* was riding the wave of public eating to its glorious future and business could only improve.

After the Stock Market Crash of 1929, public eating, for those who could afford it, became a form of escapism. The small family-run restaurant was overshadowed by the appearance of large corporate-driven restaurant enterprises. The modest Jewish restaurant of the East Side was a commercial embarrassment. The hard, personal labor involved in the operation of a small restaurant was something restaurateurs of the early twentieth century hoped their children would not have to endure; only as managers of a large establishment or chain would they be freed from the physical labor involved. The new organizational science applied to the restaurant business led to a boring standardization and sterility.

In 1947, Ernest M. Fleischman in his *Modern Luncheonette*

Bellow and blintzes

Management outlined the simple rules for a successful luncheonette: location ("If it is possible to procure a corner location of the right size and price, do so. You are fortunate"); store layout ("There are three general types of layout: 1. The long counter with the kitchen behind the counter if the store is wide enough; if not, at the end. 2. The single U-shaped counter. 3. The multiple U-shaped counter"); provisions ("Whenever a store smells of fine coffee, you can rest assured that most of the aroma is in the air and not in the coffee where it belongs"); kitchen equipment ("Two small refrigerators might be more convenient. Keep one about 40 degrees for vegetables, dairy items, eggs . . . another somewhat colder, about 36 degrees, for meats and fish"); and qualifications and duties of employees ("Do not brush crumbs onto the floor. . . . Do not place your pencil in your mouth. Instruct your waitress to leave totaled checks face down at the customer's place immediately after the service of dessert and beverage. It is annoying to wait for the check when one is ready to leave"). The young Jews of that generation would rather turn to the pure sciences or law as the hours were less arduous and earnings higher. They wanted to enjoy restaurants, not work in them.

On Kosher Style Dining, 1950

Within the commercial spectrum of world cuisines available in America, the dishes of European Jews were consolidated into a Jewish cuisine — a cuisine shaped, in part, by dietary laws, but now independent of them. On a 1950s menu for Cohen's Delicatessen, Pot Roast of Beef ($1.55) sits one inch above Vegetables with Sour Cream ($1.50) and Fried or Boiled Cheese Kreplekh ($1.35).

Signs stating, "We sell both Kosher and non-Kosher products," or "Our Kosher products become non-Kosher when they are sliced," appeared in delicatessens and luncheonettes.

For the theater crowd at the Cafe Royal on Second Avenue, butter was reportedly served "under the table" upon request. As one informant explained, "Artists could not be bothered by religious laws." A restaurant reviewer of 1949 remarked upon its Hungarian meat cuisine and famous cheesecake.

The Jewish-style restaurant operated in flagrant disregard of dietary laws, pushing the boundaries of what constituted Jewish culinary combinations. Because there were no negative theological consequences, such as eternal sin, the majority of New York Jews were willing to give up what appeared to be outdated dietary laws.

In a 1983 interview with Mimi Sheraton, Saul Bellow declared that, having lived in New York for about twenty years, he missed the city's kosher dairy restaurants. "They had wonderful cheese blintzes and not the kind adulterated with fruit or potatoes," he said. "Jewish food in Chicago is lighter and less greasy than it is in New York."

"Eat in these fine restaurants and have pleasure from a healthy, homey meal." Restaurant ads from the *Forverts*, December 9, 1956, including only three dairy restaurants

My Recollections of Dairy Restaurants

Wandering the streets of New York during my early adult years, I frequented a species of dairy restaurant that seemed to have always been there. A dairy restaurant stood in sharp contrast to a meat-based restaurant or delicatessen.

The delicatessen was the bastion of the big eater and the Bromo Seltzer dispenser. Glistening slabs of smoked meat were stacked on glass-fronted steam tables; salamis hung from the ceiling like trophies of some unspoken success. The walls and windows dripped with sweat and condensation. The floors were slick with fat. The tables were horizontal memorials to the survival of the fittest and man's conquest of the animal kingdom. The waiters were surly and wisecracking; the checks were scrawled in pencil with a beefy, insensitive hand. The momentary pleasure of devouring a thick meat sandwich was offset by the inevitable feeling of indigestion that followed. To counter the atmosphere of murder and death, some diners accompanied their meal with a celery-tonic soda.

I was not a vegetarian or an intentional observer of Jewish dietary law. Every so often during my childhood, my mother would announce that, as a break from the normal routine of meat and chicken, we'd be having milkhiks for dinner: a delicious cold borscht with sour cream and boiled potato, gefilte fish or frozen blintzes, or the less appealing, milekhdiker spaghetti — a concoction handed down from her mother, who found it in the pages of a Yiddish newspaper — a sauce of tomato paste, milk, and melted American cheese over pasta. My grandmother, from Kiev, was a homemaker of the Old World, who effortlessly produced the full range of homemade Jewish cuisine whenever we visited and was apparently intrigued by this "Italian" dish.

As for intimations of paradise, or pastoral impulses, I had few. My father's utopian-socialist leaning led me to feel that we were living in an unjust economic system that only a radical overhaul could improve. I had not read Karl Polanyi and did not know of social systems that existed before the market economy came to dominate the world. In my comic-book reading, I could not help but notice that the work of cartoonists from the 1940s was richer, less rushed, and more elaborately designed than what I saw each month in the comics at my corner candy store. I had a vague sense that something had gone wrong. And so these intimations of a better time, the possibility of a course of life different from the one we were on, a poor man's paradise, was something I felt even as a small child. And the very idea of pursuing a lost paradise was, in itself, a cause of unhappiness. I had no idea of the profound resetting of history that occurred in each of these Jewish dairy restaurants.

Although I had a taste for the Eastern European dishes that I grew up with, it was the appearance and atmosphere of these dairy restaurants that attracted me. I assumed that the resigned and forlorn air that filled these places was due to their being businesses in their final decline. Their customers had died or moved away, the cuisine they offered was no longer considered healthy or fashionable, and the owners did not want or expect their children to continue their line of work. Here are some memories.

Famous Dairy Restaurant, 222 West 72nd Street, Manhattan.

In operation from c. 1958 until 1992. Founded by Abraham Weingast (born 1892 Ternopil, Ukraine–died 1958, NYC). After arriving in New York in 1913, Abe and his brother Dave worked as waiters. In 1922, Weingast partnered with Morris Hass in a restaurant at 41 West 21st Street, then, c. 1938, opened the Famous Dairy Cafeteria in Brighton Beach (see page 400). After Abe's death, the 72nd Street branch continued under the direction of the Weingast family. In the 1980s, Eddie Izso became the manager.

I. B. Singer (1902–1991), a confirmed vegetarian (from the age of 60) and a resident of the Belnord at 86th and Broadway, was reported to have lunch here three times a week. His regular waiter of twenty years was Sam Orenstein. (Singer: What's for lunch? Sam: The soup is mushroom and barley and the [vegetarian] liver is on whole wheat bread. You'll have a little dessert and coffee and you'll be in good shape. Singer: Very good.)

After Singer won the Nobel Prize in 1978, Orenstein teased him about giving a bigger tip. "Dos Harts lust nischt," Mr. Singer replied. The expression literally means "My heart won't let me," meaning

that he'd like to, but he's not used to it. [*New York Times*, 1991]. He always sat in the back room in a booth below a "rumbling" air conditioner and usually had the $3.50 lunch special. Singer's other meals were taken at Steinberg's, the American Restaurant, a Greek-American-style coffee shop where a vegetarian meal could be pieced

together (pea soup, boiled potatoes, and rice pudding), or the Eclair, a Viennese-style bakery-cafe on 72nd Street, where he'd have an open-face tuna-salad sandwich, coffee, and occasionally a bowl of borscht with sour cream and boiled potato. His publisher, Roger Straus of Farrar, Straus and Giroux, "remembers that Mr. Singer . . . would always take him to 'greasy spoons' and have him try burgers made of chopped vegetables."

One winter evening in the 1980s, I had the urge to escape from the appetitive atmosphere of New York City and have dinner at the Famous Dairy. A few desiccated cakes and pastries slowly spun in a refrigerated glass carousel near the door. A long-suffering elderly waitress limped back and forth to the kitchen, a tiny saucer of creamed spinach in her trembling hand. There were never more than a few diners at night. The serpentine Formica counter was empty; the air was tinged with the fragrance of frying butter and sweet boiled fish. The name "Famous" — someone's pathetic business decision

to set this dairy apart from the dozens of other equally well-known dairies — only heightened, by contrast, the modest tone of the place. From my table, over a plate of gefilte fish sleeping on a bed of lettuce, I saw a party of four well-heeled, middle-aged people arrive in a taxi.

They entered the restaurant. The men hung their coats on a communal rack near the door. I ordered two side dishes: kasha varnishkes and creamed spinach.

They were seated several tables away, closer to the door. One woman held on to her full-length mink coat and draped it over the back of an empty chair.

Noticing the coat, the waitress asked the woman to please hang it on the communal rack — I could not hear the reasoning behind her request: it obstructed passage between the tables, or might offend the vegetarian patrons; after all, sixty dead minks are required to make one full-length fur coat. The woman explained that she preferred to keep her fur with her, but reluctantly obliged.

In those days, the traffic islands around Broadway and 72nd Street were frequented by drug addicts for business and relaxation. One small park on 70th Street was nicknamed Needle Park.

At some point during my meal, out of the corner of my eye, I noticed a young woman — one of the many underfed, drug-addicted individuals wandering upper Broadway in those days — enter the restaurant and ask to use the basement restroom.

RESTROOMS

The gefilte fish was wonderful that evening. It glistened in a pool of protein jelly alongside the iconic slice of boiled carrot. The communal jar of horseradish had been recently refilled. The bitter flavor reminded me of the suffering of my ancestors. I toyed with the small portion of creamed spinach and imagined living another life as a farmer. In my mouth, the warm bow-tie-shaped noodles and kasha offset the cold fish. In the quiet of this restaurant with its faint smell of frying butter and sweet baked goods, I was truly in a walled paradise of sorts.

Several minutes later, the woman screamed that her fur
coat was gone. I assumed that the young drug addict
had walked off with the valuable coat while no one was
looking, but kept this to myself.

The waitress was blamed for forcing the woman to hang it on the communal coatrack. Questions of insurance were raised. I turned to the menu to choose a dessert (rice pudding or apple strudel?) and wondered: What place did a fur coat have in a dairy restaurant?

The last owners of the Famous Dairy were Rhoda and Irving Burstein. In an attempt to attract observant Jews, the restaurant had taken on rabbinical supervision and served certified milk products. The prices rose slightly, Eastern European dairy dishes went out of style, and the restaurant eventually closed in May of 1992. The space was taken over by Dougie's Glatt-Kosher BBQ and Grill and is currently a hairdressing salon.

438

Garden Cafeteria Dairy Restaurant, 165 East Broadway. In 1903 the Jarmulowsky sons built their own bank at number 165. It failed in 1919, and the ground-floor space was taken over by Fischer's Dairy Lunch. In 1922, the space was converted into the East Broadway Self-Service Cafeteria, serving both milk and meat. Fischer's Dairy Lunch apparently moved to the corner building at Rutgers and East Broadway (number 163), which was demolished in 1933 to widen the street for subway construction. Farther down the block, number 183 was occupied by a succession of legendary dairy restaurants (see page 371). In 1941, in the space last occupied by the East Broadway Self-Service Cafeteria, Charlie Metzger (born 1896, Austria–died 1977, Miami) opened the Garden Cafeteria Dairy Restaurant.

Down the block from the *Jewish Daily Forward* building and the Educational Alliance, the Garden Cafeteria was, in its heyday, open 24 hours a day to cater to the workers of what remained of the Yiddish Newspaper Row. A front wall was covered with a mural of a long-gone neighborhood street market. A back room offered waiter service.

I ate there every Friday night in the 1970s, before meetings of the Alliance of Figurative Artists at the Educational Alliance. The men behind the cafeteria steam table were strong, serious, and dressed in white. Effortlessly, they'd reach into the farthest corner of the steam table or effortlessly assemble a salad. The decor was utterly Spartan except for the mural. I always ordered the same thing: a salad plate with gefilte fish; for dessert: noodle kugel and coffee. I was too absorbed in

thinking and talking about figurative art to take much notice of the other diners. Occasionally, I'd notice another member of the Alliance at a nearby table lost in his thoughts. These outings were in fact an excuse for not staying home and working.

They used the old cafeteria punch card system for tallying prices and paying, but when the server grabbed the small red oblong strip of cardboard out of your hand he usually scrawled the price on the back with a blunt pencil. An English friend of mine found the food unpalatably bland. One night the mayoral candidate Abe Beame worked his way through the cafeteria, preceded by a man who called out, "Say hello to Abe Beame!" Ambitious and boisterous campaigning had no place in this garden of dairy food. A few people politely shook his hand; most ignored him. Metzger kidded one campaigner, "All you politicians show up before the election. What about after?"

From 1958 until 1963, Lawrence Block, an accountant handling Metzger's finances, was stealing money from the business. Mr. Block made out checks to pay the operating expenses of the business and, unbeknownst to Mr. Metzger, always added one payable to himself.

"Although 4,000 people a day were eating heartily in his cafeteria, Mr. Metzger found he wasn't making any money, and in an effort to correct this he began raising prices three years ago." Diners wondered why they were "paying a nickel more for blintzes, an extra dime for salads and up to 15 cents more for fish dishes." [*New York Times,* April 3, 1963]

For its last twenty-five years, it was managed by Bert Feinberg, Metzger's son-in-law, as his own son was not interested in the business. Charlie Metzger was a friend and supporter of the famous Yiddish art-song interpreter Sidor Belarsky; he'd buy fifty tickets whenever Belarsky gave a concert. He was also a member of the East Broadway Boys, an East Side merchants' association that met every month in a back room at Ratner's for dinner and card playing.

Because it was open on Saturdays, the local yeshiva students considered it "unreliable" and avoided eating there.

I. B. Singer's 1971 story "The Cabalist of East Broadway" opens in an unnamed fictional version of the Garden Cafeteria. It's long past its prime, filled

Garden Cafeteria

DAIRY RESTAURANT

MENU

165 East Broadway   **New York City**

ALgonquin 4-6962-6640

"All Baking Done On Premises"

*Compliments from
Mr & Mrs Charles Metzger*

Juices and Appetizers

Tomato Juice	.55	Fried Herring	1.40
Prune Juice	.55	Kippered Herring, Potatoes	1.55
Grapefruit Juice	.55	Pickled Lox	2.20
Maatjes Herring	1.40	Pickled Herring	1.40
Baked Herring	1.40	Greek Salad	1.40

Orange Juice - squeezed to order .... .70

Soups

Monday:	Russian Cabbage .. .85	Lima Bean	.85
Tuesday:	Potato .... .85	Green Split Pea	.85
Wednesday:	Lentil .... .85	Vegetable	.85
Thursday:	Hot Borscht .... .85	Whole Green Pea	.85
Friday:	Matzoh Ball .... .85	Mushroom Barley	.85
Saturday:	Potato .... .85	Yellow Split Pea	.85
Sunday:	Consomme Noodle .. .85	Vegetable	.85

Cold: Borscht with Cream .1.00   Schave with Cream 1.00
with Vegetables or Hard Boiled Egg (40c. extra)
Thursday: Fish Chowder .... .90

Fish

BROILED FILET OF FLOUNDER	2.75
BOILED or BAKED CARP	2.60
BROILED BLUEFISH (in Season)	2.60
BROILED PORGY (in Season)	2.60
BROILED SPANISH MACKEREL (in Season)	2.60
FRIED SMELTS (in Season)	2.60
BOILED PIKE	2.60
BROILED FLOUNDER	2.60
BROILED HALIBUT	2.65
BAKED WHITEFISH	2.60
BROILED SALMON	2.75
MARINATED FISH (Hecht) .2.75 SALMON	2.75
STUFFED FISH (Hot or Cold, Wednesday & Friday)	2.70
BROILED or FRIED FLUKE	2.75

Roasts

Monday:	GARDEN CHOW MEIN	1.65
Tuesday:	MUSHROOM POT PIE	1.75
Wednesday:	MUSHROOM GOULASH	1.65
Thursday:	FRIED EGGPLANT STEAK	1.65
Friday:	FISH CAKES and SPAGHETTI	1.65
Sunday:	STUFFED CABBAGE	1.65
MATZOH BREI		1.80
MUSHROOM STEAK		1.65
FRIED MUSHROOMS with Onions		2.15
SALMON CUTLET		1.65
VEGETABLE CUTLET		1.65

Not Responsible for Personal Property Unless Checked

Vegete

ANY 3 VEGETABLES OF TH

Sa

Skinless & Boneless Sardine	1.3
Vegetable Cream Cheese	.1.
Cream Cheese & Lox Mixed	1.5
Cream Cheese & Lox Combination	2.0
Chopped Egg & Mushrooms	1.2
Chopped Egg & Spinach	.1.1
Salmon Salad	
Lox	1.9
White Fish	1.4
Muenster Cheese	1.0
Chopped Herring	1.0
Egg Plant	1.
Tunafish	1.2
Individual Can Salmon	1.9

(Mayonnaise or Russian

Dai

POTATO BLINTZES	
CHERRY or BLUEBERRY BLIN	
CHEESE BLINTZES, To Order	
POTATO PIROGEN	
CHEESE KREPLACH	
KASHA PIROGEN	
POTATO or KASHA KNISH	
NOODLES and CHEESE	
KASHA VARNISHKES	
SPAGHETTI	
Peaches and Cream	
Bananas and Cream	
Bowl of Sour Cream	
Potato Pancakes with Apple S	
Strawberries and Sour Cream	
Pot Cheese or Vegetables with	
Blueberries with Sour Cream	

O

Lox with Onions and Eggs	2.5
Spanish Omelette	1.4
Green Pea Omelette	1.3
Swiss Cheese Omelette	1.
American Cheese Omelette	
Pot Cheese or Cottage Chee	

(Vegetable inste

MINIMUM CHE

Dishes

ˮ with Bread and Butter	. . 1.50

ˮches

Sardine	1.15
Nova Scotia Salmon	2.00
with Cream Cheese	2.30
Steak Salmon	
Vegetarian Liver	1.25
Cream Cheese	.90
Cream Cheese & Jelly	1.00
Sliced Egg	.80
Fried Egg	.75
Chopped Egg with Onions	1.10
Farmer Cheese	.95
Swiss Cheese	1.05
American Cheese	.95
Lettuce and Tomato	.90
Tomato Herring	1.10
Individual Can Tuna	1.60

ˮg Served Upon Request)

ˮishes

	1.50
	1.65
Sour Cream	1.55
Boiled 1.45 Fried 1.55	
Boiled 1.45 Fried 1.55	
Boiled 1.45 Fried 1.55	
only)	.70
	1.15
	1.15
	1.15
	1.35
	1.20
1.15 with Potatoes	1.50
ˮr Sour Cream	1.45
with Heavy Sweet Cream	1.80
Cream	1.35
	1.45

ˮtes

Mushroom Omelette	2.20
Onion Omelette	1.50
Jelly Omelette	1.40
2 Eggs, Any Style	1.00
	1.55
ˮelette	1.45

ˮotatoes 10c. extra)

ˮER PERSON - .50

Salads

Chopped Egg	1.50	Tuna	1.65
Chopped Spinach & Egg	1.50	Salmon	
Chopped Mushrooms		Salmon Steak	
and Egg	1.65	Imported Sardines	1.65
Hard Boiled Egg	1.30	Vegetarian Liver	1.65
Chopped Herring	1.40	Spring Salad	1.50
Fresh Fruit Salad	1.75	Smoked Sable	1.90
Smoked Whitefish	2.20	Egg Plant	1.60
Tomato Herring	1.50	Nova Scotia Salmon	
Garden Salad	1.50	Salad	2.50
Smoked Salmon Salad			2.30
Individual Can Salmon	2.35	Individual Can Tuna	2.05
Skinless and Boneless Sardines			2.00

Fruits and Desserts

Grapefruit	.55	Honey Dew Melon	.70
Fruit Pudding	.60	Baked Apple	.55
Stewed Prunes	.50	with Cream or Milk	.65
with Cream	.60	Cantaloupe (in season)	.70
Chocolate Pudding with Whipped Cream			.50
Fruit Jello with Whipped Cream or Milk			.50
Potato Pudding	.65	Cranshaw Melon	.70
Noodle or Rice Pudding	.65	Watermelon (in season)	.55
Fruit Cocktail	.65	Peaches	.45
Sliced Pineapple	.50	Apple Sauce	.35
Cheese Pudding (Thursday)	.65	Fresh Fruit Cup	.75

Our Own Baked Cakes and Pastries

Assorted Fruit Pies	.45	Marble Cake	.45
Strawberry Cheese Pie	.55	Sponge Cake	.45
Strawberry Cake	.55	Danish Pastry	.45
Apple Strudel	.50	Strawberry Shortcake	.65
Cheese Strudel	.55	Whipped Cream Butterfly	.55
Apple Turnover	.45	Whipped Cream Eclair	.55
Apple Cake	.45	Chocolate Cream Pie	.60
Cheese Cake	.50	Napoleon	.50

Beverages

Coffee or Tea	.25	Iced Tea or Coffee	.30
Hot Chocolate	.30	Chocolate Milk	.30
Postum	.25	Buttermilk	.30
Glass of Milk	.30	Glass of Sour Milk	.50

SPECIAL ATTENTION TO OUTGOING ORDERS
CALL: AL 4-6962 - 6640

Dinner

(Served from 4 P.M. to 10 P.M. Monday to Saturday)
(Sunday 2 P.M. to 10 P.M.)

Consists of Soup or Juice, Entree, Dessert and Beverage

No. 1 - $2.80

Choice of Soup (or) Juice

Choice of One of the Following:

Salmon Cutlet	Vegetable Cutlet	Cheese Blintzes
Spanish Omelette	Chopped Tuna	Onion Omelette
Chopped Salmon Salad		Green Pea Omelette
Chopped Herring		Egg Salad

Bread or Rolls

Cake or Pudding   Coffee or Milk

No. 2 - $3.35

Choice of Soup (or) Juice

Choice of One of the Following:

Canned Salmon Steak	Skinless and Boneless Sardine Salad
Fried Mushrooms	Mushroom Omelette

Bread or Rolls

Cake or Pudding   Coffee or Milk

No. 3 - $3.40

Choice of Soup (or) Juice

Choice of One of the Following:

Baked Whitefish	Boiled Pike	Boiled Carp
Broiled Flounder		Broiled Halibut

Bread or Rolls

Cake or Pudding   Coffee or Milk

No. 4 - $3.65

Choice of Soup (or) Juice

Choice of One of the Following:

Broiled Salmon	Filet of Flounder	Marinated Fish
	Broiled Fluke	

Bread or Rolls

Cake or Pudding   Coffee or Milk

Whipped Cream Cakes 30¢ Extra

---

with Puerto Rican and black people; the Yiddish writers and other cultural operators were gone. "The voices were different, the smells were different." The one familiar face is that of Joel Yabloner, an aged and broken kabbalist scholar who had supposedly fallen into a melancholy after being forced to eat pork at a tuberculosis sanatorium in Colorado. "He ate neither fish nor meat, not even eggs or milk — only bread, vegetables and fruit. In the cafeteria he always ordered a cup of black coffee and a dish of prunes." Despite having offers to move to Israel, where he was considered something of a "spiritual father," "he would sit for hours staring at the revolving door, at the cashier's desk, or the wall where, years ago, a commercial artist had painted the market on Orchard

Looking for a table in the Garden Dairy Cafeteria.

APPETIZERS

Street, with its pushcarts and peddlers. The paint was peeling now." Years later, in Tel Aviv, the narrator stumbles upon Yabloner, by chance, in a hotel meeting hall where he's delivering a lecture on the Kabbalah in Ashkenazic Hebrew. He seems to have been miraculously reborn: elegantly dressed, sporting a goatee, a full set of dentures in his mouth. His erudite and somewhat humorous lecture is appreciated by a largely female audience. This lifelong bachelor's every move is now directed by an overly solicitous wife and a committee of admirers, who've organized a vegetarian banquet to be held in his honor. The narrator asks him why he waited so long to emigrate to Israel. His answer, "Man does not live according to reason." Back on East Broadway, a few years later, the narrator discovers Yabloner sitting alone in the cafeteria, restored to his disheveled condition and vacant stare. He refuses to enter into conversation. A few weeks later, his death is announced in the newspaper. The narrator ponders the motives behind his return. Perhaps "a power stronger than man and his calculations has driven him out of Paradise, back to Hell," or maybe some kabbalistic mission, left uncompleted, had driven him back to the cafeteria? In my reading of the story, the kabbalist had returned to the Garden Cafeteria to escape the Gehenna of an academic life in Tel Aviv.

    As an immigrant from Poland in the 1930s, Singer's first visit to a cafeteria was "a great riddle." "We did not have anything like this in Europe. No matter how poor a restaurant it was, there was always a waiter, there was no such thing as a man taking a tray and going to get food from a counter. I thought to myself: So many waiters in such a small place? How does it happen?

Why do they need so many waiters? And whenever I saw one with a tray, I gave him a sign. But these people all ignored me . . . Some of them smiled. . . . And I said to myself: What a wicked place, it almost looks to me like a dream. A little place with so many waiters and no one pays any attention to me!" In time, Singer came to understand the system and cafeterias became his second home. [Ed McCormack, "The Last Cafeteria," *New York Daily News,* October 16, 1983]

Jose Delgado who worked there for almost thirty years, remembered it as "a madhouse. It was open 24 hours a day all year round with the exception of Rosh Hashanah, Yom Kippur, and the first two days of Passover. Yes, man, every seat was taken. People lined up especially on Sundays when the theater audiences came and we also got the trade from Delancey and Orchard Streets. The big-shot editors and the workingmen printers used to have sometimes three meals a day."

The Garden Cafeteria was documented in a series of photographs by Bruce Davidson in 1975. Metzger also operated **Metzger's Bakery** and pastry shop at 555 Grand Street, NYC. Surviving matchbooks for the Garden Cafeteria feature drawings of pinup girls — a demonstration of the happy coexistence of milk and meat in the body of a woman. The Garden Cafeteria Dairy closed in 1983.

The final owner, Joseph Baumohl, a native of Romania, explained: "Business is going down. The better people who lived around here moved away and what's left is the elderly people drinking a cup of coffee and eating a piece of cake for 80 cents. They can't afford more. We have a dining room with

RATNER'S
DAIRY
RESTAURANT

RATNER'S
DAIRY RESTAURANT

ANCEY

LOEW

CRAWFORD & T
"THE GORGEOUS
TONE AND BARR
ALSO HAPPY HARMO

JOAN CRAWFORD & M
"THE GORGEOUS H

ROOMS

JUICE

138 Delancey St.
1936

240 seats and not enough people to fill them. You couldn't make a living." In 1983, he sold the place to a Chinese restaurateur.

Ratner's Dairy Restaurant, 138 Delancey Street, between Norfolk and Suffolk Streets. The last of the large-scale dairy restaurants in New York. The decor was vaguely Deco after its final renovation — cut-glass mirrors and streamlined sculptural woodwork — an atmosphere of refined industrial hygiene. The high ceilings and rambling rear party rooms were a holdover from a more luxurious and expansive restaurant culture. I knew this place in its decline but appreciated that I was eating in a place not of this world. It was staffed by waiters who had lost all sense of decorum. They were small, rough Russians and ex–delicatessen workers who had ended up at one of the last Jewish restaurants on Delancey Street.

I recall having a bowl of borscht placed on my table with such carelessness that half of it spilled onto the table — and the waiter did not notice. The onion rolls remained good to the bitter end. The borscht was unfortunately served premixed with sour cream. The lettuce in the salads consisted of pale interior leaves. The kasha varnishkes were drowned in an ancient mushroom gravy. The retail bakery counter in the front offered packaged frozen Ratner's blintzes and soups. The afterlife of this venerable dairy restaurant would be situated in the frozen-food section of suburban supermarkets. It was a vast space enjoyed by just a handful of evening diners. It seemed impossible that such a place could exist in twentieth-century Manhattan without a subsidy. The owner and/or cashier sat near the register killing time and bemoaning their bad timing.

In the 1990s, Harold H. Harmatz's sons, Robert and Fred, in an attempt to cater to the newly observant Jews of New York, hired a rabbi to supervise the kitchen and closed on Fridays at sundown in observance of the Sabbath. The hours were changed to Sunday–Thursday, 6 am–10:30 pm, and Fridays, 6 am–3 pm. From 1995 to 2000, business had dropped by half. In 1991 a serious fire closed the place for four months while the staff of one hundred collected unemployment benefits. The interior design was preserved. Marty Sacks was the night manager in those days.

In 1997, Robert and Fred opened an ersatz speakeasy, located in the rear party room, named after the Jewish gangster who frequented Ratner's. "He used to sit right at this table, surrounded by bodyguards," said Abraham Reinstein, who had been the manager of Ratner's for almost forty years. "We didn't approach, unless asked."

The Lansky Lounge, complete with secret alleyway entrance and photo murals of East Side criminals, served an upscale continental menu. As if anyone cared, a sign notified its patrons that its kitchen (which it shared with Ratner's) was "not under Chaf-K supervision. Food is prepared in Ratner's kitchen, which has Chaf-K supervision." At some point, Ratner's gave up on kosher supervision because they "didn't get support of the Jewish community." Reportedly, the Chaf-K wanted Ratner's to erect opaque partitions at the washing stations, so that its customers could not see into the Lansky Lounge, with its bar, dancing, and social scene.

When Ratner's closed in 2002, the restaurant was just breaking even.

Operating costs rose and "there was only so much they could charge for a blintz." It was sad to read of the final closing and auction sale of its contents — Ratner's had finally succumbed to the larger world.

The Harmatz brothers and Alex Ratner's history is recounted on page 342. Morris (Alex) Ratner, their brother-in-law by marriage to a Harmatz half-sister, was born in Russia (Poland) in 1878 and arrived in the U.S. in 1889 at the age of eleven. (Died September 26, 1935, in Roscoe, California.) He was by 1910 already operating his own restaurant in Harlem at 1754 Madison Avenue at 115th Street.

Small display ads in the March 15, 1912, edition of *Di Yidisher Vokhenshrift* and *Der Kibetser* from 1913 announce a Ratner's Dairy Restaurant at 179 East Broadway. A classified ad in the October 4, 1914, edition of the *Yidishes Tageblat* says, "The best dairy dishes you'll get in Ratner's Restaurant, 170 East Broadway." These may have been early locations of the Ratner's partnership or simply a downtown branch of Alex's restaurant.

RATNER'S

138 DELANCEY STREET

new york city

Visit Our Retail Cou

Salads

California Fruit Salad with Cottage Cheese	2.50
Tropical Salad	2.40
Vegetable Liver Salad with Potato Salad	2.30
Salmon Salad with Potato Salad (Steak)	2.55
Sliced Egg Salad with Potato Salad	2.00
Chopped Egg Salad with Potato Salad	2.20
Chopped Herring Salad with Potato Salad	2.25
Individual (Can) Tunafish Salad with Potato Salad	2.35
Combination Salad ....2.00 with Maatjes Herring	2.40
Imported Sardine Salad with Potato Salad	2.25
Smoked Whitefish with Potato Salad	3.05
Imported Boneless and Skinless Sardine Salad, Potato Salad	2.30

Side Order of:—
Tomato 35   Cole Slaw 35   Lettuce & omato 60   Potato Salad 35

Eggs and Omelettes

CHOICE OF FRESH JERSEY EGGS USED EXCLUSIVELY

Two Eggs, Boiled	.80
Two Eggs, Scrambled, Fried or Omelette	1.00
Shirred Eggs	1.05
Poached Eggs on Toast 1.05 Poached Egg on Spinach	1.65
Scrambled Eggs with Onions	1.25
with Lox	2.00
with Mushrooms	2.40
with Nova Scotia Salmon	2.60
Stewed Tomato or Green Pepper Omelette	1.70
Spanish or Western Omelette	2.00
Cheese Omelette	1.80
Fresh Stewed or Fried Mushroom Omelette	2.40

Above Orders Served with Potatoes Only
With Onions - 25c. additional
Substitution of Vegetable - 15c. extra
Substitution of Sliced Tomato - 35c. extra

Dairy Dishes

Noodles with Cheese and Butter	1.90
French Apple Pancake (10 minutes)	2.40
Matzo Brei, Scrambled or Pancake Style (10 minutes)	2.40
Marmaliga with Cheese and Butter	1.85
Matzo Pancakes	2.40
Cheese Pancakes with Sour Cream	1.80
Cauliflower with Butter Sauce, Boiled Potato and Carrots	1.80
Apple Fritters with Jam	2.20
French Toast with Jam or Syrup	2.30

Cream Dishes

Bowl of Sour Cream ....1.35 with Potato	1.80
Pot Cheese with Sour Cream	1.80
Peaches with Sour Cream	1.80
Bananas with Sour Cream	1.80
Vegetables with Sour Cream	1.80
Fresh Strawberries or Blueberries	2.20

All Above Orders Served with Sweet Cream 25c. extra
Blueberries or Strawberries Served in a Side Dish 80c.

SINGLE ORDER SERVED for (2) 50c. extra
CHILDREN'S SERVICE CHARGE 50c. per Child

COFFEE or TEA with Bread or Rolls and Butter 75c.

SPECIALS FOR TOD

Friday,

Fruits and Juices

Fresh Orange or Grapefruit Juice 40   Large G
MELON IN SEASON 75   Stewed Oregon Prunes
Fresh Fruit Cup 70   Half Grapefruit 65   Baked Apple
Chilled Apricot, Prune, Pineapple or Tomato Juice 35
California Vegetable Juice Cocktail 35   Large

Appetizers

Chopped Eggs and Onions 1.80	Spring Salad .....
Greek Salad	2.00	Canned Salmon
Pickled Lox	2.40	Individual Canne
Chopped Vegetarian Liver	2.00	Chopped Egg Pla
Pickled Herring	2.00	Chopped Salmon
Chopped Herring	2.00	Smoked Whitefish
Chopped Tunafish	2.00	Mixed Appetizers
Individual Canned Tunafish 2.00	Maatjes Herring
Imported Marshall Tomato Herring		
Imported Brisling Sardines in Tomato Sauce		

Above Orders Served with Lettuce and Tomat

Soups

Manhattan Fish Chowder 90   Consomme with Matzo
Rice or Noodles or Kashe with Milk 80   Barley and M
COLD BORSCHT with Cream (glass or bowl) 85   w
with Vegetables ....1.10   Combination Vegetable an
Soups without Entree or Roast 20c. extra

Fish

Baked Gefilte Fish, Vegetable and Potato	
Smoked Sable, Lettuce, Tomato, Cole Slaw and Potato Sala	
Broiled Fish with Vegetable and Potatoes	
Broiled Halibut with Vegetables and Potatoes	
Baked Boston Colfish Cakes, Tomato Sauce, Spaghetti, Gree	
STUFFED FISH (Gefilte) ....2.50 Pickled Fish (Jellie	
Baked Fish with Vegetable and Mashed Potatoes	
Broiled Kippered Herring, Potato, Onions 1.90 with Chef's	
Chilled Boiled Carp with Lettuce 3.10 Boiled Whitefish, Pota	
Fried Herring with Onions ....1.90. Pickled Salmon N	
FRIED FISH, SCALLOP STYLE, Sauce Tartare, Cole Slaw	

All Broiled Fish—To Order 15 minutes

Hot Dishes

BAKED VEGETABLE CUTLET with Carrots and Peas
Boiled or Fried Potato Pirogen with Cream
New Vegetable Dinner
Baked Brown Kashe with Gravy and Onions
Noodle Chop Suey with Kashe
KASHE VARNISHKES with Mushrooms en Casserole
Baked Mushroom Steak with Spaghetti
Boiled or Fried Cheese Kreplach with Cream
Nuttose or Protose Steak (Vegetarian Meat), Onions, Vegeta
Fried Eggplant Steak, Vegetables, French Fried Poatoes
Fresh Spinach with Poached Eggs
Spaghetti with Tomato Sauce
Potato Pancakes with Apple Sauce
Apple Cheese, Pineapple Cheese or Cherry Blintzes with Ca
Cheese, Potato or Kashe Blintzes with Sour Cream
Spinach and Egg au Gratin (to Order 10 minutes)

OLD FASHIONED POTATO PUDDING

OLEO MARGARINE SERVED ON REQUEST

SUBSTITUTIONS OF BAKED POTATO, 15c.
BAGEL OR BIALSTOKER, 15c. extra

MINIMUM CHARGE 75c. PER PERSON

Ratner's Dairy Restaurant, Delancey Street, menu, 1972

er 24, 1972

BREAD, ROLLS AND BUTTER WITHOUT APPETIZER
OR MAIN COURSE - 40c.

Mushrooms and Vegetables
BAKED IDAHO POTATO 35

Broiled Fresh Mushrooms on Toast 2.80
New Vegetable Dinner ....2.00 with Hard Boiled Egg 2.45
Fresh Stewed Mushrooms, Mashed Potatoes en Casserole 2.50
Fresh Fried Mushrooms with Mashed Potatoes en Casserole 2.60
Spinach and Mashed Potatoes 1.70
Baked Brown Kashe with Creamed Mushrooms 2.50
Mashed Potatoes 40 with Onions 60   Boiled Potatoes 45
Kashe Varnishkes with Creamed Mushrooms 2.50

Side Order of Vegetables Served with Order 25c.
Side Order of Fried or Stewed Mushrooms 60c.
Dietetic Vegetables Served with Order 25c.

Fruits and Desserts

POTATO PUDDING 65   Stewed Prunes 65   with Cream 75
MELON IN SEASON 75   Sliced Pineapple 55   Fresh Fruit Cup 70
Cream Cheese Ruglech 60   Apple Cake 65
Half Grapefruit 65   Chocolate Pudding 45   Whipped Cream 55
Crumb Cheese Cake (Cherry or Pineapple) 60   Cheese Cake 60
Baked Apple 60   with Cream 70   Stewed Figs 60   with Cream 70
Home Made Fruit Pie 55   a la Mode 95   Danish Pastry 55
Whipped Cream Layer Cake 65   Chocolate Layer Cake 55
Crumb Cake 55   Boston Cream Pie 75   Nesselrode Pie 65
Jello 40 with Cream 50   with Fruit 70
Apple or Pineapple Fritters with Jam 2.10   Victory Layer Cake 65
Coffee Cake 55   Fruit Compote 75   Chocolate Eclair 60
Strawberry Shortcake 75   Bartlett Pears 55
CREAMY RICE PUDDING (Hot or Cold) 60   with Cream 70

ICE CREAMS

Sherbet ....60 Ratner's Parfait 70
Ice Cream Cake 75
French Ice Cream 65
Peach Melba 85
1 Pineapple Ice Cream Sundae, Whipped Cream 85
2 Strawberry Ice Sundae, Whipped Cream 85
3 Peach Ice Cream Sundae, Whipped Cream 85

ASSORTED CAKES, PASTRIES and WHIPPED CREAM CAKES

Toasts

Fruit Wheat Cakes with Syrup and Butter 1.60
Devonshire Melba Toast 15   Wheat Cakes and Syrup 1.25
French Toast with Jam or Syrup 2.30

Beverages

Coffee with Cream 25   Ginger Ale 40
Pekoe Tea 25   Dr. BROWN'S Celery Tonic 40
Individual Bottle of Milk 25   Dr. BROWN'S Slim Ray 40
Individual Postum 25   Cola 40
Individual Sanka Coffee 30   Home Made Sour Milk 40
Hot Chocolate with   Individual Buttermilk 25
with Whipped Cream 35   Saratoga Vichy Water...........45
Iced Tea 35   Iced Coffee 35
Milk Chocolate with Whipped Cream 40

NOT RESPONSIBLE FOR PERSONAL PROPERTY
UNLESS CHECKED AT CASHIER'S DESK

Chef's Suggestions

Boiled or Fried Potato
  or Kashe Pirogen 2.20
Cheese, Potato or Kashe
  Blintzes with Sour Cream 2.20
Pineapple, Cherry, Blueberry,
  or Apple Cheese Blintzes
  with Sour Cream 2.40
California Fruit Salad
  with Cottage Cheese 2.50
Vegetable Liver Salad
  with Potato Salad 2.30
Chopped Egg Salad
  with Potato Salad 2.20
Smoked Whitefish Salad
  with Potato Salad 3.05

Any Order of Assorted Blintzes
                    15c. Extra

Weight Watchers Specials

California Fruit Salad 2.50
Spring Salad 1.90
Broiled Mushrooms 2.60
Asparagus on Toast 2.45

From Our Broiler

TO ORDER 10 MINUTES

Special a la Ratner, 30c. extra

Broiled Florida Pompano 7.00
BROILED CORN-FED CARP ...3.75
Broiled Sea Bass 4.20
Broiled Florida Red Snapper 4.85
Broiled Speckled Brook Trout 3.85
Broiled Salmon 4.95
Broiled Eastern Halibut Steak 3.95
Broiled Whitefish 3.90
Broiled L. I. Flounder 3.50
Broiled Filet of Sole 3.90

Fried Fish Scallop Style,
  Sauce Tartar, Cole Slaw 3.50
Fried Filet, Tartar Sauce 3.40
HOT or COLD FRIED FLOUNDER,
  Tartar Sauce 3.50

Vegetable, Potatoes and Chef's Salad Bowl
with French Dressing, Served with Above

Substitutions of Lettuce and Tomato
Instead of Salad, 35c. extra

The commonly stated opening date of 1918 for Ratner's at 138 Delancey is belied by an ad for the G & G (Goodman and Goldman's) Bakery and Dairy Restaurant opening at the same location on February 4, 1919. This may have been a short-lived lease, soon taken over by Ratner's. Alex Ratner seems to have sold out his share of the restaurant by that date. Harold L. (Harris) Harmatz took sole possession of his own "Ratner's Dairy Restaurant" on Second Avenue (see page 342).

Ratner's on Delancey was opened sometime after April 1919 by Jacob Harmatz (born 1885–died July 2, 1966, age 81) in partnership with Max and Louis Zankel. The partnership later extended to Max's son, Harry.

They eventually purchased the building and slowly, in a partnership known as the Zankel Group, began expanding their real-estate holdings. Real estate, not the restaurant, became their main source of income.

In a 1940 interview, Jacob explained that back in 1905, "stirred by recurrent epidemics of stomach ailments that had befallen unwary patrons of third rate meat establishments, and out of a desire to be helpful, he opened a dairy eating place at 87 Pitt Street with an investment of $150.00. Their first day's income amounted to $9.00." It was, he claimed, among the first dairy restaurants on the East Side. "Between 1905 and 1928 their menu consisted of some twelve items; today it includes about 150 selections none of which are known to have ever caused anybody stomach trouble."

Snacks

Plate of Nova Scotia Lox 2.45	Chopped Herring 1.90
Filet of Pickled Herring in Cream Sauce 1.90	Imp. Marshall Sardines in Tomato Sauce 1.90
Fresh Smoked Whitefish 2.70	Iceland Maatjes Herring 1.90
Imported Portuguese Boneless Sardines 1.90	Box of Imported Crosspack Brislings 1.80
Plate of Lox 2.35	Maatjes Herring in Wine Sauce 1.95
	Box of Imp. Boneless and Skinless Sardines ..1.95

(Above Orders Served with Lettuce and Tomato)

Delicacies - Platters

1. Smoked Salmon, Cream Cheese or Swiss Cheese, Lettuce and Tomato 2.70
2. Chinook Salmon, Hard Boiled Egg, Lettuce and Tomato 2.70
3. Sable Carp, Swiss Cheese, Smoked Salmon, Lettuce and Tomato 3.95
4. Combination Platter: Sable Carp, Whitefish, Nova Scotia Salmon, Cream Cheese, Lettuce and Tomato 4.45
   (for two) .....8.20   (for three) .....12.20   (for four) 15.70
5. Nova Scotia Salmon and Cream Cheese, Lettuce and Tomato 2.95

Sandwiches

1. Imported Boneless Sardines with Hard Boiled Egg 2.00
2. Smoked Salmon and Cream Cheese 2.05
3. Sable Carp and Smoked Salmon 3.65
4. Nova Scotia Salmon and Cream Cheese 2.50
5. Imported Filet of Tunafish 2.55

Hard Boiled Egg 1.15	Chopped Eggs and Onions ..1.30	Canned Tunafish 1.50
American or Cream Cheese 1.15	Smoked Salmon 1.70	Canned Salmon 1.65
Chopped Herring 1.30	Imported Sardines 1.50	Imported Boneless and
Melted Cheese 1.30	Imported Swiss Cheese 1.50	Skinless Sardines 1.55
Chopped Liver 1.30	Nova Scotia Lox 1.90	Chopped Salmon 1.35
Tomato Herring 1.30	Western 1.60	Smoked Whitefish 2.15
Chopped Tunafish 1.30	Lettuce and Tomato 1.25	
	Cream Cheese and Jelly on Toast 1.15	

(All Above Orders Served with Cole Slaw, Lettuce and Tomato)

Made to Order
SPECIAL CAKES
FOR ALL OCCASIONS

Catering

HAVING A PARTY?

We Accept Reservations for . . . Showers, Engagements, Weddings, Anniversaries, Confirmations, After Meeting Parities, Bon Voyage, Farewell Parties and all other Social Functions . . . at moderate prices.

Private rooms from 30 to 200 persons

Estimates will be furnished on request

ASK FOR MANAGER . . .

Abe Beame at Ratner's

Jacob Harmatz, already characterized as "a wealthy restaurateur" and "The King of Delancey Street," was sued in December of 1926 for $50,000 by his son-in-law, Henry G. Finger, age twenty-one, for alienation of his wife, Nathalie, age eighteen. Harmatz was stunned by the secret elopement of his underaged daughter to this poor apprentice in the garment trade and ordered an annulment of the marriage or that she live at home until she finished college. Harmatz told Mr. Finger, "I know you are not the man for my girl. She should marry a professional man or somebody with money and position."

An ad in the 1929–30 *East Side Chamber of Commerce News* announced a renovation of the Delancey Street space: "The East Side's Premier Dining Place. Ratner's Dairy Restaurant. More than $100,000 has been spent to make this famous East Side eating place bigger and better in every modern way. Larger Baking facilities on premises. Big Sanitary Kitchen. 250 Seats." In those years, the businessmen of the East Side were calling for urban redevelopment projects to bring business back to their neighborhood.

A 1934 photo of Delancey Street shows a sidewalk crowded with well-dressed Jews, the Paradise Chop Suey Chinese Restaurant, the Paramount Cafeteria (also run by Jacob Harmatz), a Woolworth's 5 & 10 Cent Store, Silver's Dress Suits to Hire, Ratner's Dairy Restaurant, and Loew's Delancey Movie Theatre running *The Mystery of Mr. X*, a pre-code crime film starring Robert Montgomery, and a newsstand filled to capacity with printed matter; the roadway carries cars and trucks to and from the Williamsburg Bridge, which dissolves in the distance. Delancey was the major artery bisecting the Jewish Lower East Side and the perfect location for a large milkhiker oasis.

Over the years, Jacob remained partners with Max and Louis Zankel, and Max's son, Harry.

In 1949, Moishe Breitbart, a recently arrived twenty-seven-year-old Polish Jew from Turka, who survived the Second World War as a partisan fighter, walked into Ratner's on Delancey Street looking for work. Jacob Harmatz hired him to work as the night cleanup man. At that time, Ratner's was open 24 hours a day, 7 days a week. In time, Breitbart moved to the bakery counter, to a short stint in the bakery (the hours were too much for him), to the night manager, and finally, in 1969, to the general manager — a job he held until two months before his death in 2002.

A conversation in 2016 with Moishe's son, William Breitbart, yielded these memories.

In the early days, Breitbart worked alongside the general manager, a Mr. Minor, a fellow who was as wide as he was tall with glasses and a cigar, and the one active owner, Jacob's son, Harold Harmatz. Zankel's son, Harry, described as something of an elderly playboy, appeared at the restaurant on occasion. The headwaiter, Mr. Hauser, and waiter Dave Keller were two among many cigar-smoking Eastern European Holocaust survivors who found employment at Ratner's. Another, Irving Weicher, worked his way through college and became the accountant for Ratner's.

Breitbart, as general manager, was responsible for the day-to-day running of the restaurant: dealing with suppliers and employees. He worked a 12-hour day. He was responsible for calculating how much food to buy in order to prepare and serve the anticipated number of meals to the 240 customers who'd fill the main dining room on a busy Sunday. He was also in charge of private parties and catering. Family-circle dinners, Israel bond drives, and bar-mitzvah parties of up to 180 people helped augment his income with tips — it was a cash business.

He occasionally dreamt of opening a diner of his own, not a dairy restaurant, with the help of Julius Merkrebs, the head baker, but, in the end, remained at Ratner's for fifty years. In those years, the restaurant increasingly became a sideline to the Zankel Group's real-estate holdings. As the demographic of the Lower East Side changed, Ratner's tried to appeal to the Orthodox community by receiving a hechsher and closing on Shabbos, but it didn't help.

Breitbart had no office but roamed around the restaurant. He ate the same meal every day — mushroom-barley soup and a basket of Ratner's beloved onion rolls. He sat alone at a table before the two automatic doors leading to the kitchen. A group of Eastern European women were hired to make a variety of pirogen, cheese kreplekh, and blintzes. The rest of the kitchen staff was divided between short-order cooks, a fish man, hot and cold kitchen chefs who made salads, assembled plates of smoked and pickled fish, and vegetarian chopped liver. Peanut butter was the secret ingredient in their vegetarian chopped liver. His management style — eternal dissatisfaction with the work of his staff — led him to do things himself and, on at least one occasion, led to a fistfight. He was, understandably, an angry man "who worked his kishkas out for his family."

Vegetarianism was of no interest to Breitbart. On his days off, he would choose to eat in one of the many delicatessens in the area — Crown Delicatessen was a favorite until it closed — or enjoy his wife's wonderful home cooking. Toward the end, his favorite eating place was his friend Abe Lowenthal's 2nd Avenue Deli. Breitbart's parents, who lived in the same building as him, were known to never eat in restaurants. Breitbart had a dim view of upscale restaurants. Taken to the Four Seasons for his anniversary, he was disgusted by the excessive number of waiters and busboys, substandard bread, and only ordered a simple plate of scrambled eggs.

Breitbart, a registered Democrat with a socially conservative outlook, was willing to pose for photos with the countless politicians who considered Ratner's

Jacob Harmatz
on
Delancey
Street

an important campaign stop. Breitbart couldn't understand his son William's opposition to the war in Vietnam. William's mother was the liberal thinker in the family who introduced her children to the arts.

There was no question of Breitbart's son, William, going into the restaurant business. "When I woke up Father was asleep, when I came home from school he was at the restaurant." Only on Mondays and Fridays did he spend time with his father. But, through his teenage years and while at college, he'd work a range of part-time jobs at Ratner's. At the bakery counter, he could wrap a dozen assorted Danish (prune, poppy, cheese) in under twenty-four seconds, prompting Harry the counterman to remark, "Now you're cooking with gas!" As a busboy, he accidentally grabbed a handful of knives from the wrong end, showering the dairy cutlery bin, to his father's dismay, with blood. As a waiter, he could rattle off the ten vegetables of the day in a single breath. He served Woody Allen cold borscht with a potato and sour cream; Mayor John Lindsay, kippered herring; of Kim Novak, he recalled only her tight sweater.

He recalled Mr. Hauser, the headwaiter, talking a customer out of ordering the Protose steak — a canned vegetable concoction with the consistency of dog food — "You don't want it."

In 1940 they employed 75 workers. Its 300 seats were filled with an average of 2,500 customers a day. Some 150 pounds of boiled and gefilte fish were sold daily, with 200 pounds on Fridays and Saturdays. Huge quantities of butter (300 pounds), eggs (15,000 dozen), vegetables (6 tons), herring (2,000), cream (600 quarts), milk (1,200 quarts), flour (4,900 pounds), cheese (500 pounds),

458

and coffee (350 pounds) were consumed each week. The restaurant never closed its door except for Rosh Hashanah, Yom Kippur, and the first two days of Passover.

Only 25 percent of their customers were from the neighborhood — they simply couldn't afford to eat out — the rest were middle- and upper-class Jews from other parts of the city and large parties on the weekend. According to Jacob Harmatz, religious Jews who wouldn't usually eat at restaurants, or, for that matter, their own children's homes, felt comfortable in his restaurant. Only 8 percent of their customers were non-Jewish.

A menu from 1940 included such specialties as mamaliga in cheese and butter (25 cents), various mock meats including chicken giblet fricassee vegetarian-style (35 cents) and a lake sturgeon sandwich (45 cents).

Jacob's son Harold (1913–2004) and his four daughters helped out at the restaurant. Harold went on to earn a law degree at NYU, but in 1944, at the request of his father, returned to manage the business. The restaurant was renovated again and had a grand reopening on December 10, 1957, with an enlarged kitchen and facelift of the dining room: new lighting fixtures and new upholstery, but the same number of tables. The contractors were proudly listed: Pollack and Sons Store Fixtures, Inc.; Salzman Sign Co., Inc.; Superior Metal Store Front Corp.; V. Foscato, terrazzo floor; and Baskin Plumbing Corp.

The announcement played on the nostalgia angle: "For over a half century expatriates from the East Side have been making pilgrimages to Delancey St. Unto the third and fourth generations they have retained the image of exotic dairy and fish dishes . . . of seductive rolls and pastries . . . that created mouthmelting memories!"

In addition, Jacob Harmatz and his partners operated two Paramount Cafeterias (American-style meat and dairy), one on Kings Highway in Brooklyn and one on Delancey Street.

According to the *New York Times,* in the mid-1950s Ratner's baked 10,000 onion rolls to feed 1,200 diners at Sunday brunch. They were irresistible, small, soft, square rolls stuffed with cooked onions. Harold expanded the restaurant to accommodate 344 seats.

On a hot August evening in 1957, a fistfight broke out in Ratner's when teenagers Frank and Edward Falco along with John Kealy made some remarks about two women escorted by Nicholas Gregoria and Dominick Capola. When the police arrived to break up the fight, they were brutally attacked by the five boys.

In April of 1956, after throwing acid in the face of the labor columnist Victor Riesel, Abe Telvi stumbled into Ratner's at 4 am to meet with Joseph Carlino, the man who hired him for $500. Telvi was holding a handkerchief to his face, where some of the acid had landed. Carlino gave him an extra $100 to cover the replacement of his acid-spotted suit.

In 1958, Ratner's was visited by Nelson A. Rockefeller campaigning for governor of New York State. Although a resident of New York City, he had never before visited Delancey Street. "Before an admiring crowd, he learned the glories of the blintz. . . . They're delicious, he said and ate with the obvious enjoyment of a vigorous man with a solid athletic build." In near disregard of Jewish dietary law, he went from Ratner's to stop at Max Weitzman's kosher delicatessen, where he posed in a butcher's apron alongside a salami.   .
[*Chicago Tribune,* October 5, 1958]

In 1964, Harold was active in opposing a plan by Robert Moses to build an expressway connecting the Williamsburg Bridge to the Holland Tunnel. Such an expressway, he maintained, would destroy the fabric of the neighborhood.

In 1965, New York City policemen were angered by a directive by Lindsay's Deputy Mayor Robert Price to pick up eighty-four danishes and eight quarts of beverages at 7:30 am from Ratner's for biweekly Cabinet meetings. When the Patrolmen's Benevolent Association complained, the order was shifted in 1971 to uniformed firemen of Engine Co. 17, located a block from Ratner's. A complaint soon followed detailing the misuse of their overworked men.

The oldest waiter at Ratner's in 2006 was Alex Hersko, age seventy; Romanian born, he came to New York via Israel in 1970. After thirty years on the job he claimed to have an intuitive sense of which customers would be good tippers.

Ratner's was open for breakfast, lunch, dinner, and supper seven days a week, twenty-four hours a day, until 1975. Harold's sons, Robert and Fred, took over management in the 1980s.

In 1981, while at his condominium in Hallandale, Florida, Harold Harmatz discovered a newly opened restaurant called Rattner's (with two "t"s) of Florida serving Jewish food "identical" to that served in his restaurant. He requested an injunction to prevent them from using the trademarked name. The owners of the Florida Rattner's at first claimed to have never heard of Ratner's, but at a second hearing admitted the infringement. They had decided to use another name in Jewish restaurant history, "Rappaport's" (*sic*), then out of business for fifteen years.

By 2002, catering to the neighborhood's shift from Jewish discount clothing stores to galleries and boutiques, the Lansky Lounge was opened seven nights a week, Ratner's only on Sundays. Fred mused, "The way this neighborhood has changed, people who come into Lansky's now, if you asked them what a bowl of borscht was they'd think you were speaking a foreign language." The Ratner's brand of frozen foods, started by Harold, was sold to King Kold of Chicago, and is now owned by the Saveur Food Group, LLC, and manufactured by Cohen's Foods of Lakewood, New Jersey — famous for their "Mini Franks in a Blanket."

The Dayton Dairy Cafeteria at 454 Broadway, two blocks above Canal Street, was, in the mid-1980s, the functioning ruin of a great New York dairy cafeteria. The generous proportions of the room (high tin ceilings, long communal tables) reflected an early-twentieth-century lower Broadway, where wholesale textile and leather-hide dealers escaped their sordid business dealings for lunch in a dairy paradise. The cafeteria tray tracks ran on forever. Business was always slow; there was little food in sight. I sat there one beautiful winter morning with friends discussing the ambitious plans of our youth over coffee, while the manager, an aged, pale man in an oversized short-sleeve shirt, wondered why we weren't eating something to nourish his dying business. A description in *New York* magazine from 1972 captures its happier days: "The food is excellent, especially the baked goods. A luxuriously leaden nut cake was particularly impressive, and there is distinguished challah on Fridays only. Prices for full-scale lunches . . . hover in the $2 area. . . .

Dayton's is open Monday to Friday from 6 am to 6 pm. The entire neighborhood lunches here, so it's very crowded from noon to 2 pm." It disappeared soon after my discovery of its existence.

Williamsburg Pizza and Restaurant (Green's Pizza & Restaurant, Green & Ackerman Restaurant & Pizza), 214–16 Ross Street, Williamsburg, Brooklyn. In this nondescript taxpayer overlooking the BQE, one can sample gefilte fish in which the chopped fish mixture is actually filled (gefüllte) back into the body of a fish.

An 1899 *New York Tribune* article explained: "The fish cook does not reach the point of perfection until she can prepare stuffed fish in the real Posen style. For this dish only large fish are selected. After the fish has been thoroughly cleaned, the skin is carefully removed, and the bones have all been taken out, the meat is hashed and mixed with spices and condiments, and put back into the skin, which is sewed up, and then, the reconstructed fish is boiled. People who have eaten it and lived have spoken highly of the dish."

Catering to the surrounding Satmar Hasidic community of Hungarian descent, they serve fish that is sweet, along with a sweet khreyn (horseradish, beets, and sugar). It's operated in a cafeteria style: you choose your dishes by surveying the ovenworn pans of cooked food spread across the counter and a menu posted on the wall above. The kugels, noodle puddings, and fish dishes are of a quality rare for twenty-first-century New York. The rear of the space is devoted to a pizzeria and

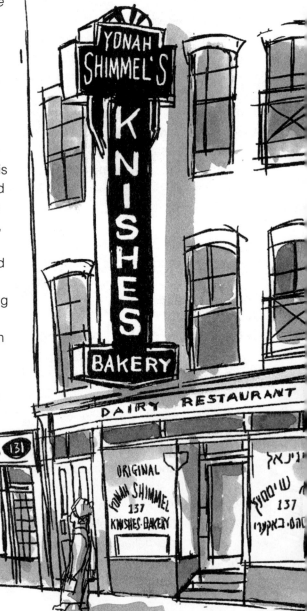

knishes. The clientele is divided between distracted Hasidic businessmen and mothers with children and baby carriages.

In recent years, this traditional Jewish dairy restaurant has adopted the mainstream DIY salad bar found in every midtown lunch place, down to the metal tossing bowls and glass-enclosed display of ingredients. We can thus understand how even traditional Jews readily adopted the eating habits of the surrounding Christian culture in Europe — it looked like a good idea.

Weiss Kosher Dairy Restaurant, a small establishment on Coney Island Avenue, near Avenue H in the Midwood section of Brooklyn, catered to an Orthodox community. They had excellent gefilte fish. Within a few years, Weiss's moved across the avenue to a cavernous space designed for large catered parties. One afternoon, I wandered in and ordered gefilte fish. The fish was served without horseradish. When I asked for some horseradish, the waiter disappeared into the kitchen and came back to tell me that they were out of horseradish.

As a lover of knishes, particularly kasha knishes, I frequently stopped at the **Yonah Shimmel Knish Bakery** at 137 Houston Street. It offered an abbreviated dairy menu of knishes, borscht, and sour milk. A counter in the front, a few tables in the rear, and a patina of Lower East Side history. The sign outside boasts that it's the "original since 1910," but the full history of Yonah Shimel (with one "m") and his knishes is more complicated.

According to the "official" version, Yonah Shimmel, a Romanian immigrant and Torah scribe/ scholar, began peddling his

137 East Houston St.
1940

wife's knishes from a pushcart in Coney Island around 1890. In partnership with his cousin Joseph Berger he opened a store at 144 East Houston. After two years Shimmel returned to his Torah studies and Berger, with his wife, Rose (Shimmel's daughter), took possession of the business under the name Yonah Shimmel, and in 1910 moved to the south side of Houston at number 137, next door to the Houston Street Hippodrome. The bakery/restaurant is currently owned by Alex Wolfman, identified in the press as a great-nephew of Yonah's.

However, evidence in the form of ads in the Yiddish press, a period photo, and city directories reveals a more convoluted history.

A great-granddaughter of Yonah's brother Leo (see page 400) reports that the Schimels were from Lvov, Poland. Jewish restaurateurs may have been exaggerating their Romanian culinary pedigree. In 1910, Alexander Ratner still occupied 137 East Houston. By 1915, two J. Shimel Bakeries were listed in the phone book: one at 144 East Houston Street (the original Houston Street location) and another at 1363 Fifth Avenue between 112th and 113th Streets, in the then Jewish neighborhood of Harlem. By 1917, a restaurant is listed at 22 West Houston and two bakeries are listed: one at 44 Avenue B, between 3rd and 4th Streets, and the Harlem branch at 1363 Fifth Avenue. The businesses are listed under two spellings: Jos. Shimel and Jonas Schimel.

The Avenue B location, now named **Yonah Shimel Milkhiger Restaurant,** closed by December 1920 and was replaced by the **Kohen and Harmatz Bakery and Kosher Milkhiger Restaurant,** which promised to continue baking tasty knishes "upon universal public demand." In 1921, an ad in *Der Morgn Zhurnal* announces: "Yonah Shimel is again here! The famous restaurant opens a magnificent **Milkhiger Restaurant** today, Tuesday, August 16th at 175 Rivington Street, near Attorney St., where there will be served the finest milkhige dishes à la Yonah Shimel with prices as in the year 1910. Come and have pleasure! Eat and be healthy!" The ad ends with the warning: "This is the only Yonah Shimel restaurant in all New York. No connection with those other restaurants." (One year earlier **Louis Driks** operated a milkhiger restaurant at this same address; see page 357.)

The accusation of restaurants fraudulently operating under Shimel's name (or a slight variation to avoid prosecution) raises the possibility that the Houston Street store and possibly other locations were operated by parties who continued to trade on the well-known name, but had no direct business relation to Mr. Shimel.

A 1973 ad for Yonah Shimmel at 137 East Houston features non-dairy party foods: Franks-in-Jackets, Steakball or Liver Puffs, and Miniature Egg Rolls. In 1995, while under the ownership of Sheldon Ketiz, the store was implicated in the operation of a loan-sharking scheme. The current owners, catering to contemporary tastes, offer "traditional vegan knishes" and even a "pizza knish."

Brighton Dairy Restaurant, located on Brighton Beach Avenue, Brooklyn. In the early 1970s, before the great influx of Russian Jews, this place catered to the elderly Jewish population that settled in Brighton Beach as a result of the white flight from Crown Heights and Flatbush. I recall a disorderly interior littered with soiled paper napkins, a self-service glass display counter on the left, and a line of hard, brightly colored Formica booths on the right. The elderly management struggled to supply a credible, but microwaved, version of Eastern European dairy cuisine on paper plates. Possibly because I had long hair in those days, an old woman in the next booth pointed me out to her friend as a being a "feygele," a Yiddish euphomism for "homosexual." I can't remember what I ate in that atmosphere of cultural collapse.

Mrs. Stahl's Knishes was located in a deep rambling storefront at 1001 Brighton Beach Avenue in the shadow of the BMT Brighton Line. Founded in the mid-1930s by Mrs. Fannie Stahl, it was, by 1960, owned and operated by Morris and Sam Weingast, sons of Dave Weingast (see page 428). I recall a long counter running along the left-hand side of the store and a collection of mismatched Formica-clad tables along the right. The smell of baked dough and its various fillings (cherry-cheese, potato, kasha, cabbage) was overwhelming. I don't recall whether their menu extended beyond knishes, as that's what I was there to eat, but a photo from its last years has a sign for "kosher frankfurters" hanging alongside the front door. They were also known for their onion pletzels and challah. Closed around 2004.

Gefen's Dairy Restaurant, 297 Seventh Avenue (Incorporated 1963, dissolved 1984). On a busy block between 26th and 27th Streets this beloved restaurant catered to the workers and bosses in the Garment and Fur Districts. The Gefens had retired and sold the restaurant in 1972. It had changed hands twice since then, but my interest in dairy restaurants led me to arrange an interview with them in their 23rd Street apartment in 1989.

Through that interview conducted with Salek (1911–90) and Pola Gefen (1920–92), the following details of the life of a postwar dairy restaurant emerged.

Although Pola and Salek Gefen could recall the names of a number of delicatessens and bars operated by Jews in their hometown of Pabianice (Łódź district of Poland) where one could have a beer, kosher meat sandwich, or hot meal, Orthodox Jews, Pola explained, did not patronize these places. Even people who were not Orthodox bought kosher meat and kept a kosher kitchen. Her Orthodox friends and family did, however, frequent an ice-cream parlor in Pabianice. Neither Pola nor Salek Gefen could recall the existence of dairy restaurants in their town.

Because of its industrial activity, the city of Pabianice was known as "Little America." Mr. Gefen's family owned a bread bakery and there he learned the trade. Mrs. Gefen recalled that the main meal of the day served at 1 or 2 o'clock would be meat-based. To hold oneself over for six hours until the evening meal of dairy, one had tea with challah rolls made with cinnamon, sugar, and raisins.

In Łódź, the restaurant culture included dining rooms set up in private apartments where dinners were served. There were also street vendors of hot bagels. People where ashamed to eat in

the street; they took food home to eat. Mr. Gefen quotes in Hebrew from the Talmud: "The Sages taught: One who eats in the marketplace is comparable to a dog."

"Over there, five years were lost," Pola Gefen explained. The Germans invaded Pabianice in September 1939. Mr. Gefen was in the Polish Army, and upon their liquidation was incarcerated in Auschwitz from 1941 to January 1945. He worked on the construction of runways and coal mines.

They returned to Pabianice to reclaim their bakery business but were met with hostility from the Polish population. In December 1945 they left for Berlin, where they lived in a displaced-persons camp and managed a cake bakery for the United States Army, producing blueberry tarts, apple cakes, and éclairs. With the help of the HIAS, they were assigned a sponsor in Cleveland, and with their two children left for America in July of 1950.

After a short, unsuccessful time in Cleveland, they moved, with the help of relatives, to Teaneck, New Jersey.

Mrs. Gefen was struck by the difference in taste of fish and poultry in America. To her, carp never tasted as sweet as it did in Europe. After a failed attempt to start a bakery,

Mr. Gefen found work as a dishwasher in a Jewish-style diner on Route 4 run by a Hungarian named Weiss — this was his introduction to the restaurant business.

In 1953, after a year of observing the operation of a restaurant, the Gefens moved to 109th Street and Amsterdam Avenue in New York City. Salek took a job in a Jewish luncheonette at Sixth Avenue and 29th Street as a counterman and cook. After a week's vacation, he was summarily fired, and then decided they must have their own business regardless of how little money it made. They borrowed money from friends and through a broker on 42nd Street discovered a small dairy luncheonette called Halpern's that was for sale. It had been in operation for over forty years. (Samuel Halpern had been operating two restaurants since 1915, one at 146 Forsyth and the second at 233 Sixth Avenue.)

By 1939, Halpern's Dairy Lunch was at 297 Seventh Ave. (See page 385.) It was a long, narrow store with a counter and a couple of tables in the front. The dairy restaurant was unknown to them from Europe, but they soon discovered

the well-known dairies of New York: Rapoport's, Ratner's, and Gross's.

They did not eat in Halpern's before deciding to buy it. Mrs. Gefen looked at it and then called her husband at work and said, "I am in a place that will be good for us." It was, she felt, small enough for two people to manage. They gave a deposit and after observing the luncheonette for a full 5-am-to-11-pm day Mr. Gefen had misgivings.

"They used to sell for 40¢ breakfast. They used to give fresh orange juice, butter, and cream cheese on the tables, bagels, bread, challah, rye bread, white bread, bialys, eggs, cereal, coffee with heavy cream, six glasses of water. 40¢ in 1957. And what they couldn't eat, you know the tough guys with the baykher [bellies] they put in their pockets. Lunch — you didn't see them. He already took his lunch. So, you lost on every customer money. I said, Pola, it's busy, it's good, but you lose money."

Mrs. Gefen explained: "You see, they were shrewd. They wanted to make it busy. We found out later that they paid off customers to come in to make it look busy and to have some money in the cash register. They were there for forty years. They came from Hungary. So, my husband said, come home, it's not for you, it's not for us. Come home.

"So, I went home. I wouldn't argue in the store. At home I started to talk to him. I said, 'Listen, something has to be done. I want that business and I think we can make a go out of it.' We went back the next morning, and it was as I told you.

"Mrs. Halpern, let her rest in peace, she was a peculiar person. She knew that our English was very limited at that time and we never were in business here, especially in a dairy restaurant, and she promised that she would stay with me as long as we need her. She will show us how to make in the kitchen. When she came in the first day, it was all right. The second day, she started to manipulate me, because she told me completely different from what she told me the first day.

"For example, she used string beans, green peas, and corn from cans. So, the first day, she told me, Put out one can, if you're short you have another. The second day, she said put in two, then she said three. From three cans was too much left over. Then also, when she told me how to make the vegetable cutlets, she took all the lettuce that's supposed to be thrown out, she chopped it up and made vegetable cutlets out of it. It was plain garbage. We put nicer lettuce in the garbage. No, I said, that's not for me, because I wouldn't eat it and I cannot get it in me to serve it to a customer. She said, 'They will eat everything.'

"Anyway, after three or four days, I saw that she is doing completely not good. I felt it. She said she would stay a month or two, then she wants to go to Florida. So, on the fourth day, I said, 'Mrs. Halpern, you know what? I would appreciate if you go to Florida and rest up.'"

The Gefens discovered later that Mrs. Halpern had a bet with her next-door neighbor that they wouldn't last three months in the dairy restaurant business.

"She had sold the business three times before and they had to take it back, and they got a lot of money — deposits — which she didn't give back. So, she said, this time for sure she will have a catch, because I don't know how to run it. So, when she left, I started to work. It was hard, it didn't come out the way I wanted it to, because I wanted to do it too good, so I put in too much butter or too much eggs. It came out too soft. But it was delicious. They liked it even though it was soft, the puddings, or whatever. So then, in time, I . . ."

Starting out was hard work. They started at five o'clock in the morning and worked until eleven at night. Pola "worked like three people. She baked, she cooked, she stood at the counter."

The Gefens adopted the existing menu and in time added some of their own dishes. "You had an appetizer, you had a soup, you had a main dish, whatever you wanted. From salmon croquettes to loaf or to vegetable meatballs or vegetable cutlets or mushroom cutlets. . . . We had mushroom sauce, spaghetti sauce, creamed spinach, kasha varnishkes, plain kasha."

As Mrs. Gefen explained, these were not dishes familiar to her from Pabianice. "At home, I don't recall my mother making vegetables, because in Europe we were not used to vegetables so much.

"I never put a recipe on a paper and I never looked up in a cookbook. Whatever I made at home or in the restaurant, I just used my imagination. The way I would like to have it, to eat, or the way I want it to taste." Scaling the dishes up to restaurant quantities was no problem, as Pola was used to cooking for at least eight people in Berlin — concentration camp survivors who had lost their families.

Halpern's had no sign, the name was known by word of mouth, but when the Gefens took over, they put up a sign with their name, but never with the word "kosher." "If they don't believe me, from my heart, then the sign wouldn't help." Salek added, "We never had a mashgiyekh."

"No," opined Mrs. Gefen, "I wonder for what a restaurant needs a mashgiyekh. It's only dairy. . . . For a lot of things, the Board of Health is watching, even by us. They came in and asked, 'Why don't you have a sign "Kosher"?' I don't want it. If they

Lemon Squeezer

don't trust me, that sign doesn't mean a thing."

And Mr. Gefen added, "I never had a kosher dairy. I would have a little sign in the window, Shomer Shabbos. That we're closed on Saturday and the holidays. How does it look, you have a kosher restaurant — filthy?"

In the early 1960s, they advertised that they had a sukkah in the backyard that could accommodate five people. This was expanded each year until it took over the entire backyard.

Mrs. Gefen made a point of buying whole fish from Mouser and Jaffee at the Fulton Fish Market and filleting them herself. The Gefens introduced Jewish "scallops" made of halibut. They offered gefilte fish, boiled and baked, boiled carp, whitefish, and pike; marinated pike; baked halibut, whitefish, and carp, broiled salmon, fried "scallops," and fillet of sole. "Ten kinds of fish every day."

At home Mrs. Gefen made a sweet gefilte fish, but in the restaurant not so sweet, as people didn't like it.

As for milk and cream, Mr. Gefen explained: "At the beginning was not like it is now. Now you have Cholov Yisroel; in 1957, we didn't.

Later it came from Williamsburg. So, we had both regular milk and Cholov Yisroel."

They introduced doughnuts and butter cookies that Mr. Gefen baked every morning.

At the beginning they served mamaliga, but as it didn't move, they removed it from the menu. As for gefilte (filled) fish, at home and in Poland the minced fish was stuffed back into a fish body, but not in the restaurant, because people did not like the center bone. Raw onions were never used, because they're burped up after eating. Gefilte fish was served both hot and cold. Red and white horseradish were bought from Gold's.

The smoked fish was Nova Scotia, lox, smoked whitefish, and carp. Mrs. Gefen made her own chopped-whitefish salad with apples and small onions and a special herring soaked to bring out the salt. She also made her own potato salad and coleslaw.

Their vegetarian "chopped liver" was made with a base of Protose, a commercial nut-and-vegetable concoction, and eggs, oil, fried onions, and salt. Protose was also used for goulash, Protose steaks, and Western omelets. Mrs. Gefen recalled a vegetarian chopped liver in Poland made from nuts and string beans, but "it's not the same."

Eggplant dishes consisted of eggplant parmigiana, plain cutlets, and eggplant salad (baked eggplant mashed with oil and vinegar, served with chopped onions and tomatoes on the side).

Squash was not served. Mixed vegetables — radishes, scallions, and cucumbers — were served with sour cream. Bananas or strawberries with sour cream. The rye and white bread was supplied by Fink; and pumpernickel by Moishe's.

Their noodle kugel was sweet with fruit and raisins, sour cream, cheese, and butter. They also served rice pudding and farina pudding and potato pudding.

Their stuffed cabbage was made with rice and tomato sauce. A popular favorite, served only Wednesdays as a main course or side dish, was potato noodles with mushroom sauce or just fried onions.

Every day they served potato latkes, from raw potatoes, and matzo meal pancakes. Kremslach — a fried pancake made with eggs and mashed potatoes or matzo meal — was not on the menu; they called it a matzo-meal pancake.

Kasha varnishkes as well as kasha with milk or onions were served.

At some point they hired a short-order cook and two dishwashers (automatic dishwashers were installed in 1963) in the kitchen, two countermen, three at lunch, and two Greek waiters in jackets and tie. Mr. Gefen was stationed at the cash register. On the difficulty of finding Jewish waiters, Mrs. Gefen explained: "Years ago, the Jewish man went in for waiters, for countermen, but when they had children, the children grew up, they didn't want to take them in their business. They tried to educate them. And that's why it was hard to get a waiter already in the late 1960s. As I told you, we had Greek fellows as waiters. And countermen, we had a Puerto Rican man or a colored fellow. But don't forget, even if we were not prejudiced, there were customers who didn't like to be served by them. Because they thought, 'It's a Jewish restaurant, it has to be run by Jewish people' — which is just impossible.

"We had two unions when we started off. But because I was alone in the kitchen, they didn't bother me. But then we had one dishwasher who went to the union to complain that we had no union. And once we had a court case, but it passed by. But the second time, two or three years later, we had to take in a kitchen union man. I said, 'Good, I will take in the kitchen union if you bring me in a cook, but you don't have a cook. A dishwasher I can get a dime a dozen.' But it didn't help we had to take in a union dishwasher, because they wanted to picket the store. So, we had three unions. But a cook, they could never manage to give me one.

"The waiters and countermen were all union workers who could not be told how to behave — only occasionally reminded to increase the food on a salad plate so as to make it worth its price. Irving Halfin, a waiter of ours, still works at the Grand Street Dairy." Other waiters were Harold, Moishe Rosenbaum, and Nat Orbach. One waiter, after working at Halpern's for forty years, remained on after the Gefens took over and retired at the age of eighty-four.

The fish dishes, including gefilte fish, were made fresh every morning; borscht and schav once a week, fruit soup twice a week.

To make blintzes (nalesniki in Polish), Mrs. Gefen worked ten frying pans at once. "I rotated them to make the bletlekh — and you could look through each and every one, not thick." After she folded in the ends, the bletlekh were rolled lengthwise. "Oh, we had delicious blintzes! Cheese, fresh blueberry and strawberry in season, kasha and potato."

They offered a soft, yeasty blueberry cake — a kolacz in Polish — as well as cheese, potato, kasha, and cherry pirogen.

They baked their own cheesecake with pot cheese, cream cheese, butter, and eggs — something they didn't know in Poland — and made cheese knishes for Purim and Shavuot.

Mrs. Gefen prided herself on giving the customer their money's worth — big portions and ingredients of the best quality.

Since they were in a business area, their store hours were 6 am to 8 pm. "When we took over in 1957, soup was 20¢. A piece of pudding 20¢. And a coffee 10¢. And if you had a check, 50¢. It was a lunch."

Mrs. Gefen described the operation of the kitchen: "I worked at everything. The dishwasher who came in at six o'clock in the morning did the dishes to two o'clock. Then he went down [to the basement] to peel for the next day. He peeled carrots, potatoes, onions, everything I needed for the next day. We had a walk-in box in the basement.

"Five o'clock in the morning, the dishwasher who left at night had to put down the big pots: forty gallons, two pots for two soups [each day]. The smaller pots I could take down myself. So, I put up the water. I cooked the broth for the soup. Not just dump it in the pot. Cook a good broth with all kinds of chopped vegetables in it. Cook it out for an hour, hour and a half, then I put in the ingredients that I want. The lima beans or Yankee beans or barley — mushroom or cabbage soup. And always a borscht — that was cold. I put in eggs and sour cream. Also, on the table, sour cream.

"Then I'd fry the onions in a giant frying pan. Then I put up the pot for kasha, then the pot for rice. Then for the mushroom sauce and the tomato sauce. Whatever I needed.

"[The short order cooks] worked at the counter on a grill with two flames [to cook eggs]. One pot for boiled fish, one pot for gefilte fish. And baked fish, halibut, salmon, or fillet—were broiled to order.

"The sour cream came in twenty-quart cans. The supplier was Soiffer. We made our own sour milk. You mix a tablespoon of sour cream with the milk. You mix it and put it away — it makes sour milk. In the summer, the next day, it would be ready. It has to stay until it gets thick. The [yogurt] culture was not kosher, but now they have yogurt with the 'U.'"

The baking consisted mostly of individual Danish and large trays of apple cake, cheesecake, and homentashen. Mr. Gefen made the dough and his wife made them up and baked them. No bread, just egg challah rolls.

"Later we put in a seltzer machine. People like it, they get free seltzer." When they expanded the restaurant into the adjoining store in the early 1960s, they put in two machines: one in the back and one behind the counter.

By the summer of 1956 the restaurant was air conditioned. In the summer they made larger amounts of cold soup: borscht, schav, and fruit.

More baked goods were produced in the summer because customers took food with them to the country.

For two years in a row, they attempted to keep the restaurant open during Chol Hamoed Pesach. "A rabbi came in and said it wouldn't be right if we close because we will force people to eat chometz. One day, two days they will drag along a piece of matzo, but four days! So, we were open. Then we had to have a mashgiyekh. Before Erev Pesach, at night, the mashgiyekh came in with workers, everything was cleaned, kashered — completely new dishes, everything new."

When asked if anyone ever asked for something not on the menu, Mrs. Gefen explained, "Once in a blue moon someone came in: 'Do you have mamaliga?' "

January and February were slow months as their clientele went to Florida. Their regular customers came from the Flower District and the Garment District, but many people came from uptown just to eat.

A regular customer was the Garment Union Local 99. "We served them a lot. They'd call down, 'Pola, I need for this afternoon 500 Danish — 700 Danish, 700 coffees.' One time only we opened for Labor Day because they had a big parade and they ordered hundreds and hundreds of Danish and coffee, so we had to open. Not to the public, but just to give them fresh Danish and coffee." Celebrity diners included Barry Farber, Zero Mostel (whose painting studio was in the neighborhood), Rodgers and Hammerstein ("both of them came when they wanted Jewish food"), Elia Kazan ("loved the carp I made"), Patty Duke, Frank Sinatra Jr., Celeste Holm, and the Rothschilds from Switzerland.

Their clientele was mostly Jewish, but not too many Orthodox Jews. "You'd hear Hungarian, Russian, Polish, Yiddish."

Mrs. Gefen explained: "The decor was made the way I would like to have it. We didn't put in too many seats to be cramped. But ninety seats comfortable. And I like it. Everybody who came in, they never saw behind a counter should be so much space. I am a heavy person. I could go through and not disturb another one with a knife.

"And when we built it, that was in my mind. I designed everything. I gave the contractor a layout and I said, I want to have it this and this way, don't change it. If you have to do something, you have to ask me. But everything was the way I laid it out on paper. And also, in the kitchen — I made a big kitchen.

"Many times, I said I kept it cleaner than my house, because we lived there a whole week. And I knew what it is when a customer will come and see that it's dirty. It's awful. I was not ashamed for the Board of Health, for customers, for no one, to come into the kitchen to see how it looked."

Mrs. Gefen's favorite dish was the chopped herring. "I cooked it every day. One day I took a half a pickled herring, one day a little chopped herring. Many times in the summer, I ate the Jersey tomatoes stuffed with cottage cheese. Or plain, a piece of Melba toast with farmer cheese. Or, a farmer cheese and coffee. As you see, I drink black coffee, no sugar, no milk — with farmer cheese, it was all right."

The Gefens ate all week in the restaurant; Shabbos, she cooked meat at home.

They had little time to visit other dairy restaurants but were friends with the Herschenfelds of Hershey's Dairy Restaurant on 29th Street and Mr. Hammer of Hammer's Dairy on 14th Street.

They sold the restaurant because their children did not want to go into the business. "We thought we built it for our children, but they didn't want to work as hard as we did. Sure, restaurant work is a hard work."

Asked if they have a favorite restaurant, Mrs. Gefen answered, "No, we don't eat out." Mr. Gefen pointed to the kitchen table, "Yeah, right here."

Grand Street Dairy, 341 Grand Street, corner of Ludlow. Owner: Sol Guberman. Of my rare visits to this lively luncheonette catering to East Side shoppers I remember only the hairy forearm of the counterman in white, the bowl set before me, and sunlight streaming through the windows. The cold-borscht season was here declared to begin just after Passover. A food writer revealed that the secret ingredient filling the core of their baked apples was Coca-Cola.

In the mid-1980s, **Friedman's Canal Street Kosher Dairy Restaurant,** 43 Canal, was based in a modest storefront amid the Jewish bookstores and religious-supply companies on the eastern end of Canal Street. It was a dimly lit, ramshackle place, littered with prayer booklets and drooping paper signage. It catered to the struggling businessmen and exhausted shoppers in the area. It had Orthodox certification and served Cholov Yisroel products. Although I ate there several times, I have no memory of the food. It was closed Saturdays and Jewish holidays and is now closed forever.

Diamond Dairy Kosher Luncheonette, 4 West 47th Street. Opened approximately 1944, closed December 2009. The manager, Shmuel Strauss, fifty-five, who had run the business for the past eighteen years, confessed that its closing "was very disappointing. It really was a little

piece of New York."

Wandering in midtown, I'd often stop for cold borscht or gefilte fish at the Diamond Dairy — a serpentine counter and table service squeezed onto the rear, low-ceilinged mezzanine level overlooking the National Jewelers Exchange on 47th Street. It was run by a fair-haired, yarmulke-wearing Jew of Hungarian descent and catered to the Jews working in and around the Diamond Center. The gefilte fish was sweet and served with sweetened khreyn. The kitchen was staffed by Hispanic men, the counter by a buxom blonde woman possibly hired for being the perfect embodiment of a "Poylishe shiksa." The Diamond Dairy, when I knew it in the 1980s, was clearly operated under rabbinical supervision. The activity below, men and women waiting for customers for their archaic merchandise and by extension all business, seemed particularly hopeless as viewed from the table of a dairy luncheonette. The bread, challah or rye, tasted as though it was imported from Monsey, New York, and was served with ice-cold sweet butter. The Diamond Dairy was one of the few places in midtown Manhattan where one could overhear a conversation in Yiddish. For some time, the opposite side of the mezzanine housed a meat restaurant as well; at other times that space was used as a gathering place for prayer: weekdays after 3:30 pm participants could "choose one of six 15-minute services of mincha, the afternoon prayer." Mr. Strauss boasted that "anytime you come up you always have a minyan."

In 2012, a new restaurant opened in the same space — the Dairy

Lunch. The serpentine counter was straightened out; the menu now features panini and kosher sushi.

In the 1980s, while wandering in the West 20s, the Fur District of Manhattan, I stumbled upon **Hershey's Dairy Restaurant** at 167 West 29th Street. This was clearly a restaurant in decline. The walls were clad in worn "wood-grain" formica, the chairs bore sour-cream stains, the menus were battered from heavy use. I recall a warm, comforting smell of cooking coming from the kitchen. It felt more like a clubhouse than a public restaurant. I don't remember what I ordered: either gefilte fish — that endangered species of Jewish fish — or matzo brei. A uniformed Latino waiter went through the motions of taking my order, but his mind seemed to be somewhere else.

On the wall was a large, ornate plaque, like something from a synagogue, bearing the title "Hershey's Breakfast Club." In columns, it held three hundred or so small nameplates, one for each of the restaurant's regulars. Some were marked by a brass floret, indicating a deceased member.

A few articles about Hershey's from the 1970s and '80s describe a lively and beloved restaurant catering to the fur industry. The waiter Jack Weinblatt

kibitzed with the regulars, poker games took place between meals, and funds were raised for regulars down on their luck. The owner Roy Herschenfeld (born 1924, New York – died 1987, Boca Raton) oversaw the operation of 150 tightly packed seats from the 1950s until the late 1980s. In the 1970s, the menu featured a fish soup with noodles, an unusual item for a dairy restaurant. "Breadbaskets are filled with light and dark pumpernickel, rye bread, salt sticks, onion rolls, seeded rolls, hard rolls, soft rolls and pumpernickel rolls. . . . The cold gefilte fish served in its own gelatin with crisp lettuce and first-grade tomatoes (a rarity these days) is as good as any we've had ($2.85)." The matzo brei was served pancake-style. Sandwiches could be split onto two small rolls for an extra 10 cents. "The cheese cake is the thick yellow variety that sticks to the roof of your mouth," and "counter to the Jewish restaurant tradition of bad coffee, Hershey's has a singularly good coffee (20 cents). . . . It is the deft and experienced hand of the female chef (whose name the management was reluctant to reveal) that distinguishes Hershey's from other dairy restaurants. [*New York Magazine,* August 24, 1970]

For people who handled and sewed the pelts of dead animals for a living, the need to escape into a dairy environment would seem to have had a special urgency. This may account for the restaurant's popularity.

Dairy Restaurant, 4801 16th Avenue, Brooklyn, Borough Park. Opened in 1968 by Tillie and Jacob Lieberman. Currently operated by their son Shloimie Lieberman and his wife Roz. A popular corner breakfast and lunch place with tables for twelve and a counter for ten features omelets, soups, and sandwiches. Angelo Saavedra, who came from Mexico, started as their egg chef in 2000 and uses individual frying pans, not a grill. Like most dairy restaurants, they never felt the need for official certification, and to this day, there hangs in their window a statement of their own devising that attests to their compliance with dietary laws.

The B&H Dairy Lunch, 127 Second Avenue, New York, opened 1937 or 1938. A remnant of the Second Avenue Yiddish rialto, the B&H catered to a new generation of young Lower East Siders who appreciated its inexpensive vegetarian fare. The sign outside reads "dairy lunch"; a neon sign in the window seems to explain that B&H means "Better health." They were actually the initials of the original owners, Abie Bergson and Jack Heller, who opened the lunch counter around 1937. Bergson was an aspiring actor and the B&H, during the tail end of Yiddish theater on Second Avenue, was patronized by stars such as Molly Picon and Maurice Schwartz. Mr. Heller was succeeded in the partnership by Sol Hausman. Bergson sold the luncheonette in the early 1970s, and by September of 1978, it went bankrupt. In May of that year, Bob Sherman, a partner in a lower-Manhattan construction company, bought the assets, fixtures, and name with a ten-year lease.

It's a small, narrow store that seats twenty-six, with a counter that accommodates thirteen, yet Leo Ratnofsky, a counterman since 1940, estimated at least one thousand customers on a typical day. He was part of a five-man team of countermen serving affordable food — breakfast starting at 5:30 am — and acting as social directors for the ever-changing neighborhood. Customers who left tips over 25 cents received a public shout-out of "Jumbo jockey!" Ratnofsky recalled Maurice Schwartz, of the Yiddish Art Theatre, complaining "that there were more people at the counter of the B&H than in

his theater." In the late 1970s the cook was a Ukrainian woman, Ksenia Pylyp. Ratnofsky worked a fourteen-hour day. [Talk of the Town, *The New Yorker,* May 15, 1978]

In the 1980s, it was the last remaining dairy restaurant on Second Avenue, Ratner's and Rapoport's having closed. Dave Schornstein, a middle-aged Jewish, wisecracking ventriloquist (producing a flirtatious woman's voice

when a cop sat down at the counter: "You must be Lana Turner's brother, Stomach") worked the counter since the 1960s with an automatism developed over decades of repeated motion.

Between his moments onstage during a run of *Little Shop of Horrors* in the Orpheum Theatre (1982–87) just across the street, Fyvush Finkel would step out into the street, toss his cigar in the gutter, and cross over to the B&H for a bowl of soup. He'd check his wristwatch and abruptly leave to make his next entrance onstage. Finkel was a child star in the Yiddish theater in the 1930s.

The matzo brei at the B&H was served in the scrambled style (supposedly the Galitsyaner preference), as opposed to a pancake (Litvak). Before cooking, the matzo was dampened with boiling water. To the culinary Jew, the texture is everything.

The B&H menu hanging above the counter still strongly reflected Eastern European dairy cuisine: gefilte fish, borscht, blintzes, kasha varnishkes, and pirogen. They served no meat and displayed no rabbinical certification. What was the origin of the red citrus sauce spooned over their noodle pudding — the same sauce served at the 2nd Avenue Deli?

Otherwise, it offered an American luncheonette menu of meatless salads, sandwiches, and soup. Besides Dave, the other countermen were Latinos, whose cultural attachment to the food they were serving seemed to be on a purely business level. A variety of Polish or Ukrainian women worked in the cramped kitchen in the rear.

In my late twenties, I stopped there for gefilte fish, soup, or a "special" omelet (chopped peppers, onion, mushrooms) with kasha every night before visiting the neighborhood bars. One evening, in 1981, a woman happened to sit on the one empty stool at the counter next to mine and asked me what I was eating (it was a plate of gefilte fish). We left together to take a walk and several years later got married. She explained that

she had left a nearby movie theater and, while waiting in the cold for a bus, decided to go into the B&H for a bowl of hot soup. She knew exactly what it was that I was eating.

In 1995, having lost the print venue for my weekly comic strip, *Julius Knipl, Real Estate Photographer,* I constructed an 18 x 24–inch illuminated Plexiglas box to display the ongoing episodes of the strip in public and somehow convinced Beatrice Poznanski, the then owner of the B&H, to allow me to place that box in the window of her restaurant. Each week, I washed down the box and posted the latest strip for passersby to read. It remained on display there, and at a Papaya King stand on East 86th Street, for close to a year.

My Discovery of Falafel in America

In those years, the discovery of a wonderful dairy restaurant was soon followed by its closing. That the Jewish delicatessen, a vital eating place in every New York neighborhood, was also in steep decline didn't bother me as much.

From the preceding account, it might seem as though dairy restaurants comprised a major section of the New York restaurant scene. Snapshots of the various boroughs will demonstrate just how few there were in relation to other restaurants. The Brooklyn Classified Telephone Directory of Winter 1938–39 lists 2,991 restaurants. Of those only 13 were specifically identified as being dairy/vegetarian restaurants, while 550 were listed as delicatessens (including restaurants and stores). The specialized retail dairy store was still a big business: there were 1,638 retail grocery stores and an additional 768 specializing in dairy (butter, cheese, eggs, and milk).

The Manhattan Red Book for February 1941 lists 7,098 restaurants and only 34 were identifiable by name as dairy/vegetarian. There were 1,062 cigar stores, 708 confectionery stores, 472 retail dairy stores, and 708 delicatessens, including restaurants and stores.

Today, most people don't know what a dairy restaurant is or was. If they're observant Jews, they might think of one of the many rabbinically certified pizzerias in New York serving a strictly milekhdike menu.

My first encounter with a kosher pizzeria was during my years at Erasmus Hall High School in Flatbush, Brooklyn. From the outside, it seemed to be modeled on the many other Italian pizza places in Brooklyn — a storefront open to the street, a self-service counter before a stack of large pizza ovens, and a few tables in the rear. In the Jewish eating places that I was familiar with the food preparation was hidden behind swinging kitchen doors. Here, as in an Italian pizzeria, the ovens were in full view and manned by muscular young men in short-sleeved shirts with tiny, almost invisible yarmulkes bobby-pinned to their stylishly coiffed hair. At the time, I did not know that flatbread covered with melted cheese was part of Abrahamic cuisine or that the words "pita" and "pizza" may have a shared etymology.

They also served falafel sandwiches in pita breads. The falafel sandwich was an unknown concoction to me. It was an acquired taste. In flavor and texture, it had nothing to do with any Jewish food that I had ever eaten; its very name was Arabic, not Yiddish or English. The walls and windows bore

signs proclaiming its kosher certification. The few Eastern European dishes that were on the menu (knishes, kugel) seemed to be offered for the benefit of the elderly Jews in the neighborhood as an embarrassing afterthought. With their Middle Eastern dishes — falafel, hummus, baba ghanoush, and pizza made with kosher cheese — these places faced modern Israel, not the Pale of Settlement.

If the Zionist project in the nineteenth century offered an alternative to the constrained urban life of European Jews — a supposed return to the agricultural possibilities of life in Palestine — the implementation of this pastoral dream happened to include all the brutal trappings of a modern nation state. The falafel/pizzeria offered a dairy cuisine, but in the

486

atmosphere of a harried fast-food place tinged with the macho atmosphere of an Italian pizzeria. Had these young countermen left a socialist kibbutz to man this outpost of Israeli culture as an alternative form of military service? Physically occupying an actual piece of Palestine, that mythical land of milk and honey, seemed to cause the need to cultivate a paradise of the imagination to vanish. With their Israeli-inflected names — Matamin, Hadar, Taam-Tov, etc. — these places try to distance themselves from New York Yiddish culture. As the dairy restaurants that I enjoyed went out of business through the 1970s and '80s, these kosher pizzerias sprang up wherever observant Jews worked or lived.

Some have upscale culinary aspirations. Today, even an Orthodox Jew does not want to be confined to the culinary tastes of his ancestors — the cuisines of the world can be prepared according to strict dietary law. What would Moshe Sofer say about this turn of events?

In the 1990s, on every Saturday night after Sabbath observance, the **Jerusalem II Dairy Restaurant** on Broadway near Macy's became a popular social scene. This busy midtown cafeteria-style dairy/pizzeria in the Israeli mode, with Middle Eastern decor and food, was packed with young observant

Jews, standing shoulder to shoulder as in any Manhattan singles bar, but nibbling on falafel and kosher pizza. If a romantic meeting at the B&H was an accident propelled through subterfuge and misdirection, at Jerusalem II it was a blatant singles scene fueled by the aphrodisiac power of Israeli travel posters, olive oil, and tahini sauce.

The **Garden of Eat-In**, in Midwood, Brooklyn, boasts special creations by Head Chef Harvey Pearlman. In this highly certified and supervised restaurant, the Eastern European offerings have been reduced to blintzes and pirogen (vegetarian chopped liver and a vegetable cutlet are thrown in for good measure) — otherwise the menu is indistinguishable from an Italian-oriented American-style mid-priced restaurant.

Dozens of these kosher "dairy" restaurants serve a growing number of Orthodox, and newly observant, Jews a menu of popular non-meat dishes. Opened in 1976, **The Milky Way** on West Pico Boulevard in Los Angeles (moved in 1981 from its original location on Beverly Boulevard) was owned and operated by Leah Adler, the mother of the filmmaker Steven Spielberg. All the food is rabbinically approved, the doorways bear mezuzahs, and a sink is available for ritual hand-washing. According to an interview, it was the yellow tablecloths in the original location that made Mrs. Adler think of "dairy." The menu includes crêpes filled with ratatouille, a vegetable soup, a guacamole dip on tortilla — "an eclectic menu containing a hit-parade of American and continental favorites — all kosher, spinach salad, pasta primavera, lasagna, fried mozzarella, pita sandwiches, fish steaks and kebabs . . . trout amandine, Creole-style fish, stuffed won tons, fish and chips." Cheese blintzes and herring appetizer are among the few menu items associated with Eastern European Jewish cuisine. Steven Spielberg's favorite dish was fried smelts. Adler died in 2017. [*Los Angeles Times,* August 29, 1985]

The menu of **Milk 'n Honey,** another kosher dairy restaurant located on West Pico Boulevard, "largely resembles the most trendy and popular menus in Los Angeles: pizza, pasta, salads," and entrées consisting entirely of fish.

The Professionalization of Jewish Cuisine

Psychologists in the 1950s had recognized and studied the eternal conflict between Jewish mothers and daughters over control of the kitchen. Many young women were banned from the kitchen by their mothers, who felt threatened by a younger woman usurping this central area of expertise and familial pleasure. Did a similar threat arise with the professionalization of Jewish-style cuisine in restaurants? For those more complicated dairy dishes husbands would turn to their favorite restaurant, where they'd be expertly and effortlessly produced by Puerto Rican and black cooks hidden behind swinging

515 Seventh Ave.
c.1970

doors. The waiters, plodding-middle aged Jews, were merely the deliverymen. The daughters were vindicated in their power struggle, but the mothers felt an increased worthlessness as their physical beauty faded; even a package of the most mediocre frozen blintzes posed a terrible threat.

The Second Expulsion

Through the 1970s, the dairy restaurant had seemed to be an eternal presence in the restaurant culture of New York. The remarkable fragility of their existence — dependent upon the rare confluence of ancient Jewish dietary law and the eighteenth-century invention of the restaurant — was completely taken for granted. Now that they are almost completely gone, I understand that the Jews in those years had experienced a second expulsion from a kind of paradise.

The causes for the demise of the Jewish dairy restaurant are clear. Six million people with a taste for the Eastern European dairy dishes mentioned in this book were murdered in Europe during World War II. The remaining Jews and their children had a complex relationship to this cuisine. It may have been the beloved food of their childhood but it was often associated with the

490

embarrassments of immigrant life, suffocating family relations, economic failure, or making them fat. With access to the world's cuisine, in all its glorious variety, what chance does a plate of egg noodles and farmer's cheese have? One's choice of restaurant has always been loaded with social and political meaning.

The latest scientific evidence of the detrimental effects of dairy, and other high-cholesterol foods, struck a blow to all historical eating habits of Europe. The advent, in the 1940s, of so-called Jewish-style restaurants that serve both meat and dairy dishes cut into the dairy restaurant business as well. Dubrow's cafeteria at 515 Seventh Avenue at 38th Street, called "the culinary hub of the Garment District," served a mélange of blintzes, pirogen, kasha, and kugels along with roast chicken, breast of lamb, and whipped-cream cake. Part of a chain of four cafeterias started in 1932 (two in Brooklyn and one in Miami), the Garment District branch opened in 1952 and closed in 1985. It was a cavernous space of modern stainless-steel-and-Formica decor with a 140-foot-long self-service cafeteria.

Overnight, it was the religiously observant Jew who seemed to be the real customer for a dedicated dairy restaurant — who else would care? Ratner's and the Famous Dairy, places that never had, or cared about, kosher certification, felt obliged to satisfy this supposedly booming market. As this history makes clear, the dairy restaurant catered to all Jews with a taste for Eastern European dairy dishes; the preparation and serving of these dishes had transcended the mere fulfillment of a dietary law. The cuisine had become separated from the religious laws and holiday meals that brought it into existence. Some restaurants were great, some mediocre, some awful.

Our survey of dairy restaurants of the past reveals that most were small family operations. Like succeeding waves of immigrant-run businesses, they were satisfied with a small or subsistence level of profit. The urban real-estate market and other forces of gentrification over the past thirty years have driven retail store rents to levels that make it impossible for a small restaurant, or any other small business, to exist.

The growth of an Orthodox and Hasidic population in America since the Second World War and, more recently, the renewed interest in organizational Jewish life among children and grandchildren of secular Jews, has led to a boom in the kosher-certification business. In the 1920s and '30s, offshoots of disputing Orthodox groups each ran their own kosher-certification business. A visual collection of mid-twentieth-century hechsher seals would overwhelm an eighteenth-century kabbalist. The Union of Orthodox Jewish Congregations of America places its hechsher today on more than 400,000 products. The

Organized Kashruth Laboratories (OK Labs) certifies 140,000 products; Star-K Kosher of Baltimore a mere tens of thousands, and they even have a special dairy certificate (Star-D) for products and establishments that contain or serve non–Cholov Yisroel ingredients. The outlandish satire of that late-nineteenth-century editorial writer in *Der Volksadvokat,* concerning rabbinical certification of ice cream and snuff, has come to pass on a grand scale.

The increased cost of buying kosher-certified products and having an on-site supervisor was, in part, blamed for the demise of the Famous Dairy on 72nd Street. When kosher certification was adopted in the 1980s, menu prices had to be set far above those of other luncheonettes in the neighborhood. Kosher certification did not help business at Ratner's — it hastened its end.

The kosher-certification business has not only had an effect on the dairy restaurant business, it's had an effect on eating altogether.

The response of Lithuanian Orthodox Rabbi Moses Feinstein (Yoreh Deah I:47 Sivan 5714, June 1954) and the opinion of Modern Orthodox Rabbi Soloveitchik make it permissible for Jews in America to consume milk that has been supervised and approved by the U.S. Department of Agriculture. The argument for this leniency is based upon three points: no non-kosher animals are to be found in herds being milked; we can rely on the United States Department of Agriculture to guarantee that the milk is from cows (a federal law prohibits the use of the term "milk" for any substance other than cow's milk; milk from other animals must be clearly marked); and since most milk is obtained by machine, the question of whether a non-Jew is milking the animal is no longer relevant. This lenient position was contested by many rabbis. The strict opinion maintains the necessity to uphold rabbinic supervision of milk based on the idea that a rabbinic edict (Shulchan Arukh in Yoreh Deah 115: If a Jew does not monitor the milking process done by a non-Jew, the milk is unfit for Jewish consumption) applies even if its reason no longer applies.

In the case of conflicting opinions, they argue, it's best to follow the strictest rule — just to ensure that one is not inadvertently violating the right decision — and drink only certified Cholov Yisroel milk, milked and bottled in the presence of a mashgiyekh.

In the complex debate upon the permissibility of opening a sealed cardboard container of milk on the Sabbath, Rav Soloveitchik believed that it

492

was okay, as "the spout already exists but that it is temporarily closed so that the contents do not leak from the container. It is deemed 'an old hole that was sealed.'" [*Halakhic Positions of Rabbi Joseph B. Soloveitchik,* Volume 3]

Today, according to certain kosher-certifying organizations, only Grade A and U.S. Fancy Grade fruits and vegetable should be bought. In one kosher pizzeria I saw a hand-painted sign proclaiming that all the lettuce and vegetables served were inspected and certified by a local rabbinical authority.

It's a complicated procedure. "Because of a Shabbos prohibition on selecting, Borrer, whenever an insect is found on a vegetable the insect alone may not be removed. Rather, part of the vegetable containing the insect and an additional portion should be cut away. . . . The surface of the vegetable should be inspected in proper lighting. If the leaf is translucent, backlighting may also be used.

"In the spring and summer, each leaf must be washed well and carefully inspected on both sides. In the fall and winter, when infestation is not as prevalent, the leaves should be soaked in a vinegar solution and flushed in water. Three leaves should be randomly selected and then inspected to determine if the soaking procedure did in fact remove all insects. If these three leaves prove to be insect-free, the remaining leaves do not need to be inspected. If, however, even one of these three leaves is contaminated, then all the leaves of the vegetable must be inspected. Others hold

that under all circumstances, all the leaves must be visually inspected." [Rabbi Beryl Broyde of Vaad Harabonim of Greater Detroit]

The guide offers four other methods of inspection to be used on different vegetables. Artichokes: "Each leaf down to the heart of the plant must be inspected" [Rabbi Pinchas Bodner]. To employ a trained and certified worker to inspect the leaf of each vegetable will understandably affect the profitability, if not possibility, of selling tuna-salad plates.

The Yoreh Deah [84,36], a section of a compilation of Jewish law c. 1300, explains that the Torah does not forbid things the eye cannot see — it was not given to angels, but human beings. If, as scientists claim, the air is filled with minute creatures, then it's unavoidable that they'll be swallowed when

a person opens his mouth. Nevertheless, the "discovery" in 2004 of microscopic copepods, a harmless form of non-kosher crustacean, in NYC tap water was of great interest to those in the Orthodox-certification business. In certain Orthodox neighborhoods, the water-filtration business is booming.

In the early years of the current century, I met an observant friend for lunch. The only place in the neighborhood that satisfied his standards for kosher supervision was the Date Palm Cafe in the Center for Jewish History on 16th Street in New York City. When the small cafe opened in 2001, it served a Mediterranean dairy menu of soups, sandwiches, and hot entrées, and so it must have been equipped with a kitchen to cook, or at least warm, foods. Over the years, there was a change of mashgikhem and caterers and, at some point, a lawsuit was filed accusing the Center of religious discrimination. The mashgiyekh had been asked to trim his long beard and not have his tsitses openly hanging from his shirt. It was implied that the Orthodox audience patronizing the cafe was not in line with the clientele, and potential donors, that the Center wanted to attract. All mashgikhem were accused of being thieves and extortionists. By the time of my visit, no food was produced on the premises.

A glance behind the counter revealed an unused sink and workspace. Everything was delivered in securely shrink-wrapped plastic containers from a kosher provider agreeable to the most observant visitor. The small menu consisted of wraps of egg and tuna salad and prepacked salads. The effort required to tear open the heavy-gauge, heat-sealed plastic wrap worked up my appetite. Sadly, the soggy contents tasted of plastic and factory production. Could the Jews of history, as represented in the archive upstairs, have ever accomplished what they did on such unpalatable fare?

For every dairy restaurateur it was not simply a matter of following a particular form of religious or cultural dietary law — it was a matter of how that law was carried out in the details of running a restaurant. Observance of a dietary law became incidental to an aesthetic law of one's own design. Pola Gefen's daily concerns went far beyond anything specified in Jewish dietary law. The realization of one's taste in food on a commercial scale is a complex and fragile pursuit. When I ordered a cold borscht at the B&H and saw the counterman reach into the refrigerator for a bottle of commercially produced borscht, it did not matter that he was following the ancient Jewish dietary laws; he was disappointing my expectations as to what a bowl of cold borscht could be, based upon a lifetime of eating experience.

And how do we explain this strange impulse to understand the world via scale models? The temple and paradise garden as a scale model of heaven; Czernowitz as a Little Vienna; the Lower East Side of Manhattan as an Eastern Europe in miniature. Should this tendency be seen as a paucity of imagination — to only understand a new thing as a reconfiguration of something familiar — or as a form of resignation in a world of endless diversity?

Were Adam and Eve in the Garden of Eden aware of their paradisiacal situation, or must they have taken it for granted? Wouldn't the very awareness of being in paradise taint the experience? We see this happening at the most exclusive vacation resorts; the practical problems of maintaining even an approximation of paradise must ruin the pleasure of being there. Customers of the dairy restaurants of the twentieth century never for a moment thought that they were actually in paradise, just eating from a version of its menu and in a place that set itself apart from the larger restaurant culture. As revealed in these pages, the operators of these restaurants could not escape the brutalities of the business world.

And each customer embodies a complex blend of impulses: the traditional, the radical, the pastoral, the industrial. How else can we explain the sight of a yarmulke-wearing young man in a business suit dining at night with his Asian girlfriend in a dark corner of a non-kosher Thai restaurant in Manhattan?

It's easy to see how Jewish dietary law, once set in motion, could continue to be obeyed with no regard for the law or the authority that set it. Other, more compelling reasons arose — gustatory considerations, homesickness, love of feeding people — while compliance with the law incidentally continued. The restaurateur has arranged a walled garden with a menu in which the violation of the milk/meat taboo is not possible. One can continue to eat from the tree of knowledge without shame or banishment as long as the fragile business arrangement remains intact.

To the young vegan reader, the ethical distinctions between meat and dairy eating are quaint issues of the past. The dairy industry, with its heavy need of grazing land, is as deeply implicated in the earth's environmental death spiral as the meat industry.

When I mentioned the idea of writing a history of the dairy restaurant to a professional historian, he acknowledged the vast range of the subject. He said, "Get a grant, hire the best graduate students conversant in the histories and languages of the many cultures involved, and put them to work."

Instead, I took the milekhdike approach and ruminated over the subject for many years. Through chance readings and suggestions of friends, I'd come across interesting tidbits of information that might, somehow, fit into this vast history. In compiling notes over the years, I learned many things, but also forgot an equal number. To unravel the countless misunderstandings upon which this history is built seemed like a hopeless task and I risked putting myself in the position of compounding those confusions and thus increasing human misery.

My editor and publisher indulged me in those years of aimless reading in the libraries of New York and on the pages of the Internet. But the publishing industry has fallen upon hard times; the last unfulfilled advances and wandering manuscripts had, at last, to be called home. My collected discoveries are here assembled and illuminated with drawings. There are still countless fields of research to graze, and the complete history of the dairy restaurant remains to be written.

Et in Arcadia ego.

Acknowledgments

Jean Strouse and the Cullman Center
    for Writers and Scholars at the New
    York Public Library
Eddy Portnoy
Dr. William S. Breitbart
Czernowitzers: Marta and Sydney Collins
Luca Ginsberg and Beyle Gottesman
Pola and Selek Gefen
Itzik Gottesman
Kurt Ottenheimer
Daniel Epner
Gertrude Frankel
Samuel Klausner
Lawry Bluth
Jeremiah Moss
Jeffrey Levinton
Ben Feingold's "Broadway Tales" column
    in the *B'nai B'rith Messenger*
The Center for Jewish History, New York
    City
Follow and contribute to the ongoing
    history of dairy restaurants at
    http://dairyrestauranthistory.com